INTELLECTUALS
AND
SOCIETY

INTELLECTUALS

AND

SOCIETY

THOMAS SOWELL

BASIC
BOOKS

A Member of the Perseus Books Group
New York

Copyright © 2009 by Thomas Sowell

Published by Basic Books,
A Member of the Perseus Books Group

All rights reserved. Printed in the United States of America. No part of this book may be reproduced in any manner whatsoever without written permission except in the case of brief quotations embodied in critical articles and reviews. For information, address Basic Books, 387 Park Avenue South, New York, NY 10016-8810.

Books published by Basic Books are available at special discounts for bulk purchases in the United States by corporations, institutions, and other organizations. For more information, please contact the Special Markets Department at the Perseus Books Group, 2300 Chestnut Street, Suite 200, Philadelphia, PA 19103, or call (800) 810-4145, ext. 5000, or e-mail special.markets@perseusbooks.com.

A CIP catalog record for this book is available from the Library of Congress.

LCCN: 2009937004
ISBN: 978-0-465-01948-9

10 9 8 7 6 5 4 3 2 1

CONTENTS

PREFACE

There has probably never been an era in history when intellectuals have played a larger role in society. When those who generate ideas, the intellectuals proper, are surrounded by a wide penumbra of those who disseminate those ideas— whether as journalists, teachers, staffers to legislators or clerks to judges, and other members of the intelligentsia— their influence on the course of social evolution can be considerable, or even crucial. That influence has of course depended on the surrounding circumstances, including how free intellectuals have been to propagate their own ideas, rather than being instruments of state propaganda, as in totalitarian countries. There would of course be little point in studying the ideas expressed by prominent writers like Ilya Ehrenburg during the era of the Soviet Union, for these were simply the ideas permitted or advocated by the Soviet dictatorship. In short, the study of the influence of intellectuals is here a study of their influence where they have been freest to exert that influence, namely in modern democratic nations.

For very different reasons, this study of patterns among intellectuals will pay less attention to such an intellectual giant as Milton Friedman as to any number of intellectuals of lesser eminence, simply because Professor Friedman was in many ways very atypical of the intellectuals of his time, both in his scholarly work that won him a Nobel Prize and in his work as a popular commentator on issues of the day. A "balanced" general intellectual history of our times would have to give Professor Friedman a far larger amount of attention than a study which focuses on general patterns to which he was an outstanding exception. Aleksandr Solzhenitsyn was another landmark figure in the intellectual, moral and political history of his age who was likewise too atypical of contemporary intellectuals to be included in a study of the general patterns of the profession.

Many books have been written about intellectuals. Some take in-depth looks at particular prominent figures, Paul Johnson's *Intellectuals* being an especially incisive example. Other books on intellectuals focus on the ideas of particular eras. Richard A. Posner's *Public Intellectuals* is about those intellectuals who directly address the public, while the focus in *Intellectuals and Society* is about intellectuals who influence— sometimes shape— public attitudes and beliefs, whether or not they are widely read by the population at large. As J.A. Schumpeter said, "there are many Keynesians and Marxians who have never read a line of Keynes or Marx."[1] They have gotten their ideas second- or third-hand from the intelligentsia.

Among the many things said by those who have studied intellectuals, a comment by Professor Mark Lilla of Columbia University in his book *The Reckless Mind* is especially striking:

> Distinguished professors, gifted poets, and influential journalists summoned their talents to convince all who would listen that modern tyrants were liberators and that their unconscionable crimes were noble, when seen in the proper perspective. Whoever takes it upon himself to write an honest intellectual history of twentieth-century Europe will need a strong stomach.
>
> But he will need something more. He will need to overcome his disgust long enough to ponder the roots of this strange and puzzling phenomenon.[2]

While *Intellectuals and Society* is not an intellectual history of twentieth-century Europe— that would be a much larger project for someone much younger— it does attempt to unravel some of the puzzling phenomena in the world of the intellectuals, as that world impacts society at large. Rather than simply generalizing from the writings or behavior of particular intellectuals, this book will analyze both the vision and the incentives and constraints behind the general patterns found among contemporary members of the intelligentsia, as well as what they have said and its impact on the societies in which they said it.

Although we already know much about the biographies or ideologies of particular prominent intellectuals, systematic analyses of the nature and role of intellectuals as a group in society are much less common. This book seeks to develop such an analysis and to explore its implications for the direction in which the intelligentsia are taking our society and Western civilization in general.

Preface

Although this book is about intellectuals, it is not written *for* intellectuals. Its purpose is to achieve an understanding of an important social phenomenon and to share that understanding with those who wish to share it, in whatever walk of life they might be. Those among the intelligentsia who are looking for points to score or things at which to take umbrage will be left to their own devices. This book is written for those readers who are willing to join with me in a search for some understanding of a distinct segment of the population whose activities can have, and have had, momentous implications for nations and civilizations.

Thomas Sowell
Hoover Institution
Stanford University

ACKNOWLEDGMENTS

Like other books of mine, this one owes much to the dedicated work of my outstanding research assistants, Na Liu and Elizabeth Costa. Ms. Liu, having worked with me for twenty years, has not only ferreted out many facts but contributed many insights to this book, as she has to others. Now she also creates the computer files from which my books can be printed directly. My other assistant, Ms. Costa, does the copy-editing and fact-checking for me, and seldom does a lapse on my part escape her scrutiny. I have also benefitted from information or comments supplied by Dr. Gerald P. O'Driscoll of the Cato Institute, Professor Lino A. Graglia of the University of Texas at Austin and Dr. Victor Davis Hanson of the Hoover Institution. Any errors or shortcomings which survive despite their efforts can only be my responsibility.

Chapter 1

Intellect and Intellectuals

Intelligence is quickness to apprehend as distinct from ability, which is capacity to act wisely on the thing apprehended.

Alfred North Whitehead [1]

Intellect is not wisdom. There can be "unwise intellect," as Thomas Carlyle characterized the thinking of Harriet Taylor,[2] the friend and later wife of John Stuart Mill. Sheer brainpower— intellect, the capacity to grasp and manipulate complex concepts and ideas— can be put at the service of concepts and ideas that lead to mistaken conclusions and unwise actions, in light of all the factors involved, including factors left out of some of the ingenious constructions of the intellect.

Karl Marx's *Capital* was a classic example of an intellectually masterful elaboration of a fundamental misconception— in this case, the notion that "labor," the physical handling of the materials and instruments of production, is the real source of wealth. Obviously, if this were true, countries with much labor and little technology or entrepreneurship would be more prosperous than countries with the reverse, when in fact it is blatantly obvious that the direct opposite is the case. Similarly with John Rawls' elaborate and intricate *A Theory of Justice*, in which justice becomes categorically more important than any other social consideration. But, obviously, if any two things have any value at all, one cannot be categorically more valuable than the other. A diamond may be worth much more than a penny but enough pennies will be worth more than any diamond.

1

INTELLIGENCE VERSUS INTELLECT

The capacity to grasp and manipulate complex ideas is enough to define intellect but not enough to encompass intelligence, which involves combining intellect with judgment and care in selecting relevant explanatory factors and in establishing empirical tests of any theory that emerges. Intelligence minus judgment equals intellect. Wisdom is the rarest quality of all— the ability to combine intellect, knowledge, experience, and judgment in a way to produce a coherent understanding. Wisdom is the fulfillment of the ancient admonition, "With all your getting, get understanding." Wisdom requires self-discipline and an understanding of the realities of the world, including the limitations of one's own experience and of reason itself. The opposite of intellect is dullness or slowness, but the opposite of wisdom is foolishness, which is far more dangerous.

George Orwell said that some ideas are so foolish that only an intellectual could believe them, for no ordinary man could be such a fool. The record of twentieth century intellectuals was especially appalling in this regard. Scarcely a mass-murdering dictator of the twentieth century was without his intellectual supporters, not simply in his own country, but also in foreign democracies, where people were free to say whatever they wished. Lenin, Stalin, Mao, and Hitler all had their admirers, defenders, and apologists among the intelligentsia in Western democratic nations, despite the fact that these dictators each ended up killing people of their own country on a scale unprecedented even by despotic regimes that preceded them.

Defining Intellectuals

We must be clear about what we mean by intellectuals. Here "intellectuals" refers to an *occupational* category, people whose occupations deal primarily with ideas— writers, academics, and the like.* Most of us do not think of brain surgeons or engineers as intellectuals, despite the demanding mental training that each goes through, and virtually no one

---

* For those few people whose wealth enables them to pursue a career that is not the source of their livelihood, "occupation" need not mean a paying occupation.

regards even the most brilliant and successful financial wizard as an intellectual.

At the core of the notion of an intellectual is the dealer in ideas, as such— not the personal application of ideas, as engineers apply complex scientific principles to create physical structures or mechanisms. A policy wonk whose work might be analogized as "social engineering" will seldom personally administer the schemes that he or she creates or advocates. That is left to bureaucrats, politicians, social workers, the police or whoever else might be directly in charge of carrying out the ideas of the policy wonk. Such labels as "applied social science" may be put on the policy wonk's work but that work is essentially the application of general ideas only to produce more specific ideas about social policies, to be turned into action by others.

The policy wonk's work is not personally carrying out those specific ideas, as a physician applies medical science to particular flesh-and-blood human beings or as an engineer stands in hip boots on a construction site where a building or a bridge is being built. The output— the end product— of an intellectual consists of ideas.

Jonas Salk's end product was a vaccine, as Bill Gates' end product was a computer operating system. Despite the brainpower, insights, and talents involved in these and other achievements, such individuals are not intellectuals. *An intellectual's work begins and ends with ideas*, however influential those ideas may be on concrete things— in the hands of others. Adam Smith never ran a business and Karl Marx never administered a Gulag. They were intellectuals. Ideas, as such, are not only the key to the intellectual's function, but are also the criteria of intellectual achievements and the source of the often dangerous seductions of the occupation.

The quintessential intellectuals of the academic world, for example, are those in fields which are more pervaded by ideas, as such. A university's business school, engineering school, medical school, or athletics department is not what usually comes to mind when we think of academic intellectuals. Moreover, the prevailing ideologies and attitudes among academic intellectuals are usually least prevalent in these particular parts of an academic campus. That is, sociology departments have generally been found to be more one-sidedly to the left politically compared to medical schools, psychology departments more to the left than engineering schools, English departments to the left of economics departments, and so on.[3]

The term "pseudo-intellectual" has sometimes been applied to the less intelligent or less knowledgeable members of this profession. But just as a bad cop is still a cop— no matter how much we may regret it— so a shallow, confused, or dishonest intellectual is just as much a member of that occupation as is a paragon of the profession. Once we are clear as to whom we are talking about when we speak of intellectuals— that it is an occupational description rather than a qualitative label or an honorific title— then we can look at the characteristics of such occupations and the incentives and constraints faced by the people in those occupations, in order to see how those characteristics relate to how such people behave. The larger question, of course, is how their behavior affects the society in which they live.

The impact of an intellectual, or of intellectuals in general, does not depend on their being so-called "public intellectuals" who directly address the population at large, as distinct from those intellectuals whose ideas are largely confined to others in their respective specialties or to other intellectuals in general. Books with some of the biggest impacts on the twentieth century were written by Karl Marx and Sigmund Freud in the nineteenth century— and seldom read, much less understood, by the general public. But the conclusions— as distinguished from the intricacies of the analyses— of these writers inspired vast numbers of intellectuals around the world and, through them, the general public. The high repute of these writings added weight and provided confidence to many followers who had not personally mastered these writings or perhaps had not even tried to.

Even intellectuals whose very names have been little known to the general public have had worldwide impacts. Friedrich Hayek, whose writings— notably *The Road to Serfdom*— began an intellectual counter-revolution later joined by Milton Friedman, reaching a political climax with the rise of Margaret Thatcher in Britain and Ronald Reagan in the United States, was little known or read even in most intellectual circles. But he inspired many public intellectuals and political activists around the world, who in turn made his ideas the subject of wider discourse and an influence on the making of government policies. Hayek was a classic example of the kind of intellectual described by Justice Oliver Wendell Holmes as a thinker who, "a hundred years after he is dead and forgotten, men who never heard of him will be moving to the measure of his thought."[4]

The Intelligentsia

Around a more or less solid core of producers of ideas there is a penumbra of those whose role is the use and dissemination of those ideas. These latter individuals would include those teachers, journalists, social activists, political aides, judges' clerks, and others who base their beliefs or actions on the ideas of intellectuals. Journalists in their roles as editorial writers or columnists are both consumers of the ideas of intellectuals and producers of ideas of their own, and so may be considered intellectuals in such roles, since originality is not essential to the definition of an intellectual, so long as the end product is ideas. But journalists in their roles as reporters are supposed to be reporting facts and, in so far as these facts are filtered and slanted in accordance with the prevailing notions among intellectuals, these reporters are part of the penumbra surrounding intellectuals. They are part of the *intelligentsia*, which includes but is not limited to the intellectuals. Finally, there are those whose occupations are not much impacted by the ideas of the intellectuals, but who are nevertheless interested as individuals in remaining *au courant* with those ideas, if only for discussion on social occasions, and who would feel flattered to be considered part of the intelligentsia.

IDEAS AND ACCOUNTABILITY

Because of the enormous impact that intellectuals can have, both when they are well known and when they are unknown, it is critical to try to understand the patterns of their behavior and the incentives and constraints affecting those patterns.

Ideas are of course not the exclusive property of intellectuals. Nor is the complexity, difficulty or qualitative level of ideas the crucial factor in determining whether those who produce these ideas are or are not considered to be intellectuals. Engineers and financiers deal with ideas at least as complex as those of sociologists or professors of English. Yet it is these latter who are more likely to come to mind when intellectuals are discussed. Moreover, it is the latter who most exhibit the attitudes, beliefs, and behavior associated with intellectuals.

Verifiability

The standards by which engineers and financiers are judged are external standards, beyond the realm of ideas and beyond the control of their peers. An engineer whose bridges or buildings collapse is ruined, as is a financier who goes broke. However plausible or admirable their ideas might have seemed initially to their fellow engineers or fellow financiers, the proof of the pudding is ultimately in the eating. Their failure may well be registered in their declining esteem in their respective professions, but that is an effect, not a cause. Conversely, ideas which might have seemed unpromising to their fellow engineers or fellow financiers can come to be accepted among those peers if the empirical success of the ideas becomes manifest. The same is true of scientists and athletic coaches. But the ultimate test of a deconstructionist's ideas is whether other deconstructionists find those ideas interesting, original, persuasive, elegant, or ingenious. There is no external test.

In short, among people in mentally demanding occupations, the fault line between those most likely to be considered intellectuals and those who are not tends to run between those whose ideas are ultimately subject to internal criteria and those whose ideas are ultimately subject to external criteria. The very terms of admiration or dismissal among intellectuals reflect the non-empirical criteria involved. Ideas that are "complex," "exciting," "innovative," "nuanced," or "progressive" are admired, while other ideas are dismissed as "simplistic," "outmoded" or "reactionary." But no one judged Vince Lombardi's ideas about how to play football by their plausibility *a priori* or by whether they were more complex or less complex than the ideas of other football coaches, or by whether they represented new or old conceptions of how the game should be played. Vince Lombardi was judged by what happened when his ideas were put to the test on the football field.

Similarly, in the very different field of physics, Einstein's theory of relativity did not win acceptance on the basis of its plausibility, elegance, complexity or novelty. Not only were other physicists initially skeptical, Einstein himself urged that his theories not be accepted until they could be verified empirically. The crucial test came when scientists around the world observed an eclipse of the sun and discovered that light behaved as Einstein's theory said it would behave, however implausible that might have seemed beforehand.

The great problem— and the great social danger— with purely internal criteria is that they can easily become sealed off from feedback from the external world of reality and remain circular in their methods of validation. What new idea will seem plausible depends on what one already believes. When the only external validation for the individual is what other individuals believe, everything depends on who those other individuals are. If they are simply people who are like-minded in general, then the consensus of the group about a particular new idea depends on what that group already believes in general— and says nothing about the empirical validity of that idea in the external world.

Ideas sealed off from the outside world in terms of their origin or their validation may nevertheless have great impact on that external world in which millions of human beings live their lives. The ideas of Lenin, Hitler, and Mao had enormous— and often lethal— impact on those millions of people, however little validity those ideas had in themselves or in the eyes of others beyond the circles of like-minded followers and subordinate power-wielders.

The impact of ideas on the real world can hardly be disputed. The converse, however, is not nearly as clear, despite fashionable notions that major changes in ideas are generated by great events. As the late Nobel Prizewinning economist George J. Stigler pointed out, "A war may ravage a continent or destroy a generation without posing new theoretical questions."[5] Wars have all too often done both these things in the course of many centuries, so this hardly presents a new phenomenon for which some new explanation is required.

While one might regard Keynesian economics, for example, as a system of ideas particularly relevant to the events of the era in which it was published— namely, the Great Depression of the 1930s— what is remarkable is how seldom that can be said of other landmark intellectual systems. Were falling objects more common, or more fraught with social impact, when Newton's laws of gravity were developed? Were new species appearing, or old ones disappearing, more often or more consequentially when Darwin's *Origin of Species* was written? What produced Einstein's theory of relativity, other than Einstein's own thinking?

Accountability

Intellectuals, in the restricted sense which largely conforms to general usage, are ultimately unaccountable to the external world. The prevalence and presumed desirability of this are confirmed by such things as academic tenure and expansive concepts of "academic freedom" and academic "self-governance." In the media, expansive notions of freedom of speech and of the press play similar roles. In short, unaccountability to the external world is not simply a happenstance but a principle. John Stuart Mill argued that intellectuals should be free even from social standards— while setting social standards for others.[6] Not only have intellectuals been insulated from material consequences, they have often enjoyed immunity from even a loss of reputation after having been demonstrably wrong. As Eric Hoffer put it:

> One of the surprising privileges of intellectuals is that they are free to be scandalously asinine without harming their reputation. The intellectuals who idolized Stalin while he was purging millions and stifling the least stirring of freedom have not been discredited. They are still holding forth on every topic under the sun and are listened to with deference. Sartre returned in 1939 from Germany, where he studied philosophy, and told the world that there was little to choose between Hitler's Germany and France. Yet Sartre went on to become an intellectual pope revered by the educated in every land.[7]

Sartre was not unique. Environmentalist Paul Ehrlich said in 1968: "The battle to feed all of humanity is over. In the 1970's the world will undergo famines— hundreds of millions of people are going to starve to death in spite of any crash programs embarked upon now."[8] Yet, after that decade— and later decades— had come and gone, not only had nothing of the sort happened, a growing problem in a growing number of countries was obesity and unsalable agricultural surpluses. But Professor Ehrlich continued to receive not only popular acclaim but also honors and grants from prestigious academic institutions.

Similarly, Ralph Nader first became a major public figure with the 1965 publication of his book *Unsafe at Any Speed*, which depicted American cars in general, and the Corvair in particular, as accident-prone. Yet, despite the fact that empirical studies showed the Corvair to be at least as safe as other cars of its day,[9] Nader not only continued to have credibility but acquired a reputation for idealism and insight that made him something of a secular saint. Innumerable other wrong predictions, about everything from the price of gasoline to the outcome of Cold War policies, have left innumerable other false prophets with just as much honor as if they had been truly prophetic.

In short, constraints which apply to people in most other fields do not apply even approximately equally to intellectuals. It would be surprising if this did not lead to different behavior. Among those differences are the ways they see the world and the way they see themselves in relation to their fellow human beings and the societies in which they live.

Chapter 2

Knowledge and Notions

From an early age, smart people are reminded of their intelligence, separated from their peers in gifted classes, and presented with opportunities unavailable to others. For these and other reasons, intellectuals tend to have an inflated sense of their own wisdom.

Daniel J. Flynn [1]

Like everyone else, intellectuals have a mixture of knowledge and notions. For some intellectuals in some fields, that knowledge includes knowledge of the systematic procedures available to test notions and determine their validity as knowledge. Since ideas are their life's work, intellectuals might be expected to more thoroughly or more systematically subject notions to such tests. Whether or to what extent they do so in practice is, of course, itself a notion that needs to be tested. There are, after all, other skills in which intellectuals also tend to excel, including verbal skills that can be used to evade the testing of their favorite notions.

In short, the various skills of intellectuals can be used either to foster intellectual standards or to circumvent those standards and promote non-intellectual or even anti-intellectual agendas. In other words, intellectuals— defined as an occupational category— may or may not exemplify the intellectual process. Indeed, it is possible for people *not* defined as intellectuals— engineers, financiers, physicians— to adhere to intellectual procedures more often or more rigorously than some or most intellectuals. The extent to which this is true is another empirical question. What is important here is that the mere word "intellectual," applied to an occupational category, not be allowed to insinuate the presence of intellectual principles or standards which may or may not in fact be present.

However important rigorous intellectual principles may be within particular fields in which some intellectuals specialize, when people operate as "public intellectuals," espousing ideas and policies to a wider population beyond their professional colleagues, they may or may not carry over intellectual rigor into these more general, more policy-oriented, or more ideologically charged discussions.

Bertrand Russell, for example, was both a public intellectual and a leading authority within a rigorous field. But the Bertrand Russell who is relevant here is not the author of landmark treatises on mathematics but the Bertrand Russell who advocated "unilateral disarmament" for Britain in the 1930s while Hitler was re-arming Germany. Russell's advocacy of disarmament extended all the way to "disbanding the army and navy and air force"[2]— again, with Hitler re-arming not far away. The Noam Chomsky who is relevant here is not the linguistics scholar but the Noam Chomsky of similarly extravagant political pronouncements. The Edmund Wilson who is relevant is not the highly regarded literary critic but the Edmund Wilson who urged Americans to vote for the Communists in the 1932 elections. In this he was joined by such other intellectual luminaries of the time as John Dos Passos, Sherwood Anderson, Langston Hughes, Lincoln Steffens and many other well-known writers of that era.[3]

Visiting the United States in 1933, George Bernard Shaw said, "You Americans are so fearful of dictators. Dictatorship is the only way in which government can accomplish anything. See what a mess democracy has led to. Why are you afraid of dictatorship?"[4] Leaving London for a vacation in South Africa in 1935, Shaw declared, "It is nice to go for a holiday and know that Hitler has settled everything so well in Europe."[5] While Hitler's anti-Jewish actions eventually alienated Shaw, the famous playwright remained partial to the Soviet dictatorship. In 1939, after the Nazi-Soviet pact, Shaw said: "Herr Hitler is under the powerful thumb of Stalin, whose interest in peace is overwhelming. And every one except myself is frightened out of his or her wits!"[6] A week later, the Second World War began, with Hitler invading Poland from the west, followed by Stalin invading from the east.

The list of top-ranked intellectuals who made utterly irresponsible statements, and who advocated hopelessly unrealistic and recklessly dangerous things, could be extended almost indefinitely. Many public intellectuals have been justly renowned within their respective fields but the point here is that many *did not stay within their respective fields*. As George J. Stigler said of some of his fellow Nobel Laureates, they "issue stern ultimata to the public on almost a monthly basis, and sometimes on no other basis."[7]

The fatal misstep of such intellectuals is assuming that superior ability within a particular realm can be generalized as superior wisdom or morality over all. Chess grandmasters, musical prodigies and others who are as remarkable within their respective specialties as intellectuals are within theirs, seldom make that mistake. Here it is sufficient to make a sharp distinction between the intellectual occupation and intellectual standards which members of that occupation can and do violate, especially in their roles as public intellectuals, making pronouncements about society and advocating government policies. What was said of John Maynard Keynes by his biographer and fellow economist Roy Harrod could be said of many other intellectuals:

> He held forth on a great range of topics, on some of which he was thoroughly expert, but on others of which he may have derived his views from the few pages of a book at which he had happened to glance. The air of authority was the same in both cases.[8]

COMPETING CONCEPTS OF KNOWLEDGE

The way the word knowledge is used by many intellectuals often arbitrarily limits what verified information is to be considered knowledge. This arbitrary limitation of the scope of the word was expressed in a parody verse about Benjamin Jowett, master of Balliol College at Oxford University:

> My name is Benjamin Jowett.
>   If it's knowledge, I know it.
> I am the master of this college.
>   What I don't know isn't knowledge.

Someone who is considered to be a "knowledgeable" person usually has a special kind of knowledge— perhaps academic or other kinds of knowledge not widely found in the population at large. Someone who has even more knowledge of more mundane things— plumbing, carpentry, or baseball, for example— is less likely to be called "knowledgeable" by those intellectuals for whom what they don't know isn't knowledge. Although the special kind of knowledge associated with intellectuals is usually valued more, and those who have such knowledge are usually accorded more prestige, it is by no means certain that the kind of knowledge mastered by intellectuals is necessarily more consequential in its effects in the real world. The same is true even of expert knowledge. No doubt those in charge of the *Titanic* had far more expertise in the many aspects of seafaring than most ordinary people had, but what was crucial in its consequences was the mundane knowledge of where particular icebergs happened to be located on a particular night. Many major economic decisions are likewise crucially dependent on the kind of mundane knowledge that intellectuals might disdain to consider to be knowledge in the sense in which they habitually use the word.

Location is just one of those mundane kinds of knowledge, and its importance is by no means confined to the location of icebergs. For example, the mundane knowledge of what is located at Broadway and 23rd Street in Manhattan, and what the surrounding neighborhood is like, may not be considered relevant to determining whether a given individual should be regarded as a knowledgeable person. But, for a business seeking a place to open a store, that knowledge can be the difference between going bankrupt and making millions of dollars.

Enterprises invest much time and money in determining where to locate their operations, and these locations are by no means random. It is not accidental that filling stations are often located on street corners, and often near other filling stations, just as automobile dealers are often located near other automobile dealers, but stationery stores are seldom located near other stationery stores. People knowledgeable about business have cited, as one of the factors behind the spectacular rise of Starbucks, the Starbucks management's careful attention to choosing the locations of their outlets—

and one of the factors cited in Starbucks having to close hundreds of outlets in 2008 has been their straying from that practice.[9] It is a cliché among realtors that the three most important factors in determining the value of a house are location, location, and location.

Location is just one of many mundane facts with major, and often decisive, consequences. A nurse's mundane knowledge of whether a particular patient is allergic to penicillin can be the difference between life and death. When a plane is coming into an airport for a landing, the control tower's observation that the pilot has forgotten to lower the landing gear is information whose immediate conveyance to the pilot can likewise be crucial, even though such knowledge requires nothing more intellectually challenging than eyesight. Foreknowledge that the D-Day invasion of Europe would take place at Normandy, rather than at Calais where Hitler expected it, would have led to a wholly different concentration of the Nazis' military forces, costing thousands more lives among the troops hitting the beach, perhaps dooming the whole operation and changing the course of the war.

In short, much of the special kind of knowledge concentrated among intellectuals may not have as weighty consequences as much mundane or intellectually unimpressive knowledge, scattered among the population at large. In the aggregate, mundane knowledge can vastly outweigh the special knowledge of elites, both in its amount and in its consequences. While special knowledge is almost invariably articulated knowledge, other kinds of knowledge need not be articulated to others nor even be consciously articulated to ourselves. Friedrich Hayek included in knowledge "all the human adaptations to environment in which past experience has been incorporated." He added:

> Not all knowledge in this sense is part of our intellect, nor is our intellect the whole of our knowledge. Our habits and skills, our emotional attitudes, our tools, and our institutions— all are in this sense adaptations to past experience which have grown up by selective elimination of less suitable conduct. They are as much an indispensable foundation of successful action as is our conscious knowledge.[10]

Concentration and Dispersion of Knowledge

When both special knowledge and mundane knowledge are encompassed within the concept of knowledge, it is doubtful whether the most knowledgeable person on earth has even one percent of the total knowledge on earth, or even one percent of the consequential knowledge in a given society.

There are many serious implications of this which may, among other things, help explain why so many leading intellectuals have so often backed notions that proved to be disastrous. It is not simply with particular policies at particular times that intellectuals have often advocated mistaken and dangerous decisions. Their whole general approach to policy-making— their ideology— has often reflected a crucial misconception about knowledge and its concentration or dispersion.

Many intellectuals and their followers have been unduly impressed by the fact that highly educated elites like themselves have far more knowledge per capita— in the sense of special knowledge— than does the population at large. From this it is a short step to considering the educated elites to be superior guides to what should and should not be done in a society. They have often overlooked the crucial fact that the population at large may have vastly more *total* knowledge— in the mundane sense— than the elites, even if that knowledge is scattered in individually unimpressive fragments among vast numbers of people.

If no one has even one percent of the knowledge currently available, not counting the vast amounts of knowledge yet to be discovered, the imposition from the top down of the notions in favor among elites, convinced of their own superior knowledge and virtue, is a formula for disaster.

Sometimes it is economic disaster, which central planning, for example, turned out to be in so many countries around the world during the twentieth century that even most governments run by communists and socialists began replacing such top-down economic planning by freer markets by the end of that century. No doubt central planners had far more expertise, and far more statistical data at their command, than the average person making transactions in the market. Yet the vastly greater mundane knowledge brought to bear by millions of ordinary people making their own mutual accommodations among themselves almost invariably produced higher economic growth rates and higher standards of living after central planning was jettisoned, notably in China and India, where rates of poverty declined dramatically as their economies grew at accelerated rates.

Central planning is just one of a more general class of social decision-making processes dependent on the underlying assumption that people with more per capita knowledge (in the special sense) should be guiding their societies. Other forms of this general notion include judicial activism, urban planning, and other institutional expressions of the belief that social decisions cannot be left to be determined by the actions and values of the less knowledgeable population at large. But if no one has even one percent of all the knowledge in a society— in the larger sense in which many different kinds of knowledge are consequential— then it is crucial that the other 99 percent of knowledge, scattered in small and individually unimpressive amounts among the population at large, be allowed the freedom to be used in working out mutual accommodations among the people themselves. These innumerable interactions and mutual accommodations are what bring the other 99 percent of knowledge into play— and generate new knowledge in the process of back and forth bids, reflecting changes in supply and demand.

That is why free markets, judicial restraint, and reliance on decisions and traditions growing out of the experiences of the many— rather than the presumptions of an elite few— are so important to those who do *not* share the social vision prevalent among intellectual elites. In short, ideological fault lines divide those who have different conceptions of the meaning of knowledge, and who consequently see knowledge as being concentrated or dispersed. "In general, 'the market' is smarter than the smartest of its individual participants,"[11] is the way the late Robert L. Bartley, editor of the *Wall Street Journal*, expressed his belief that systemic processes can bring into play more knowledge for decision-making purposes, through the interactions and mutual accommodations of many individuals, than any one of those individuals possesses.

Systemic processes are essentially trial-and-error processes, with repeated or continuous— and consequential— feedback from those involved in these processes. By contrast, political and legal processes are processes in which initial decisions are harder to change, whether because of the high cost to political careers of admitting a mistake or— in the law— the legal precedents that are set. Why the transfer of decisions from those with personal experience and a stake in the outcome to those with neither can be expected to lead to better decisions is a question seldom asked, much less answered. Given the greater cost of correcting surrogate decisions, compared to correcting individual decisions, and the greater cost of persisting in mistaken decisions by those making decisions for themselves, compared to the lower cost of making mistaken decisions for others, the economic success of market economies is hardly surprising and neither are the counterproductive and often disastrous results of various forms of social engineering.

People on both sides of the ideological fault line may believe that those with the most knowledge should have the most weight in making decisions that impact society, but they have radically different conceptions of just where in society there is in fact the most knowledge. If knowledge is defined expansively, including much mundane knowledge whose presence or absence is consequential and often crucial, then individuals with Ph.D.s are as grossly ignorant of most consequential things as other individuals are, since no one can be truly knowledgeable, at a level required for consequential decision-making for a whole society, except within a narrow band out of the vast spectrum of human concerns.

The ignorance, prejudices, and groupthink of an educated elite are still ignorance, prejudice, and groupthink— and for those with one percent of the knowledge in a society to be guiding or controlling those with the other 99 percent is as perilous as it is absurd. The difference between special knowledge and mundane knowledge is not simply incidental or semantic. Its social implications are very consequential. For example, it is far easier to concentrate power than to concentrate knowledge. That is why so much social engineering backfires and why so many despots have led their countries into disasters.

Where knowledge is conceived of as Hayek conceived of it, to include knowledge unarticulated even to ourselves, but expressed in our individual habits and social customs, then the transmission of such knowledge from millions of people to be concentrated in surrogate decision-makers becomes very problematic, if not impossible, since many of those operating with such knowledge have not fully articulated such knowledge even to themselves, and so can hardly transmit it to others, even if they might wish to.

Since many, if not most, intellectuals operate under the implicit assumption that knowledge is already concentrated— in people like themselves— they are especially susceptible to the idea that a corresponding concentration of decision-making power in a public-spirited elite can benefit society. That assumption has been the foundation for reform movements like Progressivism in the United States and revolutionary movements in various other countries around the world. Moreover, with sufficient knowledge being considered already concentrated, those with this view often conceive that what needs to be done is to create an accompanying will and power to deal collectively with a wide array of social problems. Emphasis on "will," "commitment," "caring" or "compassion," as crucial ingredients for dealing with social issues essentially assumes away the question whether those who are presumed to have these qualities also have sufficient knowledge.

Sometimes the sufficiency of knowledge is explicitly asserted and any questions about that sufficiency are then dismissed as reflecting either ignorance or obstruction. John Dewey, for example, spelled it out: "Having the knowledge we may set hopefully at work upon a course of social invention and experimental engineering."[12] But the ignored question is: Who— if anybody— has that kind of knowledge?

Since intellectuals have every incentive to emphasize the importance of the special kind of knowledge that they have, relative to the mundane knowledge that others have, they are often advocates of courses of action which ignore the value, the cost, and the consequences of mundane knowledge. It is common, for example, for the intelligentsia to deplore many methods of sorting and labeling things and people, often saying in the case of people that "each person should be judged as an individual." The cost of the knowledge necessary to do that is almost never considered. Lower cost substitutes for that knowledge of individuals— ranging from credit reports to IQ tests— are used precisely because judging "the whole person" means acquiring and weighing vast amounts of knowledge at vast costs that can include delayed decisions in circumstances where time is crucial. Depending on how expansively "judging the whole person" is defined, the time required can exceed the human lifespan, which would make it impossible for all practical purposes.

Armies sort people into ranks, colleges sort applicants into ranges of SAT scores, and virtually everyone else sorts people by innumerable other criteria. Many, if not most, of these sorting methods are criticized by the intelligentsia, who fail to appreciate the scarcity and high cost of knowledge— and the necessity of making consequential decisions despite that scarcity and high cost, which necessarily includes the costs of mistakes. The risks of making decisions with incomplete knowledge (there being no other kind) are part of the tragedy of the human condition. However, that has not stopped intellectuals from criticizing the inherent risks that turn out badly in everything from pharmaceutical drugs to military operations— nor does it stop them from helping create a general atmosphere of unfulfillable expectations in which "the thousand natural shocks that flesh is heir to" become a thousand bases for lawsuits.

Without some sense of the tragedy of the human condition, it is all too easy to consider anything that goes wrong as being somebody's fault.

It is common for intellectuals to act as if their special kind of knowledge of generalities can and should substitute for, and override, the mundane specific knowledge of others. This emphasis on the special knowledge of intellectuals often leads to the dismissing of mundane, first-hand knowledge as "prejudices" or "stereotypes," in favor of abstract beliefs common among the intelligentsia, who may have little or no first-hand knowledge of the individuals, organizations or concrete circumstances involved. Moreover, such attitudes are not only disseminated far beyond the ranks of the intelligentsia, they have become the basis of policies, laws, and judicial decisions.

One small but revealing example of the social consequences of this attitude is that many company policies of establishing retirement ages for their employees have been made illegal as "age discrimination" because those policies are said to be based on stereotypes about the elderly, who can be productive beyond the age of "mandatory retirement." In other words, third parties with no stake in the outcome, no direct experience in the particular companies or industries, and no knowledge of the particular individual employees involved, are assumed to have superior understanding of the effects of age than those who do have such experience, such a stake, and such direct knowledge, mundane though that knowledge may be. Moreover, employers have economic incentives to hang on to productive employees, especially since they must pay costs to recruit their replacements and invest in bringing those replacements up to speed, while surrogate decision-makers pay no cost whatever for being mistaken.

The very phrase "mandatory retirement" shows the verbal virtuosity of the intelligentsia— and what a fatal talent that can be in obscuring, rather than clarifying, rational analysis. There has seldom, if ever, been any such thing as mandatory retirement. Particular employers had set an age beyond which they automatically ceased to employ people. Those people remained free to go work elsewhere and many did. Even within a company with an automatic retirement policy, those particular employees who clearly remained productive and valuable could find the retirement policy waived, either for a particular span of time or indefinitely. But such waivers would be based on specific knowledge of specific individuals, not abstract generalities about how productive older people can be.

Virtually all adverse conclusions about any ethnic minority are likewise dismissed as "prejudices," "stereotypes" and the like by the intelligentsia. For example, a biographer of Theodore Roosevelt said, "During his years as a rancher, Roosevelt had acquired plenty of anti-Indian prejudice, strangely at odds with his enlightened attitude to blacks."[13] Here was a writer, nearly a hundred years removed from the particular Indians that Theodore Roosevelt dealt with personally in the west, declaring *a priori* that Roosevelt's conclusions were mistaken and based on prejudice, even while conceding that racial prejudice was not a general feature of TR's outlook.

It would probably never occur to that writer that it was he who was reaching a conclusion based on prejudgment— prejudice— even if it was a prejudice common among intellectuals, while Theodore Roosevelt's conclusions were based on his own direct personal experience with particular individuals. Many intellectuals seem unwilling to concede that the man on the scene at the time could reach accurate conclusions about the particular individuals he encountered or observed— and that the intellectuals far removed in space and time could be mistaken when reaching conclusions based on their own shared preconceptions.

Another writer, even further removed in space and time, dismissed as prejudice Cicero's advice to his fellow Romans not to buy British slaves because they were so hard to teach.[14] Considering the enormous difference between the primitive, illiterate, tribal world of the Britons of that era and the sophisticated world of the Romans, it is hard to imagine how a Briton taken in bondage to Rome could comprehend the complex circumstances, methods, and expectations of such a radically different society. But the very possibility that Cicero might have known what he was talking about from direct experience received no attention from the writer who dubbed him prejudiced without further ado.

A much more recent example of intellectuals dismissing the first-hand experience of others, in favor of prevailing assumptions among themselves, involved nationally publicized charges of rape filed against three students at Duke University in 2006. These students were members of the men's lacrosse team and, in the wave of condemnation that instantly swept the campus and the media, the only defenders of these students at the outset were members of the women's lacrosse team. These particular women had long associated socially with the accused men and were adamant from the beginning that the three young men in question were not the kind of people to do what they were accused of. Since this case involved race as well as rape, it should also be noted that a black woman on the lacrosse team took the lead in defending these men's character.[15]

In the absence of any evidence on either side of the issue at the outset, there was no reason why unsubstantiated statements for or against the accused should have been uncritically accepted or uncritically rejected. But the statements of members of the women's lacrosse team were not merely dismissed but denounced.

The Duke women lacrosse players were characterized as "stupid, spoiled little girls" in remarks quoted in the *Atlanta Journal-Constitution*, people who "negate common sense" according to a *New York Times* writer, who were "dumb" according to a writer in the *Philadelphia Daily News*, and "ignorant or insensitive" according to a *Philadelphia Inquirer* writer.[16]

In other words, members of the intelligentsia, hundreds of miles away, who had never laid eyes on the men in question, were so convinced of their guilt, on the basis of commonly shared *a priori* notions among the intelligentsia, that they could assail young women who had had direct personal knowledge of the individuals in question, including their attitudes and behavior toward women in general and a black woman in particular. It was a classic example of the presumption of superior knowledge on the part of intellectuals with less knowledge than those whose conclusions they dismissed and denounced. Unfortunately, it was not the only example, nor even a rare example.

Experts

A special occupation which overlaps that of intellectuals, but is not wholly coincident with it, is that of the expert. One may, after all, be an expert on Spanish literature or existentialist philosophy— where one's end product in either case consists of ideas— or one may be an expert on repairing automobile transmissions or extinguishing oil field fires, where the end product is a service rendered. Obviously only the former experts would fit our definition of intellectuals.

Experts of whatever sort are especially clear examples of people whose knowledge is concentrated within a narrow band out of the vast spectrum of human concerns. Moreover, the interactions of innumerable factors in the real world mean that, even within that narrow band, factors from outside that band can sometimes affect outcomes in ways that mean an expert whose expertise does not encompass those other factors can be an amateur when it comes to making consequential decisions, even within what is normally thought of as that expert's field of expertise. For example, in early twentieth century America, experts on forestry predicted a "timber famine" that never materialized because these forestry experts did not know enough economics to understand how prices allocate resources over time, as well as allocating resources among alternative users at a given time.[17]

Similar hysteria about an impending exhaustion of other natural resources, such as oil, has flourished for well over a century, despite repeated predictions that we had only enough oil reserves to last for a dozen or so years and repeated experiences that there were more known oil reserves at the end of the dozen or so years than there were at the beginning.[18]

With experts, as with non-profit organizations or movements with idealistic-sounding names, there is often an implication of disinterested endeavors, uncorrupted by the bias of self-interest. This is one of many perceptions which cannot survive empirical scrutiny— but which is seldom subjected to such scrutiny. Quite aside from the vested interest that experts have in the use of expertise— rather than other economic or other social mechanisms— to shape consequential decisions, there is much empirical evidence of their biases. City planners are a typical example:

> Planners often call for visioning sessions in which the public are consulted about their desires for their regions.
> In a typical visioning session, members of the public are asked leading questions about their preferences. Would you like to have more or less pollution? Would you like to spend more or less time commuting? Would you like to live in an ugly neighborhood or a pretty one? Planners interpret the answers as support for their preconceived notions, usually some form of smart growth. If you want less pollution, you must want less auto driving. If you want to spend less time getting to work, you must want a denser city so you live closer to work. If you want apple pie, you must oppose urban sprawl that might subdivide the apple orchard.[19]

Quite aside from the tendentiousness of the questions, even an honest attempt to get meaningful input into a decision-making process from answers to questions that neither cost anything to answer nor even include any notion of costs in the questions, would be relevant only to a costless world, while the crucial fact of the world we live in is that all actions or inactions entail costs which have to be taken into account in order to reach a rational decision. "Rational" is used here in its most basic sense— the ability to make a ratio, as in "rational numbers" in mathematics— so that rational decisions are decisions that weigh one thing against another, a trade-off as distinguished from a crusade to achieve some "good thing" without weighing costs.

City planners, like other experts, are also well aware that their own incomes and careers depend on providing ideas that are saleable to those who employ them, including politicians, whose goals and methods become the experts' goals and methods. Even where experts go through the formality of weighing costs against benefits, that can remain only a formality in a process where a goal has been chosen politically. For example, after a planning expert was ordered by a politician who wanted a rail system built to "revise rail ridership estimates upward and costs downward," later cost over-runs and revenue shortfalls became a public scandal. But the politician was able to say: "It's not my fault; I relied on forecasts made by our staff, and they seem to have made a big mistake."[20]

In other words, experts are often called in, not to provide factual information or dispassionate analysis for the purpose of decision-making by responsible officials, but to give political cover for decisions already made and based on other considerations entirely. The shifting of socially consequential decisions from systemic processes, involving millions of people making mutual accommodations— at their own costs and risks— to experts imposing a master plan on all would be problematic even if the experts were free to render their own best judgment. In situations where experts are simply part of the window dressing concealing arbitrary and even corrupt decisions by others, reliance on what "all the experts" say about a given issue is extremely risky. Even where the experts are untrammeled, what "all the experts" are most likely to agree on is the need for using expertise to deal with problems.

Experts have their place and can be extremely valuable in those places, this no doubt being one reason for the old expression, "Experts should be on tap, not on top." For broader social decision-making, however, experts are no substitute for systemic processes which engage innumerable factors on which no given individual can possibly be expert, and engage the 99 percent of consequential knowledge scattered in fragments among the population at large and coordinated systemically during the process of their mutual accommodations to one another's demand and supply.

The simple fact that central planners in the Soviet Union had more than 24 million prices to set shows the absurdity of the task undertaken by central planning. That central planning has failed repeatedly in countries around the world, among both democracies and dictatorships, can hardly be surprising because the central planners could not possibly be experts— or even competent— on all the things under their control. The fact that central planning was abandoned by country after country in the late twentieth century— even in countries with communist or socialist governments— suggests the depth and undeniability of that failure.

Economic central planning is just one aspect of top-down social engineering in general, but bad outcomes in other fields are not always so blatantly obvious, so readily quantifiable, and so undeniable as in the economy, though these other social outcomes may be just as bad or worse.[21] While lawyers and judges are experts on legal principles, and have valuable roles to play within their expertise, both have over the years increasingly moved beyond those roles to using law "as an instrument of social change"— which is to say, making amateur decisions on complex matters extending far beyond the narrow boundaries of their professional expertise. Moreover, the consensus of like-minded experts on matters beyond their expertise has emboldened many legal experts— like experts in other fields— to imagine that the difference between their elite group perceptions and those of other people is almost axiomatically a difference between knowledgeable people and the uninformed masses.

Among the many examples of this attitude was a 1960s judicial conference where a retired police commissioner attempted to explain to the judges and law professors present how the courts' recent expansions of criminals' legal rights undermined the effectiveness of law enforcement. Among those present were Supreme Court Justice William J. Brennan and Chief Justice Earl Warren, both of whom remained "stony-faced" during the police commissioner's presentation, according to a *New York Times* account, but later "roared with laughter" after a law professor arose to pour ridicule on what the police commissioner had just said.[22] Yet such scornful dismissal was not based on any factual evidence— and evidence subsequently accumulating over the years made painfully clear that law enforcement was in fact breaking down, to an accompanying skyrocketing of crime rates.

Prior to the revolution in judicial interpretations of criminal law in the early 1960s, the murder rate in the United States had been going down for decades, and was by 1961 less than half of what it had been back in 1933.[23] But this long downward trend in murder rates suddenly reversed during the 1960s, and by 1974 the murder rate was double what it was in 1961.[24]

Yet here, as elsewhere, the first-hand observations and years of personal day-to-day experience— in this case, by a retired police commissioner— were not merely dismissed but ridiculed by people who relied instead on shared but unsubstantiated assumptions among the elite. Neither this issue nor this episode was unique as an example of those with the vision of the anointed scornfully dismissing alternative views instead of answering them.

THE ROLE OF REASON

There are as many conceptions of reason and its social role as there are conceptions of knowledge and its social role. Both merit scrutiny.

Reason and Justification

The implicit assumption of superior knowledge among intellectual elites underlies one of the demands of intellectuals that goes back at least as far as the eighteenth century— namely, that actions, policies, or institutions "justify themselves before the bar of reason." The words in which this demand is expressed have changed since the eighteenth century, but the basic premise has not. Many intellectuals today, for example, find it a weighty consideration that they do not understand how corporate executives can be worth such high salaries as they receive— as if there is any inherent reason why third parties should be expected to understand, or why their understanding or acquiescence should be necessary, in order for those who are directly involved in hiring and paying corporate executives to proceed on the basis of their own knowledge and experience, in a matter in which they have a stake and intellectuals do not.*

Similarly, many of the intelligentsia express not only surprise but outrage at the number of shots fired by the police in some confrontation with a criminal, even if many of these intellectuals have never fired a gun in their lives, much less faced life-and-death dangers requiring split-second decisions. Seldom, if ever, do the intelligentsia find it necessary to seek out any information on the accuracy of pistols when fired under stress, before venting their feelings and demanding changes. In reality, a study by the New York City Police Department found that, even within a range of only six feet, just over half the shots fired by police missed completely. At distances from 16 to 25 yards— less than the distance from first base to second base on a baseball diamond— only 14 percent of the shots hit.[25]

However surprising such facts might be to those who have never fired a pistol, even at a stationary target in the safety and calm of a pistol range, much less in the scramble and stress of life-and-death dangers with moving targets, what is crucial here is that so many of the intelligentsia and those whom they influence have seen no reason to seek such factual information before venting their outrage, in utter ignorance of the facts. Moreover, even a criminal who is hit by a bullet is not necessarily rendered instantly harmless, so there is no reason to stop firing, so long as that criminal continues to be a danger. But such mundane knowledge has been of no interest to those joining elite group expressions of indignation over things beyond their experience or competence.**

To demand that things justify themselves before the bar of reason, in a world where no one has even one percent of all consequential knowledge, is

---

* Some try to claim that, as consumers who buy the products of the companies whose executives receive high pay, they are affected in the prices of the products they buy. However, if all the executives of oil companies, for example, agreed to work for no salary at all, that would not be enough to reduce the price of a gallon of gasoline by a dime, since the total profits of the oil companies are a small fraction of the price of a gallon of gasoline— usually much less than the taxes levied by governments at state and national levels. For a fuller discussion of executives' pay see my *Economic Facts and Fallacies* (New York: Basic Books, 2008), pp. 141-145.

** As a personal note, I once taught pistol shooting in the Marine Corps and have not been at all surprised by the number of shots fired by the police.

to demand that ignorance be convinced and its permission obtained. How can a brain surgeon justify what he does to someone who knows nothing about the brain or about surgery? How can a carpenter justify his choice of nails and woods to people who know nothing about carpentry, especially if the carpenter is being accused of wrongdoing by lawyers or politicians, whose articulation skills may greatly exceed those of the carpenter, while their knowledge of carpentry is far less? The confidence born of their generally superior special knowledge may conceal from these elites themselves the extent of their ignorance and their resulting misconception of the issue at hand. Moreover, arguments against the carpenter by articulate but ignorant elites to a general public that is equally ignorant on this subject— whether the public are on juries or in election booths— may easily prove to be convincing, even if those same arguments would seem absurd to other carpenters.

It is one thing for the population at large to make their own individual transactions and accommodations on matters pertaining to themselves individually, and something quite different for them to make collective decisions for the society at large. Collective decision-making, whether through democratic processes or through top-down commands, involves people making decisions for other people rather than for themselves. The same problem of inadequate knowledge afflicts both these processes. To revert for a moment to central planning as a proxy for surrogate decision-making in general, when central planners in the days of the Soviet Union had to set more than 24 million prices it was an impossible task for any manageably sized group of central planners, but far less of a problem in a country with hundreds of millions of people, each making decisions about the relatively few prices relevant to their own economic transactions.

Incentives as well as knowledge are different. There are far more incentives to invest time and attention in decisions with major direct personal consequences to oneself than to invest similar amounts of time and attention to casting one vote among millions in decisions that will affect mostly other people, and whose effect on oneself is unlikely to be changed by how one's own single vote among millions is cast.

The notion that things must justify themselves before the bar of reason opens the floodgates to sweeping condemnations of things not understood by people with credentialed ignorance. Differences in incomes and occupations not understood by intellectual elites, usually without much knowledge of either the mundane specifics or of economics in general, readily become "disparities" and "inequities" without further ado, just as intellectuals who have never fired a gun in their lives do not hesitate to express their outrage at the number of bullets fired by the police in a confrontation with a criminal. In these and other ways, notions trump knowledge— when these are notions prevalent among intellectuals.

This key fallacy— and the bad social consequences to which it can lead— is not limited to intellectual elites. The squelching of individual decision-making by the imposition of collective decisions arrived at by third parties, whether those third parties are elites or masses, usually means essentially allowing ignorance to overrule knowledge. A public opinion poll or a popular vote on an issue involving carpentry would be as irrelevant as the views prevalent in elite circles. The only saving grace is that the masses are much less likely than the elites to think that they should be overruling people whose stake and whose relevant knowledge for the issue at hand are far greater than their own. Moreover, the masses are less likely to have the rhetorical skills to conceal from others, or from themselves, that this is what they are doing.

The intellectuals' exaltation of "reason" often comes at the expense of experience, allowing them to have sweeping confidence about things in which they have little or no knowledge or experience. The idea that what they don't know isn't knowledge may also be a factor in many references to "earlier and simpler times" by people who have made no detailed study of those times, and who are unlikely even to suspect that it is their knowledge of the complexities of those times which is lacking, not the complexities themselves. Oliver Wendell Holmes pointed out that Roman law contained "a set of technicalities more difficult and less understood than our own."[26]

Central planners are not the only elites whose special knowledge has proved less effective in practice than the vastly greater amount of mundane knowledge in the population at large, nor is the economic marketplace the only place where the knowledge imbalance between the elites and the masses can be the opposite of the way this imbalance is perceived by the elites. If, as Oliver Wendell Holmes said, the life of the law has not been logic but experience,[27] then here too it is the millions— and especially the successive generations of millions— who have vastly more knowledge in the form of personal experience than do the relatively small circles of experts in the law. This is not to say that experts have no role to play, whether in the law or in other aspects of life. But the nature of that role is very different when both elite expertise and mass experience must be combined.

Within a sufficiently circumscribed area of decision-making, experts on that particular circumscribed area can have a vital role to play. The few with legal expertise can make court decisions applying the laws that developed out of the experiences of the many. But that is fundamentally different from creating or changing the law to suit the notions of judges or the notions in vogue among law school professors. Likewise, someone with the special talents and skills to collect information and convey it to the public through the media can be an indispensable part of the functioning of a democratic society, but that is wholly different from journalists taking on the role of filtering and slanting the news to buttress conclusions reflecting notions common within journalistic circles, as will be documented in Chapter 5.

The difference between the carrying out of circumscribed roles and using those roles to exert power or influence to try to shape wider social decisions also applies to those teachers who are classroom indoctrinators or those religious leaders promoting liberation theology, as well as generals who displace civilian government with military coups. What the various non-military ambitious elites are doing is creating smaller and more numerous coups, pre-empting social decisions that others have been authorized to make, in order to acquire power or influence in matters for which they have neither expertise nor, in many cases, even simple competence.

In short, whether one stays within a circumscribed role, based on one's expertise, or ventures beyond that role into areas beyond one's expertise, depends in part on whether one presumes oneself to have more knowledge than those whose decisions are being preempted. How knowledge is seen affects how society is seen, and how one's own role within that society is seen.

"One Day at a Time" Rationalism

Intellectuals' faith in "reason" sometimes takes the form of believing themselves capable of deciding each issue ad hoc as it arises. In principle, reason can be applied to as limited or as expansive a time period as one wishes— a day, a year, a generation, or a century, for example— by analyzing the implications of decisions over whatever span of time may be chosen. One-day-at-a-time rationalism risks restricting its analysis to the immediate implications of each issue as it arises, missing wider implications of a decision that may have merit as regards the issue immediately at hand, considered in isolation, but which can be disastrous in terms of the ignored longer-term repercussions. A classic example was a French intellectual's response to the Czechoslovakian crisis that led to the Munich conference of 1938:

> An eminent French political scientist, Joseph Barthélemy, who taught constitutional law at the University of Paris and was French representative at the League of Nations, asked in *Le Temps* the question French leaders had to answer: "Is it worthwhile setting fire to the world in order to save the Czechoslovak state, a heap of different nationalities? Is it necessary that three million Frenchmen, all the youth of our universities, of our schools, our countryside and our factories would be sacrificed to maintain three million Germans under Czech sovereignty?"[28]

Since it was not France that was threatening to set fire to the world, but Hitler, the larger question was whether someone who was threatening to set fire to the world if he didn't get his way was someone who should be appeased in this one-day-at-a-time approach, without regard to what this appeasement could do to encourage a never-ending series of escalating demands. By contrast, Winston Churchill had pointed out, six years earlier, that "every concession which has been made" to Germany "has been followed immediately by a fresh demand."[29] Churchill clearly rejected one-day-at-a-time rationalism.

By the time that Barthélemy addressed the Czechoslovakian crisis, Hitler had already taken the crucial step toward preparing for war by remilitarizing the Rhineland, in defiance of treaty commitments, had initiated military conscription when there was no military threat against Germany, and had seized Austria by force. As Winston Churchill said at the time, "Europe is confronted with a program of aggression, nicely calculated and timed, unfolding stage by stage." This raised the longer run question posed by Churchill: "How many friends would be alienated, how many potential allies should we see go, one by one, down the grisly gulf, how many times would bluff succeed, until behind bluff ever-gathering forces had accumulated reality?"[30]

In short, the handwriting was on the wall for anyone who wanted to read it, and presenting the immediate Czechoslovakian crisis in isolation was one way of not facing the implications of a series of actions over a longer span of time, leading toward a growing threat, as more and more resources came under the control of Nazi Germany, increasing its military potential. That threat would be even greater with the significant resources of Czechoslovakia under Hitler's control— as France would discover just two years later, when an invading German army battered them into quick submission, using among other things tanks manufactured in Czechoslovakia.

The one-day-at-a-time approach has been applied to numerous issues, foreign and domestic. At the heart of this approach is the implicit notion that intellectuals can define an issue in ways they find convenient— and that what happens in the real world will remain within the confines of their definition. But time is just one of the many things that can move beyond the boundaries of man-made definitions and conceptions. For example, however humane it may seem to have "forgiveness" of loans to Third World countries, at least in a one-day-at-a-time perspective, what happens today affects how people will behave tomorrow. In this case, Third World countries repeatedly borrow money that they repeatedly do not repay, either because of explicit "forgiveness" or because international aid agencies allow them to repeatedly borrow ever larger amounts, using the proceeds of later loans to pay off previous loans, but with no end in sight as far as ever paying off any loan with their own resources. Fiscal irresponsibility has seldom provided a way out of poverty, whether for individuals or for nations.

Hurricanes in Florida and wildfires in southern California are likewise recurrent phenomena over the years but each individual natural catastrophe is treated as an immediate and discrete crisis, bringing not only government rescue efforts but also vast amounts of the taxpayers' money to enable people who live in these places to rebuild in the known path of these dangers.* Any administration which might refuse to saddle taxpayers with the huge costs of subsidizing the rebuilding would no doubt be roundly condemned, not only by its political opponents but also by much of the media and the intelligentsia, looking at each particular hurricane or wildfire in a one-day-at-a-time perspective, rather than as part of an on-going sequence with a long history and a predictable future.

---

* An economist has estimated that the cost of rebuilding New Orleans was enough to instead give every New Orleans family of four $800,000, which they would be free to use to relocate to some safer place. But the idea of *not* rebuilding New Orleans has been seen as part of "the apparently heartless reaction of many urban economists to the devastation of New Orleans." Tim Harford, *The Logic of Life* (New York: Random House, 2008), p. 170.

Chapter 3

Intellectuals and Economics

Whether one is a conservative or a radical, a protectionist or a free trader, a cosmopolitan or a nationalist, a churchman or a heathen, it is useful to know the causes and consequences of economic phenomena.

George J. Stigler[1]

Most intellectuals outside the field of economics show remarkably little interest in learning even the basic fundamentals of economics. Yet they do not hesitate to make sweeping pronouncements about the economy in general, businesses in particular, and the many issues revolving around what is called "income distribution." Famed novelist John Steinbeck, for example, commented on the many American fortunes which have been donated to philanthropic causes by saying:

> One has only to remember some of the wolfish financiers who spent two thirds of their lives clawing a fortune out of the guts of society and the latter third pushing it back.[2]

Despite the verbal virtuosity involved in creating a vivid vision of profits as having been clawed out of the guts of society, neither Steinbeck nor most other intellectuals have bothered to demonstrate how society has been made poorer by the activities of Carnegie, Ford, or Rockefeller, for example— all three of whom (and many others) made fortunes by reducing the prices of their products below the prices of competing products. Lower prices made these products affordable to more people, simultaneously increasing those people's standard of living and creating fortunes for sellers who greatly expanded the numbers of their customers. In short, this was a process in which wealth was created, not a process by which some could get rich only by making others poorer.

Nevertheless, negative images of market processes have been evoked with such phrases as "robber barons" and "economic royalists"— without answering such obvious questions as "Just who did the robber barons rob when they lowered their prices?" or "How is earning money, often starting from modest circumstances (or even poverty-stricken circumstances in the case of J.C. Penney and F.W. Woolworth) the same as simply inheriting wealth and power like royalty?" The issue here is not the adequacy or inadequacy of intellectuals' answers to such questions because, in most cases, such questions are not even asked, much less answered. The vision, in effect, serves as a substitute for both facts and questions.

This is not to suggest that nobody in business ever did anything wrong. Saints have been no more common in corporate suites than in government offices or on ivy-covered campuses. However, the question here is not one of individual culpability for particular misdeeds. The question raised by critics of business and its defenders alike has been about the merits or demerits of alternative *institutional processes* for serving the economic interests of society at large. Implicit in many criticisms of market processes by intellectuals is the assumption that these are zero-sum processes, in which what is gained by some is lost by others. Seldom is this assumption spelled out but, without it, much of what is spelled out would have no basis.

Perhaps the biggest economic issue, or the one addressed most often, is that of what is called "income distribution," though the phrase itself is misleading, and the conclusions about income reached by most of the intelligentsia are still more misleading.

"INCOME DISTRIBUTION"

Variations in income can be viewed empirically, on the one hand, or in terms of moral judgments, on the other. Most of the contemporary intelligentsia do both. But, in order to assess the validity of the conclusions they reach, it is advisable to assess the empirical issues and the moral issues separately, rather than attempt to go back and forth between the two, with any expectation of rational coherence.

Empirical Evidence

Given the vast amounts of statistical data on income available from the Census Bureau, the Internal Revenue Service and innumerable research institutes and projects, one might imagine that the bare facts about variations in income would be fairly well known by informed people, even though they might have differing opinions as to the desirability of those particular variations. In reality, however, the most fundamental facts are in dispute, and variations in what are claimed to be facts seem to be at least as great as variations in incomes. Both the magnitude of income variations and the trends in these variations over time are seen in radically different terms by those with different visions as regards the current reality, even aside from what different people may regard as desirable for the future.

Perhaps the most fertile source of misunderstandings about incomes has been the widespread practice of confusing statistical categories with flesh-and-blood human beings. Many statements have been made in the media and in academia, claiming that the rich are gaining not only larger incomes but a growing share of all incomes, widening the income gap between people at the top and those at the bottom. Almost invariably these statements are based on confusing what has been happening over time in statistical categories with what has been happening over time with actual flesh-and-blood people.

A *New York Times* editorial, for example, declared that "the gap between rich and poor has widened in America."[3] Similar conclusions appeared in a 2007 *Newsweek* article which referred to this era as "a time when the gap is growing between the rich and the poor— and the superrich and the merely rich,"[4] a theme common in such other well-known media outlets as the *Washington Post* and innumerable television programs. "The rich have seen far greater income gains than have the poor," according to *Washington Post* columnist Eugene Robinson.[5] A writer in the *Los Angeles Times* likewise declared, "the gap between rich and poor is growing."[6] According to Professor Andrew Hacker in his book *Money*: "While all segments of the population enjoyed an increase in income, the top fifth did twenty-four times better than the bottom fifth. And measured by their shares of the aggregate, not just the bottom fifth but the three above it all ended up losing ground."[7]

Although such discussions have been phrased in terms of *people*, the actual empirical evidence cited has been about what has been happening over time to *statistical categories*— and that turns out to be the direct opposite of what has happened over time to flesh-and-blood human beings, most of whom *move* from one category to another over time. In terms of statistical categories, it is indeed true that both the amount of income and the proportion of all income received by those in the top 20 percent bracket have risen over the years, widening the gap between the top and bottom quintiles.[8] But U.S. Treasury Department data, following specific individuals over time from their tax returns to the Internal Revenue Service, show that in terms of *people*, the incomes of those particular taxpayers who were in the bottom 20 percent in income in 1996 rose 91 percent by 2005, while the incomes of those particular taxpayers who were in the top 20 percent in 1996 rose by only 10 percent by 2005— and those in the top 5 percent and top one percent actually declined.[9]

While it might seem as if both these radically different sets of statistics cannot be true at the same time, what makes them mutually compatible is that flesh-and-blood human beings *move* from one statistical category to another over time. When those taxpayers who were initially in the lowest income bracket had their incomes nearly double in a decade, that moved many of them up and out of the bottom quintile— and when those in the top one percent had their incomes cut by about one-fourth, that may well have dropped them out of the top one percent. Internal Revenue Service data can follow particular individuals over time from their tax returns, which have individual Social Security numbers as identification, while data from the Census Bureau and most other sources follow what happens to statistical categories over time, even though it is not the same individuals in the same categories over the years.

Many of the same kinds of data used to claim a widening income gap between "the rich" and "the poor"— names usually given to people with different incomes, rather than different wealth, as the terms rich and poor might seem to imply— have led many in the media to likewise claim a growing income gap between the "super-rich" and the "merely rich." Under the headline "Richest Are Leaving Even the Rich Far Behind," a front-page *New York Times* article dubbed the "top 0.1 percent of income earners— the top one-thousandth" as the "hyper-rich" and declared that they "have even left behind people making hundreds of thousands of dollars a year."[10] Once again, the confusion is between what is happening to statistical categories over time and what is happening to flesh-and-blood individuals over time, as they move from one statistical category to another.

Despite the rise in the income of the top 0.1 percent of taxpayers as a statistical category, both absolutely and relative to the incomes in other categories, as flesh-and-blood human beings those individuals who were in that category initially had their incomes actually *fall* by a whopping 50 percent between 1996 and 2005.[11] It is hardly surprising if people whose incomes are cut in half drop out of the top 0.1 percent. What happens to the income of the category over time is not the same as what happens to the people who were in that category at any given point in time. But many among the intelligentsia are ready to seize upon any numbers that seem to fit their vision.

Behind many of those numbers and the accompanying alarmist rhetoric is a very mundane fact: Most people begin their working careers at the bottom, earning entry-level salaries. Over time, as they acquire more skills and experience, their rising productivity leads to rising pay, putting them in successively higher income brackets. These are not rare, Horatio Alger stories. These are common patterns among millions of people in the United States and in some other countries. More than three-quarters of those working Americans whose incomes were in the bottom 20 percent in 1975 were also in the *top* 40 percent of income earners at some point by 1991. Only 5 percent of those who were initially in the bottom quintile were still there in 1991, while 29 percent of those who were initially at the bottom quintile had risen to the top quintile.[12] Yet verbal virtuosity has transformed a transient cohort in a given statistical category into an enduring class called "the poor."

Just as most Americans in statistical categories identified as "the poor" are not an enduring class there, studies in Britain, Canada, New Zealand and Greece show similar patterns of transience among those in low-income brackets at a given time.[13] Just over half of all Americans earning at or near the minimum wage are from 16 to 24 years of age[14]— and of course these individuals cannot *remain* from 16 to 24 years of age indefinitely, though that age category can of course continue indefinitely, providing many intellectuals with data to fit their preconceptions.

Only by focussing on the income brackets, instead of the actual people moving between those brackets, have the intelligentsia been able to verbally create a "problem" for which a "solution" is necessary. They have created a powerful vision of "classes" with "disparities" and "inequities" in income, caused by "barriers" created by "society." But the routine rise of millions of people out of the lowest quintile over time makes a mockery of the "barriers" assumed by many, if not most, of the intelligentsia.

Far from using their intellectual skills to clarify the distinction between statistical categories and flesh-and-blood human beings, the intelligentsia have instead used their verbal virtuosity to equate the changing numerical relationship between statistical categories over time with a changing relationship between flesh-and-blood human beings ("the rich" and "the poor") over time, even though data that follow individual income-earners over time tell a diametrically opposite story from that of data which follow the statistical categories which people are moving into and out of over time.

The confusion between statistical categories and flesh-and-blood human beings is compounded when there is confusion between income and wealth. People called "rich" or "super-rich" have been given these titles by the media on the basis of income, not wealth, even though being rich means having more wealth. According to the Treasury Department: "Among those with the very highest incomes in 1996— the top 1/100 of 1 percent— only 25 percent remained in this group in 2005."[15] If these were genuinely super-rich people, it is hard to explain why three-quarters of them are no longer in that category a decade later.

A related, but somewhat different, confusion between statistical categories and human beings has led to many claims in the media and in academia that Americans' incomes have stagnated or grown only very slowly over the years. For example, over the entire period from 1967 to 2005, median real household income— that is, money income adjusted for inflation— rose by 31 percent.[16] For selected periods within that long span, real household incomes rose even less, and those selected periods have often been cited by the intelligentsia to claim that income and living standards have "stagnated."[17] Meanwhile, real per capita income rose by 122 percent over that same span, from 1967 to 2005.[18] When a more than doubling of income is called "stagnation," that is one of the many feats of verbal virtuosity.

The reason for the large discrepancy between growth rate trends in household income and growth rate trends in individual income is very straightforward: The number of persons per household has been declining over the years. As of 1966, for example, the U.S. Bureau of the Census reported that the number of households was increasing faster than the number of people and concluded: "The main reason for the more rapid rate of household formation is the increased tendency, particularly among unrelated individuals, to maintain their own homes or apartments rather than live with relatives or move into existing households as roomers, lodgers, and so forth."[19] Increasing individual incomes made this possible.

Despite such obvious and mundane facts, household or family income statistics continue to be widely cited in the media and in academia— and per capita income statistics widely ignored, despite the fact that households are variable in size, while per capita income always refers to the income of one person. However, the statistics that the intelligentsia keep citing are much more consistent with their vision of America than the statistics they keep ignoring.

Just as household statistics understate the rise in the American standard of living over time, they *overstate* the degree of income inequality, since lower income households tend to have fewer people than upper income households. While there are 39 million people in households whose incomes are in the bottom 20 percent, there are 64 million people in households whose incomes are in the top 20 percent.[20] There is nothing mysterious about this either, given the number of low-income mothers living with fatherless children, and low-income lodgers in single room occupancy hotels or rooming houses, for example.

Even if every *person* in the entire country received exactly the same income, there would still be a significant "disparity" between the average incomes received by *households* containing 64 million people compared to the average income received by households containing 39 million people. That disparity would be even greater if only the incomes of working adults were counted, even if those working adults all had identical incomes. There are more adult heads of household working full-time and year-around in even the top *five* percent of households than in the bottom *twenty* percent of households.[21]

Many income statistics are misleading in another sense, when they leave out the income received in kind— such as food stamps and subsidized housing— which often exceeds the value of the cash income received by people in the lower-income brackets. In 2001, for example, transfers in cash or in kind accounted for more than three-quarters of the total economic resources at the disposal of people in the bottom 20 percent.[22]

Moral Considerations

The difference between statistical categories and actual people affects moral, as well as empirical, issues. However concerned we might be about the economic fate of flesh-and-blood human beings, that is very different from being alarmed or outraged about the fate of statistical categories. Michael Harrington's best-selling book *The Other America*, for example, dramatized income statistics, lamenting "the anguish" of the poor in America, tens of millions "maimed in body and spirit" constituting "the shame of the other America," people "caught in a vicious circle" and suffering a "warping of the will and spirit that is a consequence of being poor."[23] But investing statistical data with moral angst does nothing to establish a connection between a transient cohort in statistical categories and an enduring class conjured up through verbal virtuosity.

There was a time when such rhetoric might have made some sense in the United States, and there are other countries where it may still make sense today. But most of those Americans now living below the official poverty line have possessions once considered part of a middle class standard of living, just a generation or so ago. As of 2001, three-quarters of Americans with incomes below the official poverty level had air-conditioning (which only one-third of Americans had in 1971), 97 percent had color television (which fewer than half of Americans had in 1971), 73 percent owned a microwave oven (which fewer than one percent of Americans had in 1971) and 98 percent of "the poor" had either a videocassette recorder or a DVD player (which no one had in 1971). In addition, 72 percent of "the poor" owned a motor vehicle.[24] None of this has done much to change the rhetoric of the intelligentsia, however much it may reflect changes in the standard of living of Americans in the lower income brackets.

Typical of the mindset of many intellectuals was a book by Andrew Hacker which referred to the trillions of dollars that become "the personal income of Americans" each year, and said: "Just how this money is apportioned will be the subject of this book."[25] But this money is not *apportioned* at all. It becomes income through an entirely different process.

The very phrase "income distribution" is tendentious. It starts the economic story in the middle, with a body of income or wealth existing *somehow*, leaving only the question as to how that income or wealth is to be distributed or "apportioned" as Professor Hacker puts it. In the real world, the situation is quite different. In a market economy, most people receive income as a result of what they produce, supplying other people with some goods or services that those people want, even if that service is only labor. Each recipient of these goods and services pays according to the value which that particular recipient puts on what is received, choosing among alternative suppliers to find the best combination of price and quality— both as judged by the individual who is paying.

This mundane, utilitarian process is quite different from the vision of "income distribution" projected by those among the intelligentsia who invest that vision with moral angst. If there really were some pre-existing body of income or wealth, produced *somehow*— manna from heaven, as it were— then there would of course be a moral question as to how large a share each member of society should receive. But wealth is *produced*. It does not just exist *somehow*. Where millions of individuals are paid according to how much what they produce is valued subjectively by millions of other individuals, it is not at all clear on what basis third parties could say that some goods or services are over-valued or under-valued, that cooking should be valued more or carpentry should be valued less, for example, much less that not working at all is not rewarded enough compared to working.

Nor is there anything mysterious in the fact that at least a thousand times as many people would pay to hear Pavarotti sing as would pay to hear the average person sing.

Where people are paid for what they produce, one person's output can easily be worth a thousand times as much as another person's output to those who are the recipients of that output— if only because thousands more people are interested in receiving some products or services than are interested in receiving other products and services— or even the same product or service from someone else. For example, when Tiger Woods left the golf tournament circuit for several months because of an injury, television audiences for the final round of major tournaments declined by varying amounts, ranging up to 61 percent.[26] That can translate into millions of dollars' worth of advertising revenue, based on the number of television viewers.

The fact that one person's productivity may be a thousand times as valuable as another's does not mean that one person's *merit* is a thousand times as great as another's. Productivity and merit are very different things. An individual's productivity is affected by innumerable factors besides the efforts of that individual— being born with a great voice being an obvious example. Being raised in a particular home with a particular set of values and behavior patterns, living in a particular geographic or social environment, merely being born with a normal brain, rather than a brain damaged during the birth process, can make enormous differences in what a given person is capable of producing.

Moreover, third parties are in no position to second-guess the felt value of someone's productivity to someone else, and it is hard even to conceive how someone's merit could be judged accurately by another human being who "never walked in his shoes." An individual raised in terrible home conditions or terrible social conditions may be laudable for having become an average, decent citizen with average work skills as a shoe repairer, while someone raised from birth with every advantage that money and social position can confer may be no more laudable for becoming an eminent brain surgeon. But that is wholly different from saying that repairing shoes is just as valuable to others as being able to repair maladies of the brain.

To say that merit may be the same is not to say that productivity is the same. Nor can we logically or morally ignore the discrepancy in the relative urgency of those who want their shoes repaired versus those in need of brain surgery. In other words, it is not a question of simply weighing the interest of one income recipient versus the interest of another income recipient, while ignoring the vastly larger number of other people whose well-being depends on what these individuals produce.

If one prefers an economy in which income is divorced from productivity, then the case for that kind of economy needs to be made explicitly. But that is wholly different from making such a large and fundamental change on the basis of verbal virtuosity in depicting the issue as being simply that of one set of "income distribution" statistics today versus an alternative set of "income distribution" statistics tomorrow.

As for the moral question, whether any given set of human beings can be held responsible for disparities in other people's productivity— and consequent earnings— depends on how much control any given set of human beings has maintained, or can possibly maintain, over the innumerable factors which have led to existing differences in productivity. Since *no* human being has control over the past, and many deeply ingrained cultural differences are a legacy of the past, limitations on what can be done in the present are limitations on what can be regarded as moral failings by society. Still less can statistical differences between groups be automatically attributed to "barriers" created by society. Barriers exist in the real world, just as cancer exists. But acknowledging that does not mean that all deaths— or even most deaths— can be automatically attributed to cancer or that most economic differences can be automatically attributed to "barriers."

Within the constraints of circumstances, there are things which can be done to make opportunities more widely available, or to help those whose handicaps are too severe to expect them to utilize whatever opportunities are already available. In fact, much has already been done and is still being done in a country like the United States, which leads the world in philanthropy, not only in terms of money but also in terms of individuals donating their time to philanthropic endeavors. But only by assuming that everything that has not been done could have been done, disregarding costs and risks, can individuals or societies be blamed because the real world does not match some vision of an ideal society. Nor can the discrepancy between the real and the vision of the ideal be automatically blamed on the existing reality, as if visionaries cannot possibly be mistaken.

The Poor as Consumers

Although most people in the lower income brackets as of a given time do not remain there permanently, some people do. Moreover, particular neighborhoods may remain the homes of poor people for generations, no matter how many people from those neighborhoods move out to a better life as they move up from one income bracket to another. Complete racial turnovers in neighborhoods— Harlem having once been a middle-class Jewish community[27]— are just one sign of such economic mobility.

Low-income neighborhoods tend to have their own economic characteristics, one of the most salient of which is that prices tend to be higher there than in other neighborhoods. Intellectuals' discussions of the fact that "the poor pay more" are often indignant indictments and condemnations of those who charge higher prices to people who can least afford to pay them. The *causes* of those high prices are implicitly assumed to originate with those who charge them, and in particular to be due to malign dispositions such as "greed," "racism" and the like. Seldom is the possibility even mentioned, much less investigated, that whoever or whatever *conveys* high prices may not be the same as whoever or whatever *causes* those prices to be higher than in other neighborhoods. Confusing conveyance with causation is at the heart of many intellectuals' discussions of "social problems." In many very different contexts, prices often convey an underlying reality without being the cause of that reality.

Among the underlying realities in many low-income neighborhoods are higher rates of crime, vandalism, and violence, as well as a lack of the economic prerequisites for the economies of scale which enable big chain stores to charge lower prices and make profits on higher rates of inventory turnover in more affluent neighborhoods. But such mundane considerations do not present intellectuals with either an opportunity to display their special kind of knowledge or an opportunity to display their presumptions of superior virtue by condemning others. If stores in low-income neighborhoods were in fact making higher rates of profit on their investments, it would be hard to explain why national store chains and many other businesses avoid locating in such places, which are often painfully lacking in many businesses that are common in more affluent neighborhoods.

The underlying costs of providing financial services to people in low-income neighborhoods are likewise ignored by much, if not most, of the intelligentsia. Instead, the high rates of interest charged on personal loans to the poor are enough to set off orgies of denunciation and demands for government intervention to put an end to "exploitative" and "unconscionable" interest rates. Here verbal virtuosity is often used by stating interest rates in *annual* percentage terms, when in fact loans made in low-income neighborhoods are often made for a matter of weeks, or even days, to meet some exigency of the moment. The sums of money lent are usually a few hundred dollars, lent for a few weeks, with interest charges of about $15 per $100 lent. That works out to annual interest rates in the hundreds— the kind of statistics that produce sensations in the media and in politics.

The costs behind such charges are seldom, if ever, investigated by the intelligentsia, by so-called "consumer advocates" or by others in the business of creating sensations and denouncing businesses that they know little or nothing about. The economic consequences of government intervention to limit the annual interest rate can be seen in a number of states where such limits have been imposed. After Oregon imposed a limit of 36 percent annual interest, three-quarters of its "payday loan" businesses closed down.[28] Nor is it hard to see why— if one bothers to look at facts. At a 36 percent limit on the annual interest rate, the $15 in interest charged for every $100 lent would be reduced to less than $1.50 for a loan payable in two weeks— an amount not likely to cover even the cost of processing the loan, much less the risks of making the loan.*

As for the low-income borrower, supposedly the reason for the concern of the moral elites, denying the borrower the $100 needed to meet some exigency must be weighed against the $15 paid to meet that exigency. Why that trade-off decision should be forcibly removed by law from the person most knowledgeable about the situation, as well as most affected by it, and transferred to third-parties far removed in specific knowledge and general circumstances, is a question that is seldom answered or even asked. With intellectuals who consider themselves knowledgeable, as well as compassionate, it would seldom occur to them to regard themselves as interfering with things of which they are very ignorant— and doing so at costs imposed on people far less fortunate than themselves.

A *New York Times* editorial, for example, denounced the payday loan providers' "triple-digit annual interest rates, milking people's desperation" and "profiteering with the cloak of capitalist virtue." It described a 36 percent interest rate ceiling as something needed to prevent "the egregious exploitation of payday loans."[29] How much good it may have done the *New York Times* to say such things tells us nothing about whether it did any good for the poor to have one of their already limited options taken off the table.

ECONOMIC SYSTEMS

The most fundamental fact of economics, without which there would be no economics, is that what everybody wants always adds up to more than there is. If this were not true, then we would be living in a Garden of Eden, where everything is available in unlimited abundance, instead of in an economy with limited resources and unlimited desires. Because of this

---

* One of the problems is that what is called "interest" includes processing costs— and these processing costs tend to be a higher percentage of the total costs for smaller loans. In other words, the processing cost is not likely to vary much between a one hundred dollar loan and a thousand dollar loan.

inherent scarcity— regardless of whether a particular economic system is one of capitalism, socialism, feudalism, or whatever— an economy not only organizes production and the distribution of the resulting output, it must by its very nature also have ways to *prevent* people from completely satisfying their desires. That is, it must *convey* the inherent scarcity, without which there would be no real point to economics, even though the particular economy does not *cause* that scarcity.

In a market economy, prices convey the inherent scarcity through competing bids for resources and outputs that are inherently inadequate to supply all the bidders with all that they want. This may seem like a small and obvious point, but even such renowned intellectuals as the philosopher John Dewey have grossly misconceived it, blaming the particular economic system that *conveys* scarcity for *causing* the scarcity itself. Dewey saw the existing market economy as one "maintaining artificial scarcity" for the sake of "personal profit."[30] George Bernard Shaw likewise saw "restricting output" as the principle on which capitalism was founded.[31] Bertrand Russell depicted a market economy as one in which "wealthy highwaymen are allowed to levy toll upon the world for the use of indispensable minerals."[32]

According to Dewey, to make "potential abundance an actuality" what was needed was to "modify institutions."[33] But he apparently found it unnecessary to specify any alternative set of economic institutions in the real world which had in fact produced greater abundance than the institutions he blamed for "maintaining artificial scarcity." As in many other cases, the utter absence of factual evidence or even a single step of logic often passes unnoticed among the intelligentsia, when someone is voicing a view common among their peers and consistent with their general vision of the world.

Similarly, a twenty-first century historian said in passing, as something too obvious to require elaboration, that "capitalism created masses of laborers who were poverty stricken."[34] There were certainly many such laborers in the early years of capitalism, but neither this historian nor most other intellectuals have bothered to show that capitalism *created* this poverty. If in fact those laborers were more prosperous before capitalism, then not only would such a fact need to be demonstrated, what would also need to be explained is why laborers gave up this earlier and presumably higher standard of living to go work for capitalists for less. Seldom is either of these tasks undertaken by intellectuals who make such assertions— and seldom do their fellow intellectuals challenge them to do so, when they are saying things that fit the prevailing vision.

Chaos versus Competition

Among the other unsubstantiated notions about economics common among the intelligentsia are that there would be chaos in the economy without government planning or control. The order created by a deliberately controlled process may be far easier to conceive or understand than an order emerging from an uncontrolled set of innumerable interactions. But that does not mean that the former is necessarily more common, more consequential or more desirable in its consequences.

Neither chaos nor randomness is implicit in uncontrolled circumstances. In a virgin forest, the flora and fauna are not distributed randomly or chaotically. Vegetation growing on a mountainside differs systematically at different heights. Certain trees grow more abundantly at lower elevations and other kinds of trees at higher elevations. Above some altitude no trees at all grow and, at the summit of Everest, no vegetation at all grows. Obviously, none of this is a result of any decisions made by the vegetation but depends on variations in surrounding circumstances, such as temperature and soil. It is a *systemically* determined outcome with a pattern, not chaos.

Animal life also varies with environmental differences and, while animals like humans (and unlike vegetation) have thought and volition, that thought and volition are not always the decisive factors in the outcomes. That fish live in the water and birds in the air, rather than vice versa, is not strictly a matter of their choices, though each has choices of behavior within their respective environments. Moreover, what kinds of choices of behavior will survive the competition that weeds out some kinds of responses to the environment and lets others continue is likewise not wholly a matter of volition. In short, between individual volition and general outcomes are systemic factors which limit or determine what will survive, creating a pattern, rather than chaos.

None of this is difficult to understand in the natural environment. But the difference between individual, volitional causation and constraining systemic causation is one seldom considered by intellectuals when discussing economies, unless they happen to be economists. Yet that distinction has been commonplace among economists for more than two centuries. Nor has this been simply a matter of opinion or ideology. Systemic analysis was as common in Karl Marx as in Adam Smith, and it existed in the eighteenth century school of French economists called the Physiocrats before either Marx or Smith wrote about economics.

Even the analogy between systemic order in nature and in an economy was suggested by the title of one of the Physiocratic writings of the eighteenth century, *L'Ordre Naturel* by Mercier de la Rivière. It was the Physiocrats who coined the phrase *laissez-faire*, later associated with Adam Smith, based on their conviction that an uncontrolled economy was not one of chaos but of order, emerging from systemic interactions among the people competing with, and accommodating to, one another.

Karl Marx, of course, had a less benign view of the pattern of outcomes of market competition than did the Physiocrats or Adam Smith, but what is crucial here is that he too analyzed the market economy in terms of its systemic interactions, rather than its volitional choices, even when these were the choices of its economic elites, such as capitalists. Marx said that "competition" creates economic results that are "wholly independent of the will of the capitalist."[35] Thus, for example, while a new technology with lower production costs *enables* the capitalist to lower his prices, the spread of that technology to competing capitalists *compels* him to lower his prices, according to Marx.[36]

Likewise in his analysis of downturns in the economy— depressions or economic "crises" in Marxian phraseology— Marx made a sharp distinction between systemic causation versus volitional causation:

> A man who has produced has not the choice whether he will sell or not. He *must* sell. And in crises appears precisely the circumstance that he cannot sell, or only below the price of production, or even that he must sell at a positive loss. What does it avail him or us, therefore, that he has produced in order to sell? What concerns us is precisely to discover what has cut across this good intention of his.[37]

Neither in his theory of economics nor in his theory of history did Marx make end results simply the carrying out of individual volition, even the volition of elites. As his collaborator Friedrich Engels put it, "what each individual wills is obstructed by everyone else, and what emerges is something that no one willed."[38] Economics is about the pattern that emerges. Historian Charles A. Beard could seek to explain the Constitution of the United States by the economic interests of those who wrote it but that volitional approach was not the approach used by Marx and Engels, despite how often Beard's theory of history has been confused with the Marxian theory of history. Marx dismissed a similar theory in his own day as "facile anecdote-mongering and the attribution of all great events to petty and mean causes."[39]

The question here is not whether most intellectuals agree with systemic analysis, either in economics or elsewhere. Many have never even considered, much less confronted, that kind of analysis. Those who reason in terms of volitional causation see chaos from conflicting individual decisions as the alternative to central control of economic processes. John Dewey said, "comprehensive plans" are required "if the problem of social organization is to be met."[40] Otherwise, there will be "a continuation of a regime of accident, waste and distress."[41] To Dewey, "dependence upon intelligence" is an alternative to "drift and casual improvisation"[42]— that is, chaos— and those who are "hostile to intentional social planning" are in favor of "atomistic individualism."[43]

Here, as in other cases, verbal virtuosity transforms the arguments of people with opposing views into mere emotions. In this case the emotion is *hostility* to social planning. That hostility is presumably due to the leftover notions of a by-gone era that society can depend on "the unplanned coincidence of the consequences of a vast multitude of efforts put forth by isolated individuals without reference to any social end,"[44] according to Dewey's characterization of those with whom he disagreed. By the time John Dewey said all this—1935— it was more than a century and a half since the French Physiocrats first wrote their books explaining how competitive markets systemically coordinate economic activities and allocate resources through supply and demand adjustments to price movements.

Whether or not one agrees with the Physiocrats' explanations, or the similar and more sophisticated explanations of later economists, these are the arguments that would have to be answered if such arguments were not so widely evaded by reducing them to emotions or by using other arguments without arguments. Professor Ronald Dworkin of Oxford, for example, simply dismissed arguments for systemic causation in general, whether in the economy or elsewhere, as "the silly faith that ethics as well as economics moves by an invisible hand, so that individual rights and the general good will coalesce, and law based on principle will move the nation to a frictionless utopia where everyone is better off than he was before."[45]

Here again, verbal virtuosity *transforms* an opposing argument, rather than answering it with either logic or evidence. Moreover, as of the time when Professor Dworkin made this claim, there were numerous examples of countries whose economies were primarily market economies and others whose economies clearly were not, so that empirical comparisons were readily available, including comparisons of countries composed of the same peoples— East Germany versus West Germany or North Korea versus South Korea, for example. But verbal virtuosity made both analytical and empirical arguments unnecessary.

Economic competition is what forces innumerable disparate individual decisions to be reconciled with one another, as transactions terms are forced to change in response to changes in supply and demand, which in turn change economic activities. This is not a matter of "faith" (as Dworkin would have it) or of ideology (as Dewey would have it), but of economic literacy. John Dewey could depict businesses as controlling markets but that position is not inherent in being ideologically on the left. Karl Marx was certainly on the left, but the difference was that he had studied economics, as deeply as anyone of his time.

Just as Karl Marx did not attribute what he saw as the detrimental effects of a market economy to individual capitalists, so Adam Smith did not attribute what he saw as the beneficial effects of a market economy to individual capitalists. Smith's depictions of businessmen were at least as negative as those of Marx,[46] even though Smith is rightly regarded as the patron saint of free market economics. According to Smith, the beneficial social effects of the businessman's endeavors are "no part of his intention."[47] Both in Adam Smith's day and today, more than two centuries later, arguments for a free market economy are based on the systemic effects of such economies in allocating scarce resources which have alternative uses through competition in the marketplace. Whether one agrees or disagrees with the conclusions, this is the argument that must be confronted— or evaded.

Contrary to Dewey and many others, systemic arguments are independent of any notions of "atomistic individualism." These are *not* arguments that each individual's well-being adds up to the well-being of society. Such an argument would ignore the systemic interactions which are at the heart of economic analysis, whether by Adam Smith, Karl Marx or other economists. These economic arguments need not be elaborated here, since they are spelled out at length in economics textbooks.[48] What is relevant here is that those intellectuals who see chaos as the alternative to government planning or control have seldom bothered to confront those arguments and have instead misconceived the issue and distorted the arguments of those with different views.

Despite the often expressed dichotomy between chaos and planning, what is called "planning" is the forcible *suppression* of millions of people's plans by a government-imposed plan. What is considered to be chaos are systemic interactions whose nature, logic and consequences are seldom examined by those who simply assume that "planning" by surrogate decision-makers must be better. Herbert Croly, the first editor of the *New Republic* and a major figure in the Progressive era, characterized Thomas Jefferson's conception of limited government as "the old fatal policy of drift," as contrasted with Alexander Hamilton's policy of "energetic and intelligent assertion of the national good." According to Croly, what was needed was "an energetic and clear-sighted central government."[49] In this conception, progress depends on surrogate decision-makers, rather than on millions of others making their own decisions and exerting their own efforts.

Despite the notion that scarcity is contrived for the sake of profit in a market economy, that scarcity is at the heart of *any* economy— capitalist, socialist, feudal or whatever. Given that this scarcity is inherent in the system as a whole— any system— that scarcity must be conveyed to each individual in some way. In other words, it makes no sense for any economy to produce as much as physically possible of any given product, because that would have to be done with scarce resources which could be used to produce other products, whose supply is also inherently limited to less than what people want.

Markets in capitalist economies reconcile these competing demands for the same resources through price movements in both the markets for consumer goods and the market for the resources which go into producing those consumer goods. These prices make it unprofitable for one producer to use a resource beyond the point where that resource has a greater value to some competing producer who is bidding for that same resource.

For the individual manufacturer, the point at which it would no longer be profitable to use more of some factor of production— land, labor, machinery, etc.— is indeed the point which provides the limit of that manufacturer's output, even when it would be physically possible to produce more. But, while profitability and unprofitability *convey* that limit, they are not what *cause* that limit— which is due to the scarcity of resources inherent in any economic system, whether or not it is a profit-based system. Producing more of a given output in disregard of those limits does not make an economy more prosperous. On the contrary, it means producing an excess of one output at the cost of a shortage of another output that could have been produced with the same resources. This was a painfully common situation in the government-run economy of the Soviet Union, where unsold goods often piled up in warehouses while dire shortages had people waiting in long lines for other goods.[50]

Ironically, Marx and Engels had foreseen the economic consequences of fiat prices created by government, rather than by supply and demand, long before the founding of the Soviet Union, even though the Soviets claimed to be following Marxian principles. When publishing a later edition of Marx's 1847 book, *The Poverty of Philosophy*, in which Marx rejected fiat pricing, Engels spelled out the problem in his editor's introduction. He pointed out that price fluctuations have "forcibly brought home to the individual commodity producers what things and what quantity of them society requires or does not require." Without such a mechanism, he demanded to know "what guarantee we have that necessary quantity and not more of each product will be produced, that we shall not go hungry in regard to corn and meat while we are choked in beet sugar and drowned in potato spirit, that we shall not lack trousers to cover our nakedness while trouser buttons flood us in millions."[51] On this point, the difference between Marx and Engels, on the one hand, and most other intellectuals of the left on the other, was simply that Marx and Engels had studied economics and the others usually had not.

A volitional view of economics enables the intelligentsia, like politicians and others, to dramatize economics, explaining high prices by "greed" and low wages by a lack of "compassion," for example. While this is part of an ideological vision, an ideology of the left is not sufficient by itself to explain this approach. "I paint the capitalist and the landlord in no sense *couleur de rose*," Karl Marx said in the introduction to the first volume of *Capital*. "My stand-point," he added, however, "can less than any other make the individual responsible for relations whose creature he socially remains, however much he may subjectively raise himself above them."[52] In short, prices and wages were not determined volitionally but systemically.

Understanding that was not a question of being on the left or not, but of being economically literate or illiterate. The underlying notion of volitional pricing has, in our own times, led to at least a dozen federal investigations of American oil companies over the years, in response to either gasoline shortages or increases in gasoline prices— with none of these investigations turning up facts to support the sinister explanations abounding in the media and in politics when these investigations were launched. Many people find it hard to believe that negative economic events are not a result of villainy, even though they accept positive economic events— the declining prices of computers that are far better than earlier computers, for example— as being just a result of "progress" that happens *somehow*.

In a market economy, prices convey an underlying reality about supply and demand— and about production costs behind supply, as well as innumerable individual preferences and trade-offs behind demand. By regarding prices as merely arbitrary social constructs, some can imagine that existing prices can be replaced by prices controlled by government, reflecting wiser and nobler notions, such as "affordable housing" or "reasonable" health care costs. A history of price controls going back for centuries, in countries around the world, shows negative and even disastrous consequences from treating prices as mere arbitrary constructs, rather than as symptoms and conveyances of an underlying reality that is not nearly as susceptible to control as the prices are.*

As far as many, if not most, intellectuals are concerned, history *would* show that but does not, because they often see no need to consult history or any other validation process beyond the peer consensus of other similarly disposed intellectuals when discussing economic issues.

The crucial distinction between market transactions and collective decision-making is that in the market people are rewarded according to the value of their goods and services to those particular individuals who receive those goods and services, and who have every incentive to seek alternative sources, so as to minimize their costs, just as sellers of goods and services have every incentive to seek the highest bids for what they have to offer. But collective decision-making by third parties allows those third parties to superimpose their preferences on others at no cost to themselves, and to become the arbiters of other people's economic fate without accountability for the consequences.

Government Intervention

Among the consequences of the economic illiteracy of most intellectuals is the zero-sum vision of the economy mentioned earlier, in which the gains of one individual or one group represent a corresponding loss to another individual or another group. According to Harold Laski, "the interests of capital and labor are irreconcilable in fundamentals— there's a sum to divide and each wants more than the other will give."[53] This assumption is seldom spelled out this plainly, perhaps not even in the minds of most of those whose conclusions require such an implicit zero-sum assumption as a

---

* See, for example, Chapter 3 of my *Basic Economics*, third edition (New York: Basic Books, 2007).

foundation. But the widespread notion, coalescing into a doctrine, that one must "take sides" in making public policy or even in rendering judicial decisions, ignores the fact that economic transactions would not continue to take place unless *both* sides find these transactions preferable to not making such transactions.

Each side would of course prefer to have the terms favor themselves more but both sides must be willing to accept some mutually agreeable terms or no such transaction will take place at all, much less continue. Far from being an "irreconcilable" situation, as Laski claimed, it is a situation reconciled millions of times each day. Otherwise, the economy could not function. Indeed, a whole society could not function without vast numbers of both economic and non-economic decisions to cooperate, despite the fact that no two sets of interests, even among members of the same family, are exactly the same.

Contrary to Laski and many others with similar views, there is no given "sum to divide," as there would be with manna from heaven. It is precisely the cooperation of capital and labor which *creates* a wealth that would not exist otherwise, and that both sides would forfeit if they did not reconcile their conflicting desires at the outset, in order to produce it. It is literally preposterous (putting in front what comes behind) to begin the analysis with "a sum to divide"— that is, wealth— when that wealth can be created only *after* capital and labor have reconciled their competing claims and agreed to terms on which they can operate together in the production of wealth. The habit of many intellectuals to largely ignore the prerequisites, incentives and constraints involved in the production of wealth has many ramifications that can lead to many fallacious conclusions, even if their verbal virtuosity conceals these fallacies from others and even from themselves.

Intervention by politicians, judges, or others, in order to impose terms more favorable to one side— minimum wage laws or rent control, for example— reduces the overlapping set of mutually agreeable terms and, almost invariably, reduces the number of mutually acceptable transactions, as the party disfavored by the intervention makes fewer transactions subsequently. Countries with generous minimum wage laws, for example, often have higher unemployment rates and longer periods of unemployment than other countries, as employers offer fewer jobs to inexperienced and low-skilled workers, who are typically the least valued and lowest paid— and who are most often priced out of a job by minimum wage laws.

It is not uncommon in European countries with generous minimum wage laws, as well as other worker benefits that employers are mandated to pay for, to have inexperienced younger workers with unemployment rates of 20 percent or more.[54] Employers are made slightly worse off by having to rearrange their businesses and perhaps pay for more machinery to replace the low-skilled workers whom it is no longer economic to hire. But those low-skilled, usually younger, workers may be made much worse off by not being able to get jobs as readily, losing both the wages they could make otherwise and sustaining the perhaps greater loss of not acquiring the work experience that would lead to better jobs and higher pay.

In short, "taking sides" often ends up making both sides worse off, even if in different ways and to different degrees. But the very idea of taking sides is based on treating economic transactions as if they were zero-sum events. This zero-sum vision of the world is also consistent with the disinterest of many intellectuals in what promotes or impedes the *creation* of wealth, on which the standard of living of a whole society depends, even though the creation of wealth has lifted "the poor" in the United States today to economic levels not reached by most of the American population in past eras or in many other countries even today.

Just as minimum wage laws tend to reduce employment transactions with those whose pay is most affected, increasing their unemployment, so rent control laws have been followed by housing shortages in Cairo, Melbourne, Hanoi, Paris, New York and numerous other places around the world. Here again, attempts to make transactions terms better for one party usually lead the other party to make fewer transactions. Builders especially react to rent control laws by building fewer apartment buildings and, in some places, building none at all for years on end.

Landlords may continue to rent existing apartments but often they cut back on ancillary services such as painting, repairs, heat and hot water— all of which cost money and all of which are less necessary to maintain at previous levels needed to attract and keep tenants, once there is a housing shortage. The net result is that apartment buildings that receive less maintenance deteriorate faster and wear out, without adequate numbers of replacements being built. In Cairo, for example, this process led to families having to double up in quarters designed for only one family. The ultimate irony is that such laws can also lead to *higher* rents on average— New York and San Francisco being classic examples— when luxury housing is exempt from rent control, causing resources to be diverted to building precisely that kind of housing.

The net result is that renters, landlords, and builders can all end up worse off than before, though in different ways and to different degrees. Landlords seldom end up living in crowded quarters or on the street, and builders can simply devote more of their time and resources to building other structures such as warehouses, shopping malls and office buildings, as well as luxury housing, all of which are usually not subject to rent control laws. But, again, the crucial point is that both sides can end up worse off as a result of laws and policies based on "taking sides," as if economic transactions were zero-sum processes.

One of the few writers who has explicitly proclaimed the zero-sum vision of the economy— Professor Lester C. Thurow of M.I.T., author of *The Zero-Sum Society*— has also stated that the United States has been "consistently the industrial economy with the worst record" on unemployment. He spelled it out:

> Lack of jobs has been endemic in peacetime during the past fifty years of American history. Review the evidence: a depression from 1929 to 1940, a war from 1941 to 1945, a recession in 1949, a war from 1950 to 1953, recessions in 1954, 1957-58, and 1960-61, a war from 1965 to 1973, a recession in 1969-70, a severe recession in 1974-75, and another recession probable in 1980. This is hardly an enviable economic performance.[55]

Several things are remarkable about Professor Thurow's statement. He reaches sweeping conclusions about the record of the United States *vis-à-vis* the record of other industrial nations, based solely on a recitation of events within the United States— *a one-nation international comparison* when it comes to facts, rather than rhetoric. Studies which in fact compare the unemployment rate in the United States versus Western European nations, for example, almost invariably show Western European nations with *higher* unemployment rates, and longer periods of unemployment, than the United States.[56] Moreover, the wars that Professor Thurow throws in, in what is supposed to be a discussion of unemployment, might leave the impression that wars contribute to unemployment, when in fact unemployment virtually disappeared in the United States during World War II and has been lower than usual during the other wars mentioned.[57]

Professor Thurow's prediction about a recession in 1980 turned out to be true, though that was hardly a daring prediction in the wake of the "stagflation" of the late 1970s. What turned out to be false was the idea that large-scale government intervention was required to head off more unemployment— that, in Thurow's words, the government needed to "restructure the economy so that it will, in fact, provide jobs for everyone."[58] What actually happened was that the Reagan administration took office in 1981 and did the exact opposite of what Lester Thurow advocated— and, after the recession passed, there were twenty years of economic growth, low unemployment and low inflation.[59]

Professor Thurow was not, and is not, some fringe kook. According to the material on the cover of the 2001 reprint of his 1980 book *The Zero-Sum Society*, "Lester Thurow has been professor of management and economics at MIT for more than thirty years." He is also the "author of several books, including three *New York Times* best sellers, he has served on the editorial board of the *New York Times*, as a contributing editor of *Newsweek*, and as a member of *Time* magazine's Board of Economics." He could not be more mainstream— or more wrong. But what he said apparently found resonance among the elite intelligentsia, who made him an influence on major media outlets.

Similar prescriptions for active government intervention in the economy have abounded among intellectuals, past and present. John Dewey, for example, used such attractive phrases as "socially organized intelligence in the conduct of public affairs,"[60] and "organized social reconstruction"[61] as euphemisms for the plain fact that third-party surrogate decision-makers seek to have their preferences imposed on millions of other people through the power of government. Although government is often called "society" by those who advocate this approach, there is no concrete institution called "society," and what is called "social" planning are in fact *government orders* over-riding the plans and mutual accommodations of millions of other people.

Despite whatever vision may be conjured up by euphemisms, government is not some abstract embodiment of public opinion or Rousseau's "general will." Government consists of politicians, bureaucrats, and judges— all of whom have their own incentives and constraints, and none of whom can be presumed to be any less interested in the promotion of their own interests or notions than are people who buy and sell in the marketplace. Neither sainthood nor infallibility is common in either venue. The fundamental difference between decision-makers in the market and decision-makers in government is that the former are subject to continuous and consequential feedback which can force them to adjust to what others prefer and are willing to pay for, while those who make decisions in the political arena face no such inescapable feedback to force them to adjust to the reality of other people's desires and preferences.

A business with red ink on the bottom line knows that this cannot continue indefinitely, and that they have no choice but to change whatever they are doing that produces that red ink, for which there is little tolerance even in the short run, and which will be fatal to the whole enterprise in the long run. In short, financial losses are not merely informational feedback but *consequential* feedback which cannot be ignored, dismissed or spun rhetorically through verbal virtuosity.

In the political arena, however, only the most immediate and most attention-getting disasters— so obvious and unmistakable to the voting public that there is no problem of "connecting the dots"— are comparably consequential for political decision-makers. But laws and policies whose consequences take time to unfold are by no means as consequential for those who created those laws and policies, especially if the consequences emerge after the next election. Moreover, there are few things in politics as unmistakable in its implications as red ink on the bottom line is in business. In politics, no matter how disastrous a policy may turn out to be, if the causes of the disaster are not understood by the voting public, those officials responsible for the disaster may escape any accountability, and of course they have every incentive to deny having made mistakes, since admitting mistakes can jeopardize a whole career.

Why the transfer of economic decisions from the individuals and organizations directly involved— often depicted collectively and impersonally as "the market"— to third parties who pay no price for being wrong should be expected to produce better results for society at large is a question seldom asked, much less answered. Partly this is because of rhetorical packaging by those with verbal virtuosity. To say, as John Dewey did, that there must be "social control of economic forces"[62] sounds good in a vague sort of way, until that is translated into specifics as the holders of political power forbidding voluntary transactions among the citizenry.

BUSINESS

The organizations, large and small, which produce and distribute most of the goods and services that make up a modern standard of living— businesses— have long been targets of the intelligentsia. Accusations against businesses have been as specific as charging excessively high prices and as nebulous as failing to live up to their social responsibilities.

Management

Intellectuals who have never run any business have been remarkably confident that they know when businesses have been run wrongly or when their owners or managers are overpaid. John Dewey, for example, declared, "Industrial entrepreneurs have reaped out of all proportion to what they sowed."[63] Evidence? None. This is one of many assertions that can pass unchallenged among the intelligentsia, its familiarity and its consonance with the prevailing vision being substitutes for evidence or analysis.

The ease of running a business has been a common belief going back at least as far as Edward Bellamy's *Looking Backward* in the nineteenth century.[64] Lenin said that running a business involved "extraordinarily simple operations" which "any literate person can perform," so that those in charge of such enterprises need not be paid more than any ordinary worker.[65] Just three years after taking power, however, and with his post-capitalist economy facing what Lenin himself later called "ruin, starvation and devastation,"[66] he reversed himself and declared to the 1920 Communist Party Congress: "Opinions on corporate management are all too frequently imbued with a spirit of sheer ignorance, an antiexpert spirit."[67] Lenin reversed himself in deeds as well as words, creating his New Economic Policy which allowed more leeway for markets to function, and the Soviet economy began to recover.

In short, the first time that the theory of how easy it is to run a business was put to a test, it failed that test disastrously. As the twentieth century unfolded, that theory would fail repeatedly in other countries around the world, to the point where even most communist and socialist governments began to free up markets by the end of the twentieth century, usually leading to higher economic growth rates, as in China and India.

When judging those who run businesses, the criteria applied, either implicitly or explicitly, by many intellectuals are often remote from any relevance to the operation of an economic enterprise. Theodore Roosevelt, for example, said: "It tires me to talk to rich men. You expect a man of millions, the head of a great industry, to be a man worth hearing; but as a rule they don't know anything outside their own businesses."[68]

That certainly could not be said of Theodore Roosevelt himself. In addition to his experience as a politician at municipal, state, national, and international levels, TR was not only a well-educated and widely read man but also a scholar in his own right, whose naval history of the war of 1812 was required reading at naval academies on both sides of the Atlantic for decades. The author of fifteen books,[69] he was for many years an intellectual in our sense, as someone who earned his living from his writings, especially during the years when his pay as a municipal or state official was inadequate to support his family, and during the years when his business ventures on the western frontier were losing money.

"Few, if any Americans could match the breadth of his intellect," according to a biographer of Theodore Roosevelt.[70] Certainly few, if any, business leaders were at all comparable to TR in intellectual scope or depth. *Nor was there any reason why they should be.* In many fields, it is often the specialist— sometimes the monomaniac— who is most likely to produce the peak achievements. No one expected Babe Ruth or Bobby Fischer to be a Renaissance Man, and anyone who might have would have been very badly disappointed. The judging of people in non-intellectual fields by intellectual criteria will almost inevitably find them unworthy of the rewards they receive— which would be a legitimate conclusion only if non-intellectual endeavors were automatically less worthy than intellectual endeavors. Few would argue explicitly for this premise but, as John Maynard Keynes pointed out, conclusions often continue on without the premises on which they were based.[71]

Another common misconception among the intelligentsia is that individual business entrepreneurs should— or could— be "socially responsible" by taking into account the wider consequences of the entrepreneur's business decisions. This idea goes back at least as far as Woodrow Wilson, another intellectual in our sense, because of his academic career before entering politics:

> We are not afraid of those who pursue legitimate pursuits, provided they link those pursuits in at every turn with the interest of the community as a whole; and no man can conduct a legitimate business if he conducts it in the interest of a single class.[72]

In other words, it is not considered sufficient if a manufacturer of plumbing fixtures produces high-quality faucets, pipes and bathtubs, and sells them at affordable prices, if this entrepreneur does not also take on the role of philosopher-king and try to decide how this business affects "the interest of the community," however that nebulous notion might be conceived. It is a staggering requirement which few, if any, people in business, academia, politics, or other occupations could meet. John Dewey likewise lamented that workers, like their employers, had "no social outlook upon the consequences and meaning of what they are doing."[73] Intellectuals may choose to imagine what are the wider social consequences of their own actions, inside or outside their fields of professional competence, but there is little or no consequential feedback when they are wrong, no matter how wrong or for how long. That both business owners and workers usually avoid taking on such a cosmic task suggests that they may have a more realistic assessment of human limitations.

Business "Power" or "Control"

One of the many signs of verbal virtuosity among intellectuals is the repackaging of words to mean things that are not only different from, but sometimes the direct opposite of, their original meanings. "Freedom" and "power" are among the most common of these repackaged words. The basic concept of freedom as not being subjected to other people's restrictions, and of power as the ability to restrict other people's options, have both been stood on their heads in some of the repackaging of these words by intellectuals discussing economic issues. Thus business enterprises which *expand* the public's options, either quantitatively (through lower prices) or qualitatively (through better products) are often spoken of as "controlling" the market, whenever this results in a high percentage of consumers choosing to purchase their particular products rather than the competing products of other enterprises.

In other words, when consumers decide that particular brands of products are either cheaper or better than competing brands of those products, third parties take it upon themselves to depict those who produced these particular brands as having exercised "power" or "control." If, at a given time, three-quarters of the consumers prefer to buy the Acme brand of widgets to any other brand, then Acme Inc. will be said to "control" three-quarters of the market, even though consumers control 100 percent of the market, since they can switch to another brand of widgets tomorrow if someone else comes up with a better widget, or stop buying widgets altogether if a new product comes along that makes widgets obsolete.

Any number of companies that have been said to "control" a majority of their market have not only lost that market share but have gone bankrupt within a few years of their supposed dominance of the market. Smith Corona, for example, sold over half the typewriters and word processors in the United States in 1989 but, just six years later, it filed for bankruptcy, as the spread of personal computers displaced both typewriters and word processors. Yet the verbal packaging of sales statistics *ex post* as market "control" *ex ante* has been common, not only in the writings of the intelligentsia but even in courts of law in anti-trust cases. Even at its peak, Smith Corona controlled nothing. Every consumer was free to buy any other brand of typewriter or word processor, or refrain from buying any.

The verbal packaging of consumer choice as business "control" has become so widespread that few people seem to feel a need to do anything so basic as thinking about the meaning of the words they are using, which transform an *ex post* statistic into an *ex ante* condition. By saying that businesses have "power" because they have "control" of their markets, this verbal virtuosity opens the way to saying that government needs to exercise its "countervailing power" (John Kenneth Galbraith's phrase) in order to protect the public. Despite the verbal parallels, government power is in fact power, since individuals do not have a free choice as to whether or not to obey government laws and regulations, while consumers are free to ignore the products marketed by even the biggest and supposedly most "powerful" corporations in the world. There are people who have never set foot in a Wal-Mart store and there is nothing that Wal-Mart can do about it, despite being the world's largest retailer.

One of John Kenneth Galbraith's earliest and most influential books, *American Capitalism: The Concept of Countervailing Power*, declared that "power on one side of a market creates both the need for, and the prospect of reward to, the exercise of countervailing power from the other side."[74] Thus, according to Professor Galbraith, the rise of big corporations gave them an oppressive power over their employees, which led to the creation of labor unions in self-defense.[75] As a matter of historical fact, however, it was not in large, mass-production industries that American labor unions began but in industries with numerous smaller businesses, such as construction, trucking and coal mining— all of which were unionized years before the steel or automobile industries.

But, whatever the genesis of union power, the crucial countervailing power for Galbraith was that of the government, both in support of private countervailing power with such legislation as the National Labor Relations

Act of 1935 and legislation to help coal producers and others supposedly oppressed by the "power" of big business.[76] Such government "countervailing power performs a valuable— indeed an indispensable— regulatory function in the modern economy,"[77] according to Galbraith. But this formulation depends crucially on redefining "power" to include its opposite— the expansion of consumer options by businesses, in order to increase sales.

John Kenneth Galbraith was perhaps the most prominent, and certainly one of the most verbally gifted, of the advocates of a theory of volitional pricing. According to Professor Galbraith, the output of a given industry tends to become more concentrated over time in the hands of a few producers, who acquire decisive advantages that make it difficult for a new company without the same amount of experience to enter the industry and compete effectively against the leading incumbents. Therefore, according to Galbraith, "sellers have gained authority over prices," which are "tacitly administered by a few large firms."[78] In reality, one of the most common reasons for buyers buying disproportionately from a particular seller is that this seller has a lower price. After Galbraith has redefined power as a concentration of sales and of resulting profits and size, he is able to depict that "power" of the seller as a reason why that seller can now set prices different from— and implicitly higher than— those of a competitive market.

In this formulation, "the size of the corporation which the individual heads is again a rough index of the power the individual exercises."[79] However plausible all this might seem, Galbraith did not venture very far in the direction of empirical verification. The *insinuation* of Galbraith's— and many others'— discussions of the "power" of big business is that the growth of ever larger businesses means the growth of their power to raise prices. This insinuation— as distinguished from either a demonstrated fact or even a testable hypothesis— was a staple among the intelligentsia long before Galbraith's time, and provided the impetus for the Sherman Anti-Trust Act of 1890, among other attempts to contain the "power" of big business.

In reality, the era leading up to the Sherman Act was not an era of rising prices imposed by monopolies, even though it was an era of growing sizes of businesses in many industries, often through consolidation of smaller businesses into giant corporations. Far from leading to higher prices, however, this was an era of *falling* prices charged by these larger businesses, whose size created economies of scale, which meant lower production costs that enabled them to profit from *lower* prices, thereby expanding their sales. Crude oil, which sold for $12 to $16 a barrel in 1860, sold for less than one dollar a barrel in every year from 1879 to 1900. Railroad freight costs fell by 1887 to 54 percent of what they had been in 1873. The price of steel rails fell from $68 in 1880 to $32 in 1890. The prices of sugar, lead, and zinc all fell during this period.[80]

Henry Ford pioneered in mass production methods and had some of the highest paid workers of his day— decades before the industry was unionized— and the lowest priced cars, notably the legendary Model T, which made the automobile no longer a luxury confined to the wealthy. But none of these plain facts prevailed against the vision of the Progressive era intelligentsia, who in this case included President Theodore Roosevelt. His administration launched anti-trust prosecutions against some of the biggest price-cutters, including Standard Oil and the Great Northern Railroad. Theodore Roosevelt sought the power, in his words, to "control and regulate all big combinations."[81] He declared that "of all forms of tyranny the least attractive and the most vulgar is the tyranny of mere wealth, the tyranny of a plutocracy."[82]

No doubt it was true, as TR said, that Standard Oil created "enormous fortunes" for its owners "at the expense of business rivals,"[83] but it is questionable whether consumers who paid lower prices for oil felt that they were victims of a tyranny. One of the popular muckraking books of the Progressive era was *The History of the Standard Oil Company* by Ida Tarbell, which said among other things that Rockefeller "should have been satisfied"[84] with what he had achieved financially by 1870, implying greed in his continued efforts to increase the size and profitability of Standard Oil.

A study done a century later, however, pointed out: "One might never know from reading *The History of Standard Oil* that oil prices were actually falling."[85] That fact had been filtered out of the story. The question whether Rockefeller's pursuit of a larger fortune actually made the consuming public worse off was seldom even addressed. How consumers would have been better off if a man who introduced extraordinary efficiencies into the production and distribution of oil had ended his career earlier, leaving both the cost of producing oil and the resulting prices higher, is a question not raised, much less answered.

One of the common complaints against Standard Oil was that it was able to get railroads to charge them less for shipping their oil than was charged to competing businesses shipping oil. Such an inequality was of course anathema to those who thought in terms of abstract people in an abstract world— ignoring what there was specifically about Standard Oil that was different, which was the very reason why John D. Rockefeller amassed a fortune in an industry in which many others went bankrupt. Standard Oil's tank cars were easier to transport than oil shipped in barrels by other companies.[86] Yet Theodore Roosevelt— who knew little or no economics and had lost a large portion of his inheritance in his one business venture— said that discount shipping rates were discriminatory and should be forbidden "in every shape and form."[87] Senator John Sherman, author of the Sherman Anti-Trust Act, also introduced legislation to ban differential shipping rates, apparently at the prompting of a refinery that shipped its oil in barrels.[88]

Businesses which charge lower prices often lead to losses by competing businesses which charge higher prices. But, obvious as this might seem, it has not stopped outcries over the years from the intelligentsia, legislation from politicians and adverse court decisions from judges, aimed not only at Standard Oil in the early twentieth century but also later at other businesses that reduced prices in other industries, ranging from the A&P grocery chain in the past to Microsoft today.

In short, the verbal transformation of lower prices and larger sales into an exercise of "power" by business that has to be counteracted by more government power has more than purely intellectual implications. It has led to many laws, policies and court decisions that punish lower prices in the name of protecting consumers.

As a result of the spread of globalization, even if a particular company is the only producer of a given product in a given country, that monopoly means little if foreign producers of the same product compete in supplying that product to the consumers. Eastman Kodak has long been the only major American producer of film but camera stores across the United States also sell film produced in Japan (Fuji) and sometimes in England (Ilford), and in other countries, quite aside from the competition from digital cameras, produced primarily overseas. In short, Kodak's ability to jack up film prices without suffering lost sales is hemmed in by substitutes. The fact that Eastman Kodak is a huge enterprise does not change any of that, except in the visions and rhetoric of the intelligentsia.

The straining of words to depict businesses as exercising "power" in situations where consumers simply buy more of their products, has been used to justify depriving people who run businesses of the rights exercised by other people. As we shall see in Chapter 6, this attitude can even extend to putting the burden of proof on businesses to rebut accusations in certain anti-trust cases and civil rights cases. A somewhat similar mindset was expressed in a question asked in *The Economist* magazine: "Why should companies be allowed to dodge taxes and sack workers by shifting operations overseas?"[89] In free countries, no one else's right to relocate for their own benefit is treated as something requiring some special justification. Indeed, workers who relocate to other countries in violation of immigration laws are often defended by those who consider it wrong for businesses to relocate legally.

RECESSIONS AND DEPRESSIONS

Nothing established the idea that government intervention in the economy is essential like the Great Depression of the 1930s. The raw facts tell the story of that historic tragedy: National output fell by one-third between 1929 and 1933, thousands of banks failed, unemployment peaked at 25 percent, corporations as a whole lost money two years in a row. Prior to this time, no president had attempted to have the federal government intervene to bring a depression to an end.

Many saw in the Great Depression the failure of free market capitalism as an economic system and a reason for seeking a radically different kind of economy— for some Communism, for some Fascism and for some the New Deal policies of Franklin D. Roosevelt's administration. Whatever the particular alternative favored by particular individuals, what was widely believed then and later was that the stock market crash of 1929 was a failure of the free market and the cause of the massive unemployment that persisted for years during the 1930s. Given the two most striking features of that era— the stock market crash and a widespread government intervention in the economy— it is not immediately obvious which was more responsible for the dire economic conditions. But remarkably little effort has been made by most of the intelligentsia to try to sort out the cause or causes. It has been largely a foregone conclusion that the market was the cause and government intervention was the saving grace.

While unemployment went up in the wake of the stock market crash, it never went as high as 10 percent for any month during the 12 months following that crash in October 1929. But the unemployment rate in the wake of subsequent government interventions in the economy never fell below 20 percent for any month over a period of 35 consecutive months.[90] In short, though the stock market crash has been conceived of as the "problem" and government intervention as the "solution," in reality the unemployment rate following the economic problem was less than half of the unemployment rate following the political solution.

One of the few things on which people across the ideological spectrum are agreed upon today is that the Federal Reserve System mishandled its job during the Great Depression. Looking back at that period, Milton Friedman called the people who ran the Federal Reserve "inept" and John Kenneth Galbraith said that Federal Reserve officials showed "startling incompetence."[91] For example, as the country's money supply declined by one-third in the wake of massive bank failures, the Federal Reserve raised the interest rate, creating further deflationary pressures.

In order to try to save American jobs by limiting imports that competed with American-made goods, Congress in 1930 passed the Smoot-Hawley tariffs, the highest in more than a century, despite a public appeal signed by more than a thousand economists and a warning from them as to the consequences. Other nations retaliated, as the economists had warned, drastically reducing American exports and the jobs dependent on those exports, so that the unemployment rate went up rather than down. In the wake of these tariffs, unemployment rose far more dramatically than in the wake of the stock market crash. The unemployment rate stood at 6.3 percent in June, 1930— eight months after the stock market crash— when the Smoot-Hawley tariffs were passed. A year later, the unemployment rate was 15 percent— and a year after that it was 25.8 percent.[92]

All of this unemployment need not be attributed to the tariffs but the point is that the tariffs were supposed to reduce unemployment. The unemployment rate was already trending generally *downward* for several months when the Smoot-Hawley bill was passed, a trend that reversed itself just five months after the new tariffs went into effect. Once the unemployment rate rose into double digits in November 1930, an unemployment rate as low as 6.3 percent was not seen again for the remainder of the decade.[93] The Smoot-Hawley tariffs under Herbert Hoover were simply one of the first massive government interventions of the 1930s, including many more under Franklin D. Roosevelt.* There is little empirical evidence to suggest that these interventions helped the economy and much evidence to suggest that they made matters worse.

Congress also passed laws more than doubling the tax rates on the upper income brackets under Hoover and raised them still higher under FDR. President Hoover urged business leaders not to reduce workers' wage rates during the depression, even though the greatly reduced money supply made the previous wage-rates unpayable with full employment. Both Hoover and his successor, President Franklin D. Roosevelt, sought to keep prices from falling, whether the price of labor or of farm produce, assuming that this would keep purchasing power from falling. However, purchasing power depends not only on what prices are charged but on how many transactions will actually be made at those prices. With a reduced money supply, neither the previous amount of employment of labor nor the previous sales of farm or industrial products could continue at the old prices.

---

* For details, see *FDR's Folly* by Jim Powell, which also mentions some of Hoover's folly.

Neither Hoover nor FDR seemed to understand this nor to have thought this far. However, columnist Walter Lippmann pointed out the obvious in 1934 when he said, "in a depression men cannot sell their goods or their service at pre-depression prices. If they insist on pre-depression prices for goods, they do not sell them. If they insist on pre-depression wages, they become unemployed."[94]

In short, many things that the Federal Reserve, Congress and the two Presidents did were counterproductive. Given these multiple failures of government policy, it is by no means clear that it was the market economy which failed. There is of course no way to re-run the stock market crash of 1929 and have the federal government let the market adjust on its own to see how that experiment would turn out. The closest thing to such an experiment was the 1987 stock market crash, similar in size but not in duration to the 1929 collapse. The Reagan administration did nothing, despite outrage in the media at the government's failure to act.

"What will it take to wake up the White House?" the *New York Times* asked, declaring that "the President abdicates leadership and courts disaster."[95] *Washington Post* columnist Mary McGrory said that Reagan "has been singularly indifferent" to the country's "current pain and confusion."[96] The *Financial Times* of London said that President Reagan "appears to lack the capacity to handle adversity" and "nobody seems to be in charge."[97] A former official of the Carter administration criticized President Reagan's "silence and inaction" following the 1987 stock market crash and compared him unfavorably to President Franklin D. Roosevelt, whose "personal style and bold commands would be a tonic" in the current crisis.[98]

The irony in this was that FDR presided over an economy with seven consecutive years of double-digit unemployment, while Reagan's policy of letting the market recover on its own, far from leading to another Great Depression, led instead to one of the country's longest periods of sustained economic growth, low unemployment and low inflation, lasting twenty years.[99]

Like many other facts at variance with the prevailing vision, this one received remarkably little attention at the time or since. While it might be possible to debate the wisdom or effectiveness of various government responses or non-responses to economic crises, there is remarkably little awareness of anything to debate by intellectuals outside the economics profession. Histories of the Great Depression by leading historians such as Arthur M. Schlesinger, Jr. and Henry Steele Commager have made FDR the hero who came to the rescue, though Schlesinger himself admitted that he— Schlesinger— "was not much interested in economics,"[100] despite his willingness to make historic assessments of how FDR's policies affected the economy. However, Professor Schlesinger was by no means unusual among intellectuals for reaching sweeping conclusions about economic issues without feeling any need to understand economics.

Chapter 4

Intellectuals and Social Visions

At the core of every moral code there is a picture of human nature, a map of the universe, and a version of history. To human nature (of the sort conceived), in a universe (of the kind imagined), after a history (so understood), the rules of the code apply.

Walter Lippmann[1]

Intellectuals do not simply have a series of isolated opinions on a variety of subjects. Behind those opinions is usually some coherent over-arching conception of the world, a social vision. Intellectuals are like other people in having visions— some intuitive sense of how the world works, what causes what. The vision around which most contemporary intellectuals tend to coalesce has features that distinguish it from other visions prevalent in other segments of contemporary society or among elites or masses in earlier times.

While visions differ, a vision of some kind or other underlies attempts to explain either physical or social phenomena, whether by intellectuals or by others. Some visions are more sweeping and dramatic than others, as well as differing in the particular assumptions on which they are based, but all kinds of thinking, whether formal or informal, must start somewhere with a hunch, a suspicion, or an intuition of some sort— in short, with a vision of causal connections. Systematically working out the implications of that vision can produce a theory, which in turn can be refined into specific hypotheses that can be tested against empirical evidence. But "the preconceived idea— supposedly 'unscientific'— must nearly always be there," as British historian Paul Johnson put it.[2] Economist J.A. Schumpeter defined a vision as a "preanalytic cognitive act."[3]

What then is the prevailing vision of the intelligentsia, including both the solid core of intellectuals and the surrounding penumbra of those who follow their lead? And what alternative vision opposes them?

A CONFLICT OF VISIONS

At the heart of the social vision prevalent among contemporary intellectuals is the belief that there are "problems" created by existing institutions and that "solutions" to these problems can be excogitated by intellectuals. This vision is both a vision of society and a vision of the role of intellectuals within society. In short, intellectuals have seen themselves not simply as an elite— in the passive sense in which large landowners, rentiers, or holders of various sinecures might qualify as elites— but as an *anointed* elite, people with a mission to lead others in one way or another to better lives.

John Stuart Mill, who epitomized the intellectual in many ways, expressed this view explicitly, when he said that the "present wretched education" and "wretched social arrangements" were "the only real hindrance" to attaining general happiness among human beings.[4] Moreover, Mill saw the intelligentsia— "the most cultivated intellects in the country," the "thinking minds," "the best and wisest"— as guides to a better world in their role of "those who have been in advance of society in thought and feeling."[5] This has been the role of the intelligentsia, as seen by the intelligentsia, both before and after Mill's time— that of intellectual leaders whose deeper insights can liberate people from the needless restrictions of society.

Jean-Jacques Rousseau's famous declaration— "Man was born free, and he is everywhere in chains"[6] summarizes the heart of the vision of the anointed, that social contrivances are the root cause of human unhappiness and explain the fact that the world we see around us differs so greatly from the world that we would like to see. In this vision, oppression, poverty, injustice and war are all products of existing institutions— problems whose solutions require changing those institutions, which in turn require changing the ideas behind those institutions. In short, the ills of society are seen as ultimately an intellectual and moral problem, for which intellectuals are especially equipped to provide answers, by virtue of their greater knowledge and insight, as well as their not having vested economic interests to bias them in favor of the existing order and still the voice of conscience.

Large, unmerited differences in the economic and social prospects of people born into different social circumstances have long been a central theme of intellectuals with the vision of the anointed. Contrasts between the grinding poverty of some and the luxurious extravagance of others, compounded by similar unmerited contrasts in social status, are among the problems that have long dominated the agenda of those with the vision of the anointed. More general sources of unhappiness among people across the social spectrum— the psychic problems created by moral stigma, as well as the horrors of war, for example— are also things for which intellectual solutions are sought.

This vision of society, in which there are many "problems" to be "solved" by applying the ideas of morally anointed intellectual elites is by no means the only vision, however much that vision may be prevalent among today's intellectuals. A conflicting vision has co-existed for centuries— a vision in which the inherent flaws of human beings are the fundamental problem and social contrivances are simply imperfect means of trying to cope with that problem— these imperfections themselves being products of the inherent shortcomings of human beings. A classical scholar has contrasted modern visions of the anointed with "the darker picture" painted by Thucydides of "a human race that escaped chaos and barbarism by preserving with difficulty a thin layer of civilization," based on "moderation and prudence" growing out of experience.[7] This is a tragic vision of the human condition that is very different from the vision of the anointed.

"Solutions," are not expected by those who see many of the frustrations, ills, and anomalies of life— the tragedy of the human condition— as being due to constraints inherent in human beings, singly and collectively, and in the physical world in which they live. In contrast to the vision of today's anointed, where existing society is discussed largely in terms of its inadequacies and the improvements which the anointed have to offer, the tragic vision regards civilization itself as something that requires great and constant efforts merely to be preserved— with these efforts to be based on actual experience, not on "exciting" new theories.

In the tragic vision, barbarism is always waiting in the wings and civilization is simply "a thin crust over a volcano." This vision has few solutions to offer and many painful trade-offs to ponder. Commenting on Felix Frankfurter's references to the success of various reforms, Oliver Wendell Holmes wanted to know what the costs— the trade-offs— were. Otherwise, while lifting up society in one respect, "how the devil can I tell whether I am not pulling it down more in some other place," he asked.[8] This constrained vision is thus a tragic vision— not in the sense of believing that life must always be sad and gloomy, for much happiness and fulfillment are possible within a constrained world, but tragic in limitations that cannot be overcome merely by compassion, commitment, or other virtues which those with the vision of the anointed advocate or attribute to themselves.

In the tragic vision, social contrivances seek to restrict behavior that leads to unhappiness, even though these restrictions themselves cause a certain amount of unhappiness. It is a vision of trade-offs, rather than solutions, and a vision of wisdom distilled from the experiences of the many, rather than the brilliance of a few. The conflict between these two visions goes back for centuries.[9] Those with the tragic vision and those with the vision of the anointed do not simply happen to differ on a range of policy issues. They *necessarily* differ, because they are talking about very different worlds which exist inside their minds. Moreover, they are talking about different creatures who inhabit that world, even though both call these creatures human beings, for the nature of those human beings is also fundamentally different as seen in the two visions.[10]

In the constrained vision, there are especially severe limits on how much any given individual can know and truly understand, which is why this vision puts such emphasis on systemic processes whose economic and social transactions draw upon the knowledge and experience of millions, past and present. In the vision of the anointed, however, far more knowledge and intelligence are available to some people and the difference between them and the masses is far greater than in the constrained vision.[11]

These opposing visions differ not only in what they believe exists and in what they think is possible, but also in what they think needs explaining. To those with the vision of the anointed, it is such evils as poverty, crime, war, and injustice which require explanation. To those with the tragic vision, it is prosperity, law, peace, and such justice as we have achieved, which require not only explanation but constant efforts, trade-offs, and sacrifices, just to maintain them at their existing levels, much less promote their enhancement over time. While those with the vision of the anointed seek the causes of war,[12] for example, those with the tragic vision say such things as "No peace keeps itself,"[13] that peace "is an unstable equilibrium, which can be preserved only by acknowledged supremacy or equal power,"[14] that a nation "despicable by its weakness, forfeits even the privilege of being neutral,"[15] and that "nations in general will make war whenever they have a prospect of getting anything by it."[16]

A tragic vision is a sort of zero-based vision of the world and of human beings, taking none of the benefits of civilization for granted. It does not assume that we can begin with what we already have and simply tack on improvements, without being concerned at every step with whether these innovations jeopardize the very processes and principles on which our existing level of well-being rests. It does not assume that the chafing restrictions conveyed to us by social contrivances— from prices to stigmas— are *caused* by those contrivances. Above all, it does not assume that untried theories stand on the same footing as institutions and practices whose very existence demonstrate their ability to survive in the world of reality, however much that reality falls short of what can be imagined as a better world. As Professor Richard A. Epstein of the University of Chicago put it: "The study of human institutions is always a search for the most tolerable imperfections."[17]

The two visions differ fundamentally, not only in how they see the world but also in how those who believe in these visions see themselves. If you happen to believe in free markets, judicial restraint, traditional values and other features of the tragic vision, then you are just someone who believes in free markets, judicial restraint and traditional values. There is no personal exaltation resulting from those beliefs. But to be for "social justice" and "saving the environment," or to be "anti-war" is more than just a set of beliefs about empirical facts. This vision puts you on a higher moral plane as someone concerned and compassionate, someone who is for peace in the world, a defender of the downtrodden, and someone who wants to preserve the beauty of nature and save the planet from being polluted by others less caring. In short, one vision makes you somebody special and the other vision does not. These visions are not symmetrical.

While the conflicts between the tragic vision and the vision of the anointed can lead to innumerable arguments on a wide range of issues, these can also lead to presentations of views that take the outward form of an argument without the inner substance of facts or analysis— in other words, arguments without arguments.

ARGUMENTS WITHOUT ARGUMENTS

Although many intellectuals are especially well equipped by talent and training to engage in logically structured arguments using empirical evidence to analyze contending ideas, many of their political or ideological views are promoted by verbal virtuosity in *evading* structured arguments and empirical evidence. Among the many arguments without arguments are claims that opposing views are "simplistic" and opposing individuals unworthy, as well as assertions of "rights" and attributing to adversaries a belief in panaceas or golden ages.

"Simplistic" Arguments

Related to the assumption of the unworthiness of opponents is the assumption that certain arguments are unworthy because they are "simplistic"— not as a conclusion from counter-evidence or counter-arguments, but in lieu of counter-evidence or counter-arguments. It is a very effective debating tactic, however questionable it may be logically. With one word, it preempts the intellectual high ground without offering anything substantive. It is insinuated, rather than demonstrated, that a more complex explanation is more logically consistent or more empirically valid.

That one argument may be simpler than another says nothing about which argument reaches conclusions that turn out to be validated by empirical evidence more often. Certainly the explanation of many physical phenomena— the sun setting over the horizon, for example— by the argument that the earth is round is simpler than the more complex explanations of the same phenomena by members of the Flat Earth Society. Evasions of the obvious can become very complex.

Before an explanation can be *too* simple, it must first be wrong. But often the fact that some explanation seems too simple becomes a *substitute* for showing that it is wrong. For example, when Professor Orley Ashenfelter, an economist at Princeton University, began to predict the prices of particular vintages of wine, based solely on weather statistics during the growing season, without bothering to taste the wines or to consult experts who had tasted the wines, his method was dismissed as simplistic by wine connoisseurs, one of whom referred to the "self-evident silliness"[18] of this method. However, Professor Ashenfelter's predictions have turned out to be substantiated more often than those of wine experts.[19]

Only after a given method has turned out to be wrong is it legitimate to call it "simplistic." Otherwise, its use of smaller amounts of information to produce validated conclusions is greater efficiency. But use of the term "simplistic" has become a widely used argument without an argument, a way of dismissing opposing views without confronting them with either evidence or analysis.

Virtually any answer to virtually any question can be made to seem simplistic by *expanding* the question to unanswerable dimensions and then deriding the now inadequate answer as simplistic. For example, in the 1840s, an Austrian doctor collected statistics showing a substantial difference in mortality rates among women in maternity clinics in Vienna when they were examined by doctors who had washed their hands before examining them and doctors who had not. He sought to get all doctors to wash their hands before examining patients. But his suggestion was rejected, essentially as being simplistic, using a kind of argument that is still with us today. He was challenged to explain *why* washing one's hands would affect maternal mortality— and, since this was before the germ theory of diseases was developed and accepted, he could not do so.[20] In short, the question was expanded to the point where it could not be answered (at the current state of knowledge), thereby making any answer seem "simplistic." However, the real issue was not whether the statistically minded doctor could explain the larger question but whether his evidence on the more modest and mundane question was valid— and could therefore save lives, based on empirical facts alone. The danger of committing the *post hoc* fallacy could have been easily avoided by continuing to collect data on whether more washing of hands by more doctors reduced current maternal mortality rates.

Today, those who reject stronger police action and more severe punishment as ways of dealing with crime, and who prefer social programs and rehabilitation efforts, often stigmatize the traditional "law and order" approach by *expanding* the question to that of finding the "root causes" of crime, a question that police action and punishment cannot answer. Neither may alternative theories provide an answer that is convincing to those who require something more than an answer whose only basis is consonance with the prevailing vision. But the substitution of a much larger and more sweeping question for the more pragmatic and empirical question of which alternative approach to crime control has a better track record accomplishes the tactical purpose of derailing an alternative to the prevailing vision by making the alternative seem simplistic.

Ironically, many of those who emphasize the complexities of real-world problems and issues nevertheless often also regard people with opposing views of those problems and issues as either intellectually or morally unworthy. In other words, despite an emphasis on the complexities involved, these problems or issues are not regarded as being so complex that a different person could weigh the various probabilities or values differently and legitimately arrive at a different conclusion.

A variation on the theme of opponents' "simplistic" arguments is to say that whatever they advocate is "no panacea"— as indeed nothing is a panacea or else, by definition, all the problems of the world would already have been solved. When the collapse of the Communist bloc in Eastern Europe left Czechoslovakia celebrating its freedom, *New York Times* columnist Tom Wicker cautioned that freedom is "not a panacea; and that

Communism has failed does not make the Western alternative perfect, or even satisfying for millions of those who live under it."[21] That millions more people fled from the Communist bloc to the West than went in the other direction might suggest where there was more satisfaction. But of course nothing human has ever achieved perfection, so the fact that intellectuals can always imagine something better than the best that exists in reality is hardly surprising. Clearly, however, Tom Wicker's vision is not the same as the vision of Richard Epstein, for whom the most we can hope for is "a search for the most tolerable imperfections."[22]

A related assertion is that there was never a "golden age," often said in answer to people who never claimed that there was, but who happen to think that some past practice produced better results than some present practice. Instead of offering evidence that the present practice produces better results, panaceas and golden ages are dismissed. Sometimes the same notion is expressed by saying that we cannot or should not "turn back the clock." But unless one accepts as dogma that all things subsequent to some arbitrary date are automatically better than all things prior to that date, this is another evasion of specifics, another argument without an argument.

Unworthy Opponents

Because the vision of the anointed is a vision of themselves as well as a vision of the world, when they are defending that vision they are not simply defending a set of hypotheses about external events, they are in a sense defending their very souls— and the zeal and even ruthlessness with which they defend their vision are not surprising under these circumstances. But for people with opposite views, who may for example believe that most things work out better if left to free markets, traditions, families, etc., these are just a set of hypotheses about external events, and there is no such huge personal ego stake in whether those hypotheses are confirmed by empirical evidence. Obviously everyone would prefer to be proved right rather than proved wrong, but the point here is that there are no such comparable ego stakes involved among believers in the tragic vision.

This difference may help explain a striking pattern that goes back at least two centuries— the greater tendency of those with the vision of the anointed to see those they disagree with as enemies who are morally lacking. While there are individual variations in this, as with most things, there are nevertheless general patterns, which many have noticed, both in our times and in earlier centuries. For example, a contemporary account has noted:

> Disagree with someone on the right and he is likely to think you obtuse, wrong, foolish, a dope. Disagree with someone on the left and he is more likely to think you selfish, a sell-out, insensitive, possibly evil.[23]

Supporters of both visions, by definition, believe that those with the opposing vision are mistaken. But that is not enough for those with the vision of the anointed. It has long been taken for granted by those with the vision of the anointed that their opponents were lacking in compassion. Moreover, there was no felt need to test that belief empirically. As far back as the eighteenth century, the difference between supporters of the two visions in this regard was apparent in a controversy between Thomas Malthus and William Godwin. Malthus said of his opponents, "I cannot doubt the talents of such men as Godwin and Condorcet. I am unwilling to doubt their candour."[24] But when Godwin referred to Malthus, he called Malthus "malignant," questioned "the humanity of the man," and said "I profess myself at a loss to conceive of what earth the man was made."[25]

Edmund Burke was a landmark figure among those with the tragic vision but, despite his all-out attacks on the *ideas* and *deeds* of the French Revolution, Burke nevertheless said of those with the opposing vision that they "may do the worst of things, without being the worst of men."[26] It would be hard, if not impossible, to find similar statements about ideological adversaries from those with the vision of the anointed, either in the eighteenth century or today. Yet such a view of opponents— as mistaken or even dangerously mistaken, but not necessarily evil personally— has continued to be common among those with the tragic vision. When Friedrich Hayek in 1944 published *The Road to Serfdom*, his landmark challenge to the prevailing social vision among the intelligentsia, setting off an intellectual and political counter-revolution later joined by Milton Friedman, William F. Buckley and others intellectually and by Margaret Thatcher and Ronald Reagan politically, he characterized his adversaries as "single-minded idealists" and "authors whose sincerity and disinterestedness are above suspicion."[27]

Clearly, however, sincerity was not considered sufficient to prevent opponents from being considered to be not only mistaken but dangerously mistaken, as illustrated by Hayek's belief that they were putting society on "the road to serfdom." Similarly, even in the midst of a political campaign in 1945, when Winston Churchill warned of authoritarian rule if the opposing Labor Party won, he added that this was not because they wanted to reduce people's freedom but because "they do not see where their theories are leading them."[28] Similar concessions to the sincerity and good intentions of opponents can be found in Milton Friedman and other exponents of the constrained or tragic vision. But such a view of ideological opponents has been much rarer among those with the vision of the anointed, where the presumed moral and/or intellectual failings of opponents have been more or less a staple of discourse from the eighteenth century to the present.[29]

While sincerity and humane feelings are often denied to ideological opponents by those with the vision of the anointed, whether or not opposition to minimum wage laws or rent control laws, for example, is in fact due to a lack of compassion for the poor is irrelevant to the question whether the arguments for or against such policies have either empirical or analytical validity. Even if it could be proved to a certainty that opponents of these and other "progressive" policies were veritable Scrooges, or even venal, that would still be no answer to the arguments they make. Yet claims that opponents are racist, sexist, homophobic or "just don't get it" are often advanced by the intelligentsia in lieu of specific refutations of their specific arguments.

"What often distinguishes liberals from others," according to best-selling author Andrew Hacker, is that they are "ready to share some of what they have with others less fortunate than themselves."[30] This is not a view peculiar to Professor Hacker. It reflects an opinion that was widespread among those with the vision of the anointed before he was born. But here, as elsewhere, the power of a vision is shown not by the evidence offered in favor of it but precisely by the lack of any sense of need for evidence— in this case, evidence of the lesser humanitarianism among conservatives opposed to "progressive" policies. However, an empirical study by Professor Arthur C. Brooks of Syracuse University, to test the extent to which liberals and conservatives in America donated money, blood, and time to philanthropic endeavors showed that conservatives donated on average both a larger amount of money and a higher percentage of their incomes (which were slightly lower than liberals' incomes) to philanthropic causes, that they donated more hours of their time as volunteers, and that they donated far more blood.[31]

This, of course, in no way proves that conservatives' arguments on social or political issues are more valid. What it does show is how far wrong people can go when they believe what is convenient for their vision and see no need to test such convenient assumptions against any empirical evidence. The fact that the assumption that conservatives were less concerned about other people's well-being prevailed so strongly and so unquestioningly for so long— literally for centuries— before even being tested reinforces the point.

Similarly, when those with the vision of the anointed advocate disarmament and international agreements among potential adversary nations as the way to preserve peace, and are opposed by those with the tragic vision who advocate military deterrence and military alliances as the way to preserve peace, these are seldom seen as simply different hypotheses about prospects and risks in the external world. Those with the vision of the anointed have far more often, for a very long time, seen such differences as signs of internal defects in those who disagree with them. Those who rely on stronger military forces, rather than disarmament or international agreements, to deter war have often been depicted by intellectuals as being in *favor* of war. Bertrand Russell, for example, said:

> If you address an audience of unselected men on the prevention of war, you are sure to come up against the middle-aged man who says, with a sneer: "Wars will never stop; it would be contrary to human nature." It is quite obvious that the man who says this delights in war, and would hate a world from which it had been eliminated.[32]

Nor was Bertrand Russell the only internationally known philosopher to make this kind of argument, as he did in 1936, against those who wanted Britain to rearm in the face of Hitler's massive buildup of military forces that would be unleashed just three years later to begin the Second World War. Earlier, back in the 1920s, when many intellectuals were in favor of international agreements renouncing war, such as the Kellogg-Briand Pact of 1928, those who opposed this approach were depicted by John Dewey as people exhibiting "the stupidity of habit-bound minds,"[33] suffering from "mental inertia,"[34] people whose reasons were "psychological rather than practical or logical"[35] or else people "who believe in the war system."[36]

British writer J.B. Priestley likewise explained the failure of the pacifism common among his fellow intellectuals in the 1930s to catch on with the general public by saying that the public *favored war* out of "boredom," a boredom leading to "the widespread desire for some grand piece of excitement, for fiery speeches and flag-waving, for special editions, troop trains, casualty lists."[37] While acknowledging "the enormous sales" of the anti-war novel *All Quiet on the Western Front*, Priestley said of the people who read it, "The very horrors fascinated them," that the book was "too good a show as a tragic spectacle."[38]

In short, no matter what the empirical facts might be, they would simply be interpreted to fit Priestley's vision. The desires arbitrarily attributed to the public made it unnecessary for Priestley to confront opposing arguments or to confront the possibility that there were gaps or flaws in the arguments advanced by pacifists like himself, which left the public unconvinced that the pacifists' approach— disarmament and treaties— was likely to reduce the dangers of war. There has been a long history of a similar approach to issues of war and peace by intellectuals, going back at least as far as Godwin and Condorcet in the eighteenth century, and often depicting those who disagreed with them as people who favored war for some malign or irrational reason.[39]

The contrast between how those with the tragic vision and those with the vision of the anointed see opponents has been too widespread and too long-lasting to be attributed simply to differences in particular personalities, even if there are individual variations on both sides. The very nature of the visions themselves involve very different personal ego stakes. To believe in the vision of the anointed is to be oneself one of the anointed, something that many find too precious to risk forfeiting. As T.S. Eliot put it:

> Half of the harm that is done in this world is due to people who want to
> feel important. They don't mean to do harm— but the harm does not
> interest them. Or they do not see it, or they justify it because they are
> absorbed in the endless struggle to think well of themselves.[40]

The Rhetoric of "Rights"

Much advocacy by intellectuals involve assertions of "rights" for which
no basis is asked or given. Neither constitutional provisions, legislative
enactments, contractual obligations, nor international treaties are cited as
bases for these "rights." Thus there are "rights" to "a living wage," "decent
housing," "affordable health care," and numerous other benefits, material
and psychic. That such things may be desirable is not the issue. The real
issue is why such things are regarded as obligations— the logical corollary
of rights— upon other people who have agreed to no such obligation. If
someone has a right, someone else has an obligation. But the proposed right
to a "living wage," for example, is not based on any obligation agreed to by
an employer. On the contrary, this "right" is cited as a reason why
government should force the employer to pay what third parties would like
to see paid.

"Rights," as the term is used ideologically, imply no mutual agreement
of any kind, whether among individuals, enterprises or nations. Captured
terrorists, for example, have been deemed by some to have the right to the
same treatment prescribed for prisoners of war by the Geneva Convention,
even though terrorists have neither agreed to the terms of the Geneva
Convention nor are among those whom the signers of that convention
designated as covered by the convention. Again, "rights," as the term is used
ideologically, are ultimately assertions of arbitrary authority by third parties
to prescribe what others have never agreed to.

The same principle is expressed when terms like "social responsibility"
or "social contract" are used to describe what third parties want done,
regardless of whether any others have agreed to do it. Thus business is said

to have a "social responsibility" to provide various benefits to various individuals or to society at large, regardless of whether those businesses have chosen to assume such a responsibility. Nor are these responsibilities necessarily based on laws that have been enacted. On the contrary, the asserted "responsibilities" are the basis for advocating the passing of such laws, even though the responsibilities have no basis themselves, other than the fact that third parties want them imposed.

The same principle can be seen in assertions of figurative "promises," as in the title of *The Promise of American Life* by Herbert Croly, the Progressive-era first editor of the *New Republic*— where these "promises" are found nowhere except in the desires of Herbert Croly and like-minded Progressives. Similarly with "contracts" that no one has signed or even seen. Thus Social Security is often described as a "contract" between the generations when, by definition, generations yet unborn could not have agreed to any such contract.

Legal obligations can of course be imposed on unborn generations, whether through Social Security or the national debt, but the argument is not about what is physically possible but what has any logical or empirical foundation. To say that it has a moral foundation, without providing any specifics, is only to say that some people feel that way. But there would be no issue in the first place unless other people felt differently. Nor are the asserted "rights," "social responsibilities," or fictitious "contracts" or "promises" necessarily based on claims of demonstrable majorities favoring such things. On the contrary, they are asserted as reasons why the majority or political leaders or the courts *ought* to impose what third parties want imposed. They are arguments without arguments.

Sometimes the term "social justice" is used to provide the semblance of a basis for these arbitrary assertions. But "justification," even as the term is used in carpentry or printing, means aligning one thing with another. But what are these assertions to be aligned with, other than the feelings, visions or groupthink that happen to prevail currently among the intelligentsia? The groupthink of the intelligentsia is still groupthink and their prejudices are still prejudices.

Justice Oliver Wendell Holmes said, "the word 'right' is one of the most deceptive of pitfalls" and "a constant solicitation to fallacy."[41] While he rejected abstract rights, he regarded those rights actually "established in a given society" to have a different basis.[42] Holmes was particularly concerned about the notion that judges should be enforcing abstract rights for which there was no basis:

> There is a tendency to think of judges as if they were independent mouthpieces of the infinite, and not simply directors of a force that comes from the source that gives them their authority. I think our court has fallen into the error at times and it is that that I have aimed at when I have said that the Common Law is not a brooding omnipresence in the sky and that the U.S. is not subject to some mystic overlaw that it is bound to obey.[43]

Holmes' original statement that the common law "is not a brooding omnipresence in the sky" was in the 1917 U.S. Supreme Court case of *Southern Pacific Co. v. Jensen*, where he explained that law is "the articulate voice of some sovereign or quasi-sovereign that can be identified."[44] Assertions of abstract "rights" by intellectuals in effect transform themselves into sovereigns with neither identification nor authorization.

THE LEFT-RIGHT DICHOTOMY

One of the fertile sources of confusion in discussions of ideological issues is the dichotomy between the political left and the political right. Perhaps the most fundamental difference between the left and the right is that only the former has even a rough definition. What is called "the right" are simply the various and disparate opponents of the left. These opponents of the left may share no particular principle, much less a common agenda, and they can range from free-market libertarians to advocates of monarchy, theocracy, military dictatorship or innumerable other principles, systems and agendas.

To people who take words literally, to speak of "the left" is to assume implicitly that there is some other coherent group which constitutes "the right." Perhaps it would be less confusing if what we call "the left" would be designated by some other term, perhaps just as *X*. But the designation as being on the left has at least some historical basis in the views of those deputies who sat on the left side of the president's chair in France's Estates General in the eighteenth century. A rough summary of the vision of the political left today is that of collective decision-making through government, directed toward— or at least rationalized by— the goal of reducing economic and social inequalities. There may be moderate or extreme versions of the left vision or agenda but, among those designated as "the right," the difference between free market libertarians and military juntas is not simply one of degree in pursuing a common vision, because there is no common vision among these and other disparate groups opposed to the left— which is to say, there is no such definable thing as "the right," though there are various segments of that omnibus category, such as free market advocates, who can be defined.

The heterogeneity of what is called "the right" is not the only problem with the left-right dichotomy. The usual image of the political spectrum among the intelligentsia extends from the Communists on the extreme left to less extreme left-wing radicals, more moderate liberals, centrists, conservatives, hard right-wingers, and ultimately Fascists. Like so much that is believed by the intelligentsia, it is a conclusion without an argument, unless endless repetition can be regarded as an argument. When we turn from such images to specifics, there is remarkably little difference between Communists and Fascists, except for rhetoric, and there is far more in common between Fascists and even the moderate left than between either of them and traditional conservatives in the American sense. A closer look makes this clear.

Communism is socialism with an international focus and totalitarian methods. Benito Mussolini, the founder of Fascism, defined Fascism as *national* socialism in a state that was totalitarian, a term that he also coined. The same idea was echoed in the name of the National Socialist German Workers' Party in Germany, Hitler's party, now almost always abbreviated as Nazis, thereby burying its socialist component. Viewed in retrospect, the most prominent feature of the Nazis— racism in general and anti-Jewish racism in particular— was not inherent in the Fascist vision, but was an obsession of Hitler's party, not shared by the Fascist government of Mussolini in Italy or that of Franco in Spain.

At one time, Jews were in fact over-represented among Fascist leaders in Italy. Only after Mussolini became Hitler's junior partner in the Axis alliance of the late 1930s were Jews purged from Italy's Fascist party. And only after Mussolini's Fascist government in Rome was overthrown in 1943, and was replaced by a rump puppet government that the Nazis set up in northern Italy, were Jews in that part of Italy rounded up and sent off to concentration camps.[45] In short, official and explicit government racist ideology and practice distinguished the Nazis from other Fascist movements.

What distinguished Fascist movements in general from Communist movements was that Communists were officially committed to government ownership of the means of production, while Fascists permitted private ownership of the means of production, so long as government directed the private owners' decisions and limited what profit rates they could receive. Both were totalitarian dictatorships but Communists were officially internationalist while Fascists were officially nationalist. However, Stalin's proclaimed policy of "socialism in one country" was not very different from the Fascists' proclaimed policy of national socialism.

When it came to practice, there was even less difference, since the Communist International served the *national* interests of the Soviet Union, despite whatever internationalist rhetoric it used. The way Communists in other countries, including the United States, reversed their opposition to Western nations' military defense efforts in World War II, within 24 hours after the Soviet Union was invaded by Hitler's armies, was only the most dramatic of many examples that could be cited.

As regards Fascists' supposed restriction of their interests to those within their own respective countries, that was belied by both Hitler's and Mussolini's invasions of other countries and by Nazi international networks, operating among Germans living in other countries ranging from Brazil to Australia[46]— all focused on Germany's national interest, as distinguished from seeking ideological hegemony or the interests of Germans living in these other countries. Thus the grievances of the Sudeten Germans in Czechoslovakia were pressed during the Munich crisis of 1938 as part of Germany's national expansion, while Germans living in Italy were told to squelch their grievances, since Mussolini was Hitler's ally.[47]

While the Soviet Union proclaimed its internationalism as it set up various officially autonomous nations within its borders, the people who wielded the real power in those nations— often under the official title of "Second Secretary" of the Communist Party in these ostensibly autonomous nations— were typically Russians,[48] just as in the days when the czars ruled what was more candidly called the Russian Empire.

In short, the notion that Communists and Fascists were at opposite poles ideologically was not true, even in theory, much less in practice. As for similarities and differences between these two totalitarian movements and liberalism, on the one hand, or conservatism on the other, there was far more similarity between these totalitarians' agendas and those of the left than with the agendas of most conservatives. For example, among the items on the agendas of the Fascists in Italy and/or the Nazis in Germany were (1) government control of wages and hours of work, (2) higher taxes on the wealthy, (3) government-set limits on profits, (4) government care for the elderly, (5) a decreased emphasis on the role of religion and the family in personal or social decisions and (6) government taking on the role of changing the nature of people, usually beginning in early childhood.[49] This last and most audacious project has been part of the ideology of the left— both democratic and totalitarian— since at least the eighteenth century, when Condorcet and Godwin advocated it, and it has been advocated by innumerable intellectuals since then,[50] as well as being put into practice in various countries, under names ranging from "re-education" to "values clarification."[51]

These are of course things opposed by most people who are called "conservatives" in the United States, and they are things much more congenial to the general approach of people who are called "liberals" in the American political context. It should be noted also that neither "liberal" nor "conservative," as those terms are used in the American context, has much relationship to their original meanings. Milton Friedman, one of the leading

American "conservative" intellectuals of his time, advocated radical changes in the country's school system, in the role of the Federal Reserve System, and in the economy in general. One of his books was titled *The Tyranny of the Status Quo*. He, like Friedrich Hayek, called himself a "liberal" in the original sense of the word, but that sense has been irretrievably lost in general discussions in the United States, though people with similar views are still called liberals in some other countries.

Despite this, even scholarly studies of intellectuals have referred to Hayek as a defender of the "status quo," and as one of those whose "defense of the existing state of affairs" has "furnished justifications for the powers that be."[52] Whatever the merits or demerits of Hayek's ideas, those ideas were far more distant from the status quo than were the ideas of those who criticized him. In general, people such as Hayek, who are referred to in the American context as "conservatives," have a set of ideas which differ not only in degree, but in kind, from the ideas of many others who are said to be on the right politically. Perhaps if liberals were simply called *X* and conservatives were called *Y* there would be less confusion.

Conservatism, in its original sense, has no specific ideological content at all, since everything depends on what one is trying to conserve. In the last days of the Soviet Union, those who were trying to preserve the existing Communist regime were rightly referred to as "conservatives," though what they were trying to conserve had nothing in common with what was advocated by Milton Friedman, Friedrich Hayek or William F. Buckley in the United States, much less Cardinal Joseph Ratzinger, a leading conservative in the Vatican who subsequently became Pope. Specific individuals with the "conservative" label have specific ideological positions, but there is no commonality of specifics among "conservatives" in different venues.

If we attempt to define the political left by its proclaimed goals, it is clear that very similar goals have been proclaimed by people whom the left repudiates and anathematizes, such as Fascists in general and Nazis in particular. Instead of defining these (and other) groups by their proclaimed goals, we can define them by the specific institutional mechanisms and policies they use or advocate for achieving their goals. More specifically, they can be defined by the institutional mechanisms they seek to establish for making decisions with impacts on society at large. In order to keep the discussion manageable, the vast sweep of possible decision-making mechanisms can be dichotomized into those in which individuals make decisions individually for themselves and those in which decisions are made collectively by surrogates for society at large.

In market economies, for example, consumers and producers make their own decisions individually and the social consequences are determined by the effect of those individual decisions on the way resources are allocated in the economy as a whole, in response to the movements of prices, incomes, and employment— which in turn respond to supply and demand.

While this vision of the economy is often considered to be "conservative" (in the original sense of the word), in the long view of the history of ideas it has been revolutionary. From ancient times to the present, and in highly disparate societies around the world, there have been the most varied systems of thought— both secular and religious— seeking to determine how best the wise and virtuous can influence or direct the masses, in order to create or maintain a happier, more viable or more worthy society. In this context, it was a revolutionary departure when, in eighteenth-century France, the Physiocrats arose to proclaim that, for the economy at least, the best that the reigning authorities could do would be to leave it alone— *laissez-faire* being the term they coined. To those with this vision, for the authorities to impose economic policies would be to give "a most unnecessary attention," in Adam Smith's words,[53] to a spontaneous system of interactions that would go better without government intervention— not perfectly, just better.

Variations of this vision of spontaneous order can also be found in other areas, ranging from language to the law. No elites sat down and planned the languages of the world or of any given society. These languages evolved from the systemic interactions of millions of human beings over the generations, in the most varied societies around the world. Linguistic scholars study and codify the rules of language— but after the fact. Young children learn words and usage, intuiting the rules of that usage before they are taught these things explicitly in schools. While it was possible for elites to create languages such as Esperanto, these artificial languages have never caught on in a way that would displace historically evolved languages.

In law, a similar vision was expressed in Justice Oliver Wendell Holmes' statement that "The life of the law has not been logic: it has been experience."[54] In short, whether in the economy, language, or the law, this vision sees social viability and progress as being due to systemic evolution rather than elite prescription. Reliance on systemic processes, whether in the economy, the law, or other areas, is based on the constrained vision— the tragic vision— of the severe limitations on any given individual's knowledge and insight, however knowledgeable or brilliant that individual might be, compared to other individuals. Systemic processes which tap vastly more knowledge and experience from vastly more people, often including traditions evolved from the experiences of successive generations, are deemed more reliable than the intellect of the intellectuals.

By contrast, the vision of the left is one of surrogate decision-making by those presumed to have not only superior knowledge but sufficient knowledge, whether these surrogates are political leaders, experts, judges or others. This is the vision that is common to varying degrees on the political left, whether radical or moderate, and common also to totalitarians, whether Communist or Fascist. A commonality of purpose in society is central to collective decision-making, whether expressed in town-meeting democracy or totalitarian dictatorship or other variations in between. One of the differences between the commonality of purposes in democratic systems of government and totalitarian systems of government is in the range of decisions infused with that commonality of purpose and in the range of decisions reserved for individual decision-making outside the purview of government.

The free market, for example, is a huge exemption from government power. In such a market, there is no commonality of purpose, except among such individuals and organizations as may choose voluntarily to coalesce into groups ranging from bowling leagues to multinational corporations. But even these aggregations typically pursue the interests of their own respective constituents and compete against the interests of other aggregations. Those who advocate this mode of social decision-making do so because they believe that the systemic results of such competition are usually better than a society-wide commonality of purpose imposed by surrogate decision-makers superintending the whole process in the name of "the national interest."

The totalitarian version of collective surrogate decision-making by government was summarized by Mussolini, who defined "totalitarianism" in the motto: "Everything in the State, nothing outside the State, nothing against the State."[55] Moreover, the state ultimately meant the political leader of the state, the dictator. Mussolini was known as *Il Duce*— the leader— before Hitler acquired the same title in German as the *Führer*. Democratic versions of collective surrogate decision-making by government choose leaders by votes and tend to leave more areas outside the purview of government. However, the left seldom has any explicit principle by which the boundaries between government and individual decision-making can be determined, so that the natural tendency over time is for the scope of government decision-making to expand, as more and more decisions are taken successively from private hands.

Preferences for collective, surrogate decision-making from the top down are not all that the democratic left has shared with the original Italian Fascists and with the National Socialists (Nazis) of Germany. In addition to political intervention in economic markets, the democratic left shared with the Fascists and the Nazis the underlying assumption of a vast gap in understanding between ordinary people and elites like themselves. Although both the totalitarian left— that is, the Fascists, Communists and Nazis— and the democratic left have widely used in a positive sense such terms as "the people," "the workers" and "the masses," these are the ostensible beneficiaries of their policies, but *not* autonomous decision-makers. Although much rhetoric on both the democratic left and the totalitarian left has long papered over the distinction between ordinary people as beneficiaries and as decision-makers, it has long been clear that decision-making has been seen as something reserved for the anointed in these visions.

Rousseau, for all his emphasis on "the general will," left the interpretation of that will to elites. He likened the masses of the people to "a stupid, pusillanimous invalid."[56] Godwin and Condorcet, also on the eighteenth century left, expressed similar contempt for the masses.[57] Karl Marx said, "The working class is revolutionary or it is nothing"[58]— in other words, millions of human beings mattered only if they carried out his vision. Fabian socialist George Bernard Shaw included the working class among the "detestable" people who "have no right to live." He added: "I should despair if I did not know that they will all die presently, and that there is no need on earth why they should be replaced by people like themselves."[59] As a young man serving in the U.S. Army during the First World War, Edmund Wilson wrote to a friend: "I should be insincere to make it appear that the deaths of this 'poor white trash' of the South and the rest made me feel half so bitter as the mere conscription or enlistment of any of my friends."[60]

The totalitarian left has been similarly clear that decision-making power should be confined to a political elite— the "vanguard of the proletariat," the leader of a "master race," or whatever the particular phrase that might become the motto of the particular totalitarian system. In Mussolini's words, "The mass will simply follow and submit."[61]

The similarity in underlying assumptions between the various totalitarian movements and the democratic left was openly recognized by leaders of the left themselves in democratic countries during the 1920s, when Mussolini was widely lionized by intellectuals in the Western democracies, and even Hitler had his admirers among prominent intellectuals on the left. It was only as the 1930s unfolded that Mussolini's invasion of Ethiopia and Hitler's violent anti-Semitism at home and military aggression abroad made these totalitarian systems international pariahs that they were repudiated by the left— and were thereafter depicted as being on "the right."[*]

During the 1920s, however, radical writer Lincoln Steffens wrote positively about Mussolini's Fascism as he had more famously written positively about Soviet Communism.[62] Nor was he the only prominent

---

[*] The Nazis' street battles with the Communists in 1920s Germany were internecine warfare among groups competing for the allegiance of the same constituency, much as the Communists killed socialists during the Spanish civil war and as Stalin purged Trotskyites in the Soviet Union.

American radical or progressive to do so.[63] As late as 1932, famed novelist and Fabian socialist H.G. Wells urged students at Oxford to be "liberal fascists" and "enlightened Nazis."[64] Historian Charles Beard was among Mussolini's apologists in the Western democracies, as was the *New Republic* magazine.[65] The poet Wallace Stevens even justified Mussolini's invasion of Ethiopia.[66]

W.E.B. Du Bois was so intrigued by the Nazi movement in the 1920s that he put swastikas on the covers of a magazine he edited, despite protests from Jews.[67] Even though Du Bois was conflicted by the Nazis' anti-Semitism, he said in the 1930s that creation of the Nazi dictatorship had been "absolutely necessary to get the state in order" in Germany, and in a speech in Harlem in 1937 he declared that "there is today, in some respects, more democracy in Germany than there has been in years past."[68] More revealing, Du Bois saw the Nazis as part of the political left. In 1936, he said, "Germany today is, next to Russia, the greatest exemplar of Marxian socialism in the world."[69]

The heterogeneity of those later lumped together as the right has allowed those on the left to dump into that grab-bag category many who espouse some version of the vision of the left, but whose other characteristics make them an embarrassment to be repudiated. Thus the popular 1930s American radio personality Father Coughlin— who was, among other things, an anti-Semite— has been verbally banished to "the right," even though he advocated so many of the policies that became part of the New Deal that many Congressional Democrats at one time publicly praised him and some progressives urged President Franklin D. Roosevelt to make him a Cabinet member.[70]

During this early period, it was common on the left, as well as elsewhere, to compare as kindred experiments Fascism in Italy, Communism in the Soviet Union and the New Deal in the United States.[71] Such comparisons were later as completely rejected as the inclusion of Father Coughlin as a figure of the left was. These arbitrary changes in classifications not only allowed the left to distance themselves from embarrassing individuals and groups, whose underlying assumptions and conclusions bore many similarities to their own, these classification changes also allowed the left to verbally transfer these embarrassments to their political opponents. Moreover, such changes in nomenclature greatly reduced the likelihood that observers would see the negative potential of the ideas and agendas being put forth by the left in its bid for influence or power.

The kinds of concentrations of government power sought by the left may be proclaimed to be in the service of various sorts of lofty goals, but such concentrations of power also offer opportunities for all sorts of abuses, ranging up to mass murder, as Hitler, Stalin, Mao, and Pol Pot demonstrated. These leaders did *not* have a tragic vision of man, such as that underlying what is called "conservative" thought in America today. It was precisely these dictators' presumptions of their own vastly greater knowledge and wisdom than that of ordinary people which led to such staggering tragedies for others.

"CHANGE" VERSUS THE STATUS QUO

The intelligentsia often divide people into those who are for "change" and those who are for the status quo. John Dewey's *Liberalism and Social Action*, for example, begins with these words:

> Liberalism has long been accustomed to onslaughts proceeding from those who oppose social change. It has long been treated as an enemy by those who wish to maintain the *status quo*.[72]

As already noted, even such landmark "conservative" figures as Milton Friedman and Friedrich Hayek advocated policies radically different from those in existing institutions or societies. No book was more completely based on the tragic vision than *The Federalist*— and yet its authors had not only rebelled against British colonial rule but had created a new form of government, radically at variance with the autocracies that prevailed around the world at the time. To call such people defenders of the status quo is to completely divorce words from realities.

Similarly among their contemporaries in eighteenth century England, where Edmund Burke and Adam Smith were towering figures among those with the tragic vision. Both Burke and Smith advocated such drastic changes as freeing the American colonies instead of fighting to retain them, as the British government did, and both also opposed slavery at a time when few others did in the Western world and virtually no one did outside the West. Burke worked out a plan for preparing slaves for freedom and providing them with property to begin their lives as free people.[73] Adam Smith not only opposed slavery but also dismissed with contempt the theory that black slaves in America were inferior to the whites who enslaved them.[74]

Calling those with the tragic vision defenders of the status quo is a triumph of verbal virtuosity over plain and demonstrable facts. That such a lazy way of evading critics should have prevailed unchallenged from the eighteenth century to the present, among those who consider themselves "thinking people," is a sobering sign of the power of a vision and rhetoric to shut down thought.

More generally, it is doubtful whether there are many— if any— individuals in a free society who are completely satisfied with all the policies and institutions of their society. In short, virtually everybody is in favor of some changes. Any accurate and rational discussion of differences among them would address which particular changes are favored by which people, based on what reasons, followed by analysis and evidence for or against those particular reasons for those particular changes. All of this is by-passed by those who simply proclaim themselves to be in favor of "change" and label those who disagree with them as defenders of the status quo. It is yet another of the many arguments without arguments.

People who call themselves "progressives" assert not merely that they are for changes but that these are beneficial changes— that is, progress. But other people who advocate other very different changes likewise proclaim those to be changes for the better. In other words, *everybody* is a "progressive" by their own lights. That some people should imagine that they are peculiarly in favor of progress is not only another example of self-flattery but also of an evasion of the work of trying to show, with evidence and analysis, where and why their particular proposed changes would produce better end results than other people's proposed changes. Instead, proponents of other changes have been dismissed by many, including John Dewey, as "apologists for the *status quo*."[75]

Despite such dismissals in lieu of arguments, anyone with a knowledge of eighteenth-century Britain must know that Adam Smith's *The Wealth of Nations* was hardly a defense of the status quo, and in fact went completely counter to the vested interests of the political, economic, and social elites of his time. It would be hard even to imagine why Adam Smith, or anyone else, would spend a whole decade writing a 900-page book to say how contented he was with the way things were. The same could be said of the voluminous writings of Milton Friedman, Friedrich Hayek, William F. Buckley, and many other writers labeled "conservative."

The very concept of change used by the intelligentsia of the left— which is to say, most of the intelligentsia— is arbitrarily restrictive and tendentious. It means in practice the particular kinds of changes, through the particular kinds of social mechanisms that they envision. Other changes— no matter how large or how consequential for the lives of millions of people— tend to be ignored if they occur through other mechanisms and in ways not contemplated by the intelligentsia. At the very least, such unprescribed developments outside the scope of the vision of the anointed are denied the honorific title of "change."

The 1920s, for example, were a decade of huge changes for the people of the United States: the change from a predominantly rural to a predominantly urban society, the spread of electricity, automobiles, and radios to vastly more millions of Americans, the beginning of commercial air travel, the revolutionizing of retail selling with resulting lower prices by the rapid spread of chain stores. Yet when intellectuals refer to eras of "change," they almost never mention the 1920s— because these sweeping changes in the way millions of Americans lived their lives were not the particular kinds of changes envisioned by the intelligentsia, through the particular kinds of social mechanisms envisioned by the intelligentsia. In the eyes of much of the intelligentsia, the 1920s (when that decade is thought of at all) are seen as a period of a stagnant status quo, presided over by conservative administrations opposed to "change."

RHETORIC VERSUS REVEALED
PREFERENCES

To understand intellectuals' role in society, we must look beyond their rhetoric, or that of their critics, to the reality of their revealed preferences.

How can we tell what anyone's goals and priorities are? One way might be to pay attention to what they say. But of course outward words do not always accurately reflect inward thoughts. Moreover, even the thoughts which people articulate to themselves need not reflect their actual behavior pattern. Goals, preferences and priorities articulated either inwardly or outwardly need not be consistent with the choices actually made when confronted with the options presented by the real world. A man may claim or believe that keeping the lawn mowed is more important than watching television but, if he is found spending hours in front of the TV screen, day in and day out for weeks on end, while weeds and tall grass take over the lawn, then the preferences revealed by his behavior are a more accurate indicator of that individual's priorities than either his expressed words or even whatever beliefs he may have about himself.

What preferences are revealed by the actual behavior of intellectuals—and how do such revealed preferences compare with their rhetoric? The professed beliefs of intellectuals center about their concern for others—especially for the poor, for minorities, for "social justice" and for protecting endangered species and saving the environment, for example. Their rhetoric is too familiar and too pervasive to require elaboration here. The real question, however, is: What are their revealed preferences?

The phrase "unintended consequences" has become a cliché precisely because so many policies and programs intended, for example, to make the situation of the less fortunate better have in fact made their situation worse that it is no longer possible to regard good intentions as automatic harbingers of good results. Anyone whose primary concern is in improving the lot of the less fortunate would therefore, by this time, after decades of experience with negative "unintended consequences," see a need not only to invest time and efforts to turn good intentions into policies and programs, but also to invest time and efforts afterwards into trying to ferret out answers as to the actual consequences of those policies and programs.

Moreover, anyone whose primary concern was improving the lot of the less fortunate would also be alert and receptive to other factors from *beyond* the vision of the intellectuals, when those other factors have been found empirically to have helped advance the well-being of the less fortunate, even if in ways not contemplated by the intelligentsia and even if in ways counter to the beliefs or visions of the intelligentsia. In short, one of the ways to test whether expressed concerns for the well-being of the less fortunate represent primarily a concern for that well-being or a use of the less fortunate as a means to condemn society, or to seek either political or moral authority over society, would be to see the revealed preferences of intellectuals in terms of how much time and energy they invest in promoting their vision, as compared to how much time and energy they invest in scrutinizing (1) the actual consequences of things done in the name of that vision and (2) benefits to the less fortunate created outside that vision and even counter to that vision.

Crusades for a "living wage" or to end "sweatshop labor" in the Third World, for example, invest enormous amounts of time and energy promoting those goals but virtually none in scrutinizing the many studies done in countries around the world to discover the actual consequences of minimum wage laws in general or of "living wage" laws in particular. These consequences have included such things as higher levels of unemployment and longer periods of unemployment, especially for the least skilled and least experienced segments of the population. Whether one agrees with or disputes these studies, the crucial question here is *whether one bothers to read them at all.*

If the real purpose of social crusades is to make the less fortunate better off, then the actual consequences of such policies as wage control become central and require investigation, in order to avoid "unintended consequences" which have already become widely recognized in the context of many other policies. But if the real purpose of social crusades is to proclaim oneself to be on the side of the angels, then such investigations have a low priority, if any priority at all, since the goal of being on the side of the angels is accomplished when the policies have been advocated and then instituted, after which social crusaders can move on to other issues. The revealed preference of many, if not most, of the intelligentsia has been to be on the side of the angels.

The same conclusion is hard to avoid when looking at the response of intellectuals to improvements in the condition of the poor that follow policies or circumstances which offer no opportunities to be on the side of the angels against the forces of evil. For example, under new economic policies beginning in the 1990s, tens of millions of people in India have risen above that country's official poverty level. In China, under similar policies begun earlier, a million people a month have risen out of poverty.[76] Surely anyone concerned with the fate of the less fortunate would want to know how this desirable development came about for such vast numbers of very poor people— and therefore how similar improvements might be produced elsewhere in the world. But these and other dramatic increases in living standards, based ultimately on the production of more wealth, arouse little or no interest among most intellectuals.

However important for the poor, these developments offer no opportunities for the intelligentsia to be on the side of the angels against the forces of evil— and that is what their revealed preferences show repeatedly to be their real priority. Questions about what policies or conditions increase or decrease the rate of growth of output seldom arouse the interest of most intellectuals, even though such changes have done more to reduce poverty— in both rich and poor countries— than changes in the distribution of income have done. French writer Raymond Aron has suggested that achieving the ostensible goals of the left without using the methods favored by the left actually provokes resentments:

> In fact the European Left has a grudge against the United States mainly because the latter has succeeded by means which were not laid down in the revolutionary code. Prosperity, power, the tendency towards uniformity of economic conditions— these results have been achieved by private initiative, by competition rather than State intervention, in other words by capitalism, which every well-brought-up intellectual has been taught to despise.[77]

Similarly, despite decades of laments in the United States about the poor quality of education in most black schools, studies of particular schools where black students meet or exceed national norms[78] arouse little or no interest among most intellectuals, even those who are active in discussions of racial issues. As with people rising out of poverty in Third World countries, a lack of interest in academically successful black schools by people who are otherwise vocal and vehement on racial issues suggests a revealed preference for the condemnation of unsuccessful schools and of the society that maintains such schools. Investigating successful black schools could offer hope of finding a possible source of knowledge and insights into how to improve education for a group often lagging far behind in educational achievement and in the incomes and occupations that depend on education. But it would not offer an opportunity for the anointed to be on the side of the angels against the forces of evil.

That many, if not most, of these successful black schools do not follow educational notions in vogue among the intelligentsia may be part of the reason for the lack of interest in such schools, just as the lack of interest in how India and China managed to raise the living standards of many millions of poor people may be in part because it was done by moving away from the kinds of economic policies long favored by the left.

It has often been said that intellectuals on the left are "soft on criminals" but, even here, the question is whether those people accused of crime or convicted and in prison are the real objects of intellectuals' beneficence or are incidental props in a larger picture— and expendable like others who are used as props. For example, one of the horrific experiences of many men in prison is being gang-raped by other male prisoners. Yet any attempt to reduce the incidence of such lasting traumatic experiences by building more prisons, so that each prisoner could be housed alone in a single cell, is bitterly opposed by the same people who are vehement in defense of prisoners' "rights." Those rights matter as a means of condemning "society" but so does opposition to the building of more prisons. When the actual well-being of prisoners conflicts with the symbolic issue of preventing more prisons from being built, prisoners become just another sacrifice on the altar to a vision.

In many ways, on a whole range of issues, the revealed preference of intellectuals is to gain moral authority— or, vicariously, political power— or both, over the rest of society. The desires or interests of none of the ostensible beneficiaries of that authority or power— whether the poor, minorities, or criminals in prison— are allowed to outweigh the more fundamental issue of gaining and maintaining the moral hegemony of the anointed.

YOUTH AND AGE

Given the very different conceptions of knowledge by those with the tragic vision and those with the vision of the anointed, it is virtually inevitable that they would have different conceptions of the role and competence of the young. Where knowledge is conceived of as more or less the kinds of things taught in schools and universities, and intelligence is conceived of as sheer brainpower in manipulating concepts and articulating conclusions, there is no inherent reason why the young would not be at least as accomplished in such things as the old, since brain development is said to reach its peak in early adulthood. But, to those with the tragic vision, where consequential knowledge is often mundane knowledge, accumulated by experience, and wisdom is also primarily distilled from experience, then almost by definition the younger generation is not usually in as good a position to make wise decisions— for themselves, much less for society— as those who have much more experience to draw upon.

Accordingly, those with the vision of the anointed have for centuries put great hopes in the young, while those with the tragic vision have relied far more on those with mature experience.

The 1960s notion that "we should learn from our young people" had antecedents going back to the eighteenth century. Such subsidiary social phenomena as lowering the voting age, and reducing the deference to the older generation in general and parents in particular, are likewise very consistent with, if not inescapable corollaries from, the over-all conception of knowledge and intelligence prevalent among those with the vision of the anointed. Where social problems are seen as being consequences of existing institutions and prejudices, the young are often seen as less wedded to the status quo, and thus as hopes for the future.

Back in the eighteenth century, William Godwin articulated this argument when he said, "The next generation will not have so many prejudices to subdue."[79] Children, according to Godwin, "are a sort of raw material put into our hands."[80] Their minds "are like a sheet of white paper."[81] At the same time, they are oppressed by their parents and must go through "twenty years of bondage" before they receive "the scanty portion of liberty, which the government of my country happens to concede to its adult subjects!"[82] Clearly the young have been seen as candidates for "liberation," both of themselves and of society, in this view— a view still very much alive among intellectuals, more than two centuries later.

All these conclusions change completely, however, if knowledge and wisdom are conceived as they are conceived by those with the tragic vision. Adam Smith, for example, said, "The wisest and most experienced are generally the least credulous." In short, the old are generally not as susceptible to heady notions, according to Smith: "It is acquired wisdom and experience only that teach incredulity, and they very seldom teach it enough."[83] The zeal and enthusiasm of the young, much praised by many of those with the vision of the anointed, have long been seen very differently by those with the tragic vision. Burke, for example, said: "It is no excuse for presumptuous ignorance that it is directed by insolent passion."[84] Some have even referred to a perennial invasion of civilization by barbarians, namely the new-born whom families and social institutions must civilize, because they enter the world no different from babies born in the days of the caveman.

People with opposing visions of the world do not simply happen to reach different conclusions about the young and the old. On these and innumerable other issues, the conclusions reached by each are entailed as corollaries of their underlying assumptions about knowledge and wisdom. The education of the young has long been a battleground between adherents of the two visions of the nature of human beings and the nature of knowledge and wisdom. William Godwin's notion that the young "are a sort of raw material put into our hands" remains, after two centuries, a powerful temptation to classroom indoctrination in schools and colleges. In the twentieth century, Woodrow Wilson wrote of his years as an academic administrator when he felt "I should like to make the young gentlemen of the rising generation as unlike their fathers as possible."[85]

This indoctrination can start as early as elementary school, where students are encouraged or required to write about controversial issues, sometimes in letters to public officials. More fundamentally, the indoctrination process habituates them to taking sides on weighty and complex issues after hearing just one side of those issues. Moreover, they are habituated to venting their emotions instead of analyzing conflicting evidence and dissecting conflicting arguments. In short, they are led to prepackaged conclusions, instead of being equipped with the intellectual tools to reach their own conclusions, including conclusions different from those of their teachers. In colleges and universities, whole academic departments are devoted to particular prepackaged conclusions— whether on race, the environment or other subjects, under such names as black, women's or environmental "studies." Few, if any, of these "studies" include conflicting visions and conflicting evidence, as educational rather than ideological criteria might require.

Critics of ideological indoctrination in schools and colleges often attack the particular ideological conclusions, but that is beside the point educationally. Even if we assume, for the sake of argument, that all the conclusions reached by all the various "studies" are both logically and factually valid, that does not get to the heart of the educational issue. Even if students were to leave these "studies" with 100 percent correct conclusions about issues A, B and C, that would in no way equip them intellectually with the tools needed to confront very different issues X, Y and Z that are likely to arise over the course of their future years.

NOTIONS VERSUS PRINCIPLES

Ideally, the work of intellectuals is based on certain principles— of logic, of evidence, and perhaps of moral values or social concerns. However, given the incentives and constraints of the profession, intellectuals' work need not be. There is ample room for attitudes, rather than principles, to guide the work of intellectuals, especially when these are attitudes prevalent among their peers and insulated from consequential feedback from the outside world.

While logic and evidence are ideal criteria for the work of intellectuals, there are many ways in which much of what is said and done by intellectuals has less to do with principles than with attitudes. For example, intellectuals who are receptive to claims of mitigation on the part of murderers who claim to have been battered wives, or others who are said to have had traumatic childhoods of one sort or another, or the less fortunate in general, are seldom receptive to claims that policemen who had a split second to make a life-and-death decision, at the risk of their own lives, should be cut some slack.

Some intellectuals who have been opposed to the principle of racism have nevertheless remained either silent or apologetic when black community leaders have made racist attacks on Asian storekeepers in black ghettos, or on whites in general or Jews in particular. Some intellectuals have even redefined racism in a way to make blacks ineligible for the label*— another exercise in verbal virtuosity. Many among the intelligentsia have denounced "greed" among corporate executives whose incomes are a fraction of the incomes of professional athletes or entertainers who are seldom, if ever, accused of greed.

The intelligentsia have led outraged outcries when oil companies' profits rose, though the amount of profits in the price of a gallon of gasoline is much less than the amount of taxes. But the concept of "greed" is almost never applied to government, whether in the amount of taxes it collects or even when working class homes, often representing the labors and sacrifices of a lifetime, are confiscated wholesale for "redevelopment" of an area in ways that will bring in more taxes, enabling politicians to do more spending to enhance their chances of being reelected.

---

* On grounds that only those with power can be racists— a proviso never part of the definition before and one which would imply that Nazis were not racists during the 1920s, before they took power.

Such responses and non-responses by intellectuals not only represent attitudes rather than principles, often they represent attitudes that over-ride principles. Nor are such biases confined to reactions to particular groups of human beings. They apply even to concepts, such as risk, for example.

Intellectuals who are highly critical of any risks associated with particular pharmaceutical drugs, and consider it the government's duty to ban some of these drugs because of risks of death, see no need for the government to ban sky-diving or white-water rafting, even if the latter represent higher risks of death for the sake of recreation than the risks from medicines that can stave off pain or disability, or which may save more lives than they cost. Similarly, when a boxer dies from a beating in the ring, that is almost certain to set off demands in the media or among the intelligentsia that boxing be banned, but no such demands are likely to follow deaths from skiing accidents, even if these are far more common than deaths from boxing. Again, it is not the principle but the attitude.

While attitudes can vary from individual to individual, the attitudes of intellectuals are largely group attitudes. Moreover, these attitudes change collectively over time, becoming transient moods of a given era, rather than permanent attitudes, much less permanent principles. Thus in the Progressive era of the early twentieth century, racial and ethnic minorities were viewed in largely negative terms, and Progressive support of the eugenics movement was not unrelated to the presumed desirability of preventing these minorities from propagating too many of their own kind. This mood had largely passed by the 1930s, and afterwards racial and ethnic minorities became objects of special solicitude. After the 1960s, this solicitude became virtually an obsession, however inconsistent it was with earlier and opposite obsessions about the same people among intellectuals considered "progressive" in the early twentieth century.

During the earlier era, when farmers and workers were the special focus of solicitude, no one paid much attention to how what was done for the benefit of these groups might adversely affect minorities or others. Likewise, in a later era, little attention was paid by "progressive" intellectuals to how affirmative action for minorities or women might adversely affect others. There is no principle that accounts for such collective mood swings. There are simply mascots du jour, much like adolescent fads that are compulsive badges of identity for a time and afterwards considered passé— but not treated as subject to logic or evidence during either the period of their obsession or the period of their dismissal. Back in the 1920s, when the Sacco-Vanzetti case was an international cause célèbre because of the presumed injustice of their trial, Justice Oliver Wendell Holmes wrote in a letter to Harold Laski about the arbitrary focus of that time:

> I cannot but ask myself why this so much greater interest in red than black. A thousand-fold worse cases of negroes come up from time to time, but the world does not worry over them. It is not a mere simple abstract love of justice that has moved people so much.[86]

ABSTRACT PEOPLE IN
AN ABSTRACT WORLD

Mistaken beliefs about society by intellectuals are not random errors. In practice, their misunderstandings or mischaracterizations promote the overall vision of a deeply flawed society, urgently in need of political intervention to carry out the vision prevalent among the intelligentsia. One of the bases for intellectuals' sweeping pronouncements about whole societies is conceiving of people in the abstract, without the specific, concrete characteristics found in flesh-and-blood human beings as they exist in the real world. For example, the intellectuals' consuming preoccupation with economic inequalities is understandable if the individuals or groups that differ in their economic and other outcomes do not differ in the things which produce those outcomes— as they would not with abstract people. Abstract people can be aggregated into statistical categories such as households, families, and income brackets, without the slightest concern for whether those statistical categories contain similar people, or even the same number of people, or people who differ substantially in age, much less in such finer distinctions as whether or not they are working or whether they are the same people in the same categories over time.

Abstract people have an immortality which flesh-and-blood people have yet to achieve. Thus, a historian writing about the newly-created state of Czechoslovakia after the First World War, said that its policies regarding the ethnic groups within it were designed "to correct social injustice" and to "put right the historic wrongs of the seventeenth century,"[87] despite the fact that actual flesh-and-blood people from the seventeenth century had died long before, putting the redressing of their wrongs beyond the reach of human control. Much the same kind of reasoning has continued to be ideologically powerful among the intelligentsia in twenty-first century America, who speak of "whites" and "blacks" as intertemporal abstractions with centuries-old issues to be redressed, rather than as flesh-and-blood people who take their sins and their sufferings with them to the grave.

Unlike real people, abstract people can be sent "back" to places where they have never been. Thus German families who had lived for centuries in parts of Eastern Europe and the Balkans were sent "back" to Germany after the Second World War, as the majority populations of these regions reacted bitterly to having been mistreated during Nazi occupation by imposing a massive ethnic cleansing of Germans from their midst after the war. Many of these flesh-and-blood people of German ancestry had never laid eyes on Germany, to which they were being sent "back." Only as intertemporal abstractions had they come from Germany.

It was much the same story with so-called Indian Tamils in Sri Lanka who in the 1960s were sent "back" to India, from which their ancestors had emigrated in the nineteenth century. Similarly, when people of Indian and Pakistani heritage were expelled from Uganda in the 1970s, most of them had been born in Uganda and more of them resettled in Britain than in India or Pakistan. Perhaps the most persistent efforts to repatriate intertemporal abstractions were nineteenth-century American proposals to free the slaves and then send them "back to Africa"— a continent which in most cases neither they nor their grandparents had ever seen.

When real differences among real people are mentioned or taken into account in actions or policies by others, intellectuals are quick to declare these differences to be mere "perceptions" or "stereotypes." Evidence for this sweeping conclusion is seldom asked for or given. Abstract equality is the default setting in their assumptions. There is no reason for abstract people to have different outcomes when all their real-world differences in inputs have been abstracted away.

Abstract people are above all equal, though flesh-and-blood people are remote from any such condition or ideal. Inequalities of income, power, prestige, health, and other things have long preoccupied intellectuals, both as things to explain and things to correct. The time and effort devoted to these inequalities might suggest that equality is so common or so automatic that its absence requires an explanation. Many intellectuals have approached equality in much the same spirit as Rousseau approached freedom: "Man was born free, and he is everywhere in chains." To much of the modern intelligentsia, man is regarded as having been born equal but as having mysteriously become everywhere unequal.

Various causes of this otherwise inexplicable inequality have been suggested— exploitation, socially constructed disadvantages, racism, sexism, or class bias, for example. But seldom is it considered necessary to demonstrate the automatic equality which makes an explanation of its absence necessary. Anyone who suggests that individuals— or, worse yet, groups— are unequal is written off intellectually and denounced morally as biased and bigoted toward those considered less than equal. Yet the empirical case for equality ranges from feeble to non-existent.

Does anyone seriously believe that whites in general play professional basketball as well as blacks? How then can one explain the predominance of blacks in this lucrative occupation, which offers fame as well as fortune? For most of the period of black predominance in professional basketball, the owners of the teams have all been white, as have most of the coaches. Then by what mechanism could blacks have contrived to deny access to professional basketball to whites of equal ability in that sport? Even those who concede that blacks, as of this moment, and under existing social and cultural circumstances, may turn out more highly skilled basketball players as a matter of empirical fact, nevertheless insist that whites could play the game equally well if circumstances— including alternative careers available— were the same for both races.

Assuming this to be true only reveals what conception of equality is implicit in much of what intellectuals say. It is not *empirical* equality that they are talking about but equality of *potential*, equality in the abstract. This is not a small difference, even when it is a difference that is often ignored or glided over in the course of discussions. Even if abstract potentiality is the same, on average, between such large aggregations of people as races or social classes, that abstract potentiality exists only at the moment of conception. But nobody chooses a career or applies for college admission at the moment of conception. By the time real people in the real world reach such decision-making points, a lot has happened since conception and it has seldom happened the same for everybody. Even between conception and birth, things have happened so differently as to produce different rates of infant mortality and different diseases and medical conditions (including narcotic drug withdrawal symptoms) among babies born to women with different behavior patterns, such as smoking and intakes of junk food, alcohol and narcotics.

The distinction between abstract potential and developed capabilities is not trivial, even though it is often lost sight of or is finessed by intellectuals who speak in generalities about "equality." Abstract potential carries very little weight anywhere in the real world, when people are making decisions for themselves. Performance is what matters. What most people want to know is: What can you actually deliver? Not what you *could have* delivered under other circumstances or might deliver after different institutions or different policies have been created, but what you can do here and now, in the real world. What we want to know is what real people can actually do, not what abstract potential there is in abstract people.

The exceptional facility of intellectuals with abstractions does not eliminate the difference between those abstractions and the real world. Nor does it guarantee that what is true of those abstractions is necessarily true of reality, much less that intellectuals' sophisticated visions about these abstractions should over-ride other people's very different direct experiences in the real world. Intellectuals may indeed dismiss the "perceptions" of others and label them "stereotypes" or "myths," but that is not the same as proving them wrong empirically, even if a remarkable number of intellectuals act as if it does. Behind the widespread practice of regarding group differences in demographic "representation" in various occupations, institutions, or income levels as evidence of discrimination, there is the implicit notion that the groups themselves cannot be different or that any differences are the fault of "society," which must correct its own mistakes or sins.

Since there is no one named "society," what such intellectuals usually turn to for redress is the government. Implicit in all this is the assumption that there is something wrong about individuals and groups being different in their empirical abilities, since their abstract potentials have been presumed to be the same.

Once the focus shifts from abstract potential to empirical capabilities, the notion of equality is not merely unproven but unlikely to the point of being absurd. How could people living in the Himalayas develop the seafaring skills of people living in ports around the Mediterranean or on the Atlantic? How could Polynesians know as much about how to handle camels as the Bedouins of the Sahara— or the Bedouins know as much about fishing as the Polynesians?

Empirically observable skills have always been grossly unequal— which is to say, real people have never been even close to the equality of abstract people. For centuries the English sheared their sheep and sent the wool to Flanders to be made into cloth. Would they have gone to this trouble if they themselves were equally good at weaving wool into cloth? Eventually, the English did master the making of woolen cloth, much to the economic discomfort of Flanders, *but it took centuries*. It likewise took centuries for the English to become masters of modern financial institutions. Before then, much of their finance was in the hands of Lombards and Jews. There is a reason why there is a Lombard Street in London's financial district today and another street there named Old Jewry. Whole industries have been dominated by particular minorities in particular countries around the world for centuries— for example, Germans in brewing beer in China, Brazil, Australia, and the United States; the overseas Chinese in retailing in Malaysia, Indonesia, the Philippines, Jamaica, and Panama; the Jains from India in diamond cutting for the world market, whether in India or in

Amsterdam; Italians in both classical and popular music around the world—and so on and on. But none of these empirical facts affect the over-riding vision of abstract equality that pervades the thinking of the intelligentsia.

Age and occupational skills are among the things which differ radically from group to group, country to country, and civilization to civilization. Rates of alcoholism vary by multiples between groups in countries around the world. So do crime rates and infant mortality rates, among many other things. But none of these empirical facts disturbs the vision of abstract equality. Outrage in the media and among the intelligentsia over the fact that blacks have been turned down for mortgage loans more often than whites wholly disregards many of the factors used in determining who will and will not get such loans. Nor have they given much attention to ferreting out the facts on how such factors differ among different groups.

Much was made of the fact that blacks and whites with the same income still had different rates of rejection of mortgage loan applications— as if income was the only factor that differed, or as if other factors not studied could be assumed to be equal or comparable.[88] Where concrete information is lacking or unstudied, equality tends to be the default assumption, no matter how many inequalities have been found in how many factors that have been studied. The fundamental flaw in such reasoning can be illustrated in a non-controversial area such as baseball. There were two players on the 1927 New York Yankees with identical batting averages of .356, but one has remained famous to this day while the other is almost completely forgotten. Their equality in one dimension in no way implied equality in other dimensions. In this case, one .356 hitter hit 6 home runs that year (Earle Combs) and the other hit 60 (Babe Ruth).

Similarly, when Lewis Terman's famous decades-long study of unusually high-IQ children assessed their achievements in adulthood, many had very high achievements but, as a later writer observed, "almost *none* of the genius children from the lowest social and economic class ended up making a name for themselves." Almost a third of these high-IQ children "from the other side of the tracks" had "a parent who had dropped out of school before the eighth grade."[89] They were like the other children in the sense of having IQs of 140 or above, but not in terms of the cultural factors involved in high achievements.

The same principle applies in innumerable contexts, not only in American society but in countries around the world. University students in India who came from families with similar incomes were found to come from families with very different levels of literacy when comparing students who were Dalits[90] (formerly "untouchables") with students who were caste Hindus— illiteracy being higher in the families of the Dalits. Equality of income did not imply equality of other consequential characteristics. In other countries, people with the "same" education— measured quantitatively— have had very different qualities of education, whether measured by their own choice of specialties, their performances as students or by the quality ranking of the institutions in which they were educated. Only abstract people in an abstract world are the same.

The point here is not that the intelligentsia were mistaken or ill-informed on particular issues. The more fundamental point is that, by thinking in terms of abstract people in an abstract world, intellectuals evade the responsibility and the arduous work of learning the real facts about real people in the real world— facts which often explain the discrepancies between what intellectuals see and what they would prefer to see. Many of what are called social problems are differences between the theories of intellectuals and the realities of the world— differences which many intellectuals interpret to mean that it is the real world that is wrong and needs changing. Moreover, these changes are to be made to the institutions of society, not to the cultures of groups, which are pronounced to be equal by the doctrine of multiculturalism.

Empirical equality never has to be demonstrated in the world of contemporary intellectuals. Equality is the default setting by assumption and the burden of proof to the contrary is put on others.

Chapter 5

Optional Reality in the Media and Academia

A screen has been fashioned through which our contemporary age reads its filtered information.

Jean-François Revel [1]

The preservation of the vision of the anointed has led many among the intelligentsia to vigorous and even desperate expedients, including the filtering out of facts, the redefinition of words and— for some intellectuals— challenging the very idea of truth itself.

FILTERING REALITY

Many among the intelligentsia create their own reality— whether deliberately or not— by filtering out information contrary to their conception of how the world is or ought to be.

Some have gone further. J.A. Schumpeter said that the first thing a man will do for his ideals is lie.[2] It is not necessary to lie, however, in order to deceive, when filtering will accomplish the same purpose. This can take the form of reporting selective and atypical samples, suppressing some facts altogether, or filtering out the inconvenient meanings or connotations of words.

Selective Samples

Filtering the sample of information available to the public can take many forms. For example, Bennett Cerf, the founder of Random House

119

publishers, at one time during the Second World War suggested that books critical of the Soviet Union be withdrawn from circulation.[3]

When the American economy was recovering from a recession in 1983 and unemployment was down in 45 out of the 50 states, ABC News simply chose to feature a report on one of the five states where that was not so or, as they put it, "where unemployment is most severe,"[4] as if these states were just more severe examples of a more general condition, when in fact they were very atypical.

Filtering can also take the form of incessantly reporting data showing blacks or other non-white groups as being worse off than whites in income, rejection of mortgage loan applications or lay-offs during economic downturns— and *not* reporting that whites are in all these same respects worse off than another non-white group, Asian Americans.[5] Even when data are available for all these groups, Asian Americans tend to be filtered out in "news" stories that are de facto editorials, whose clear thrust is that white racism is the reason for the lower incomes or lower occupational status, or other misfortunes, of non-white groups.

Including Asian Americans in these comparisons would not only introduce a discordant note, it would raise the possibility that these various groups differ in their own behavior or performances— contrary to implicit assumptions— and that such differences are reflected in the outcomes being studied. In short, the performance of Asian Americans has implications going far beyond Asian Americans themselves, for it is a threat to a whole vision of American society in which many have a large stake— ideologically and sometimes politically and economically.*

Homelessness is another area where much of the media filters what kind of reality gets through to their audience. During his time at CBS News, Bernard Goldberg noticed the difference between what he saw on the street and what was being broadcast on television:

---

* One of the small but revealing signs of the high stakes that many have in the prevailing vision is the adverse reaction of many among the intelligentsia to Asian Americans being called a "model minority." Considering all the things that various minorities have been called at various times and places, the fierceness of the reaction against this particular label suggests far more at stake than the felicity of a phrase.

In the 1980s, I started noticing that the homeless people we showed on the news didn't look very much like the homeless people I was tripping over on the sidewalk.

The ones on the sidewalk, by and large, were winos or drug addicts or schizophrenics. They mumbled crazy things or gave you the evil eye when they put paper coffee cups in your face and "asked" for money. . . .

But the ones we liked to show on television were different. They looked as if they came from your neighborhood and mine. They looked like us. And the message from TV news was that they didn't just *look* like us— they *were* like us! On NBC, Tom Brokaw said that the homeless are "people you know."[6]

If the homeless tend to be sanitized in television news, businessmen tend to be demonized in movies and television dramas, as another study found:

Only 37 percent of the fictional entrepreneurs played positive roles, and the proportion of "bad guy businessmen" was almost double that of all other occupations. What's more, they were *really* nasty, committing 40 percent of the murders and 44 percent of the vice crimes. . . Only 8 percent of prime-time criminals were black. . . [7]

In real life, as well as in fiction, what was presented to television audiences was highly atypical of what existed in the real world:

■ During the period studied, 6 percent of the people with AIDS shown on the evening news were gay men. But in real life 58 percent were gay men.
■ On TV, 16 percent were blacks and Hispanics. But in real life 46 percent were black or Hispanic.
■ On TV, 2 percent of the AIDS sufferers were IV drug users. In real life 23 percent were.[8]

This creation of a picture reflecting the vision of the anointed, rather than the realities of the world, extends to textbooks used in schools. Publishers such as McGraw-Hill, for example, have percentage guidelines as to how many of the people shown in photographs in their textbooks have to be black, white, Hispanic and disabled. Moreover, the way these individuals are portrayed must also reflect the vision of the anointed. According to the *Wall Street Journal,* "one major publisher vetoed a photo of a barefoot child in an African village, on the grounds that the lack of footwear reinforced the stereotype of poverty on that continent."[9] In short, the painfully blatant reality of desperate poverty in much of Africa is waved aside as a "stereotype" because it does not fit the vision to be portrayed, even if it does fit the facts.

Suppressing Facts

One of the historic examples of suppressing facts was the reporting and non-reporting of the Soviet Union's government-created famine in the Ukraine and the North Caucasus that killed millions of people in the 1930s. *New York Times* Moscow correspondent Walter Duranty wrote, "There is no famine or actual starvation, nor is there likely to be."[10] He received a Pulitzer Prize, the Pulitzer panel commending him for his reports, "marked by scholarship, profundity, impartiality, sound judgment and exceptional clarity."[11] Meanwhile, British writer Malcolm Muggeridge reported from the Ukraine that peasants there were in fact starving: "I mean starving in its absolute sense; not undernourished as, for instance, most Oriental peasants. . . and some unemployed workers in Europe, but having had for weeks next to nothing to eat."[12] Muggeridge wrote in a subsequent article that the man-made famine was "one of the most monstrous crimes in history, so terrible that people in the future will scarcely be able to believe it ever happened."[13] Decades later, a scholarly study by Robert Conquest, *The Harvest of Sorrow*, estimated that six million people had died in that famine over a period of three years.[14] Still later, when the official archives were finally opened in the last days of the Soviet Union under Mikhail Gorbachev, new estimates of the deaths from the man-made famine were made by various scholars who had studied material from those archives. Most of their estimates equalled or exceeded Dr. Conquest's earlier estimates.[15]

At the time of the famine, however, this was one of the most successful filtering operations imaginable. What Muggeridge said was dismissed as "a hysterical tirade" by Beatrice Webb, co-author with her husband Sidney Webb of an internationally known study of the Soviet Union.[16] Muggeridge was vilified and was unable to get work as a writer, after his dispatches from the Soviet Union, and was so financially strapped that he, his wife and two small children had to move in with friends. There is no need to believe that there was any conspiracy among editors or journalists to silence and ostracize Malcolm Muggeridge. Nor is a conspiracy necessary for successfully filtering out things that do not fit the prevailing vision— either then or now.

Except for Muggeridge and a very few other people, a famine deliberately used to break the back of resistance to Stalin— killing a comparable or larger number of people as those who died in the Nazi Holocaust— would have been filtered completely out of history, instead of being merely ignored, as it usually is today. This was not a matter of honest mistakes by Duranty and others. What Duranty said privately to some other journalists and to diplomats at the time was radically different from what he said in his dispatches to the *New York Times*. For example, in 1933 a British diplomat reported to London: "Mr. Duranty thinks it quite possible that as many as 10 million people may have died directly or indirectly from lack of food in the Soviet Union during the past year."[17]

Statistical data can also be filtered, whether by omitting data that go counter to the desired conclusion (such as data on Asian Americans) or by restricting the release of data to only those researchers whose position on the issue at hand is in accord to that of those who control the data. For example, a statistically based study by former college presidents William Bowen and Derek Bok was widely hailed for its conclusions supporting affirmative action in college admissions.[18] But when Harvard Professor Stephan Thernstrom, whose views on affirmative action did not coincide with theirs, sought to get the raw data on which the study's conclusions were based, he was refused.[19] Similarly, when UCLA professor of law Richard Sander sought to test competing theories about the effect of affirmative action in law schools by getting data on bar examination pass rates by race in California, supporters of affirmative action threatened to sue if the state bar released such data— and the state bar then refused to release the data.[20]

In these and other cases, statistics are filtered at the source, even when these are taxpayer-financed statistics, collected for the ostensible purpose of providing facts on which informed policy choices can be made, but in practice treated as if their purpose is to protect the prevailing vision.

Rummaging through numbers can turn up statistical data consistent with a given vision and rummaging through other numbers— or perhaps even the same numbers viewed or selected differently— can produce data consistent with the opposite vision. But only when numbers are in accord with a prevailing vision are they likely to be accepted uncritically, without considering other statistics that tell a very different story. For example, much of what is said about the effect of gun control on crime rates in general, or on the murder rate in particular, is based on what kinds of statistics are repeated endlessly and what kinds of data seldom, if ever, reach the general public.

It has, for example, been repeated endlessly in the media and in academia that Britain and various other countries with stronger gun control laws than those in the United States have murder rates that are only a fraction of the murder rate in the United States— the clear implication being that it is the gun control which accounts for the difference in murder rates. Having reached this conclusion, most of the intelligentsia have seen no reason to proceed further. But a serious attempt to test the hypothesis of an inverse relationship between restricted gun ownership and the murder rate would make other comparisons and other breakdowns of statistical data necessary. For example:

1. Since we know that murder rates are lower in some countries with stronger gun control laws than in the United States, are there other countries with stronger gun control laws than the United States that have *higher* murder rates?
2. Are there countries with widespread gun ownership which have lower murder rates than some other countries with lower gun ownership rates?
3. Did the murder rate differential between the United States and Britain originate with the onset of gun control laws?

Those who were content to stop when they found the kinds of statistics they were looking for were unlikely to ask such questions. The answers to these three questions, incidentally, are yes; yes; and no.

Russia and Brazil have tougher gun control laws than the United States and much higher murder rates.[21] Gun ownership rates in Mexico are a fraction of what they are in the United States, but Mexico's murder rate is more than double that in the United States. Handguns are banned in Luxembourg but not in Belgium, France or Germany; yet the murder rate in Luxembourg is several times the murder rate in Belgium, France or Germany.[22] An international statistical study found that Switzerland, Israel and New Zealand "have relatively lax gun control laws and/or high firearms availability, yet have homicide rates that differ little from those in England or Japan"[23]— which is to say, homicide rates a fraction of those in the United States.

New York City has had a murder rate some multiple of the murder rate in London for more than two centuries— and for most of those two centuries *neither* place had serious gun control laws.[24] Murders committed without guns have also been several times as high in New York as in London.[25] Nevertheless, the fact that the murder rate in England is lower than that in the United States continues to be cited as proof that gun control laws reduce the murder rate.

Considering how many intellectuals have not only supported existing gun control laws, but have actively promoted more and stronger gun control laws, it can hardly be supposed that all these highly educated and very brainy people were incapable of performing very straightforward tests of the hypothesis of an inverse correlation between gun control and murder rates. Nor need we suppose that they knew better and were deliberately lying. What seems far more likely is that, once they found statistics to support their preconception, they had no incentive to go any further.

Just as it is hard to find any consistent correlation between gun ownership and violent crime rates internationally, it is hard to find any such correlation from historical statistics within the United States. As one study noted:

> The United States experienced an extraordinary increase in violent crime in the 1960s and 1970s and a remarkable drop in violent crime in the 1990s. The number of firearms, especially handguns, in private hands increased by several million every year during this period. The relentless growth in the privately held stock of firearms cannot explain both the crime wave of the first period and the crime drop of the second period.[26]

Individual ad hoc filtering of what gets through the media to the public can readily add up to as complete a distortion of reality as if there were a conscious coordination by a heavy-handed censorship or propaganda agency— if those individual journalists and editors who do the filtering share the same general vision of what is and what ought to be. What seems plausible to those who share that vision can become the criterion of both believability and newsworthiness. Plausibility, however, is the most treacherous of all criteria, for what will seem plausible in a particular case depends on what one already believes in general.

It is not necessary for either individuals or a cabal to work out a plan of deliberate deception for filtering of information to produce a distorted picture that resembles the vision of the anointed rather than the reality of the world. All that is necessary is that those in a position to filter— whether as reporters, editors, teachers, scholars, or movie-makers— decide that there are certain aspects of reality that the masses would "misunderstand" and which a sense of social responsibility requires those in a position to filter to leave out.

Data showing the poverty rate among black married couples in America to have been in single digits for every year since 1994 are unlikely to get much, if any, attention in most of the media. Still less is it likely to lead to any consideration of the implications of such data for the view that the high poverty rate among blacks reflects the larger society's racism, even though married blacks are of the same race as unmarried mothers living in the ghetto on welfare, and would therefore be just as subject to racism, if that was the main reason for poverty. Still less are such data likely to be examined as to their implications for the notion that marriage is just one "lifestyle" choice among many, with no weightier implications for individual or social consequences.

No factual information that could reflect negatively on homosexuals is likely to find its way through either media or academic filters, but anything that shows gays as victims can get massive coverage. A search by journalist William McGowan found more than 3,000 media stories about a gay man in Wyoming who was beaten unconscious by thugs and left to die, but fewer than 50 media stories about a teenage boy who was captured and repeatedly raped for hours by two homosexual men, who likewise left him to die. McGowan's search indicated that the second story was not mentioned at all in the *New York Times* or the *Los Angeles Times*, nor was it broadcast on CBS, NBC, ABC or CNN.[27]

Despite an abundance of statistical data being published on virtually every conceivable comparison among groups, no data on the average lifespan of homosexuals compared to the national average, the cost of AIDS to the taxpayers compared to the cost of other diseases, much less a comparison of the incidence of child molestation among heterosexual and homosexual men, is likely to find its way through the filters of the intelligentsia to reach the public, even though there is a well-known national organization openly promoting homosexual relations between men and boys. Conceivably, data on such matters might lay to rest some concerns about homosexuality expressed in some quarters,[28] but few among the intelligentsia seem prepared to risk what the data might show if not filtered out. In this, as in many other cases, it is too much for some to gamble the fate of a vision on a roll of the dice, which is what empirical verification amounts to for those dedicated to a vision.

This is especially true for reporters who are themselves homosexual— and there are enough such reporters to have a National Lesbian and Gay Journalists Association. One homosexual reporter, who has worked for the *Detroit News* and the *New York Times*, knew about the role of public bathhouses frequented by gay men in spreading AIDS, but decided not to write about it because "I was hesitant to do a story that would give comfort to our enemies."[29] Nor is this attitude peculiar to homosexual reporters. Journalists hired under a "diversity" rationale as representatives of blacks, Hispanics or women have the same conflict between reporting news and filtering news for the benefit of the group they were hired to represent.

A black reporter for the *Washington Post*, for example, wrote in her memoirs that she saw her role as being "a spokeswoman for the race" and she excoriated a fellow black reporter on the *Washington Post* for writing about corruption in the local D.C. government, where black officials predominate.[30] "The National Association of Hispanic Journalists has long cautioned journalists against using the word 'illegal' in copy and headlines" about people who crossed the border into the United States without authorization, according to the *Washington Times*. "The practice is 'dehumanizing' and 'stereotypes undocumented people who are in the United States as having committed a crime,' said Joseph Torres, the group's president."[31]

In short, the first loyalty of many journalists is not to their readers or television audiences who seek information from them but to protecting the image and interests of the groups they represent under a "diversity" hiring rationale. Such journalists are also under peer pressure to filter the news, rather than report the facts straight.

Conversely, information or allegations reflecting negatively on individuals or groups seen less sympathetically by the intelligentsia pass rapidly into the public domain with little scrutiny and much publicity. Two of the biggest proven hoaxes of our time have involved allegations of white men gang-raping a black woman— first the Tawana Brawley hoax of 1987 and later the false rape charges against three Duke University students in 2006. In both cases, editorial indignation rang out across the land, without a speck of evidence to substantiate either of these charges. Moreover, the denunciations were not limited to the particular men accused, but were often extended to society at large, of whom these men were deemed to be symptoms or "the tip of the iceberg." In both cases, the charges fit a pre-existing vision, and that apparently made mundane facts unnecessary.

Another widely publicized hoax— one to which the President of the United States added his sub-hoax— was a 1996 story appearing in *USA Today* under the headline, "Arson at Black Churches Echoes Bigotry of the Past." There was, according to *USA Today*, "an epidemic of church burning," targeting black churches. Like the gang-rape hoaxes, this story spread rapidly through the media. The *Chicago Tribune* referred to "an epidemic of criminal and cowardly arson"[32] leaving black churches in ruins.

As with the gang-rape hoaxes, comments on the church fire stories went beyond those who were supposed to have set these fires to blame forces at work in society at large. Jesse Jackson was quoted in the *New York Times* as calling these arsons part of a "cultural conspiracy" against blacks, which "reflected the heightened racial tensions in the south that have been exacerbated by the assault on affirmative action and the populist oratory of Republican politicians like Pat Buchanan." *Time* magazine writer Jack White likewise blamed "the coded phrases" of Republican leaders for "encouraging the arsonists." Columnist Barbara Reynolds of *USA Today* said that the fires were "an attempt to murder the spirit of black America." *New*

York Times columnist Bob Herbert said, "The fuel for these fires can be traced to a carefully crafted environment of bigotry and hatred that was developed over the last quarter century."[33]

As with the gang-rape hoaxes, the charges publicized were taken as reflecting on the whole society, not just those supposedly involved in what was widely presumed to be arson, rather than fires that break out for a variety of other reasons. *Washington Post* columnist Dorothy Gilliam said that society in effect was "giving these arsonists permission to commit these horrible crimes."[34] The climax of these comments came when President Bill Clinton, in his weekly radio address, said that these church burnings recalled similar burnings of black churches in Arkansas when he was a boy. There were more than 2,000 media stories done on the subject after the President's address.

This story began to unravel when factual research showed that (1) *no* black churches were burned in Arkansas while Bill Clinton was growing up, (2) there had been no increase in fires at black churches, but an actual decrease over the previous 15 years, (3) the incidence of fires at white churches was similar to the incidence of fires at black churches, and (4) where there was arson, one-third of the suspects were black. However, retractions of the original story— where there were retractions at all— typically were given far less prominence than the original banner headlines and heated editorial comments.[35]

Stories that reflect adversely on America can spread rapidly through the media, with little evidence and less skepticism, whether these are racial stories or not. For example, Dan Rather began the CBS News broadcast of March 26, 1991 by proclaiming "A startling number of American children in danger of starving." He added: "One out of eight American children under the age of twelve is going hungry tonight. That is the finding of a new two-year study."[36] Despite the portentous word "study," this was all based on five questions asked by a radical advocacy group which classified as "hungry" children whose parents answered "yes" to five out of eight questions. Two of these questions did not even deal with children but asked about the eating habits of adults. One of the questions about children was: "Do you ever rely on a limited number of foods to feed your children because you are running out of money to buy food for a meal?"[37] In other words, did you ever fill them up with hot dogs when you would have preferred to have given them more of a variety of foods?

It is a long way from "ever" to "every night" and a still longer way from a limited variety of foods to hunger, much less starvation. But verbal virtuosity papered over such distinctions. Nor was Dan Rather unique. "Hunger in America" became a theme of news and commentary elsewhere in the media. *Newsweek*, the Associated Press, and the *Boston Globe* were among those who repeated the one-in-eight statistic from this "study."[38]

Meanwhile, when actual flesh-and-blood people were examined by the Centers for Disease Control and the U.S. Department of Agriculture, no evidence of malnutrition among Americans with poverty-level incomes was found, nor any significant difference in their intake of vitamins and minerals from that among people in higher income brackets. The only real difference among people in different income brackets was that being overweight was much more prevalent among the poor than among the affluent.[39] But, as in other contexts, when a story fits the vision, people in the media do not always find it necessary to check whether it also fits the facts.

Fictitious People

Filtering and slanting can create not only fictitious facts but also fictitious people. This is obvious in the case of totalitarian dictatorships, where mass-murdering tyrants are depicted in official propaganda as kindly, wise and all-caring leaders of their people, while all those who might oppose the dictator at home or abroad are depicted as the lowest sorts of villains. But something very similar can happen in free, democratic nations without any official propaganda agency, but with an intelligentsia bent on seeing the world in a particular way.

Perhaps the most striking example in twentieth-century America of a fictitious persona being created for a public figure, without any conscious coordination among the intelligentsia, was that of Herbert Hoover. Hoover's misfortune was to be President of the United States when the stock market crash of 1929 was followed by the beginning of the Great Depression of the 1930s. Had he never become president, Herbert Hoover could have gone down in history as one of the greatest humanitarians of the century. It was not simply the amount of money he donated to philanthropic causes before he became president, but the way he risked his own personal fortune to rescue starving people in Europe during the First World War that made him unique.

Because the blockades, destruction and disruptions of the war had left millions of people across Europe suffering from hunger, or even starving, Hoover formed a philanthropic organization to get food to them on a massive scale. However, realizing that if he operated in the usual way, by first raising money from donations and then buying the food, people would be dying while he was raising money, Hoover bought the food first, putting his own personal fortune at risk if he could not raise the money to pay for it all. Eventually, enough donations came in to cover the cost of the food but there was no guarantee that this would happen when he began.

Hoover also served as head of the Food Administration in Woodrow Wilson's administration during the war, where he apparently sufficiently impressed supporters of another member of that administration— a rising young man named Franklin D. Roosevelt— that these FDR supporters sought to interest Hoover in becoming the Democrats' nominee for president in 1920, with FDR as his vice-presidential running mate.[40] However, only the latter came to pass, with Roosevelt being the running mate for Democratic presidential candidate James M. Cox, who lost in 1920, while Hoover went on to serve as Secretary of Commerce under Republican Presidents Warren Harding and Calvin Coolidge.

So much for the real Herbert Hoover. What whole generations have heard and read about is the fictitious Herbert Hoover— a cold, heartless man who let millions of Americans suffer needlessly during the Great Depression of the 1930s because of his supposedly doctrinaire belief that the government should leave the economy alone. In short, the image of Hoover depicted by the intelligentsia was that of a do-nothing president.[41] According to this view— widely disseminated in both the popular media and in academia, as well as repeated at election time for decades— it was only the replacement of Hoover by FDR that got the federal government involved in trying to counter the effects of the Great Depression. The falsity of this picture was exposed back during the Great Depression itself by leading columnist Walter Lippmann, and that falsity was confirmed in later years by former members of Roosevelt's own administration, who acknowledged that much— if not most— of the New Deal was simply a further extension of initiatives already taken by President Hoover.[42] Lippmann, writing in 1935, said:

> The policy initiated by President Hoover in the autumn of 1929 was something utterly unprecedented in American history. The national government undertook to make the whole economic order operate prosperously... the Roosevelt measures are a continuous evolution of the Hoover measures.[43]

Herbert Hoover was quite aware— and proud— of the fact that he was the first President of the United States to make getting the country out of a depression a federal responsibility. "No President before had ever believed there was a government responsibility in such cases," he said in his memoirs.[44] Nor was such interventionism a new departure for Hoover who, earlier as Secretary of Commerce, had urged a reduction in the hours of labor and advocated a Constitutional amendment to forbid child labor, among other interventionist initiatives.[45] As President, Hoover responded to a growing federal deficit during the depression by proposing, and later signing into law, a large increase in tax rates— from the existing rate of between 20 and 30 percent for people in the top income brackets to new rates of more than 60 percent in those brackets.[46]

None of this, of course, means that either Hoover's or FDR's interventions were helpful on net balance, nor is that the point, which is that a completely fictitious Herbert Hoover was created, not only in politics but in the writings of the intelligentsia. For example, the fictitious Hoover cared only for the rich— whose taxes the real Hoover more than doubled, taking more than half their income. The fictitious Hoover was unconcerned about ordinary working people but the real Hoover was praised by the head of the American Federation of Labor for his efforts to keep industry from cutting workers' wages during the depression.[47]

The intelligentsia of the times created the fictitious Hoover, and the intelligentsia of later times perpetuated that image. In 1932, Oswald Garrison Villard, editor of *The Nation*, said that President Hoover "failed for lack of sympathy."[48] A *New Republic* editorial said of Hoover: "He has been the living embodiment of the thesis that it is the function of the government not to govern."[49] Noted literary critic Edmund Wilson said that Hoover "made no effort to deal with the breakdown"[50] and called him "inhuman."[51] Joint columnists Robert S. Allen and Drew Pearson denounced Hoover's "do-nothingness."[52] As far away as England, Harold Laski said, "Mr. Hoover has done nothing to cope with the problem."[53]

In politics as well, the fictitious Hoover had the same image— and that image lived on. In 1936, when Herbert Hoover was no longer a candidate, FDR's Secretary of the Interior, Harold Ickes, nevertheless attacked Hoover for having been a "do-nothing" president[54]— a trend that continued for many elections in later years, as Democrats repeatedly pictured a vote for Republican presidential candidates as a vote to return to the days of Herbert Hoover. It was twenty years after Hoover left the White House before there was another Republican president.

As late as the 1980s, President Ronald Reagan was characterized by the Democrats' Speaker of the House Tip O'Neill as "Hoover with a smile" and, when Reagan's Secretary of the Treasury defended the administration's economic policies in a statement to Congress, Democratic Senator Ernest Hollings said, "That's Hoover talk, man!"[55]— even though Reagan's tax cut policy was the direct opposite of Hoover's tax increases. Even in the twenty-first century, the 2008 financial crisis provoked a *New York Times* columnist to express fear that the 50 state governors would become "50 Herbert Hoovers."[56] In short, Hoover's image was still politically useful as a bogeyman, decades after his presidency and even after his death.

One of the signs of the great sense of decency of Harry Truman was that, a month after he became president in 1945, he sent a handwritten letter to Herbert Hoover, inviting him to the White House for the first time since Hoover left it in 1933, to seek his advice on food aid to Europe after the disruptions of the Second World War.[57] Hoover was both surprised by the letter from President Truman and moved to tears when he met with Truman in the White House.[58] Later, Truman's appointment of Hoover to head a commission to investigate the efficiency of government agencies enabled this much-hated man to regain some public respect in his later years and shake off some of the opprobrium that went with the intelligentsia's creation of a fictitious Herbert Hoover.

Fictitious positive images can of course also be created, not only by propaganda agencies in totalitarian countries but also by the intelligentsia in democratic countries. No politician in the past two generations was regarded by intellectuals as more of an intellectual than Adlai Stevenson, the suave and debonair former governor of Illinois who twice ran for President of the United States against Dwight Eisenhower in the 1950s. The *New York Times* called him "the best kind of intellectual."[59] Russell Jacoby's study, *The Last Intellectuals* depicted "Eisenhower's resounding defeat of Adlai Stevenson" as showing "the endemic anti-intellectualism of American society."[60] Yet Stevenson "could go quite happily for months or years without picking up a book,"[61] according to noted historian Michael Beschloss, among others who reported Stevenson's disinterest in books.

Meanwhile, no one thought of Harry Truman as an intellectual, though he was a voracious reader, whose fare included heavyweight books like the works of Thucydides and Shakespeare, and who was "a president who enjoyed Cicero in the original Latin"[62]— someone who was able to correct Chief Justice Fred M. Vinson when Vinson quoted in Latin.[63] However, Adlai Stevenson had the rhetoric and the airs of an intellectual, and Harry Truman did not.* Many among the intelligentsia regarded the unpretentious and plain-spoken Truman as little more than a country bumpkin.**

A contemporary public figure who has had a fictitious personality created for him by the media is Supreme Court Justice Clarence Thomas. The fictitious Clarence Thomas has been described as a loner, permanently

---

* Neither was of course an intellectual in the sense defined here but the point is that intellectuals saw Stevenson as one of their own, but not Truman, who was far more involved in matters of the mind.
** Others likewise under-estimated the scope and depth of President Truman's knowledge. At a White House conference in 1946, General Dwight D. Eisenhower raised a question as to whether the president understood the grave implications of American policy as regards the Dardanelles. Undersecretary of State Dean Acheson, who was present at that meeting, later described how President Truman "reached in a drawer, took out a large and clearly much-studied map of the area" and proceeded to give an extended account of the history of that area of the world in what Acheson described as "a masterful performance"— after which Truman turned to Eisenhower to ask whether the general was satisfied that the president understood the implications of American foreign policy in that area. Merle Miller, *Plain Speaking: An Oral Biography of Harry S. Truman* (New York: Berkley Publishing Corporation, 1974), p. 243.

embittered by his controversial Senate confirmation hearings, "a virtual recluse in private life."[64] A reporter for the *Wall Street Journal* called him "Washington's most famous recluse."[65] Justice Thomas was depicted in a *New Yorker* article as someone who can really talk only to his wife and "the couple's life appears to be one of shared, brooding isolation."[66] Because Justice Thomas and Justice Antonin Scalia have voted together so often in Supreme Court cases, he has been variously described as "a clone" of Scalia by syndicated columnist Carl Rowan[67] and a "puppet" of Scalia by a lawyer from the American Civil Liberties Union.[68] Similar statements about Justice Thomas' role on the Supreme Court have been common in the media.

Those who have bothered to check out the facts, however, have discovered a flesh-and-blood Clarence Thomas the exact opposite of the fictitious Clarence Thomas portrayed in the media. Reporters for the *Washington Post*— hardly a supporter of Justice Thomas— interviewed colleagues and former clerks of his, as well as consulting notes made by the late Justice Harry Blackmun at private judicial conferences among the justices, and came up with a radically different picture of the man:

> Thomas is perhaps the court's most accessible justice— except to journalists. . . He is known to spot a group of schoolchildren visiting the court and invite the students to his chambers. Students from his alma mater, family members of former clerks, people he encounters on his drives across the country in his 40-foot Prevost motor coach— all are welcome. . .

> Thomas seems to have an unquenchable thirst for conversation. . . A planned 15-minute drop-by invariably turns into an hour, then two, sometimes three, maybe even four, according to interviews with at least a dozen people who have visited with Thomas in his chambers. . . .Washington lawyer Tom Goldstein, whose firm devotes itself primarily to Supreme Court litigation, has met all the justices and has declared Thomas "the most real person" of them all.[69]

Far from being a recluse permanently scarred by his Senate confirmation hearings, Justice Thomas frequently goes back to the Senate at mealtimes, according to the *Washington Post*:

Thomas is hardly a stranger in the Senate. He can be spotted in the Dirksen Senate Office Building cafeteria, eating the hot buffet lunch with his clerks. He is chummy with the women who cook and waitress. He has breakfasted among senators in their private dining room, just a whisper away from some of the lawmakers who virulently opposed his nomination. Who would have imagined that the U.S. Senate, the stage for Thomas's "high-tech lynching," as he angrily charged during his 1991 confirmation hearings, is where he enjoys meals? [70]

Others who have actually studied Justice Thomas and interviewed those who have worked with him or encountered him socially have likewise been struck by the difference between the public image and the man himself:

He made a point of introducing himself to every employee at the Court, from cafeteria cooks to the nighttime janitors. He played hoops with the marshals and security guards. He stopped to chat with people in the hallways. Clerks say Thomas had an uncanny ability to recall details of an employee's personal life. He knew their children's names and where they went to school. He seemed to see people who would otherwise go unnoticed. Stephen Smith, a former clerk, recalls an instance when Thomas, on a tour of the maritime courts in 1993 or 1994, was talking to a group of judges. "There was this old woman standing there in one of those blue janitor's uniforms and a bucket, a black woman," Smith recalled. "And she was looking at him, wouldn't dare go up and talk to this important guy. He left the judges there, excused himself, and went over to talk to her. He put out his hand to shake her hand, and she threw her arms around him and gave him a big bear hug."
   Among his eight colleagues, Thomas was similarly outgoing and gregarious. Justice Ginsburg said Thomas sometimes dropped by her chambers with a bag of Vidalia onions from Georgia, knowing that her husband was a devoted chef. "A most congenial colleague," said Ginsburg of Thomas. . .
   Thomas took an especially keen interest in his clerks and often developed an almost paternal relationship with them. . . When he noticed the treads on Walker's car were thin, he showed her how to measure them for wear and tear. "The next Monday," Walker recalled, "he came in and said, 'I saw some great tires at Price Club, they're a good deal. You should really get them.' And I'm sitting there thinking, here's a Supreme Court justice who's worried about whether my tires are safe."
   Many of Thomas's clerks have similar stories to tell.[71]

Another study chronicled Clarence Thomas' life away from Washington:

> Behind the wheel of his forty-foot RV, Clarence Thomas couldn't be happier. The '92 Prevost motor coach has a bedroom in the back, plush gray leather chairs, a kitchen, satellite television, and a computerized navigational system. "It's a condo on wheels," he has said— a condo from which he observes the nation and, when he chooses, engages with fellow citizens. He is drawn mostly to small towns and RV campgrounds, national parks, and historic landmarks. Thomas has told friends he has never had a bad experience traveling by motor coach. Away from urban centers, he often encounters people who don't recognize him or don't care that he's a Supreme Court justice. He loves to pull into a Wal-Mart parking lot in jeans and deck shoes, a cap pulled over his head. Plopped outside the vehicle in a lawn chair, he can sit for hours, chatting up strangers about car waxes and exterior polishes, sipping lemonade.[72]

Justice Thomas also gives talks to "audiences of thousands at major universities," according to the *Washington Times*.[73] But, since he has seldom been seen at fashionable social gatherings of Washington's political and media elites, that makes him a "recluse" as far as the intelligentsia are concerned.

What of Clarence Thomas' work as a Supreme Court justice? The fact that his votes and those of Justice Scalia often coincide says nothing about who persuaded whom, but the media have automatically assumed that it was Scalia who led and Justice Thomas who followed. To know the facts would require knowing what happens at the private conferences among the nine justices, where even their own clerks are not present. Despite sweeping assumptions that reigned for years in the media, a radically different picture emerged when notes taken by the late Justice Harry Blackmun at these conferences became available among his papers. Author Jan Crawford Greenburg, who consulted Blackmun's notes when writing a book about the Supreme Court (*Supreme Conflict*), found an entirely different pattern from that of the prevailing media vision. Moreover, that pattern emerged early, during Clarence Thomas' first year on the Supreme Court.

In only the third case in which he participated, Justice Thomas initially agreed with the rest of his colleagues and the case looked like it was headed for a 9 to nothing decision. But Thomas thought about it overnight and decided to dissent from the views of his eight senior colleagues:

> As it turned out, Thomas was not alone for long. After he sent his dissent to the other justices, Rehnquist and Scalia sent notes to the justices that they too were changing their votes and would join his opinion. Kennedy declined to join Thomas's dissent, but he also changed his vote and wrote his own dissent. . .[74]

This was something that happened several times that first year alone. Some of Justice Blackmun's notes indicated his surprise at the independence of this new member of the court.

Not only individuals, but whole nations, can be given fictitious characteristics in furtherance of a prevailing vision. With nations, as with individuals, what is exalted and what is denigrated depends far more on what fits the vision than on what fits the facts. Intellectuals' admiration for the presumed virtues of foreign nations has often served as a means of rebuke to their own country. This pattern goes back at least as far as Jean-Jacques Rousseau in the eighteenth century, whose depiction of "the noble savage" served as a rebuke to European civilization.

While it is legitimate to compare some nations to other nations, or perhaps to some ideal vision of what nations should be like, too often Western intellectuals in general, or American intellectuals in particular, make comparisons with a fictitious image of other nations— at one time, especially during the 1930s, with the image of the Soviet Union as conceived by the intelligentsia of the times, with the help of pro-Soviet writers like Walter Duranty or Sidney and Beatrice Webb. Famed literary critic Edmund Wilson, for example, called the Soviet Union "the moral top of the world"[75] at a time when there were mass starvation and slave labor camps under Stalin. When too many facts about the Soviet Union eventually became too well known and too chilling for the fictitious image to hold up, the search for other foreign nations to admire as a rebuke to their own shifted for a while to Communist China or to various Third World nations such as India or some of the newly independent nations in sub-Saharan Africa.

India has perhaps survived in this role longer than others, partly as "the world's largest democracy" and partly because its democratic socialism under Nehru and his successors was so similar to what Western intellectuals favored. The fictitious India was depicted as not being materialistic, intolerant, or violent like the United States. It was as if India was a country of Mahatma Gandhis, when in fact Gandhi was assassinated precisely because of his attempts to dampen the violent intolerance rampant among India's population. The hundreds of thousands of Hindus and Muslims killed in riots between the two groups that followed India's independence in 1947, as the subcontinent was divided into India and Pakistan, somehow faded into the mists of memory. Even lethal violence between Hindus and Muslims in India today, in the twenty-first century— hundreds killed in riots in just one state in 2002, for example[76]— has done little to change the image of the fictitious India. Nor has the treatment of untouchables.

The Indian government eventually outlawed untouchability in 1949 and the term "untouchable" was replaced in polite conversation by "Harijan"— "children of God," as Mahatma Gandhi called them— then by "Dalits" (the downtrodden) and, in official government reports, "scheduled castes." But many of the old oppressive discriminations continued, especially in the countrysides. Years after racial lynchings had become a thing of the past in the United States, the Indian publication *The Hindu* in 2001 reported that attacks "and even massacres of men, women and children belonging to the lowest rungs of the social order" were still "a regular feature in most parts of the country."[77]

Such practices are not universal across India today. An official report in 2001 found that just three states in India produced nearly two-thirds of all the thousands of atrocities committed against untouchables annually, while there were several states with none at all.[78] But, where atrocities against untouchables continue, they are indeed atrocities. A June 2003 article in *National Geographic* magazine, complete with photographs of untouchable men mutilated by acid because they dared to fish in a pond used by higher caste Indians, detailed a chilling picture of the continuing oppressions and violence against untouchables.[79]

The point here is not to make a general assessment of India, which would have to include its positive as well as negative features, but to show how, just as fictitious people have been created by the intelligentsia, a whole fictitious country can be created, totally different from the real country it is said to be. Indeed, many such fictitious countries have been created over many generations by intellectuals disdaining their own countries.[80]

Paul Hollander's book *Political Pilgrims*— a study of intellectuals whose visits to Communist countries like the Soviet Union, China and Cuba produced glowing accounts of those totalitarian societies— attributes part of the reason to an asymmetry of information. The "unavailability of unflattering visual information about the most repressive police states" visited by intellectuals contrasts with the "vivid images of the worst aspects of their societies."[81] False interpretations of facts are to some extent inevitable, given the limitations of information and the limitations of human beings. But the creation of fictitious people and fictitious nations goes beyond that, especially when the intelligentsia who are in the business of gathering and disseminating information reach sweeping conclusions in the absence of information or in defiance of information that is available.

Facts about India, including its treatment of untouchables, are freely reported in the media there, and there are even official Indian government reports on the atrocities committed against untouchables. For that matter, there were unhappy facts readily available about life in eighteenth-century Russia under the despotism of the czars, when Voltaire and others wrote favorably about that regime. The crucial factor does not seem to be what information is available but the predispositions— the vision— with which intellectuals approach the available information, whether information about nations or information about individuals. Certainly there have been no serious barriers to information about American public figures who have been either exalted or denigrated by intellectuals.

Often fictitious individuals and nations have characteristics that are not merely different from, but the direct opposite of, those of the flesh-and-blood people to whom they are supposed to correspond. With the various fictitious personas which have been created for public figures and foreign countries by the intelligentsia, the only consistency has been a consonance with the intelligentsia's vision of the world and of themselves in that world, leading them to exalt or denigrate according to whose views coincide with or differ from their own— exaltation and denigration often taking the place of facts and analysis about individuals and the issues with which they are involved.

Verbal Cleansing

The numerous filters at work in both the media and in academia are not random. They reflect a common vision and filter out innumerable things that could threaten that vision. The verbal virtuosity of the intellectuals filters words as well as facts, through what might be called verbal cleansing, much like ethnic cleansing. Words which have acquired particular connotations over the years from the experiences of millions of people in successive generations now have those connotations systematically stripped away by a relatively small number of contemporary intellectuals, who simply substitute different words for the same things until the new words replace the old in the media. Thus "bums" has been replaced by "the homeless," "swamps" by "wetlands," and "prostitutes" by "sex workers," for example.

All the things that generations of people have learned from experience about bums, swamps, and prostitutes are in effect erased by the substitution of new words, cleansed of those connotations. Swamps, for example, are often unsightly, slimy, and smelly places, where mosquitoes breed and spread diseases. Sometimes swamps are also places where dangerous creatures like snakes or alligators lurk. But "wetlands" are spoken of in hushed and reverential tones, as one might speak of shrines.

Newly coined words for old things appear in many contexts, often erasing what experience has taught us about those things. Thus "light rail" has become the fashionable term used by mass transit advocates for things that are very much like what were once called trolleys or street cars, and which were once common in hundreds of American cities. Trolleys were replaced by buses in almost all those cities— for a reason. But now the inconveniences and inefficiencies of trolleys vanish into thin air when they are presented as that new-sounding thing called "light rail," whose prospective wonders can be described in glowing terms by city planners and other advocates, secure against experience rearing its ugly head through memories or histories of the decline and fall of the trolley car.

Another significant development in the art of verbal cleansing has been changing the names used to describe people who espouse government intervention in the economy and society, as most intellectuals tend to do. In the United States, such people changed their own designation more than once during the course of the twentieth century. At the beginning of that century, such people called themselves "Progressives." However, by the 1920s, experience had led American voters to repudiate Progressivism and to elect national governments with a very different philosophy throughout that entire decade. When the Great Depression of the 1930s again brought to power people with the government intervention philosophy— many of whom had served in the Progressive Woodrow Wilson administration— they now changed their name to "liberals," escaping the connotations of their earlier incarnation, much as people escape their financial debts through bankruptcy.

The long reign of "liberalism" in the United States— which lasted, with few interruptions, from President Franklin D. Roosevelt's New Deal in the 1930s through President Lyndon B. Johnson's Great Society of the 1960s— ultimately ended with liberalism being so discredited that later Presidential and other political candidates with long records of liberalism rejected that label or rejected labeling altogether as somehow misleading or unworthy. By the end of the twentieth century, many liberals began calling themselves "progressives," thus escaping the connotations which liberalism had acquired over the years, but which connotations no longer applied to the word "progressive," which was from an era too far in the past for most people to associate any experience with that word.

On October 26, 1988, a long list of leading intellectuals— including John Kenneth Galbraith, Arthur Schlesinger, Jr., Daniel Bell, and Robert Merton, among others— signed an advertisement in the *New York Times*, protesting what they called President Ronald Reagan's "vilifying one of our oldest and noblest traditions" by making "'liberal' and 'liberalism' terms of opprobrium."[82] Reverting to the original meaning of liberalism as "the freedom of individuals to attain their fullest development," the advertisement did not even recognize— much less defend— what liberalism had come to mean in practice, widespread government interventions in the economy and social engineering.

Whatever the merits or demerits of those interventions, these were the actual policies advocated and carried out by contemporary liberals, regardless of what the original dictionary definition of the word "liberal" might have meant in times past. But the impassioned advertisement did not even consider the possibility that the actual track record of liberals when in power might have had more to do with the term becoming one of opprobrium than the criticisms made by those with a different philosophy. Moreover, it was presented as something odd and unworthy that conservatives like Ronald Reagan would criticize liberals, as liberals so often criticized conservatives like President Reagan.

Just as people who criticize liberalism on the basis of the actual behavior of liberals are accused of being against liberalism in its dictionary definition, so people who criticize the actual behavior of intellectuals are often accused of being "anti-intellectual" in the sense of being against intellectual pursuits themselves. Richard Hofstadter's well-known book *Anti-Intellectualism in American Life* equated the two things, both in its title and in its text, where he referred to "the national disrespect for mind" and "the qualities in our society that make intellect unpopular."[83] *New York Times* columnist Nicholas D. Kristof was one of many who wrote of "the anti-intellectualism that has long been a strain in American life."[84] Even distinguished scholar Jacques Barzun said: "Intellect is despised,"[85] though he himself has been critical of intellectuals, without being someone who despised intellect. Nor did he find it necessary to try to show that scientists or engineers were despised by most Americans or even by those who were highly critical of the track record of intellectuals in the sense of people whose work begins and ends with ideas.

Objectivity versus Impartiality

Verbal virtuosity has enabled many intellectuals to escape responsibility for filtering reality to create a virtual reality more closely resembling their vision. Some among the intelligentsia inflate to insoluble levels the problem of choosing between filtering and non-filtering, and then dismiss critics as expecting the impossible— namely, perfect objectivity or complete impartiality. "None of us are objective," according to the *New York Times'* public editor.[86]

Of course no one is objective or impartial. Scientific *methods* can be objective but individual scientists are not— and need not be. For that matter, mathematicians are not objective, but that does not mean that quadratic equations or the Pythagorean Theorem are just matters of opinion. Indeed, the whole point of developing and agreeing to objective scientific *methods* is to seek reliable information not dependent upon the subjective beliefs or predilections of particular individual scientists or on any hope that most scientists would be personally objective. If scientists themselves were objective, there would be little need to spend time and effort to work out and agree upon objective scientific methods.

Even the most rigorous scientist is not objective as a person or impartial in scientific pursuits. Scientists studying the growth of cancer cells in human beings are clearly not impartial as between the life of those cancers and the lives of human beings. Cancers are not studied just to acquire academic information but precisely in order to learn how best to destroy existing cancers and, if possible, prevent new cancers from coming into existence, in order to reduce human suffering and prolong human life. There could hardly be any activity more partial. What makes this activity scientific is that it uses methods devised to get at the truth, not to support one belief or another. On the contrary, scientific methods which have evolved to put competing beliefs to the test of facts, implicitly recognize how ill-advised it would be to rely on *personal* objectivity or impartiality among scientists.

Although J.A. Schumpeter said, "The first thing a man will do for his ideals is lie," he also said that what makes a field scientific are "rules of procedure" which can "crush out ideologically conditioned error" from an analysis.[87] Such rules of procedure are an implicit recognition of the unreliability of personal objectivity or impartiality.

A scientist who filtered out facts contrary to some preferred theory of cancer would be regarded as a disgrace and discredited, while an engineer who filtered out certain facts in building a bridge could be prosecuted for criminal negligence if that bridge collapsed as a result, with people on it. But those intellectuals whose work has been analogized as "social engineering" face no such liability— in most cases, no liability at all— if their filtering out of known facts leads to social disasters.

That so many intellectuals could use the unattainability of personal objectivity and impartiality as a reason to justify their own filtering of facts— and make their argument seem plausible— shows again that they have much intellect and much verbal virtuosity, even if they do not always have much wisdom. Ultimately, the issue is not, as so often misstated, a question of being "fair" to those on "both sides" of an issue. What is far more important is being *honest* with the reader, who after all has usually not paid to learn about the psyche or ideology of the writer, but to acquire some information about the real world. As Jean-François Revel put it, "I did not spend sixty pesetas to be informed of the vibrations unleashed in this Spanish correspondent's soul."[88]

Intellectuals who take it upon themselves to filter facts, in the interest of their own vision, are denying to others the right they claim for themselves, to look at the world as it is and reach their own conclusions. Having an opinion, or expressing an opinion, is radically different from blocking information from reaching others who could form their own opinions.

SUBJECTIVE TRUTH

Truth— empirical facts or compelling logic— is an enemy of dogmas, and one dealt with as an enemy by small but growing numbers of modern intellectuals, demonstrating again the divergence between intellectual standards and the self-serving interests of intellectuals. It is not simply particular truths that are attacked or evaded but in many cases the very concept of truth itself.

The discrediting of truth as a decisive criterion has been attempted systematically by some with deconstruction, or ad hoc by others with assertions of what is "my truth" versus "your truth"— as if truth could be made private property, when its whole significance is in interpersonal communication. For example, when Robert Reich was challenged on the factual accuracy of his published accounts of various meetings that had been videotaped by others, showing situations radically different from what he had described in his book, his reply was: "I claim no higher truth than my own perceptions."[89] If truth is subjective, then its entire purpose becomes meaningless. However, that may seem to some to be a small price to pay in order to preserve a vision on which many intellectuals' sense of themselves, and of their role in society, depends.

The seeming sophistication of the notion that all reality is "socially constructed" has a superficial plausibility but it ignores the various validation processes which test those constructions. Much of what is said to be socially "constructed" has been in fact socially *evolved* over the generations and socially *validated* by experience. Much of what many among the intelligentsia propose to replace it with is in fact *constructed*— that is, created deliberately at a given time and place— and with no validation beyond the consensus of like-minded peers. If facts, logic, and scientific procedures are all just arbitrary "socially constructed" notions, then all that is left is consensus— more specifically peer consensus, the kind of consensus that matters to adolescents or to many among the intelligentsia.

In a very limited sense, reality is indeed constructed by human beings. Even the world that we see around us is ultimately constructed inside our brains from two very small patches of light falling on our retinas. Like images seen in the back of a view camera, the image of the world in the back of our eyes is upside down. Our brain turns it right side up and reconciles the differences between the image in one eye with the image in the other eye by perceiving the world as three-dimensional.

Bats do not perceive the world in the same way humans do because they rely on signals sent out like sonar and bounced back. Some creatures in the sea perceive through electrical fields that their bodies generate and receive. While the worlds perceived by different creatures through different mechanisms obviously differ from one another, these perceptions are not just free-floating notions, but are subjected to validation processes on which matters as serious as life and death depend.

The specific image of a lion that you see in a cage may be a construct inside your brain, but entering that cage will quickly and catastrophically demonstrate that there is a reality beyond the control of your brain. Bats do not fly into brick walls during their nocturnal flights because the very different reality constructed within their brains is likewise subject to validation by experience in a world that exists outside their brains. Indeed, bats do not fly into plate glass windows, as birds sometimes do when relying on sight— indicating both differences in perception systems and the existence of a reality independent of those perception systems.

Even the more abstract visions of the world can often be subject to empirical validation. Einstein's vision of physics, which was quite different from that of his predecessors, was shown at Hiroshima to be not *just* Einstein's vision of physics— not just *his* truth versus somebody else's truth, but an inescapable reality for everyone present at that tragic place at that catastrophic time. Validation processes are the crucial ignored factor which allows many intellectuals to regard all sorts of phenomena— whether social, economic or scientific— as mere subjective notions, implicitly allowing them to substitute their own preferred subjective notions as to what is, as well as what ought to be.

Somewhat related to the undermining of the idea of objective truth has been the undermining of standards in various fields, including music, art and literature. "There are no hard distinctions between what is real and what is unreal, nor between what is true and what is false," according to playwright Harold Pinter.[90] Nor is this idea confined to playwrights. Distinguished British historian Paul Johnson has pointed out, for example, that a novelist has achieved "aesthetic dominance when those who cannot understand what he is doing or why he is doing it are inclined to apologize for their own lack of comprehension rather than blame his failure to convey his meaning."[91]

The same enviably self-serving result has likewise been achieved by painters, sculptors, poets and musical composers, among others, many of whom draw financial support from taxpayers whom they have no need to please, nor even to make their work comprehensible to them. In some cases, the "artistic" products of these subsidized artists are clearly intended to mock, shock or insult the public, and may even be questionable as art. But, as Will Rogers said long ago, "When you ain't nothing else, you can claim to be an artist— and nobody can prove you ain't."[92] Jacques Barzun has aptly called artists "the most persistent denouncers of Western civilization,"[93] which is perfectly understandable when there is no price to pay for such self-indulgences.

THE INVIDIOUS AND THE DRAMATIC

The invidious and the dramatic play an especially large role in the careers of intellectuals— and almost inevitably so. Although thinking is the core activity of intellectuals, thinking is something that everyone does. The only rationale or justification for there being a special class of intellectuals is that they do it better— *from an intellectual standpoint*, in terms of the originality, complexity and internal consistency of their ideas, together with a large knowledge base of a certain kind of knowledge, and the consonance of these ideas with accepted premises among intellectuals— but not necessarily from the standpoint of empirical consequences to others.

The Invidious

In an era of widespread access to higher education for those who pass through successive screenings, being in the top five or ten percent by various criteria is often crucial to getting into elite academic institutions, from which careers as intellectuals are most readily launched with the greatest promise of success. A preoccupation with the invidious is thus not simply an individual idiosyncrasy but part of a group experience that goes with the territory of becoming an intellectual and having passed through successive intellectual filters on the road to that occupation. Even those individual intellectuals who have had a more modest educational background imbibe the heady atmosphere of the leading intellectuals, and are able to believe that intellectuals as such are a very special and precious group.

A sense of superiority is not an incidental happenstance, for superiority has been essential to getting intellectuals where they are. They are in fact often very superior within the narrow band of human concerns with which they deal. But so too are not only chess grandmasters and musical prodigies but also computer software engineers, professional athletes and people in many mundane occupations whose complexities can only be appreciated by those who have had to master them. The fatal misstep of many among the intelligentsia is in generalizing from their mastery of a certain kind of knowledge to a general wisdom in the affairs of the world— which is to say, in the affairs of other people, whose knowledge of their own affairs is far greater than what any given intellectual can hope to have. It has been said that a fool can put on his coat better than a wise man can put it on for him.

Many intellectuals are so preoccupied with the notion that their own special knowledge exceeds the *average* special knowledge of millions of other people that they overlook the often far more consequential fact that their mundane knowledge is not even one-tenth of the *total* mundane knowledge of those millions. However, to many among the intelligentsia, transferring decisions from the masses to people like themselves is transferring decisions from where there is less knowledge to where there is more knowledge. That is the fatal fallacy behind much that is said and done by intellectuals, including the repeated failures of central planning and other forms of social engineering which concentrate power in the hands of people with less total knowledge but more presumptions, based on their greater average knowledge of a special kind.

As already noted, there were 24 million prices to be set by central planners in the Soviet Union[94]— an impossible task if those prices were to bear any rational relationship to one another as means of reflecting the relative scarcities or costs of goods and services or the relative desires of consumers of those 24 million goods and services, compared to one another, and allocating the resources for their production accordingly. But while this was an overwhelming task for any central planning commission, it has been a very manageable task in market economies for millions of individual consumers and producers, each keeping track of only those relatively few prices relevant to their own personal decision-making, with the coordination of the allocation of resources and the distribution of products and services in the economy as a whole being done through price competition in the market for inputs and outputs.

In short, the millions know far more than any central planning commission can possibly know, even if the central planners all have advanced degrees and most other people do not. Credentialed ignorance is still ignorance. Ironically, the big problem for supposedly knowledgeable intellectuals is that they do not have nearly enough knowledge to do what they set out to do. Nobody does. But intellectuals have every incentive to claim to be able to do more than anyone can do, and their education and that of their like-minded peers are enough to make these claims seem plausible. Yet, with the ever-narrower specialization of academic intellectuals, it becomes ever more unlikely that even the most outstanding scholars in a given specialty can comprehend all the factors that go into a practical problem in the real world, since many or perhaps most of those factors almost inevitably fall beyond the scope of a given specialty.

The moral dimensions of the invidious seem also to have a widespread attraction among the intelligentsia. Opportunities to be morally one-up on others— sometimes including their whole society— have been eagerly seized, whether in opposing stern punishment of criminals, denouncing the destruction of Hiroshima and Nagasaki, or insisting on applying the Geneva Convention to captured terrorists who neither subscribe to the Geneva Convention nor are covered by it. Moral double standards— denouncing the United States for actions that are passed over with little or no comment when other nations do the same things or worse— are defended on grounds that we should have higher moral standards. Thus an incidental comment that can be construed as "racist" can provoke more outrage in the American media than the beheading of innocent people by terrorists and the dissemination of the videotapes of these beheadings to eager audiences in the Middle East.

Seldom is there much concern expressed by the intelligentsia about the cumulative effect of such biased filtering of information and comments on the public at large or on students who receive a steady diet of such filtered information from the elementary schools to the universities. What is called "multiculturalism" is seldom a warts-and-all picture of societies around the world. Far more common is an emphasis on warts when it comes to discussing the history and current condition of the United States or of Western civilization, and a downplaying or ignoring of warts when discussing India or other non-Western societies.

Since every society is challenged from within and without, distortions that denigrate a society have consequences, including a reluctance to defend one's own society against even unreasonable demands or deadly threats. As will become clear in Chapter 7, this can include a reluctance to respond even to military dangers, sometimes giving potential enemies such as Hitler every benefit of the doubt until it is too late.

The Dramatic

What of the dramatic? The vision of the anointed lends itself to dramatic, categorical decisions— a proliferation of "rights," for example— rather than to incremental trade-offs. Whatever the benefits and losses to the general public from each of these decision-making approaches in particular instances, the benefits to the anointed come from making categorical decisions which ringingly and dramatically affirm their loftier vision, while trade-offs reduce issues to undramatic quibbling over more or less— with all of this being done on a plane of moral equality with their adversaries, at that, this itself being a violation of the vision of the anointed.

This bias toward categorical decisions has fateful consequences to the larger society. It almost doesn't matter what policy you believe in, if you believe in it categorically, because almost any policy can be pushed to the point where it becomes counterproductive. The institutions through which decisions are made can be crucial, when some institutions tend to be categorical and others incremental. Political, and especially legal, institutions tend toward categorical decisions while families and markets tend toward incremental trade-offs because of an unwillingness to sacrifice completely either love or wealth, for example. It is completely consistent with the vision of the anointed that they wish to have so many decisions made categorically as "rights."

There are other reasons for a tendency toward the dramatic. It is worth noting again that those who are intellectuals in our sense are not dealing primarily with mathematics, science, medicine or engineering, but with things like language, literature, history, or psychology. While the most routine saving of a human life by a doctor using common medical methods has a socially recognized importance, the mere recording of hum-drum events does not make history or journalism interesting, much less important in the eyes of society or a path to distinction, acclaim or influence for the individual intellectual conveying such information. It is exceptional individuals or momentous events that make history worth reading. In journalism, the adage "dog bites man is not news," but the reverse is, conveys the same point. In literature or psychology as well, it is the exceptional subject or the exceptional theory that gives importance to the practitioner or to the field itself.

By contrast, a doctor who never does a thing outside the normal practice of medical science is nevertheless accorded recognition and respect for contributing to the health, and saving the lives, of fellow human beings. There need be no claim of originality or superiority to other doctors in order to receive both the material and moral rewards of the profession. However, in most of the fields in which the intelligentsia work, no such automatic importance is accorded. Only the new, the exceptional, or the dramatic, puts the practitioner or the field on the map, as far as public recognition is concerned. Indeed, even within these fields, complete mastery of the subject matter may mean little for a career in the academic world, without some personal contribution to the development of the field. Hence the imperative among academics to "publish or perish."

Both the invidious process which gives birth to intellectuals from exceptional individuals and the incentives to continue to demonstrate one's exceptional nature contribute to a pattern summarized in Eric Hoffer's observation that "the intellectual cannot operate at room temperature."[95] The mundane cannot sustain them, as the mundane sustains people in fields where the mundane involves something widely recognized as vital in itself, such as health or economic production. Given the process which selects and rewards intellectuals, and the incentives they continue to face, it is understandable that their attention is drawn toward exceptional things that demonstrate their own specialness and away from things that may be vital to others, but are too mundane to serve the interests of intellectuals.

As noted in Chapter 3, most of the intelligentsia show little or no interest in what facilitates or impedes economic production, even though it is ultimately increased production which has relieved the mass poverty that intellectuals have been preoccupied with lamenting for centuries. Much of what is called poverty in the industrialized nations today would have been considered unbelievable prosperity by most people in times past or in some contemporary Third World nations. But contemporary intellectuals who show little interest in such things are enormously interested in the relative shares of existing wealth that go to various segments of society, and in the ways and means of redistributing existing wealth— even though, historically, the growth of the economic pie, as it were, has done far more to reduce poverty than changing the relative sizes of the slices going to different segments of the population.

Even whole societies created for the express purpose of changing the relative size of the slices— Communist countries, for example— have done much less to reduce poverty than countries whose policies have facilitated the creation of a larger pie. It is difficult, if not impossible, to explain the widespread lack of interest in the creation of wealth by intellectuals who are forever discussing and bemoaning poverty, when ultimately increased wealth is the only thing that has cured mass poverty, without understanding that mundane solutions to even vital problems are not promoted by the incentives, constraints, and habits of intellectuals.

To much of the intelligentsia, the solution to great problems like poverty involves great *intellectual* input, such as their own. H.G. Wells, for example, said that "escape from economic frustration to universal abundance and social justice" requires "a mighty intellectual effort."[96] Similarly, creating a lasting peace "is a huge, heavy, complex, distressful piece of mental engineering."[97]

The coincidence of real world challenge and intellectual challenge, which Wells and others have tended to treat as almost axiomatic, depends on the initial assumptions of one's social vision. Those with opposite assumptions reach opposite conclusions, such as that by George J. Stigler already noted in Chapter 1: "A war may ravage a continent or destroy a generation without posing new theoretical questions."[98] In short, even the gravest catastrophes are not necessarily *intellectual* challenges.

After China's communist government decided in the late twentieth century to make their economy increasingly capitalistic, the dramatically increased economic growth rate led to an estimated one million Chinese per month rising out of poverty.[99] Surely anyone genuinely interested in reducing poverty would be not only pleased but inquisitive as to how such a huge benefit could be achieved. Yet virtually none of the intellectuals who have been preoccupied with poverty for years has shown any real interest in the actual reduction of poverty through market mechanisms in China, India or anywhere else. It did not happen in either the way they predicted or the way they preferred— so it was disregarded, as if it had not happened at all.

Again, it is attitudes rather than principles that are manifested— attitudes towards the kinds of policies and institutions based on the prevailing views of intellectuals versus the kinds of policies and institutions which have produced demonstrable results without reflecting, or even considering, the views of intellectuals.

Journalists and others who write for a popular audience face additional incentives, and few constraints, to explain the world in terms which both their audience and often themselves find emotionally satisfying. Many issues are misconstrued, not because they are too complex for most people to understand, but because a mundane explanation is far less emotionally satisfying than an explanation which produces villains to hate and heroes to exalt. Indeed, the emotionally satisfying explanation may often be more complex than a mundane explanation that is more consonant with verifiable facts. This is especially true of conspiracy theories.

Perhaps the classic example of a widespread preference for emotionally satisfying explanations has been the reaction of the American media, politicians and much of the public to the changing prices— and, in the 1970s, shortages— of gasoline. None of these events has required a level of economic sophistication going beyond that in any standard introductory economics textbook. Indeed, it has not been necessary to rise even to that level of sophistication in order to understand how supply and demand operate for a standard product like oil, traded on a massive scale in a vast world market, in which even companies called "Big Oil" in the United States have little or no control of the price. Nor does it require any breakthroughs on the frontiers to knowledge to understand how price controls on oil in the 1970s led to shortages of gasoline— when price controls have led to shortages of innumerable products in countries around the world, whether in modern societies or in the Roman Empire or ancient Babylon.*

---

* See, for example, Robert L. Schuettinger and Eamonn F. Butler, *Forty Centuries of Wage and Price Controls: How Not to Fight Inflation* (Washington: Heritage Foundation, 1979) or my own *Basic Economics*, third edition (New York: Basic Books, 2007), Chapter 3.

None of these mundane explanations, however, has proved to be as popular or as prevalent in the media or in politics as the "greed" of oil companies. Over the years, numerous American oil company executives have been hauled before Congressional committees to be denounced on nationwide television for gasoline prices, gasoline shortages or whatever the issue of the moment might be. Politicians' loudly proclaimed determination to "get to the bottom of this" have launched numerous federal investigations of oil companies over the years, accompanied by banner headlines on newspapers and similar dramatic statements on television. The later anticlimactic conclusions of these investigations typically appear in small items buried deep inside newspapers or in a similarly inconspicuous way on television news programs— or do not appear at all. With the emotional catharsis now over, the mundane conclusions— that no evidence of collusion or market control has been found— may no longer be considered to be news.

Although intellectuals exist in the first place because they supposedly think better or more knowledgeably than other people, in reality their mental superiority is a superiority within a particular narrow band out of the vast spectrum of human capabilities. Intellectuals are often extraordinary within their own specialties— but so too are chess grandmasters, musical prodigies and many others. The difference is that these other exceptional people seldom imagine that their extraordinary talents in a particular endeavor entitle them to judge, pontificate to, or direct a whole society.

Many people over the years have accused intellectuals of not having common sense. But it may be expecting too much to expect most intellectuals to have common sense, when their whole role in life is based on their being uncommon— that is, saying things that are different from what everyone else is saying. Yet there is only so much genuine originality in anyone. Beyond some point, being uncommon can mean indulging in pointless eccentricities or clever attempts to mock or shock. Politically, it can mean seeking dramatic ideological "solutions" instead of prudent trade-offs. Not only Communist movements, but also Fascist and Nazi movements, had a special appeal to intellectuals, as noted by historian Paul Johnson:

The association of intellectuals with violence occurs too often to be dismissed as an aberration. Often it takes the form of admiring those 'men of action' who practise violence. Mussolini had an astonishing number of intellectual followers, by no means all of them Italian. In his ascent to power, Hitler consistently was most successful on the campus, his electoral appeal to students regularly outstripping his performance among the population as a whole. He always performed well among teachers and university professors. Many intellectuals were drawn into the higher echelons of the Nazi Party and participated in the more gruesome excesses of the SS. Thus the four *Einsatzgruppen* or mobile killing battalions which were the spearhead of Hitler's 'final solution' in Eastern Europe contained an usually high proportion of university graduates among the officers. Otto Ohlendorf, who commanded 'D' Battalion, for instance, had degrees from three universities and a doctorate in jurisprudence. Stalin, too, had legions of intellectual admirers in his time, as did such post-war men of violence as Castro, Nasser and Mao Tse-tung.[100]

It was much the same story later in the infamous killing fields of Cambodia:

> The hideous crimes committed in Cambodia from April 1975 onwards, which involved the deaths of between a fifth and a third of the population, were organized by a group of Francophone middle-class intellectuals known as the Angka Leu ('the Higher Organization'). Of its eight leaders, five were teachers, one a university professor, one a civil servant and one an economist.[101]

Eric Hoffer's claim that intellectuals "cannot operate at room temperature"[102] has had many other confirming examples.

However dramatic or attractive a particular vision may be, ultimately everyone must live in the world of reality. To the extent that reality has been filtered to fit a vision, this filtered information is a misleading guide to making decisions in an unforgiving reality, to which we must all adjust, because it is not going to adjust to us.

Chapter 6

Intellectuals and the Law

Although science is capable of linear advancement, the same is not true of law, where the same insights and mistakes tend to recur again and again.

Richard A. Epstein [1]

The law is one of the many arenas in which the ideological conflict of visions is fought out. Just as a free market economy puts severe limits on the role to be played by the vision of the intellectuals, so too does strict adherence to the rule of law, especially Constitutional law. To those whose vision casts a knowledgeable elite in the role of surrogate decision-makers for society at large, the law must have very different characteristics from what it has in the vision of those who see the vast majority of consequential knowledge scattered among millions of people, with no given individual having more than a minute fraction of that knowledge.

If the law depends on the knowledge, wisdom and virtue of surrogate decision-makers, then it is easy to imagine that it is up to those decision-makers to shape laws that are "fair," "compassionate," or guided by a sense of "social justice." But, since these are all undefined words, malleable in the hands of those with verbal virtuosity, such a concept of law is wholly incompatible with the kind of law desired by those who wish the law to provide a dependable framework of rules, within which independent decisions can be made by millions of people working out their mutual accommodations among themselves.

There can be no dependable framework of law where judges are free to impose as law their own individual notions of what is fair, compassionate or in accord with social justice. Whatever the merits or demerits of particular judges' conceptions of these terms, they cannot be known in advance to

157

others, nor uniform from one judge to another, so that they are not law in the full sense of rules known in advance to those subject to those rules. The Constitution of the United States explicitly forbids *ex post facto* laws, so that citizens cannot be punished or held liable for actions which were not illegal when those actions took place. But judges making decisions on the basis of their own conceptions of fairness, compassion or social justice are, in effect, creating laws after the fact, which those subject to such laws could not have known in advance.

Here, as in so many other situations, the fatal step is in going beyond one's expertise. While judges have specialized knowledge and skills in determining where the law sets the boundaries of citizens' discretion, that is wholly different from having judges become second-guessers as to how citizens exercise whatever discretion belongs to them within those boundaries. Individuals may, for example, choose to take on the responsibilities of marriage or to live together without taking on those responsibilities. But judges who have awarded "palimony" to one of the partners after a breakup have, in effect, retroactively forced the responsibilities of marriage on people who had in effect agreed to avoid those responsibilities when they decided to live together without availing themselves of this well-known institution.

The consequences can spread far beyond the particular cases or the particular issues in those cases. The wider penumbra of uncertainty around *all* laws, when judges indulge their own notions, encourages increased litigation by those who have no real case under the law as written, but who may be able to extort concessions from those they sue, who may not be willing to risk some judge's imaginative interpretation of the law.

CHANGING THE LAW

Laws must of course change as conditions change in society but there is a fundamental difference between laws that change by the electorate deciding to vote for officials who will pass new legislation that will then become laws announced in advance— versus laws changed individually by judges who inform those standing before them in court how the judge's new interpretation applies to them.

Justice Oliver Wendell Holmes' famous statement, "The life of the law has not been logic: it has been experience,"[2] was more than a judgment about history. It was part of his judicial philosophy. In one of his U.S. Supreme Court opinions, he said:

> Tradition and the habits of the community count for more than logic. . .
> The plaintiff must wait until there is a change of practice or at least an
> established consensus of civilized opinion before it can expect this court
> to overthrow the rules that the lawmakers and the court of his own State
> uphold.[3]

While relying more on the evolved experience of generations, embodied in law, as against the reasonings of intellectuals, Holmes did not deny that some "great intellects" had made contributions to the development of the law, "the greatest of which," he added, "is trifling when compared with the mighty whole."[4] But if the systemic evolution of the law as conceived by Holmes has not been so much a matter of intellect as of wisdom— a wisdom distilled from the experiences of whole generations, rather than from the brilliance or presumptions of an intellectual elite— then intellectuals who seek more than a "trifling" role have little choice but to try to create a very different kind of law, one more suited to their own particular endowments and aspirations.

That has in fact been the thrust of those with the vision of the anointed for more than two centuries. In the eighteenth century, the Marquis de Condorcet took a view of the law opposite to that later taken by Holmes and more consonant with that of the twentieth century intelligentsia:

> Laws are better formulated and appear less often to be the vague product
> of circumstance and caprice; they are made by learned men if not yet by
> philosophers.[5]

By the second half of the twentieth century, the view of law as something to be deliberately shaped according to the spirit of the times, as interpreted by intellectual elites, became more common in the leading law schools and among judges. Professor Ronald Dworkin of Oxford University epitomized this approach when he dismissed the systemic evolution of the law as a "silly faith,"[6] based on "the chaotic and unprincipled development of history,"[7]— systemic processes being equated with chaos, as they have been among those who promoted central economic planning rather than the systemic interactions of markets. In both cases, the preference has been for an elite to impose its vision, overriding if necessary the views of the masses of their fellow citizens, for Dworkin also said, "a more equal society is a better society even if its citizens prefer inequality."[8]

In short, this vision has sought to impose social and economic equality through a political inequality that would allow an elite to override what the population at large wants. Despite Professor Dworkin's claim, it hardly seems likely that most people really prefer inequality. What they may prefer is the freedom that systemic processes permit, rather than elite dictation, even if those systemic processes entail a certain amount of economic inequality.

Law— in the full sense of rules known in advance and applied as written— is a major restriction on surrogate decision-making, especially when it is Constitutional law, not readily changed by a simple majority of the moment. Those with the vision of the anointed must either chafe under such restrictions or else use their talents, including verbal virtuosity, to loosen the restrictions of law on government officials— which is to say, they must make law less than law and more in the nature of ad hoc decision-making by empowered elites. That has, in fact, long been the general direction taken by intellectuals who favor surrogate decision-making in general and by government officials seeking greater scope for the exercise of their power.

The Constitution and the Courts

Individual intellectuals and individual judges can take any of a number of approaches to interpreting the Constitution. However, there are certain patterns and vogues that can be traced to particular periods of history. The Progressive era, at the beginning of the twentieth century, saw the beginning of a pattern that would become dominant— first among the intellectuals and then in the courts— later in that century. These Progressive era ideas were promoted not only by such legal scholars as Roscoe Pound and Louis Brandeis but also by the only two Presidents of the United States who had for some years been intellectuals in our sense of people earning their livings from intellectual work— Theodore Roosevelt and Woodrow Wilson.

Theodore Roosevelt referred in his memoirs to his policies as President, including "my insistence upon the theory that the executive power was limited only by specific restrictions and prohibitions appearing in the Constitution or imposed by the Congress under its Constitutional powers."[9] This blithely ignored the Tenth Amendment, under which the federal government could exercise only those powers specifically granted to it by the Constitution, with all other powers belonging either to the states or to the people themselves.

Theodore Roosevelt stood the Tenth Amendment on its head, as if all powers not specifically forbidden to the President were his to use. Nor were his words mere theorizing. When Roosevelt authorized troops to seize a coal mine during a strike, he told the general in charge, "I bid you pay no heed to any other authority, no heed to a writ from a judge, or anything else excepting my commands." Nor was he willing to listen to a Congressional official from his own party, who raised questions about the Constitutionality of the President's actions:

> Exasperated, Roosevelt grabbed Watson by the shoulder and shouted, "The Constitution was made for the people and not the people for the Constitution."[10]

With this, Theodore Roosevelt verbally transformed himself into "the people" and transformed the Constitution into an optional or advisory document, defeating the whole purpose of having a Constitution as a check on the powers of government officials.

Woodrow Wilson, the other President who was an intellectual in the sense defined here, was less dramatic but just as impatient with the restrictions of the Constitution. He introduced a theme that would long outlive his presidency when he wrote, while still a scholar at Princeton, of "the simple days of 1787" when the Constitution was adopted and of how "each generation of statesmen looks to the Supreme Court to supply the interpretation which will serve the needs of the day."[11] "The courts are the people's forum," he asserted, choosing a different branch of government as a surrogate for the people and, like Theodore Roosevelt, transforming the Constitution into an advisory document, with the courts' role being to determine "the adequacy of the Constitution in respect of the needs and interests of the nation" and to be the nation's "conscience" in matters of law— in short, expecting the courts to be surrogate policy makers, rather than simply legal specialists applying laws created by others. That unelected federal judges with lifetime appointments should be depicted as "the people's forum" was yet another example of verbal virtuosity in transforming an institution specifically insulated from popular opinions into a supposed expression of those opinions.

If courts "interpreted the Constitution in its strict letter, as some proposed," Wilson said, it would turn that document into "a strait-jacket."[12] Wilson used yet another argument that would be repeated by many others, on into the next century— namely, the role of "change" in general and technological change in particular: "When the Constitution was framed there were no railways, there was no telegraph, there was no telephone,"[13] he said. Like others who would repeat this kind of argument for generations to come— citing airplanes, computers, and other new technological marvels— Wilson made no attempt whatever to show how these or other changes specifically required courts to reach new and different interpretations of the Constitution. One could go through a long list of controversial landmark Supreme Court decisions, from *Marbury v. Madison* to *Roe v. Wade*, finding few— if any— where technological change made any difference.

Abortion,[14] prayer in school,[15] the arrest of criminals,[16] the segregation of the races,[17] capital punishment,[18] the displaying of religious symbols on government-owned property,[19] and the differential weighting of votes,[20] were all things wholly familiar to those who wrote the Constitution. Melodramatic apostrophes to "change" may be triumphs of verbal virtuosity but they seldom have any relevance to the issues at hand.

Generic "change" is one of the most uncontroverted facts of life among people across the entire ideological spectrum. Nor is there any question whether laws, including sometimes the Constitution, may require changing. Indeed, the Constitution itself recognized a need for such changes and established a process for creating new Amendments. The salient question that is resolutely ignored in all the rhetoric about "change" is the central question of decision-making in general: *Who* is to decide?

There are, after all, legislative bodies and an executive branch of government, not to mention a whole galaxy of private institutions available to respond to changes. Merely repeating the mantra of "change" offers no reason why *judges* specifically are the ones to make the changes. It is another of the many arguments without arguments, unless repetition is considered an argument.

Sometimes the "difficulty" of changing laws, and especially the difficulty of amending the Constitution, is invoked as a reason why judges should become the shortcut to change. For example, Herbert Croly, first editor of the *New Republic*, said in his Progressive era classic, *The Promise of American Life*, "every popular government should in the end, and after a necessarily prolonged deliberation, possess the power of taking any action, which, in the opinion of a decisive majority of the people, is demanded by the public welfare." He added, "Such is not the case with the government organized under the Federal Constitution."[21] He deplored what he called "the practical immutability of the Constitution."[22] Many others have advanced the thesis that the Constitution is difficult to amend. But difficulty is not determined by frequency. If the people do not want a particular thing done, even if the intelligentsia consider it desirable or even imperative, that is not a difficulty. That is democracy.

If the Constitution is not amended very often, that in itself is no evidence of a difficulty in amending the Constitution. There is no difficulty in getting up in the morning and putting on one red shoe and one green shoe. It doesn't happen very often because people *don't want it to happen*. When the people wanted it to happen, the Constitution was amended four times in eight years, from 1913 through 1920.

As far back as 1908, Roscoe Pound, later to become dean of the Harvard Law School, referred to the desirability of "a living constitution by judicial interpretation."[23] He called for "an awakening of juristic activity," for "the sociological jurist," and declared that law "must be judged by the results it achieves."[24] What he called "mechanical jurisprudence" was condemned for "its failure to respond to vital needs of present-day life." When law "becomes a body of rules," that "is the condition against which sociologists now protest, and protest rightly,"[25] he said. Although Pound depicted a "gulf between legal thought and popular thought" as a reason to bring the former into line with the latter, in order to have a system of law which "conforms to the moral sense of the community," this apparently populist notion became merely a rhetorical backdrop in the end, as he called for law "in the hands of a progressive and enlightened caste whose conceptions are in advance of the public and whose leadership is bringing popular thought to a higher level."[26]

In short, Roscoe Pound advocated that an anointed elite change the nature of law to conform to what they defined as the "vital needs of present-day life,"[27] despite being at variance with ("in advance of") the public, with whose "moral sense" the law was supposedly being made to conform. Law, according to Pound, should also reflect what he repeatedly called— without definition— "social justice."[28] With Pound, as with Woodrow Wilson, what the public at large wanted faded into the background, except when used as an opaque mandate for "change." Pound lamented that "we still harp upon the sacredness of property before the law" and approvingly cited the "progress of law away from the older individualism" which "is not confined to property rights."[29]

Thus, in 1907 and 1908, Roscoe Pound set forth principles of judicial activism— going beyond interpreting the law to making social policy— that would be dominant a hundred years later. He even anticipated the later practice of referring to foreign law as justifications for judicial decisions about American law[30]— a process removing judicial decisions even further from the legislation it was supposedly interpreting, from the control of citizens subject to those decisions, and from the Constitution of the United States.

In a similar vein, Louis Brandeis spoke of "revolutionary changes" in society to which courts had been "largely deaf and blind," including a need for state governments to be able to "correct the evils of technological unemployment and excess productive capacity."[31] What would qualify judges to go beyond their legal competence to shape economic and social policies was unspecified. In an article titled "The Living Law," Brandeis asserted that there had been, "a shifting of our longing from legal justice to social justice."[32] Just whose longing this was, Brandeis did not make clear, though his praise of Roscoe Pound and other legal theorists and like-minded judges might suggest that this was the longing of intellectual elites for a broader influence on policy-making via the courts. Brandeis, like Pound, cited foreign legal theories and practices as a reason why American judges should go in that direction. He also cited "social science" as having "raised the doubt whether theft was not perhaps as much the fault of the community as of the individual."[33]

Like Pound, Brandeis argued that courts "continued to ignore newly arisen social needs" and "complacently" applied such old-fashioned notions as "the sacredness of private property."[34] Like many others then and later, Brandeis treated property rights as just special privileges for a fortunate few, rather than as a limit on the power of politicians. The culmination of the Progressives' conception of property rights came in 2005, when the Supreme Court in *Kelo v. New London* decreed that politicians could seize private property— typically the homes and businesses of working class and middle class people— and turn it over to other private parties, typically developers who would build things for more upscale people, who would pay more in taxes into coffers controlled by politicians.

Again, like Pound, Brandeis noted some recent trends toward "a better appreciation by the courts of existing social needs."[35] Why judges were qualified to be arbiters of what constituted "social needs" was not explained— which is to say, the more general question of elites going beyond the boundaries of their professional competence was not addressed. Brandeis also invoked "social justice,"[36] without definition, as Pound had done before him and as innumerable others would do after him. He also justified the kind of law he wanted as one which, as he illustrated with an example from Montenegro, "expressed the will of the people"[37]— though, in the American system of government, the will of the people is expressed through elected officials, rather than through unelected judges. This is so obvious that it is hard to see why the will of the people is invoked at all, except as rhetorical window dressing for judicial coups.

Most courts of the Progressive era rejected the kinds of arguments made by Roscoe Pound and Louis Brandeis. The most famous of these rejections came in the 1905 case of *Lochner v. New York*, which upheld the Constitution's ban on government's changing the terms of private contracts. But the passage of time brought more and more Progressive era legal doctrines into courts, including the Supreme Court to which Brandeis was appointed, and these courts overturned not only *Lochner* but other Constitutional precedents. Roscoe Pound's becoming dean of the leading law school in the country, at Harvard, likewise marked a turning point in the evolution of American legal thinking.

As with so many other issues, intellectuals have tended to dismiss, rather than answer, the objections of those with opposing views. John Dewey, for example, referred to "verbal and sentimental worship of the Constitution,"[38] once again reducing contrary views to mere emotions, requiring no substantive counter-argument.

While there are many controversies over particular aspects of the law, the most fundamental controversy has long been over who should control the law and who should change the law. American intellectuals, since at least the middle of the twentieth century, have overwhelmingly favored expansion of the role of judges beyond that of applying laws created by others to themselves remaking the law to "fit the times"— which is to say, making the law fit the prevailing vision of the times, the vision of the anointed intellectuals.

Where the Constitution of the United States is a barrier to this expanded role of judges, then judges have been urged to "interpret" the Constitution as a set of values to be applied as judges choose, or updated as they think appropriate, rather than as a set of specific instructions to be followed. That is what "judicial activism" means, though verbal virtuosity has managed to confuse that meaning with other meanings.

Judicial Activism

Those who advocate a greatly expanded latitude for judges to "interpret" laws to suit the presumed necessities or spirit of the times, rather than being bound by what the words meant when the laws were enacted, seem implicitly to assume that activist judges will bend the law in the direction preferred by such advocates— in effect, promote the vision of the anointed. But judicial activism is a blank check for going in any direction on any issue, depending on the predilections of particular judges.

While Chief Justice Earl Warren used expansive interpretations of the law to outlaw racial segregation in public schools in 1954, almost exactly a century earlier Chief Justice Roger Taney had used expansive interpretations of the law to say in the *Dred Scott* case that a black man "had no rights which the white man was bound to respect."[39] It was the dissenters in that case who insisted on following the laws as written and the legal precedents, showing that free blacks had exercised legally recognized rights in parts of the country even before the Constitution was adopted, as well as thereafter.[40]

Intellectuals of the Progressive era and later may well have correctly read the tendencies of their times for judicial activism to move the law in the direction of these intellectuals' goals and values. But that is neither inherent nor inevitable. If the principle of free-wheeling judicial law-making becomes established and accepted across the ideological spectrum, then swings of the ideological pendulum over time can unleash a judicial war of each against all, in which the fundamental concept of law itself is undermined, along with the willingness of the people to be bound by the arbitrary dictates of judges. In the meantime, the sophistry of "results"-oriented judges can make a mockery of the very concept of law, including the Constitution of the United States.

A classic case of judicial sophistry for the sake of desired social "results" was the 1942 case of *Wickard v. Filburn*, which established a precedent and a rationale that extended far beyond the issues in that particular case. Under the Agricultural Adjustment Act of 1938, the federal government had the power to control the production and distribution of many agricultural products. That power derived from the authority of Congress to regulate interstate commerce, as provided by the Constitution. Yet the law was applied to a farmer in Ohio who grew what the Supreme Court itself characterized as "a small acreage of winter wheat,"[41] for his own consumption and that of his farm animals. This farmer planted about 12 acres more than the Department of Agriculture permitted but he challenged the federal government's authority to tell him what to grow on his own farm, when that produce did not enter interstate commerce or even intrastate commerce.

The Supreme Court ruled that the federal authority extended to "production not intended in any part for commerce but wholly for consumption on the farm."[42] The reasoning of the High Court was:

> One of the primary purposes of the Act in question was to increase the market price of wheat, and to that end to limit the volume thereof that could affect the market. It can hardly be denied that a factor of such volume and variability as home-consumed wheat would have a substantial influence on price and market conditions. This may arise because being in marketable condition such wheat overhangs the market and, if induced by rising prices, tends to flow into the market and check price increases. But if we assume that it is never marketed, it supplies a need of the man who grew it which would otherwise be reflected by purchases in the open market. Home-grown wheat in this sense competes with wheat in commerce.[43]

Thus wheat which did not enter any commerce at all was ruled to be subject to federal control under the interstate commerce clause of the Constitution. Under such expansive stretching of the law, virtually anything could be called "interstate commerce," which in fact became a magic phrase justifying virtually any expansion of federal power over the years, contrary to the Tenth Amendment's limitation on federal authority. In 1995, there was consternation in some quarters when the Supreme Court voted 5 to 4 in *U.S. v. Lopez* that carrying a gun near a school was not "interstate commerce," so that Congress had no authority to ban it, though all the states had that authority and most in fact did ban it. What made the vote close and the result surprising was that it rejected the long-standing practice of courts stretching the phrase "interstate commerce" to cover— and rubber stamp— virtually anything that Congress chose to regulate.

Some judicial activists not only make rulings that stretch the law but even go directly counter to it. A classic example of this was the 1979 case of *United Steelworkers of America v. Weber*. Section 703(a) of the Civil Rights Act of 1964 made it illegal for an employer "to discriminate against any individual with respect to his compensation, terms, conditions, or privileges of employment, because of such individual's race" or various other characteristics. Section 703(d) more specifically forbade such discrimination in "any program established to provide apprenticeship or other training." Nevertheless, a white employee, Brian F. Weber, was denied admission to a training program where places were awarded on the basis of seniority, even though black employees with less seniority were admitted, because racially separate seniority lists were used and racial quotas were established.

That this was counter to the plain meaning of the Act was not explicitly denied in the U.S. Supreme Court opinion written by Justice William J. Brennan. But Justice Brennan rejected "a literal interpretation" of the Civil Rights Act, preferring instead to seek the "spirit" of the Act in Congress' "primary concern" for "the plight of the Negro in our economy."[44] Because that presumed purpose was not to protect whites from racial discrimination, the Act was deemed not to protect Brian F. Weber, who lost the case. The emergence of this decision from the clear language of the Act to the contrary was likened to the great escapes of Houdini, in the dissenting opinion of Justice William H. Rehnquist.[45]

In all three of these examples— *Dred Scott, Wickard v. Filburn* and *Weber*— the decisions reflected the "results" preferred rather than the written law. They are classic concrete examples of judicial activism. Unfortunately, the meaning of the phrase has been obfuscated in recent years and so requires some closer scrutiny.

"Judicial activism" is an idiomatic expression whose meaning cannot be determined by the separate meanings of its words, any more than the meaning of the exclamation "Hot dog!" can be determined by referring to a separate definition of "hot" and "dog." Nevertheless, in recent times, some have attempted to redefine judicial activism by how *active* a judge has been in declaring laws or government actions unconstitutional. However, the Constitution itself is a limitation on the powers of Congress, as well as on the powers of the other branches of government. Judges have been considered duty-bound to invalidate legislation that goes counter to the Constitution, ever since the landmark case of *Marbury v. Madison* in 1803, so how often they perform that duty is not solely in their hands, but depends also on how often others do things that exceed the powers granted them by the Constitution.

The real issue regarding judicial activism is over whether the *basis* of a judge's decisions is the law created by others, including the Constitution, or whether judges base their decisions on their own particular conception of "the needs of the times" or of "social justice" or of other considerations beyond the written law or the legal precedents.

There is another idiomatic expression used for the practice of a judge who confines his role to following the written law— "judicial restraint" or following the "original intent" of law. Here again, the meaning of these terms cannot be understood simply from the separate meaning of each word. Judicial restraint means making judicial rulings based on laws created by others, rather than being based on the judge's own assessment of what would be best for either the parties in the case at hand or for society at large.

Justice Oliver Wendell Holmes exemplified this legal philosophy when he said that his role as a judge "is to see that the game is played according to the rules whether I like them or not."[46] He also said: "The criterion of constitutionality is not whether we believe the law to be for the public good."[47] But, since the judge who believes in judicial restraint makes the existing law the paramount consideration in deciding cases, that often means that such a judge must be *active* in striking down new laws which violate the restrictions of the Constitution, which is "the supreme law of the land."

In short, activity is *not* what distinguishes the judicial activist from the practitioner of judicial restraint, since these are just idiomatic expressions for different philosophies of carrying out a judge's function. Judges who base their decisions on the kinds of social, economic, or other considerations of the sort urged by Roscoe Pound or Louis Brandeis are judicial activists in the sense that has stirred controversy, whether they declare many laws or few laws unconstitutional.

Although Justice William O. Douglas was a classic judicial activist in the sense of paying only the most token attention to the Constitution in making rulings based on his own policy preferences— the most famous example being basing his ruling in *Griswold v. Connecticut* on "emanations" from the "penumbras" of the Constitution— he nevertheless deferred to legislators who passed liberal social legislation, using language dear to the heart of advocates of judicial restraint, saying that the court should not be a "super-legislature" but leave social policy to Congress and state legislators.[48] But when the existing law represented social policy that he disapproved, Justice Douglas did not hesitate to intervene and declare it unconstitutional— as he did in *Griswold v. Connecticut*— even if he had nothing more on which to base his ruling than "emanations" that he somehow discerned coming from the "penumbras" of the Constitution,[49] which not even the greatest legal minds, on or off the court, had ever discerned before.

The high tide of judicial activism was the Warren Court of the 1950s and 1960s, when Chief Justice Earl Warren and a like-minded majority on the Supreme Court decided to remake social policy in both civil and criminal areas, almost invariably to the applause of the intelligentsia in the media and in academia. However, as justices with a more judicially restrained view of their role later went on the court, beginning with the Warren Burger Court in 1969, many among the intelligentsia sought to turn the previous complaints about judicial activism against the new judges, by measuring how *active* these judges were in declaring laws unconstitutional or in amending the precedents established by judicial activists such as those of the Warren Court era.

Liberal journalist Michael Kinsley accused Antonin Scalia of judicial activism when Scalia wrote an opinion as a Circuit Court of Appeals judge which, in Kinsley's words, over-ruled "a major piece of legislation passed by large majorities in both houses of Congress and signed with a flourish by a popular president"[50]— as if these were things that make a law Constitutional. Linda Greenhouse of the *New York Times* called the decision that carrying a gun near a school was not interstate commerce an exercise of "raw power" by the Supreme Court because in *U.S. v. Lopez* it "invalidated a law that two houses of Congress and the President of the United States approved"[51]— as if other laws over-ruled by the Supreme Court as unconstitutional, ever since *Marbury v. Madison* in 1803, were not also duly passed laws.

Under the title, "Dissing Congress," a *Michigan Law Review* article said that "the Court in *Lopez* had taken an important step in developing its new version of judicial activism, under which Congress was accorded less respect for its handiwork."[52] Senator Herb Kohl likewise denounced the *Lopez* decision as "a piece of judicial activism that ignores children's safety for the sake of legal nit-picking." However, the *Washington Post* took a more measured view in its editorial on the case:

> One would never guess from the senator's comment, for example, that most states already prohibit the carrying of weapons in schools. In fact, Alfonso Lopez, the San Antonio teenager whose conviction was reversed in this case, was initially arrested on state charges that were dropped only when the federal government took over the prosecution. Clearly, the invalidation of this statute does not leave the nation's children vulnerable at their desks. And it may cause federal legislators to think twice about rushing into every problem area without even considering "nit-picking" questions of federalism.[53]

Senator Kohl was by no means the only law-maker to argue in "results"-oriented terms, rather than in terms of Constitutional limitations on federal power. Senator Arlen Specter said, "I think that crime is a national problem" and "Guns and drugs are the principal instrumentalities of crime." But liberal law professor Laurence Tribe saw beyond "results"-oriented criteria in this case, as reported in the *Chicago Sun-Times*:

> "Congress has pushed the outer edge of the envelope rather carelessly," said Harvard Law School professor Laurence H. Tribe, who noted that lawmakers did not present findings of a link between interstate commerce and the dangers of guns on school grounds. He said the ruling revealed that "this court takes structural limits (to Congress' power) more seriously than people had thought... which liberals and pragmatists find dismaying."[54]

The new definition of judicial activism included not only failing to defer to Congress but also the overturning of judicial precedents. In Linda Greenhouse's words, the *Lopez* case "was the first time in 60 years that the Court had invalidated a Federal law on the ground that Congress had exceeded its constitutional authority to regulate interstate commerce."[55] But judges take an oath to uphold the Constitution, not an oath to uphold precedents. Otherwise, *Dred Scott* and *Plessy v. Ferguson* would have been set in concrete forever.

The *Lopez* case was by no means the only one that caused many among the intelligentsia to denounce the later Supreme Court for "judicial activism" on the basis of its having declared some law or policy unconstitutional. Professor Cass Sunstein of the University of Chicago lamented in 2001: "We are now in the midst of a remarkable period of right-wing judicial activism." This has produced, among other things, he said, an "undemocratic judiciary"[56]— when in fact an appellate court with the power to overrule laws passed by elected officials is inherently undemocratic, so that Professor Sunstein's complaint would apply to the Constitution of the United States itself, rather than to those who carry out their function under that Constitution.

Yet Sunstein complained again in 2003 that "the Rehnquist Court has struck down at least 26 acts of Congress since 1995," and is thereby "guilty of *illegitimate activism*" for— among other things— having "struck down a number of affirmative action programs" as well as striking down "federal legislation as beyond congressional power under the Commerce Clause." According to Professor Sunstein, the Supreme Court has "forbidden Congress from legislating on the basis of its own views" of what the Fourteenth Amendment means.[57] But if Congress can determine the extent of its own powers under the Fourteenth Amendment, or any other provision of the Constitution, then the Constitution becomes meaningless as a limit on Congressional power or on government power in general.

In a similar vein, an article in the *New Republic* titled "Hyperactive: How the Right Learned to Love Judicial Activism" claimed that conservative judges "have turned themselves into the mirror image of the judicial activists whom they have spent their careers attacking."[58] Using this new redefinition of judicial activism, a *New York Times* writer charged Chief Justice John Roberts with sometimes supporting "judicial action, even if it meant trampling on Congress and the states."[59] A later *New York Times* editorial declared "a willingness to strike down Congressional laws" to be "the most common objective criteria"[60] of judicial activism. This redefinition sidesteps the whole crucial question whether the laws over-ruled were in fact consistent or inconsistent with the Constitution of the United States. But this key issue is repeatedly left out of claims that the Supreme Court is "activist" when it fails to uphold legislation or particular precedents.

The new definition of judicial activism lends itself to a purely numerical basis for deciding who is and who is not a judicial activist— Professor Sunstein, for example, basing his charges on how many "federal laws per year" the Supreme Court has declared unconstitutional.[61] That notion has spread from the intelligentsia into politics. Thus Senator Patrick Leahy used this new definition of judicial activism when he asserted, "The two most activist judges we have right now are Justice Thomas and Justice Scalia, who have struck down and thus written laws of their own in place of congressional laws more than anybody else on the current Supreme Court."[62] Since these are the two justices most identified with judicial restraint, it was a verbal coup to turn the tables and label them conservative activists. Blurring the line between judicial activism and judicial restraint not only defuses criticism of liberal activist judges but enables points to be scored by invoking moral equivalence against judicially restrained judges who can also be called "activist" by simply redefining the term.

Genuine judicial activism, like many other social phenomena, may be more readily understood by examining the incentives and constraints facing those involved. One constraint on judges' actions that has clearly weakened over the years is the disapproval of peers, whether in the judiciary or among legal scholars in the law schools. Judicial activism for litigants or causes favored by the prevailing vision of the intellectuals can expect acceptance, at a minimum, and in many cases celebration or lionizing of activist judges. In short, incentives favor judicial activism.

Judges, like intellectuals, usually become famous among the general public only when they step out beyond the bounds of their professional competence to become philosopher-kings deciding social, economic or political issues. Not even Chief Justice Earl Warren's admirers tried to portray him as a great legal scholar.[63] Both he and Chief Justice Roger Taney a century earlier became famous for making sweeping pronouncements about society on a sociological, rather than a legal, basis for their landmark rulings. With pronouncements going beyond the range of their expertise or competence being virtually a prerequisite for popular prominence, it is hardly surprising that so many judges, like so many intellectuals, have said so many things that make no sense.

Judicial Restraint and "Original Intent"

"Judicial restraint" has sometimes been summed up in another idiomatic expression— namely, following the "original intent" of the law. Many among the intelligentsia have seized upon the word "intent" to claim that it is difficult or impossible to discern exactly what those who wrote the Constitution, or legislation for that matter, actually intended, especially after the passing of many years. Thus Professor Jack Rakove of Stanford University said: "Establishing the intention behind any action is a tricky business" and "The task grows geometrically more complex when we try to ascribe intent to groups of people— especially men who were acting two centuries ago, who left us incomplete records of their motives and concerns, and who reached their decisions through a process that fused principled debate with hard-driven bargains."[64]

The key word in all of this— and the key fallacy in this common line of reasoning— is the word "behind." Practitioners of judicial restraint are seeking to understand and apply the written law as it stands— as instructions for both judges and the citizenry— *not* discover the motivations, beliefs, hopes or fears that might have been *behind* the writing of the law. Judicial restraint means undertaking an inherently less complicated task. Even the simplest law, such as a 65 miles an hour speed limit, can be expanded into a complex question of unanswerable dimensions if looked at in terms of the attitudes, values, etc., *behind* the intentions of those who created that law, rather than being looked at as an explicit instruction, readily understood.

Looking at laws in terms of the subjective intentions of those who wrote them is not only a more complicated approach, it is an approach that seeks or claims to discern the value judgments or the "spirit" behind the laws— which gives judges far greater latitude for interpretation, and thus far more opportunities to adjust the laws to meet "the needs of the time," "social justice," or whatever other synonym for the individual predilections of particular judges. But critics of judicial restraint project such difficulties onto others who are *not* looking *behind* laws, but undertaking a far more straightforward task of reading laws as explicit instructions, rather than as general statements of values.

As Justice Antonin Scalia put it, "despite frequent statements to the contrary, we do not really look for subjective legislative intent." What he is seeking is "the original meaning of the text," adding: "Often— indeed, I dare say usually— that is easy to discern and simple to apply."[65] Nor is Justice Scalia unique in this. From William Blackstone in eighteenth century England to Oliver Wendell Holmes and Robert Bork in twentieth century America, those seeking to stick to the original meaning of laws have made it very clear that they were *not* talking about events taking place within the inner recesses of the minds of those who write laws.

For one thing, the votes which provide the political, legal and moral authority of laws are votes on what is publicly set before those who vote. In other words, *nobody voted on what was in the back of somebody else's mind.* Moreover, nobody can obey or disobey what is in the back of somebody else's mind.

It was the publicly known meaning of the words of the laws, "to be understood in their usual and most known signification" as of the time they were used, according to Blackstone,[66] that determines how a judge should interpret them. For Holmes as well, legal interpretation of what the lawmaker said did not mean trying to "get into his mind."[67] Holmes said: "We do not inquire what the legislature meant; we ask only what the statute means."[68] In a letter to British jurist Sir Frederick Pollock, Holmes said "we don't care a damn for the meaning of the writer."[69] The judge's job, according to Holmes, is to "read English intelligently— and a consideration of consequences comes into play, if at all, only when the meaning of the words used is open to reasonable doubt."[70] Judge Robert H. Bork has likewise argued that judges should render decisions "according to the historical Constitution."[71]

Despite such plain statements by advocates and practitioners of judicial restraint over a long span of years, much verbal virtuosity has been deployed by others to expand the task to unachievable dimensions by turning the question into one of discerning subjective motives, beliefs, hopes and fears *behind* the creation of the law. Professor Rakove, for example, said that at the time of the Constitutional Convention in 1787, James Madison "approached the Convention in the grip of a great intellectual passion,"[72] that he had "fear" of certain policies regarding property and religion,[73] and that he "privately described" Constitutional amendments in a particular way.[74]

Similarly, Professor Ronald Dworkin has argued at considerable length against original intent on grounds that the "mental events" in the minds of legislators or writers of the Constitution are difficult or impossible to discern,[75] that "it seems even plainer that we have no fixed concept of a group intention," nor any way of deciding "which aspects of individual mental states are relevant to a group intention."[76] Justice William J. Brennan likewise spoke of the "sparse or ambiguous evidence of the original intention" of the framers of the Constitution.[77] In a similar vein, others point out that "public statements often do not reflect actual intentions."[78]

Such attempts to change the question from the plain *meaning* of a law to an esoteric quest for discovering what was *behind* the creation of the law are often used by those who espouse judicial interpretations that go beyond what the law explicitly says— and sometimes even directly counter to the written law, as Justice William J. Brennan did in the *Weber* case. Professor Ronald Dworkin defended the *Weber* decision on grounds that "the question of how Title VII should be interpreted cannot be answered simply by staring at the words Congress used."[79] The verbal virtuosity of referring to simply "staring" at words— apparently as the only alternative to adventurous reinterpretations— contrasts sharply with Holmes' statement about simply reading English intelligently.

To Dworkin, the significance of the *Weber* decision was that it was "another step in the Court's efforts to develop a new conception of what equality requires in the search for racial justice."[80] Why judges are to preempt such decisions and rule on the basis of their own new conceptions of social issues, under the guise of interpreting the law, while going directly counter to what the law says, was a question not raised, much less answered.

Saying that it is hard or impossible to discern what was meant by a law has often been a prelude to making decisions that ignore even the plainest meanings— as in the *Weber* case— in order to impose notions currently in vogue in elite circles as the law of the land. Dworkin and others have openly advocated as much, which makes their tactical agnosticism about "intent" a red herring. For those who do not intend to follow the original meaning of laws, the ease or difficulty of discovering that meaning is irrelevant, except as a distracting talking point.

The Constitution was a very plainly written document, and when it used phrases like "an establishment of religion," for example, it referred to something well known to people who had already lived under an established church, the Church of England. The prohibition against an establishment of religion had nothing to do with a "wall of separation" between church and state, which appears nowhere in the Constitution, but was a phrase from Thomas Jefferson, who was not even in the country when the Constitution was written. There was nothing esoteric about the phrase "an establishment of religion." For more than a hundred years after the Constitution was written, it never meant that it was illegal to display religious symbols on government property, however much some people in later times might wish that this was what it meant, and however much some modern judges might be willing to accommodate that wish.

Similarly with phrases like "due process" or "freedom of speech," which had a long history in British law before those same phrases were placed in the Constitution of the United States by people who had only recently ceased to be British subjects. They were not coining new phrases for new or esoteric concepts whose meanings judges would have to divine *de novo*.

Judicial restraint involves not only upholding Constitutional provisions and the provisions of legislation that are within the authority of Congress or the states, it also involves a reluctance to over-rule prior court decisions. Without such a reluctance, laws could become so changeable with the changing personnel of courts that citizens would find it difficult to plan economic or other endeavors that take time to come to fruition, for it would be impossible to predict what the turnover of judges and their changing of laws would be in the meantime.

Needless to say, this reluctance to overturn prior court decisions cannot be absolute, but must be a matter of cautious judgment. If some legal scholar today should publish an article or book showing convincingly that *Marbury v. Madison* was wrongly decided in 1803, no court today would be likely to over-rule that decision, on which two centuries of precedents have been built and under which all sorts of endeavors and commitments have been undertaken during those centuries, relying on the legal system that evolved in the wake of *Marbury v. Madison.*

Yet, ironically, many of the same intellectuals who heartily supported the Warren Court's overturning of long-standing precedents during the 1950s and 1960s also bitterly condemned later and more conservative courts which cut back on some of the precedents established by liberal justices, especially in decisions during the Warren Court era. Thus, under the headline "The High Court Loses Restraint," a *New York Times* editorial reacted to the *Lopez* decision by saying: "In deciding that Congress lacks the power to outlaw gun possession within 1,000 feet of a school, the Supreme Court has taken an unfortunate historical turn and needlessly questioned previously settled law."[81] Citing Justice Stephen Breyer, the *Times* emphasized "the value of judicial restraint," defined by them as "deferring to Congress when Congress showed a rational basis for finding an interstate commercial impact in its law." But to *defer* to those whose powers the Constitution specifically limited would be to make a mockery of those limitations. If Congress itself is to decide how far its powers extend, what purpose can there be in Constitutional limitations on the power of Congress or of the federal government?

Inconsistent as such reactions from the intelligentsia have been, when viewed as commentary on jurisprudence, these reactions are perfectly consistent when viewed as part of a "results"-oriented role for courts, since the intelligentsia clearly preferred the social results of the Warren Court's decisions to the social results of many decisions of later courts. But court decisions based on the social results preferred by judges, rather than on the law as written, have a number of adverse effects on law as a fundamental framework within which members of society can plan their own actions. The most obvious effect is that no one can predict what social results judges will turn out to prefer in the future, leaving even the most clearly written laws surrounded by a fog of uncertainty that invites increased litigation.

The opposite of the results-oriented judge is the judge who will rule in favor of litigants that the judge may personally despise, if the law is on that side in that case. Justice Oliver Wendell Holmes, for example, voted in favor of Benjamin Gitlow in the 1925 case of *Gitlow v. New York*— and then said afterwards, in a letter to Harold Laski, that he had just voted for "the right of an ass to drool about proletarian dictatorship."[82] Likewise, Holmes dissented in *Abrams v. United States* in favor of appellants whose views he characterized in his judicial opinion itself as "a creed that I believe to be the creed of ignorance and immaturity."[83] As he told Laski, "I loathed most of the things in favor of which I decided."[84] Conversely, he could rule against litigants he personally viewed favorably. In another letter to Laski, Holmes said that he had to "write a decision against a very thorough and really well expressed argument by two colored men— one bery black— that even in intonations was better than, I should say, the majority of white discourses that we hear."[85] Holmes was not taking sides or seeking "results," but applying the law.

RESULTS OF "RESULTS" DOCTRINES

Fundamental rights of individuals guaranteed by the Constitution of the United States, and by legal traditions that go back even farther than the Constitution, can be lost as a result of judicial rulings based on seeking particular social results in accordance with a prevailing vision. In so far as the nebulous phrase "social justice" might have any discernible meaning, it seems to be that merely *formal* justice is not enough, but must be either supplemented or superseded by a kind of justice based on desirable social results. In any event, the rule of law— "a government of laws and not of men"— is the antithesis of results-oriented "social justice," for the results are to be chosen according to the preferences of particular individuals empowered to pick and choose desirable outcomes, rather than to apply rules known in advance to all and binding on both citizens and judges.

Perhaps the ultimate in results-oriented law was that dispensed by "Representatives on Mission" in revolutionary France of the 1790s. These were particular members of the ruling Convention, chosen to go about the country righting wrongs, empowered to act "above all existing laws and authorities":

> They could make arrests, create revolutionary courts, conduct trials, erect guillotines. They could nullify, extend or curtail the force of any law. They could issue decrees and proclamations on any subject. They could fix prices, requisition goods, confiscate property, collect taxes. They could purge any existing government body, or, if they chose, dissolve government bodies altogether, replacing them with committees of their own nomination.[86]

This was the ultimate in results-oriented law. While no one is advocating creating Representatives on Mission today, this is the general direction in which many are urging courts to move, by emphasizing "results" over rules. Particular judges have in fact appointed people— aptly called "masters"— to prescribe and oversee the policies and operations of prisons, schools or other governmental institutions, and have even ordered state legislators to raise taxes.

Going by results seems especially questionable in a court of law, which inherently lacks institutional mechanisms for monitoring what are in fact the results of judicial decisions as their repercussions spread in all directions throughout society— as distinguished from how judges might have imagined what the results of their decision would be. Some results have in fact been the direct opposite of what "results"-based judicial decisions sought to do.

Burdens of Proof

Perhaps nothing is more fundamental to the American legal tradition than the requirement that the burden of proof be on the prosecution in criminal cases and on the plaintiff in civil cases. Yet the zeal for "results" has led to putting the burden of proof on the accused to prove their innocence in certain arbitrarily chosen classes of cases. This principle, or lack of principle, appeared in anti-trust law before being applied in civil rights cases.

The Robinson-Patman Act, for example, made price discrimination illegal, except under certain conditions. But once a *prima facie* case was made that different prices had been charged to different customers, the accused business then had to prove that the exceptions— such as cost differences in serving those customers, sufficient to justify the price differences— applied. Since the apparently simple word "cost" conceals complexities that can keep accountants, economists and lawyers on both sides tied up in endless disputes, it may not be possible for either the accuser or the accused to prove anything conclusively. This means that the accused either loses those cases or else settles them out of court on whatever terms can be negotiated, given the impossibility of proving one's innocence.

The more fundamental problem, however, is that the burden of proof has been put on the accused, contrary to centuries-old legal traditions applied in most other kinds of cases.

The same results-oriented legal principle of putting the burden of proof on the accused reappeared later in court cases involving civil rights laws and policies. Here again, all it takes is a *prima facie* case— that is, an accusation not meeting even the civil law standard of a preponderance of evidence— based simply on statistical "under-representation" of minorities or women in an enterprise's workforce, to put the burden of proof on the employer to show that discrimination is not the reason. No burden of proof whatever is put on those who presuppose an even or random distribution of achievements or rewards between racial or other groups in the absence of discrimination, despite vast amounts of evidence from both history and contemporary life of wholly disproportionate achievements among individuals, groups and nations.[87]

An employer who has hired, paid and promoted individuals without regard to race or sex can nevertheless find it either impossible or prohibitively expensive to disprove the accusation of discrimination. For example, the Equal Employment Opportunity Commission brought a sex discrimination case against the Sears department store chain in 1973, based solely on statistics, without being able to produce even one woman, either currently or previously employed in any of Sears' hundreds of stores across the country, to claim that she had personally been discriminated against. Yet this case dragged on through the courts for 15 years, and cost Sears $20 million to litigate, before the Seventh Circuit Court of Appeals eventually ruled in Sears' favor.

Since very few employers have that kind of money to spend on litigation, or can afford the negative publicity of such a damning charge hanging over them for so many years, most settle the cases out of court on whatever terms they can get— and these numerous settlements are then cited in the media and elsewhere as proof of how much discrimination there is. Again, all of this goes back to the practice of putting the burden of proof on the accused. Had the burden of proof been put on the E.E.O.C., the case might never have gotten as far as a trial in the first place, since the E.E.O.C. did not have even one woman who claimed that she had been discriminated against. All it had were statistics that did not fit the prevailing preconception that all groups would tend to be proportionally represented in the absence of discrimination.

A similar case, one that went all the way up to the Supreme Court, again taking 15 years from the time of the original trial, produced a decision in favor of the accused employer that was subsequently overturned when Congress passed a new law restoring the burden of proof to the accused. In this case, the Wards Cove Packing Company, based in Washington state and Oregon, ran a fish canning operation up in Alaska. Since it recruited its management where the firm's main offices were located and recruited its canning workforce where the fish were caught, this led to a predominantly white management, based in Washington and Oregon, and a predominantly non-white workforce in Alaska. This statistical fact became the basis for charges of discrimination. The Ninth Circuit Court of Appeals upheld the charge of discrimination but the Supreme Court over-ruled that decision and remanded the case for reconsideration. This set off a storm of criticism in the media and among academics.

New York Times Supreme Court reporter Linda Greenhouse said that the ruling in *Wards Cove v. Atonio* "shifted the burden of proof on a central question from employers to employees charging job discrimination"[88]— expressing what happened in terms of social groups and social results, rather than in terms of legal principles and legal categories— plaintiffs and respondents— where the burden has for centuries been put on plaintiffs to back up their accusations. According to Linda Greenhouse, the *Wards Cove* decision "relieved employers of some of the burden of justifying practices that are shown to have a discriminatory impact."[89]

What Ms. Greenhouse chose to call "discriminatory impact" were employee demographics not matching population demographics— which is to say, real world facts not matching the vision of the anointed. As in other contexts, the vision was taken as axiomatically true, so that statistical deviations from an even or random distribution of members of different groups in a business' workforce could be taken as evidence of employer bias, a presumption which it was then the employer's responsibility to refute or else be judged guilty of violating federal law.

New York Times columnist Tom Wicker likewise accused the Supreme Court, in its "radical Ward's Cove decision" of "overturning established law" by having "assigned the burden of proof to an *employee* who charged an employer with discriminatory hiring and employment practices." Previously, according to Wicker, the Supreme Court, "in keeping with overall legal custom, had placed the burden on the party best able to show that the procedures at issue were fair and necessary— obviously, the *employer*." Again, legal precedents were taken as preemptive, even though the particular precedent in this case— *Griggs v. Duke Power*— was not nearly as long-lived as *Plessy v. Ferguson* was when it was overturned by *Brown v. Board of Education*.

Nothing in Wicker's discussion gave the readers any inkling that putting the burden of proof on the accused was a rare exception to legal traditions going back for centuries, an exception for certain classes of cases where social "results" were the primary concern and where the particular defendants— businesses— were out of favor with the intelligentsia, whether in anti-trust cases under the Robinson-Patman Act or in civil rights cases.

When Congress developed legislation to overturn the *Wards Cove* decision and President George H.W. Bush threatened a veto, Tom Wicker said, "he threatens to make it easier for employers to discriminate and harder for employees (often members of minority groups) to get relief in court."[90]

The *New York Times* editorials made similar arguments. The *Wards Cove* decision, it said, "placed new, heavy burdens on civil rights plaintiffs."[91] Again, there was no inkling given to the readers that what the *New York Times* called the "heavy burdens on civil rights plaintiffs" were the same burdens that most other plaintiffs in most non-civil-rights cases had been carrying for centuries, on the basis of the legal principle that the accused are not required to prove their innocence.

An op-ed column in the *Washington Post* likewise used a "results" criterion, complaining that the *Wards Cove* decision was one "making it far harder for plaintiffs to win such cases."[92] An editorial in the *Boston Globe* likewise complained that the *Wards Cove* decision was one "making it virtually impossible for employees to win discrimination suits."[93] Another *Boston Globe* editorial complained that the burden of proof "now shifts to the plaintiff"[94]— as if this were an unusual place for the burden of proof to be.

The response from academics was no less strident, no less filtered in its presentation of facts, and no less focused on "results." Professor Ronald Dworkin of Oxford wrote of the "brutal disparity" between the races in the *Wards Cove* case, which he called "structural discrimination," and of the "impossible burden" put on plaintiffs.[95] Professor Paul Gewirtz of Yale University said, "the Supreme Court has dealt body blows to two of the most important mechanisms for integrating the American work force."[96] Clearly, his focus was on social results— "integrating the American work force"— not law. Professor Reginald Alleyne of the UCLA law school was no less "results"-oriented and attributed the *Wards Cove* decision to judges who "simply dislike civil-rights legislation."[97] Professor Howard Eglit of the Chicago-Kent College of Law characterized the decision in the *Wards Cove* case as a "disingenuous revisionist treatment of the burden of proof."[98]

Another law professor, Alan Freeman of the State University of New York at Buffalo, likewise used the unworthy opponent notion, dubbing the justices who rendered the *Wards Cove* decision "reactionary apologists for the existing order" who deserved "contempt."[99] Law Professor Candace S. Kovacic-Fleischer of American University called for Congress to "restore the normal allocation of burdens of proof; that is, if plaintiff proves an employment practice or practices caused a disparate-impact, the burden then should shift to the employer to prove a business necessity for the practice."[100] But this allocation of burdens of proof was "normal" only in civil rights cases and in some anti-trust cases, contrary to centuries of normal practice elsewhere in Anglo-American law.

This burden of proof on employers was *not* mandated by the Civil Rights Act of 1964. On the contrary, in the Congressional debates preceding passage of that Act, Senator Hubert Humphrey and other leaders of the fight to pass this legislation explicitly repudiated the idea that statistical disparities would be enough to force an employer to try to prove that he was not discriminating.[101] Senator Joseph Clark, another advocate for the Civil Rights Act of 1964, said that the Equal Employment Opportunity Commission established by that Act "must prove by a preponderance that the discharge or other personnel action was because of race"[102]— a preponderance of evidence, as in other civil cases, not a *prima facie* case, with the burden of proof then shifting to the employer, as later became the standard, as a result of judicial rulings.

It was the Supreme Court's *Griggs v. Duke Power* decision in 1971 which shifted the burden of proof to the employer when there were hiring criteria which had a "disparate impact" on minority workers— in that case, a mental test or a high school diploma. The *Griggs* decision— less than 20 years old at the time of the *Wards Cove* decision— was the "established law" from which Tom Wicker saw the *Wards Cove* decision as a "radical" departure.

Apparently these journalists, academics and their like-minded peers somehow just *know* that employer discrimination is the reason for statistical disparities, so apparently it is only a matter of making it easier for courts to reach that same conclusion. What this amounts to is that those members of society who are viewed unfavorably by the anointed are not to have the same rights as the general population, much less the privileges of those whom the anointed view favorably. The idea that law is about making it harder or easier for some selected segment of society to win lawsuits against some other selected segment of society runs through many, if not most, of the criticisms of the *Wards Cove* decision by intellectuals. In short, they wanted "results"— and Congress gave it to them with the Civil Rights Restoration Act of 1991, which put the burden of proof back on the employer, unlike the original Civil Rights Act of 1964.

Property Rights

Nowhere have the actual results of "results"-oriented judicial rulings been more radically different from what was contemplated than in the case of property rights, which have long been a battleground between those with opposing social visions. As ideas of a "living Constitution," to be applied to current conditions as judges see fit, became dominant in the second half of the twentieth century, property rights have been reduced to second-class status, at best. As distinguished urban economist Edwin S. Mills put it, "the courts have virtually abolished the Fifth Amendment as it applies to urban real estate."[103]

Property rights are seen in radically different terms by those with the tragic vision and those with the vision of the anointed. Those with the tragic vision of human flaws and failings see property rights as necessary limitations on the power of government officials to seize the belongings of the populace, whether for their own use or for dispersal as largesse to various constituencies whose political or financial support the politicians seek. Such actions by power holders were common in ancient despotisms and not unknown in modern democracies. Those who founded the United States of America and wrote the Constitution saw property rights as essential for safeguarding all other rights. The right to free speech, for example, would be meaningless if criticisms of the authorities could lead to whatever you owned being seized in retaliation.

Economists have seen property rights as essential to (1) keeping economic decision-making in the hands of private individuals— that is, out of the hands of politicians, and (2) maintaining incentives for private individuals to invest time, talents and resources, in the expectation of being able to reap and retain the rewards of their efforts. However, those with the vision of the anointed, in which surrogate decision-makers are better equipped than others to make wise decisions, see property rights as obstacles to the achievement of various desirable social goals through government action. Property rights simply protect those individuals fortunate enough to own substantial property from the greater interests of society at large, according to those with this vision. Professor Laurence Tribe of the Harvard

Law School, for example, said that property rights represent simply an individual benefit to "entrenched wealth."[104]

In other words, property rights are seen in terms of their individual results, rather than in terms of the social processes facilitated by a property rights system of economic decision-making. By contrast, free speech rights are almost never seen in such narrow terms, as special interest benefits for that very small proportion of the population who are professional writers, media journalists or political activists. Instead, free speech rights are seen as rights essential to the functioning of the whole system of representative government, though property rights are seldom seen by intellectuals as similarly essential to the functioning of a market economy. Instead, property rights are readily disdained as special protections of the economically privileged, as they are by Professor Tribe and as they were before him by Roscoe Pound, Louis Brandeis, and many others.

Those who take this dismissive view of property rights not only promote their own vision but often also filter out the opposite vision of property rights, or distort it as just a defense of existing "entrenched wealth,"[105] so that much of the public does not even learn what the issue is, making the question of how to resolve the issue moot. Once property rights are reduced by verbal virtuosity to simply a special benefit for a privileged few, these rights are then seen as less important than benefits to the larger society. It follows from this that property rights must often give way in clashes with other rights, when the issue is posed as "property rights versus human rights."*

Such arguments, however, make sense only within the framework of the vision of the anointed. Otherwise, there is no clash between property rights and human rights because (1) property itself has *no* rights and (2) only human beings have rights. Any clash is between different sets of human beings. Property rights are legal barriers to politicians, judges or bureaucrats arbitrarily seizing the assets of some human beings to transfer these assets to other human beings.

---

* Such phrases goes back at least as far as Theodore Roosevelt. See, for example, Theodore Roosevelt, *The Rough Riders: An Autobiography* (New York: The Library of America, 2004), pp. 720-721.

Those who see surrogate decision-makers with both the right and the duty to make "income distribution" more equal or more just see property rights as a barrier that should not stand in the way of that over-riding goal. As the ideas of Progressive era intellectuals became dominant in the law schools and in the courts during the second half of the twentieth century, property rights have been eroded by judicial decisions, and the ability of government officials to over-ride the rights of property owners has been justified on grounds of a greater public interest, supposedly for the benefit of the less fortunate. However, here as elsewhere, because certain notions fit the vision there has been remarkably little attention paid to whether they also fit the facts. In other words, the notion that an erosion of property rights benefits those with limited incomes, who lack any substantial property, is taken as axiomatic, rather than as a hypothesis to be tested empirically.

The implicit assumption that the weakening of property rights would benefit the less fortunate, at the expense of the more fortunate, has turned out to be in innumerable cases the very opposite of what has in fact happened. Given a freer hand in confiscating property, government officials at all levels have for decades promoted massive demolitions of working class and low-income neighborhoods in "urban renewal" programs that replaced these neighborhoods with more upscale housing, shopping malls and other attractions for the more affluent members of society.

The larger amounts of taxes that such "redeveloped" areas would pay provided obvious incentives for political leaders to benefit themselves at the expense of the displaced population. These displaced populations have been predominantly low-income and minority groups, primarily blacks. The ultimate consummation of the legal trends toward reducing property rights as restrictions on government action came with the 2005 case of *Kelo v. New London,* in which the Constitution's provision that private property could be taken for "public use" was expanded to mean that such property could be taken for a "public *purpose.*" While a public use would include such things as the government's building a reservoir, a bridge or some other such facility, "public purpose" could mean almost anything— and in the *Kelo* case it meant confiscating people's homes to turn the property over to developers who would build various upscale facilities.

An even more direct benefit to the affluent and the wealthy, at the expense of people of low or moderate incomes, has resulted from the ever greater scope allowed government officials to over-ride property rights in the name of "open space," "smart growth" and other forms of arbitrary building restrictions, politically packaged under a variety of rhetorically attractive labels. Banning the building of homes or other structures in or around upscale communities greatly reduces the ability of less affluent people to move into such communities, both because of the reduction in the physical supply of land for housing and because of skyrocketing housing prices resulting from vastly increased land prices when the supply of buildable land has been artificially restricted.

The doubling, tripling, or more, of housing prices in the wake of building restrictions does not adversely affect those already living in upscale communities (except for renters) but in fact benefits homeowners by raising the value of their own homes in an artificially restricted market. The arbitrary powers of planning commissions, zoning boards and environmental agencies to restrict or forbid the use of private property in ways they choose to disapprove gives them leverage to extract concessions from those who seek to build anything under their jurisdiction. These concessions may be extracted either illegally in the form of direct personal bribes or legally through forcing the property owner to contribute part of the property to the local jurisdiction. In the town of San Mateo, California, for example, approval of a housing development was made contingent on the builders turning over to local authorities "a 12-acre plot on which the city will build a public park," contributing $350,000 toward "public art," and selling about 15 percent of the homes below their market value.[106]

Chief Justice John Marshall said that the power to tax is the power to destroy. The power of arbitrary regulation is the power to extort— just as is the power to put the burden of proof on the accused.

In the case of housing, the "concessions" extorted from builders are ultimately paid for by people who buy or rent the homes or apartments that they build. The erosion of property rights permitted by courts affect even people who own no property but who have to pay more to rent, or who are unable to afford to either rent or buy in communities where housing prices have been artificially inflated by land use restrictions to levels unaffordable to any but the affluent or wealthy, establishing a *cordon sanitaire* around upscale communities, keeping out people of moderate or low incomes. Whatever the "results" being sought by those who urged a weakening of property rights, these are the results actually achieved.

Even low- or moderate-income people already living within communities that over-ride property rights with arbitrary building restrictions can be forced out as rent rises steeply. In San Francisco, for example, the black population has been cut in half since 1970, and in some other coastal California counties it has not been uncommon for the black population to decline by 10,000 or more just between the 1990 and 2000 censuses,[107] even when the total population of these counties was growing.

One of the many problems of "results"-oriented judicial decisions is that actual results cannot be confined to the particular results that judges had in mind and that other results are seldom predictable. Given legal precedents, these "results"-oriented decisions are seldom reversible, no matter how far the actual results differ from what was expected. Burdens of proof and property rights are just two examples among many.

CRIME

The vision of crime common among intellectuals goes back at least two centuries but it gained the ascendancy in practice only during the second half of the twentieth century. Louis Brandeis' claim— that modern "social science" had raised the issue whether the surrounding community was not as much responsible for theft as the thief himself— ignored the fact that blaming crime on society was a common notion among those with the vision of the anointed, as far back as the eighteenth century— which is to say, before modern "social science,"[108] though these earlier speculations antedated the practice of wrapping themselves in the mantle of science.

The vision of the anointed has long de-emphasized punishment and emphasized prevention by getting at the social "root causes" of crime beforehand and by "rehabilitation" of criminals afterwards. Subsidiary themes in this vision include mitigation of personal responsibility on the part of criminals as a result of unhappy childhoods, stressful adulthoods or other factors assumed to be beyond the control of the individual. Conflicting theories of crime can be debated endlessly, and no doubt will be, as will many other questions expanded to unanswerable dimensions. What is relevant here, however, is what the evidence of actual results has been from the ascendancy and pervasive prevalence of the intellectuals' vision of crime— and what the intellectuals' reactions have been to that evidence.

In the United States, where murder rates had been going down for decades, and were in 1961 less than half of what they had been in 1933, the legal reforms of the 1960s— applying the ideas of intellectuals and widely applauded by the intelligentsia— were followed almost immediately by a reversal of this long downward trend, with the murder rate doubling by 1974.[109] In Britain, the ascendancy of the same vision of crime was followed by similarly sudden reversals of previous downward trends in crime rates. As one study noted:

> Scholars of criminology have traced a long decline in interpersonal violence since the late Middle Ages until an abrupt and puzzling reversal occurred in the middle of the twentieth century. . . And a statistical comparison of crime in England and Wales with crime in America, based on 1995 figures, discovered that for three categories of violent crime— assaults, burglary, and robbery— the English are now at far greater risk than Americans.[110]

The abruptness of the reversal of a long downward trend in crime rates, on both sides of the Atlantic, greatly reduces the likelihood that the results were due to the kinds of complex social changes which take years to gradually unfold. But, within a relatively short span of time, legislation, court decisions, and government policy changes in both Britain and the United States greatly reduced the likelihood that a criminal would be convicted and punished for a given crime, reduced the severity of the punishment for those who were punished, and simultaneously reduced the ability of law-abiding citizens to defend themselves when confronted with a criminal or to be armed to deter criminal attacks.[111] In Britain, the anti-gun ideology is so strong that even the use of toy guns in self-defense is opposed:

Merely threatening to defend oneself can also prove illegal, as an elderly lady discovered. She succeeded in frightening off a gang of thugs by firing a blank from a toy gun, only to be arrested for the crime of putting someone in fear with an imitation firearm. Use of a toy gun for self-defence during a housebreak is also unacceptable, as a householder found who had detained with an imitation gun two men who were burgling his home. He called the police, but when they arrived they arrested him for a firearms offence. [112]

British intellectuals have long been zealous advocates of gun control. A 1965 article in the *New Statesman* declared that firearms in private hands "serve no conceivable civilised purpose," that "the possession or use of pistols or revolvers by civilians" was something that "cannot be justified for any purpose whatsoever."[113] A 1970 article in the same publication urged laws banning "all firearms"— whether concealed or not— "from the entire civilian population."[114]

Like so many ideas among the intelligentsia, the zeal for gun control laws has defied years of mounting evidence of their futility and counterproductive consequences. For example, a scholarly study in 2001 found that "the use of handguns in crime rose by 40 per cent in the two years after such weapons were banned in the UK."[115] An earlier study found: "In homicide involving organized crime and drugs no legally-owned firearms were used at all, but forty-three illegal ones were."[116] Other studies likewise indicated that, in England as in the United States, laws against owning guns had no discernible effect on people who make their livings by breaking laws:

In 1954 there were only twelve cases of robbery in London in which a firearm was used, and on closer inspection eight of these were only "supposed firearms." But armed robberies in London rose from 4 in 1954, when there were no controls on shotguns and double the number of licensed pistol owners, to 1,400 in 1981 and to 1,600 in 1991. In 1998, a year after a ban on virtually all handguns, gun crime was up another 10 percent.[117]

As gun control laws were made ever tighter in Britain toward the end of the twentieth century, murder rates rose by 34 percent, while murder rates in Canada and the United States were falling by 34 percent and 39 percent, respectively. Murder rates in France and Italy were also falling, by 25 percent and 59 percent, respectively.[118] Britain, with its strong anti-gun ideology among the intellectual and political elites, was an exception to international trends. Meanwhile, Americans' purchases of guns increased during this same period, gun sales surging "to a peak in 1993 of nearly 8 million small arms, of which 4 million were handguns."[119] Far from leading to more murders, this was a period of declining murder rates in the United States. Altogether, there were an estimated 200 million guns in the United States, and rates of violent crime were lowest where there was the highest incidence of gun ownership. The same has been true of Switzerland.[120]

Yet none of this has caused second thoughts about gun control among either the American or British intelligentsia. In Britain, both ideology and government policy have taken a negative view of other measures of self-defense as well. Opposition to individual self-defense by law-abiding citizens extends even beyond guns or imitation guns. A middle-aged man attacked by two thugs in a London subway car "unsheathed a sword blade in his walking stick and slashed at one of them"— and was arrested along with his assailants, for carrying an offensive weapon.[121] Even putting up barbed wire around a garden and its shed that had been broken into several times was forbidden by local authorities, fearful of being sued if a thief injured himself while trying to break in.[122] That such a lawsuit would be taken seriously is another sign of the prevailing notions among British officials.

The "root causes" theory of crime has likewise remained impervious to evidence on both sides of the Atlantic. In both the United States and England, crime rates soared during years when the supposed "root causes of crime"— poverty and barriers to opportunity— were visibly lessening. As if to make a complete mockery of the "root causes" theory, the ghetto riots that swept across American cities in the 1960s were less common in Southern cities, where racial discrimination was still most visible, and the most lethal riot of that era occurred in Detroit, where the poverty rate among blacks was only half that of blacks nationwide, while the homeownership rate among blacks was higher than among blacks in any other city, and the black unemployment rate in Detroit was 3.4 percent, which was lower than the national unemployment rate among *whites*.[123]

Urban riots were most numerous during the administration of President Lyndon Johnson, which was marked by landmark civil rights legislation and a massive expansion of social programs called "the war on poverty." Conversely, such riots became virtually non-existent during the eight years of the Reagan administration, which de-emphasized such things.

It would be hard to think of a social theory more consistently and unmistakably belied by the facts. But none of this has made a dent on those who have espoused the "root causes" theory of crime or the general social vision behind it. The United States was not the only country in which the supposed "root causes" of crime showed no correlation with the actual crime rate. Britain was another:

> Against prodigious odds violent crime plummeted during the nineteenth century. From midcentury up to the First World War reported assaults fell by 71 percent, woundings by 20 percent, and homicides by 42 percent. . . The age was cursed with every ill modern society pegs as a cause of crime— wrenching poverty alongside growing prosperity, teeming slums, rapid population growth and dislocation, urbanization, the breakdown of the working family, problematic policing, and, of course, wide ownership of firearms.[124]

Even the most blatant facts can be sidestepped by saying that the causes of crime are too "complex" to be covered by a "simplistic" explanation. This verbal tactic simply expands the question to unanswerable dimensions, as a prelude to dismissing any explanation not consonant with the prevailing vision as "simplistic" because it cannot fully answer the expanded question. But no one has to master the complexities of Newton's law of gravity to know that stepping off the roof of a skyscraper will have consequences. Similarly, no one has to unravel the complexities of the innumerable known and unknown reasons why people commit crimes to know that putting criminals behind bars has a better track record of reducing the crime rate than any of the complex theories or lofty policies favored by the intelligentsia.[125]

Expanding the question to unanswerable dimensions, and then deriding any unwelcome answer as "simplistic," is just one of the ways that intellectuals' rhetorical skills have been deployed against facts. As another example, to demand a return to "law and order" was long stigmatized as a sign of covert racism, since the crime rate among blacks was higher than among whites.

As noted in Chapter 2, a retired New York police commissioner who tried to tell a gathering of judges of the dangerous potential of some of their rulings was literally laughed at by the judges and lawyers present.[126] In short, theory trumped experience, as the vision has so often trumped facts, and the benighted were treated as not even worth taking seriously by the anointed.

Similar attitudes have accompanied the same vision in Britain, where much of the media, academia and the intelligentsia in general, as well as university-trained public officials, treat the public's complaints about rising crime rates, and demands for some serious sanctions against criminals, as mere signs of the public's lesser understanding of the deeper issues involved. On both sides of the Atlantic, the elites put their emphasis on the problems experienced by the people who commit crimes, and on how various social programs to solve those problems will be the real solution to the crime problem in society. In the United States, even such things as "prompt collection" of garbage has been depicted by *New York Times* columnist Tom Wicker as part of the "social justice" needed to stem crime.[127]

No amount of hard evidence has been able to burst through the sealed bubble of this elite vision in Britain. On the contrary, data that contradict that vision have been suppressed, filtered out or spun rhetorically by British officials— so much so that the British magazine *The Economist* reported "widespread distrust of official figures"[128]— while the British media have tried to make the public feel guilty for the imprisonment of those relatively few criminals who are in fact imprisoned.[129] Typical of the disdain for public complaints has been the response, or non-response, to the experiences of people living in neighborhoods in which institutions for released criminals have been placed:

> They spoke of a living nightmare brought about by the non-stop crime, intimidation, vandalism and harassment inflicted on them by their criminal residents. All spoke of their total failure to get local politicians,

MPs, criminal justice officials, police, or indeed anyone to take any notice of their desperate situation.[130]

For many of those with the vision of the anointed, a wide difference between the beliefs and concerns of the population at large and the beliefs and concerns of themselves and like-minded peers is not a reason for reconsideration, but a source of pride in being one of the anointed with a higher vision.

Meanwhile, in the United States, after many years of rising crime rates had built up sufficient public outrage to force a change in policy, rates of imprisonment rose— and crime rates began falling for the first time in years. Those with the vision of the anointed lamented the rising prison population in the country and, when they acknowledged the declining crime rate at all, confessed themselves baffled by it, as if it were a strange coincidence that crime was declining as more criminals were taken off the streets. In 1997, for example, *New York Times* writer Fox Butterfield wrote under the headline, "Crime Keeps on Falling, but Prisons Keep on Filling"— as if there were something puzzling about this:

> It has become a comforting story: for five straight years, crime has been falling, led by a drop in murder.
>
> So why is the number of inmates in prisons and jails around the nation still going up? . . . Already, California and Florida spend more to incarcerate people than to educate their college-age populations.[131]

The irrelevant comparison of prison costs versus college costs became a staple of critics of imprisonment. A *New York Times* editorial in 2008 was still repeating this argument in its laments about a growing prison population:

> After three decades of explosive growth, the nation's prison population has reached some grim milestones: More than 1 in 100 American adults are behind bars. One in nine black men, ages 20 to 34, are serving time, as are 1 in 36 adult Hispanic men.
>
> Nationwide, the prison population hovers at almost 1.6 million, which surpasses all other countries for which there are reliable figures. The 50 states last year spent about $44 billion in tax dollars on corrections, up from nearly $11 billion in 1987. Vermont, Connecticut, Delaware,

Michigan and Oregon devote as much money or more to corrections as they do to higher education. [132]

This was by no means the first time that rising rates of imprisonment were denounced in the *New York Times*. Years earlier, in 1991, *New York Times* columnist Tom Wicker said that "crimes of violence have not decreased at all" in the wake of rising levels of imprisonment— a claim that later statistics disproved— and urged shorter sentences, as well as "improved educational and vocational services and drug treatment" in prisons, and deplored "panicky public fears and punitive public attitudes."[133] Here, as with many other issues, the differing views of others were verbally reduced to mere emotions ("panicky"), rather than arguments that had to be analyzed and answered with facts.

Within prisons themselves, the changed public attitudes toward prisoners in the United States were reflected in tougher measures against inmates who caused trouble:

> Assaults at Folsom dropped 70 percent in four years, from 6.9 for every 100 inmates in 1985 to 1.9 in 1989.
> Despite a steep rise in the nation's prison population in the 1980's and despite occasional frightening outbreaks of violence like the one at Rikers Island in New York this summer, stories like Folsom's are being repeated all over the country. Prison officials, emboldened by a public mood that brooks no patience for criminals, say they have taken greater control of their institutions.[134]

Hard evidence about the effectiveness of asserting law enforcement authority, both in prison and outside, made no discernible difference to those with the vision of the anointed, either in the United States or in Britain. Yet an inverse correlation between imprisonment rates and crime rates could also be found in Australia and New Zealand, where a trend back toward more imprisonment was likewise accompanied by a decline in crime rates.[135]

The British intelligentsia have been no more impressed with facts than their American counterparts. The British media and academia abound with people opposed to imprisonment.[136] *The Economist* magazine, for example, referred to "America's addiction to incarceration"[137]— the reduction of opposing views to mere emotions being a pattern among the intelligentsia on both sides of the Atlantic. A probation officer's revealing account of the difference between vision and reality derived from his listening to his car radio while driving to work at a prison. On the radio a government minister was being questioned by an interviewer:

> A well-known presenter introduced his question to a minister with the statement, 'We all know that we send too many people to prison in this country. . .' This introductory remark was made with great assurance and confidence; it conveyed the belief that this statement was something 'everyone knew' and was beyond question. Yet as I listened, I knew I was driving to a prison which, despite its huge catchment area (it served magistrates' courts districts from several parts of the country) was only half-full. What is more this institution took the seventeen to twenty-year-old offender age group, known to be highly prolific offenders. If any prison was going to be full, it should have been ours. Yet for some years it had only ever been half-full at the most, and was often far less occupied than that. At the very time that the *Today* programme was confidently misleading the public over the numbers of offenders being given custodial sentences, the Home Office were drawing up plans to close our prison and many more besides.[138]

In Britain, as in the United States, it is often taken as axiomatic that "prisons are ineffective," as *The Economist* put it. The reason: "They may keep offenders off the streets, but they fail to discourage them from offending. Two-thirds of ex-prisoners are re-arrested within three years of being released."[139] By this kind of reasoning, food is ineffective as a response to hunger because it is only a matter of time after eating before you get hungry again. Like many other things, incarceration only works when it is done. The fact that criminals commit crimes when they are no longer incarcerated says nothing about whether incarceration is effective in reducing crime. The empirical question of the effect on the crime rate of keeping more criminals off the streets was not even considered in this sweeping dismissal of prisons as "ineffective."

The ideology of "alternatives to incarceration" is not only a shibboleth among the British intelligentsia, but is also backed up by the self-interest of government officials in reducing expenditures on prisons. Although statements about how much it costs to keep a prisoner behind bars, as compared to the cost of keeping a student at some expensive college, have become staples in arguments against incarceration, the relevant comparison would be between the cost of keeping someone in prison versus the costs of letting a career criminal loose in society. In Britain, the total cost of the prison system per year was found to be £1.9 billion, while the financial cost alone of the crimes committed per year by criminals was estimated at £60 billion.[140] In the United States, the cost of incarcerating a criminal has been estimated as being at least $10,000 a year *less* than the cost of turning him loose in society.[141]

In Britain, the anti-incarceration ideology is so strong that only 7 percent of convicted criminals end up behind bars.[142] In December 2008, London's *Daily Telegraph*, in its on-line publication *Telegraph.co.uk*, reported: "Thousands of criminals spared prison go on to offend again." It said: "More than 21,000 offenders serving non-custodial sentences committed further crimes last year, casting doubt over Labour's pledge to make the punishments a tough alternative to jail."[143] The transformation of Britain wrought by the triumph of the vision of the anointed may be summarized by noting that Britain, which had long had one of the lowest crime rates in the world, had by the end of the twentieth century seen its crime rate in most categories rise several-fold and eventually surpass that of the United States.[144]

As a young man visiting Britain shortly after the Second World War, Lee Kuan Yew was so impressed with the orderly and law-abiding people of London that he returned to his native Singapore determined to transform it from the poverty-stricken and crime-ridden place that it was at the time. Later, as a leader of the city-state of Singapore for many years, Lee Kuan Yew instituted policies that resulted in Singapore's rise to unprecedented levels of prosperity, with an equally dramatic fall in crime. By the beginning of the twenty-first century, the crime rate per 100,000 people in Singapore was 693 and in Britain was over 10,000.[145] Singapore had, in effect, gone back in time to policies and methods now disdained by the intelligentsia as "outmoded" and "simplistic."

In light of the fact that a wholly disproportionate amount of crime is committed by a relatively small segment of the population, it is hardly surprising that putting a small fraction of the total population behind bars has led to substantial reductions in the crime rate. However, that is not sufficient for those who take a cosmic view of justice and lament that some people, through no fault of their own, are born into circumstances far more likely to result in criminal behavior than the circumstances into which others are born.

While those with this vision tend to regard those circumstances as economic or social, the same injustice— as viewed from the same cosmic perspective— is involved when people are born into *cultural* circumstances that are more likely to lead them into crime. Yet, far from taking on the daunting task of trying to change cultures or subcultures, many of the intelligentsia are adherents of the multicultural ideology, according to which cultures are all on a plane of equality, so that trying to change some cultures would be an unwarranted intrusion, cultural imperialism as it were.

Like so many other nice-sounding notions, the multicultural ideology does not distinguish between an arbitrary definition and a verifiable proposition. That is, it does not distinguish between how one chooses to use words within one's own mind and the empirical validity of those words outside in the real world. Yet consequences, for both individuals and society, follow from mundane facts in the real world, not from definitions inside people's heads. Empirically, the question whether or not cultures are equal becomes: *Equal in what demonstrable way?* That question is seldom, if ever, asked, much less answered, by most of the intelligentsia.

In addition to claims that crime can be reduced by getting at its supposed "root causes," many among the intelligentsia also advocate "rehabilitation" of criminals, "anger management" and other therapeutic approaches to reducing crime— not simply as a supplement to traditional imprisonment but also as a substitute. Like other "alternatives to incarceration," these are not treated as hypotheses to be tested but as axioms to be defended. No matter how high the rate of recidivism among those who have been through "rehabilitation" programs or how much violence continues to be committed by those who have been in "anger management" programs, these notions are never considered to be refuted. Between the suppression of evidence by officials[146] and its evasion through the verbal virtuosity of the intelligentsia, these theories can seldom be defeated by mere facts.

By the same token, none of the traditional methods of crime control that have been supplanted by newer and more fashionable methods can be resurrected on the basis of factual evidence. The very mention of "Victorian" ideas about society in general, or crime control in particular, is virtually guaranteed to evoke a sneer from the intelligentsia. The fact that the Victorian era was one of a decades-long decline in alcoholism, crime and social pathology in general, both in Britain and in the United States[147]— in contrast to more modern ideas with the opposite results in both countries— carries virtually no weight among the intelligentsia, and such facts remain largely unknown among those in the general public who depend on either the media or academia for information.

The fact that ordinary, commonsense measures against crime are effective remains a matter of surprise among many of the intelligentsia. After decades of controversy over ways of reducing crime, in 2009 such news rated a headline in the *San Francisco Chronicle*: "Homicides Plummet as Police Flood Tough Areas." The account began: "San Francisco's homicide total for the first half of 2009 hit a nine-year low— falling more than 50 percent from last year— a drop that police officials attribute to flooding high-crime areas with officers and focusing on the handful of people who commit most of the crimes."[148]

A few intellectuals— James Q. Wilson being the most prominent— have bucked the tide when it comes to crime, but most of their work consists of showing what is wrong with the work of the far more numerous intellectuals whose theories of crime and prescriptions for crime control have been pervasive and have, in practice, led only to rising crime rates. The net cost of intellectuals to society as regards crime would include not only the vast sums of money lost by the general public— greatly exceeding the cost of keeping criminals behind bars— but also the impact of policies based on their theories on the lives of ordinary law-abiding citizens, brutalized by violence, demoralized by fear or cut short by criminals or rioters. If it were possible to quantify the cost of turning the theories of the intellectuals into the law of the land, the total cost would undoubtedly be enormous, just as regards crime.

Chapter 7

Intellectuals and War

Bad ages to live through are good ages to learn from.

Eugen Weber [1]

Like virtually everyone else, intellectuals generally prefer peace to war. However, as already noted in Chapter 4, there are some very fundamental differences in ideas on how to prevent wars. Just as the vision of crime prevention among intellectuals goes back at least as far as the eighteenth century, so too does their vision of war and peace. In contrast to the tragic vision, which sees military strength as the key to deterrence, the vision of the intellectuals has long been one that relies on international negotiations and/or disarmament agreements to avoid wars.

Regardless of intellectuals' vision of war in general, there are no wars in general. The real question is: How have intellectuals reacted to particular wars, or particular threats of war, at particular times? Since our focus is on intellectuals from an era when their influence has had a major impact on public opinion and government policies, that confines the question largely to intellectuals in Western nations in recent times. Within this era, intellectuals have sometimes been strong supporters of particular wars and sometimes strong opponents of other wars. There are elements of their vision consistent with either position.

Sometimes the position of intellectuals for or against a particular war seems to have been a matter of whether the time was one of a long period of peace or one in which the horrors of war had been a recent and indelible memory. The period leading up to the First World War, for example, was one in which the United States had not experienced a major war, involving a large part of its population, for more than a generation. In Europe, it had been nearly a century since the Napoleonic wars ravaged the continent. In Germany during the mid 1890s— two decades since the Franco-Prussian war— many intellectuals, including university professors, supported the Kaiser's government in its plans to build a big and expensive navy,[2] as part of a more aggressive international stance in general, even though Germany was a land power with few overseas interests to protect.

In such a time, it was easy for many intellectuals and others to think of war in the abstract, and to find in its excitement and sense of social cohesion and national purpose positive virtues, while its devastating human costs receded into the background of their thoughts. Even those mindful of the carnage and devastation of war could speak, as William James did, of a need for "the moral equivalent of war" to mobilize people behind a common purpose and common aspirations. It was part of a long-standing assumption among many intellectuals of a *dirigiste* orientation that it is the role of third parties to bring meaning into the lives of the masses.

As already noted, the vision of the anointed is a vision of intellectual and moral elites being surrogate decision-makers, imposing an over-arching common purpose to supersede the disparate and conflicting individual purposes and individual decisions of the population at large. War creates a setting in which this vision can flourish. It also creates many other things, so that the net effect is very much influenced by the conditions of the times. In the twentieth century, the First World War presented both an opportunity for the vision of the anointed to flourish— and later, after the fact, a devastating reminder of the horrors of war which had been ignored or under-estimated.

The postwar backlash against those horrors then set in motion a radically different view of war, leading to widespread pacifism among intellectuals. But, even though many intellectuals radically changed their view of war within a relatively few years, what they did *not* change was their conviction that they as the anointed were to continue to act as guides to the masses and to take the lead in promoting government policies in line with their new anti-war vision. These various periods in the history of intellectuals' pro-war and anti-war visions need to be examined individually.

THE FIRST WORLD WAR

The First World War was a shock to many people in many ways. Nearly a century without a major war on the European continent had lulled some into a comfortable feeling that European civilization had somehow left war behind, as a thing of the past. Many on the far left believed that international working class solidarity would prevent the workers of different countries from killing each other on the battlefields, supposedly for the benefit of their exploiters. In countries on both sides, generations that had no experience with war marched off to war with great public fanfare, exhilaration, and a sense of assurance that it would all be over— victoriously— in a relatively short time.[3]

Few had any idea of how modern technology would make this the most lethal and ghastly war the world had yet seen, for both soldiers and civilians alike, how many of the survivors across the continent of Europe would end up hungry or starving amid the ruins and rubble of war, or how many centuries-old empires would be shattered into oblivion by the war, much less what a monstrous new phenomenon— totalitarianism— would be spawned in the chaotic aftermath of that war. Intellectuals were among the many whose illusions would be brutally smashed by the catastrophes of the First World War.

The Pre-War Era

At the beginning of the twentieth century, the only war that most Americans had experienced was the Spanish-American war, in which the overwhelming power of the United States had quickly driven Spain from its colonies in Cuba, Puerto Rico, and the Philippines. Looking back at the Spanish-American war, Woodrow Wilson approved of the annexation of Puerto Rico by President William McKinley, saying of those annexed, "they are children and we are men in these deep matters of government and justice." Wilson disdained what he called "the anti-imperialist weepings and wailings" of critics of these actions.[4] As for Theodore Roosevelt, even before becoming President, he was not only a supporter of the Spanish-American war, but a major participant. It was in fact his own military exploits in that war, as a leader of the men called "rough riders," that first made him a national figure.

This was an era when imperialism was seen as an international mission of America to spread democracy, and as such was supported by many Progressive-era intellectuals.[5] The Progressive-era classic, *The Promise of American Life* by *New Republic* editor Herbert Croly, argued that most Asians and Africans had little chance of developing modern democratic nations without the superintendence of Western democracies. He said: "The majority of Asiatic and African communities can only get a fair start politically by some such preliminary process of tutelage; and the assumption by a European nation of such a responsibility is a desirable phase of national discipline and a frequent source of genuine national advance."[6] More generally, "A war waged for an excellent purpose contributes more to human amelioration than a merely artificial peace," according to Croly.[7]

However much intellectuals have traditionally been opposed to imperialism for the benefit of economic interests, military interests, territorial expansion or the self-aggrandizement of reigning political leaders, interventions in other countries in the absence of these factors and for ideological reasons have by no means been so universally condemned by the intelligentsia. Indeed, the complete absence of any national interest in a particular intervention has often been treated by intellectuals as exempting that intervention from the moral condemnation applied to other cases of imperialism.

Seen in this light, substantial support from intellectuals of the Progressive era for American military interventions in poor countries, from which no serious material benefit could be expected, was quite understandable at a time when those interventions posed virtually no danger to the United States, and when a long preceding era of peace allowed the brutal realities of war to recede into the background in people's minds. In such special circumstances, imperialism was simply an extension across national boundaries of the notion that the special wisdom and virtue of the anointed should be guiding other people's lives.

Famed editor William Allen White said, "Only Anglo-Saxons can govern themselves," and declared, "It is the Anglo-Saxon's manifest destiny to go forth as a world conqueror." Crusading Progressive journalist Jacob Riis, who knew Theodore Roosevelt from the days when TR was a police commissioner in New York City, said, "Cuba is free and she thanks President Roosevelt for her freedom." He also said, "I am not a jingo; but when some things happen I just have to get up and cheer. The way our modern American diplomacy goes about things is one of them."[8] Willard D. Straight, who financed the founding of the *New Republic* magazine and Herbert Croly, its first editor, both supported the imperial adventurism of Theodore Roosevelt.

Croly declared that "the forcible pacification of one or more such centers of disorder" in the Western Hemisphere was a task for the United States, which "has already made an effective beginning in this great work, both by the pacification of Cuba and by the attempt to introduce a little order into the affairs of the turbulent Central American republics."[9] Croly saw no contradiction between the principles behind Progressive domestic reforms and Progressives' support for foreign adventurism:

> That war and its resulting policy of extra-territorial expansion, so far from hindering the process of domestic amelioration, availed, from the sheer force of the national aspirations it aroused, to give a tremendous impulse to the work of national reform. . . and it indirectly helped to place in the Presidential chair the man who, as I have said, represented both the national idea and the spirit of reform.[10]

John Dewey likewise saw war as constraining "the individualistic tradition" which he opposed, and establishing "the supremacy of public need over private possessions."[11]

As for Woodrow Wilson, not only was he a believer in the rightness of McKinley's intervention in Spain's colonies, as President he ordered a number of military interventions of his own in Latin America[12] before he made his biggest and most fateful intervention, in the First World War raging in Europe.

America at War

The ostensible cause of the entry of the United States into the stalemated carnage in Europe during the First World War was German submarines sinking passenger ships which had American passengers on board. But these were ships entering a war zone in which both the British and the Germans were maintaining naval blockades, the former with surface ships and the latter with submarines— and each with the intention of denying the other both war materiel and food.[13] Moreover, the most famous of these sinkings by German submarines, that of the *Lusitania*, was of a British passenger ship that was, years later, revealed to have been secretly carrying military supplies.

By the very nature of submarine warfare, these undersea craft could not give the warnings and pauses to let crews and passengers disembark before sinking passenger ships. This was especially so when many civilian ships entering war zones were armed and when the advent of radio meant that any ship that had been warned could immediately summon warships to the scene to sink the submarine. The sudden, surprise attacks of submarines— the only way they could operate without endangering themselves— added to the shock at the loss of innocent lives. But it was the insistence by Woodrow Wilson on a right of Americans to sail safely into blockaded ports during wartime which created the setting for these tragedies. He had on his side international conventions created before the submarine became a major factor in naval warfare. Eventually, he made Germany's submarine warfare against ships sailing to enemy ports the centerpiece of his appeal to Congress in 1917 to declare war on Germany.

Whether that was Wilson's real reason for wanting war or instead a convenient occasion for launching an international ideological crusade is not clear, especially in view of the war message itself and subsequent statements and actions by President Wilson. Woodrow Wilson could not resist inserting into his war message to Congress criticisms of the autocratic nature of the German government and a reference to "heartening things that have been happening within the last few weeks in Russia,"[14] with the overthrow of the czar's autocratic government there. This was in keeping with his more famous characterization of the First World War as a war in which "The world must be made safe for democracy"[15] and his later postwar efforts to remake nations and empires in the image of his vision of what they should be like— which was a continuation on a larger scale of his interventionist policies in Latin America.

Before the war was over, Wilson was publicly demanding "the destruction of every arbitrary power anywhere that can separately, secretly and of its single choice disturb the peace of the world." This was not just idle rhetoric. Wilson sent a note to Germany demanding that Kaiser Wilhelm abdicate.[16]

Like many other intellectuals, Wilson depicted actions taken without material motives to be somehow on a higher moral plane than actions taken to advance the economic interests of individuals or the territorial interests of nations[17]— as if sacrificing countless lives to enable the anointed to play a historic role on the world stage in furthering their vision was not at least as selfish and calloused as seeking material ends would be. In a later time, Adolf Hitler would say, "I have to attain immortality, even if the whole German nation perishes in the process."[18] Woodrow Wilson was too moralistic to say such a thing but, given the power of human rationalization, the net difference in this respect may not have been great.

Sinking the blood and treasure of a nation for ideological aggrandizement was equated with idealism by many intellectuals of the time, as well as in later times. Moreover, like many other issues addressed by intellectuals, Woodrow Wilson's policies and actions have not been judged nearly as often by their actual empirical consequences as by how well their goals fit the vision of the anointed. Among the Progressives and others on the left who rallied to President Wilson's war efforts were *New Republic* editor Herbert Croly, John Dewey, Clarence Darrow, Upton Sinclair, Walter Lippmann, John Spargo and George Creel, a former muckraker who spearheaded the wartime propaganda efforts of the Wilson administration. Dewey, for example, declared: "I have been a thorough and complete sympathizer with the part played by this country in this war, and I have wished to see the resources of this country used for its successful prosecution."[19]

Since Wilson had been, for much of his adult life, a quintessential academic intellectual, it is hardly surprising that his words as President repeatedly found resonance among many other intellectuals and evoked lavish praise from them. For example, one of Woodrow Wilson's speeches about the right of self-determination of peoples in 1916 elicited these responses:

> The president of Williams College, for instance, compared it to the Gettysburg Address. Walter Lippmann, using the Monroe Doctrine as his point of reference, wrote: "In historic significance it is easily the most important diplomatic event that our generation has known." Hamilton Holt proclaimed that the address "cannot fail to rank in political importance with the Declaration of Independence." In an editorial entitled "Mr. Wilson's Great Utterance," the *New Republic* suggested that the President might have engineered "a decisive turning point in the history of the modern world."[20]

Not only has history failed to rank President Wilson's remarks with the historic pronouncements with which they were compared, at the time his own Secretary of State, Robert Lansing, was deeply troubled by the concept of the self-determination of peoples. He wrote in his diary:

> These phrases will certainly come home to roost and cause much vexation. The President is a phrase-maker par excellence. He admires trite sayings and revels in formulating them. But when he comes to their practical application he is so vague that their worth may well be doubted. He apparently never thought out in advance where they would lead or how they would be interpreted by others. In fact he does not seem to care so that his words sound well. The gift of clever phrasing may be a curse unless the phrases are put to the test of sound, practical application before being uttered.[21]

Ten days later, Secretary Lansing returned to this subject in his diary:

> The phrase is simply loaded with dynamite. It will raise hopes which can never be realized. It will, I fear, cost thousands of lives. In the end it is bound to be discredited, to be called the dream of an idealist who failed to realize the danger until too late to check those who attempt to put the principle into force. What a calamity that the phrase was ever uttered! What misery it will cause! Think of the feelings of the author when he counts the dead who died because he coined a phrase![22]

It should be noted that Lansing did not simply reach a different conclusion from that of Wilson's admirers. He applied an entirely different criterion— concrete results, rather than resonance with a vision. The military, economic and social viability of the nations created by fiat after the First World War was not a question that the victors had sufficient time to address, much less answer. As in so many other contexts in which "the people" are invoked, the people themselves actually had little to say about the decisions involved. The so-called self-determination of peoples was in fact the determination of peoples' fate by foreigners, arrogating the role of surrogate decision-makers, while having neither the degree of knowledge nor the accountability for consequences that might have made their decisions even plausible.*

Although the concept of the self-determination of peoples has been identified with Woodrow Wilson, the idea of a sweeping redrawing of national boundaries was already in the air. H.G. Wells, as early as 1914, had written of a need for "a re-mapped and pacified Europe"[23] after the war and said: "We are fighting now for a new map of Europe."[24] In other words, his was the vision of the anointed shaping other people's lives, including the lives of whole foreign nations, the vision later expressed and carried out by Woodrow Wilson.

Writing in 1915, Walter Lippmann, who would four years later become a member of President Wilson's delegation in Paris, saw the gross lack of knowledge of the peoples who were being proposed to be dealt with as if they were chess pieces being arranged to carry out some grand design:

> We are feeding on maps, talking of populations as if they were abstract lumps, and turning our minds to a scale unheard of in history. . . When you consider what a mystery the East Side of New York is to the West Side, the business of arranging the world to the satisfaction of the people in it may be seen in something like its true proportions.[25]

The very idea of having each "people" have their own homeland ignored both history and demography, not to mention economics and military security. Locations of peoples and of national boundaries had already changed repeatedly and drastically throughout history. Much of the land in

---

* A member of the British delegation to the Paris conference that shaped the postwar world wrote to his wife describing the leaders of the victorious allies— Wilson, Britain's Prime Minister David Lloyd George and France's Premier Georges Clemenceau— as "three ignorant and irresponsible men cutting Asia Minor to bits as if they were dividing a cake." Daniel Patrick Moynihan, *Pandaemonium* (Oxford: Oxford University Press, 1993), p. 102.

the world, and most of the land in the dismembered Habsburg and
Ottoman Empires, belonged to different sovereignties at different periods of
history. The number of cities in those empires with multiple names from
different languages over the centuries should have been a tip-off, quite aside
from the mosques converted to churches and the churches converted to
mosques.

The idea of rescuing oppressed minorities ignored the prospect— since
become a reality— that oppressed minorities who became rulers of their
own nations would immediately begin oppressing other minorities under
their control. The solution sought by Wilson and applauded by other
intellectuals was as illusory as it was dangerous. Small and vulnerable states
created by the dismemberment of the Habsburg Empire were later picked
off, one by one, by Hitler in the 1930s— an operation that would have been
much more difficult and hazardous if he had to confront a united Habsburg
Empire instead. The harm done extended beyond the small states
themselves; a larger state like France was more vulnerable after Hitler took
control of the military and other resources of Czechoslovakia and Austria.
Today, NATO is in effect an attempt to consolidate individually vulnerable
states, now that the empires of which some had been part are gone.

As for Wilson's other famous sweeping phrase, "The world must be
made safe for democracy,"[26] the actual concrete results of his policies led in
the directly opposite direction— to brutal totalitarian regimes replacing the
autocratic governments in Russia, Italy, and Germany. Despite the
"heartening" news of the fall of the czarist government in Russia, to which
Wilson referred in his speech asking Congress to declare war on Germany,
the Kerensky regime that followed was then undermined by the Wilson
administration itself, which made the granting of desperately needed loans
to Russia contingent on Russia's continuing to fight a losing, disastrous, and
bitterly unpopular war, leading within a year to the Bolshevik revolution,
inaugurating one of the bloodiest totalitarian regimes of the twentieth
century.

In short, the end of autocracy, which Wilson and the intelligentsia in
general so much welcomed, was followed not by the democratic
governments which were expected to replace them, but by regimes much

worse than those they replaced. The czars, for example, did not execute as many political prisoners in 92 years as the Soviets executed in a single year.[27] As in other contexts, intellectuals tended to act as if incessant criticisms and all-out opposition to the shortcomings of existing governments will lead to "change," implicitly assumed to be a change for the better, no matter how often it has led to changes for the worse. Wilson was thus a quintessential intellectual in this as well. In later years, other autocratic governments denounced by later intellectuals— whether in China, Iran or Cuba— were followed by totalitarian regimes more brutal and repressive internally and more dangerous on the world stage.

The effects of Woodrow Wilson's administration on democracy within the United States were likewise negative, despite the rhetoric of making the world safe for democracy. Wartime restrictions on civilian liberties were much more widespread during America's relatively brief involvement in the First World War— all of it fought overseas— than during the much longer involvement of the United States in the Second World War, where the war was brought much closer to home, with Japanese attacks on Pearl Harbor and the Aleutian Islands, and German submarine attacks on American ships off the east coast. Some of the landmark Supreme Court decisions on freedom of speech grew out of the Wilson administration's attempts to silence criticisms of its conduct of the war.

During the relatively brief period of American military involvement in the First World War— little more than a year and a half— a remarkably large set of pervasive federal controls over the internal life of the United States were put into operation, confirming the Progressive intellectuals' view of war as a golden opportunity for replacing traditional American individual economic and social decision-making processes with collectivist control and indoctrination. Quickly created boards, commissions, and committees were directed by the War Industries Board, which governed much of the economy, creating rationing and fixing prices. Meanwhile, the Committee on Public Information, aptly described as "the West's first modern ministry for propaganda," was created and run by Progressive George Creel, who took it as his mission to turn public opinion into "one white-hot mass" of support for the war, in the name of "100 percent Americanism," with anyone who "refuses to back the President in this crisis" being branded "worse than a traitor."[28]

While the public was being propagandized on a mass scale— by tens of millions of pamphlets and with "war studies" created in high schools and colleges, for example— a Sedition Act was passed which forbade "uttering, printing, writing, or publishing any disloyal, profane, scurrilous, or abusive language about the United States government or the military." Even the pro-war *New Republic* was warned that it could be banned from the mails if it continued to publish advertisements by the National Civil Liberties Bureau.[29] All of this was promoted by the Progressives— not inconsistently, but very consistently with their *dirigiste* vision, the vision of the anointed taking control of the masses in the name of collective goals to supersede the individual decisions that Progressives saw as chaotic.

The ultimate irony was that all this economic, political and social repression was justified as part of the war in which "The world must be made safe for democracy"— a goal which itself was far removed from the ostensible cause of American military involvement, German submarine warfare.

Just as the international repercussions of American involvement in the First World War did not end when the war ended, so the repercussions of the domestic policies of the Wilson administration did not end when the war ended. The widespread government control of the economy demonstrated, to John Dewey for example, "the practicable possibilities of governmental regulation of private business" and that "public control was shown to be almost ridiculously easy."[30] As elsewhere, government orders were verbally transformed into the more politically acceptable euphemism "public control," and the ease of imposing such orders was equated with success at achieving their proclaimed goals. Moreover, the Wilson administration did not last long enough after wartime controls were instituted to determine their long-run effects in peacetime.

As for the public, as distinguished from those who invoked its name in euphemisms, the public repudiated Wilson's Progressivism at the polls and elected conservative administrations throughout the ensuing decade of the 1920s. But the heady experience of government intervention and control of the economy in wartime shaped the thinking of individuals who would later be supporters or participants in the New Deal administration of the 1930s, headed by Wilson's Assistant Secretary of the Navy, Franklin D. Roosevelt.

THE SECOND WORLD WAR

Intellectuals Between the World Wars

While the First World War reinforced the *dirigiste* tendencies of both the intelligentsia and of many in the political arena, it devastated the notions of those intellectuals who saw war as a beneficial social tonic domestically or as a good means to spread Progressive policies internationally. Despite those intellectuals who had rallied to the military interventionist policies of Woodrow Wilson in Latin America and in Europe, the unprecedented horrors and devastations of the First World War turned virtually the whole intellectual community of the Western world in the opposite direction, toward pacifism. Indeed, pacifism became a widespread attitude among much of the population at large and therefore a potent political force in democratic nations.

No matter how drastically intellectuals had been forced to change their minds in the wake of the First World War, they remained as convinced as ever that their views on the subject of war and peace were vastly superior to the views of the general public. Part of the reason for the spread of pacifism were circumstances— especially the grim and heart-rending experiences of the First World War— and part was due to how people reacted to circumstances, especially the intelligentsia, most severely the intelligentsia in France, which suffered most among the Western democracies. The most fundamental of these circumstances were the stark facts of that war itself:

> About 1,400,000 French lost their lives; well over 1,000,000 had been gassed, disfigured, mangled, amputated, left permanent invalids. Wheelchairs, crutches, empty sleeves dangling loosely or tucked into pockets became common sights. More than that had suffered some sort of wound: Half of the 6,500,000 who survived the war had sustained injuries. Most visible, 1,100,000, were those who had been evidently

diminished and were described as *mutilés*, a term the dictionary
translates as "maimed" or "mangled," and English usage prefers to clothe
in an euphemism: "disabled."[31]

With most of the war on the western front fought on its own territory,
France suffered tremendous casualties in the First World War. More than
one-fourth of all Frenchmen between the ages of 18 and 27 were killed in
the First World War.[32] Moreover, neither the financial nor the human costs
of the First World War ended when the war itself ended. Although the
numbers of males and females in France's population were roughly equal
before the war, the massive wartime casualties among young Frenchmen
meant that in the 1930s the number of women between the ages of twenty
and forty exceeded the number of men of those ages by more than a
million— meaning that more than a million women in the prime of life
could not fulfill traditional expectations of becoming wives and mothers.
During the 1930s, there were not enough babies born in France to replace
the people who died during that decade.[33]

The sense of faith in the French government was also devastated, as
people who had patriotically invested in bonds to help finance the First
World War saw the value of those bonds drastically reduced by inflation,
cheating some citizens out of their life's savings. No country was more fertile
soil for pacifism and demoralization, and no one created more of both than
France's intelligentsia.

Anti-war novels and the memoirs of military veterans found a vast
market in France. A translation of the anti-war classic *All Quiet on the
Western Front* sold 72,000 copies in ten days and nearly 450,000 copies by
Christmas, *L'Humanité* serialized it and *Vie intellectuelle* praised it. In 1938,
the year of the Munich appeasement of Hitler, *Echo de la Nièvre* said,
"anything rather than war."[34] Novelist Jean Giono, long critical of his own
French government, likewise urged acceptance of Hitler's terms at
Munich.[35] Very similar trends were apparent in Britain in the years between
the two World Wars:

> In the late 1920s and early 1930s, the pacifist mood was being fuelled by
> the flow of memoirs and novels exploring the horrors of the Great War—
> Richard Aldington's *Death of a Hero* and Siegfried Sassoon's *Memoirs of*

a Fox-hunting Man were published in 1928, and Robert Graves' *Goodbye to All That*, Ernest Hemingway's *Farewell to Arms* and Erich Maria Remarque's *All Quiet on the Western Front* appeared in 1929. Lewis Milestone's film of Remarque's book had a powerful impact.[36]

In addition to many anti-war novels about the First World War, eighty or more novels about the horrors of future wars were published in Britain between the First and Second World Wars.[37]

One of the remarkable developments of the 1920s was an international movement among intellectuals, promoting the idea that nations should get together and publicly renounce war. As prominent British intellectual Harold Laski put it: "The experience of what world-conflict has involved seems to have convinced the best of this generation that the effective outlawry of war is the only reasonable alternative to suicide."[38] In the United States, John Dewey spoke of those who were skeptical of this movement for the international renunciation of war that he supported, which led to the Kellogg-Briand Pact of 1928, as people with "the stupidity of habit-bound minds." He saw arguments against the renunciation of war as coming "from those who believe in the war system."[39] With Laski, Dewey and others, the issue was not simply a matter of one hypothesis about war and peace versus another but was a question of the anointed versus the benighted— the latter being dismissed with contempt, rather than having their arguments answered.

Being a pacifist in the 1920s and 1930s was a badge of honor, and pacifist phrases facilitated admission to the circles of the self-congratulatory elites. At a 1935 rally of the British Labor Party, economist Roy Harrod heard a candidate proclaim that Britain ought to disarm "as an example to the others"— a very common argument at that time. His response and the answer it provoked captured the spirit of the times:

> 'You think our example will cause Hitler and Mussolini to disarm?' I asked.
> 'Oh, Roy,' she said, 'have you lost all your idealism?'[40]

Others likewise presented pacifism in personal, rather than policy, terms. Author J.M. Murry, for example, said: "What matters is that men and women should bear their witness."[41] However, pacifist Margery South objected to pacifism becoming a "precious" doctrine "which has as its objective the regeneration of the individual rather than the prevention of war."[42] Here, as in other cases, the vision of the anointed was a vision about themselves, not just about the ostensible issue at hand. Like Margery Smith, John Maynard Keynes also objected to having national policies be based on the "urge to save *one's own soul*."[43]

Given the high personal psychic stakes for pacifists, it is not surprising that those with a contrary opinion on issues of war and peace— as on other issues— were lashed out at, as personal enemies or as people threatening their soul, and were demonized rather than answered. As noted in Chapter 4, Bertrand Russell claimed that the man who opposed pacifism was someone who "delights in war, and would hate a world from which it had been eliminated."[44] In a very similar vein, H.G. Wells spoke of a substantial portion of "human beings who definitely like war, know they like war, want it and seek it."[45]

Kingsley Martin, long-time editor of the influential *New Statesman*, likewise characterized Winston Churchill in 1931 as someone whose mind "is confined in a militaristic mould," as a psychological explanation of Churchill's advocacy of "keeping the French Army and the British Navy at full strength."[46] More generally, Kingsley Martin treated those with views different from his own regarding war and peace as having psychological defects, rather than having arguments that required being answered with other arguments:

> To have a foreign enemy in the offing enables us to hate with a good conscience. . . It is only in time of war that we get a complete moral holiday, when all the things which we have learned at our mother's knee, all the moral inhibitions imposed by education and society, can be whole-heartedly thrown aside, when it becomes justifiable to hit below the belt, when it is one's duty to lie, and killing is no longer murder.[47]

In short, the unworthiness of opponents was taken as axiomatic, making substantive arguments against their arguments unnecessary. Kingsley Martin was not alone. Churchill's colleagues in Parliament were equally dismissive.[48]

Such views were not peculiar to British and American intellectuals. The French intelligentsia played a major role in the promotion of pacifism between the two World Wars. Even before the Treaty of Versailles was signed, internationally renowned French writer Romain Rolland— recipient of France's Grand Prix de Littérature, later elected to the Russian Academy of Sciences and offered the Goethe Prize by Germany, and recipient of the Nobel Prize for Literature— issued a manifesto calling on intellectuals in all countries to oppose militarism and nationalism, in order to promote peace.[49] In 1926, prominent intellectuals from a number of countries signed an internationally publicized petition calling for "some definite step toward complete disarmament and the demilitarizing of the mind of civilized nations." Among those who signed were H.G. Wells and Bertrand Russell in England and Romain Rolland and Georges Duhamel in France.

The petition called for a ban on military conscription, in part "to rid the world of the spirit of militarism."[50] Behind such arguments was the crucial assumption that both physical and moral disarmament were necessary to sustain peace. Neither in this petition nor in other statements expressing similar views was there much, if any, expressed concern that both kinds of disarmament would leave the disarmed nations at the mercy of those nations which did not disarm in either sense, thus making a new war look more attractive to the latter because it would look more winnable. Hitler, for example, banned the anti-war classic *All Quiet on the Western Front*, as he wanted neither moral nor physical disarmament in Germany, but carefully followed both phenomena in Western democracies, as he plotted his moves against them.

Pacifists of this era seemed not to think of other nations as prospective enemies but of *war itself* as the enemy, with weapons of war and those who manufactured these weapons— "merchants of death" being the fashionable phrase of the times and the title of a best-selling 1934 book[51]— also being enemies. The "merchants of death wax fat and bloated," declared John Dewey in 1935.[52] Romain Rolland called them "profiteers of massacre."[53] H.G. Wells said, "war equipment has followed blindly upon industrial advance until it has become a monstrous and immediate danger to the community."[54] Harold Laski spoke of the "wickedness of armaments."[55] Aldous Huxley referred to a battleship as a "repulsive" insect, a "huge bug," which "squatted there on the water, all its poisonous armory enlarged into instruments of destruction, every bristle a gun, every pore a torpedo tube," and added: "Men had created this enormous working model of a loathsome insect for the express purpose of destroying other men."[56]

Pacifists did not see military forces as deterrents to other nations' military forces but as malign influences in and of themselves. J.B. Priestley, for example, said "we should distrust any increase in armaments," one reason being that "heavy competitive arming produces fear." Moreover, "Once a nation is heavily armed, it has to keep playing at war, and from playing at war to the actual waging of war is a very short step."[57] Famed author E.M. Forster (*A Passage to India*) said that he was "shocked" to realize that his stock in Imperial Chemical was stock in a company that *potentially* could produce war weapons, even though currently (1934) it was "not an armament firm"— and he promptly sold all his shares of that stock. A year later, he said, "One of my reasons for voting Labour last week was that I hoped it would arm us inadequately: would, in more decorous language, keep us out of the armament race when disaster seems assured."[58]

Such views— seeing weapons rather than other nations as the danger— were not simply intellectual fashions but created political bases for national policies and international agreements, beginning with the Washington Naval Agreements of 1921-1922 among the leading naval powers of the world to limit the number and size of warships, agreements hailed by John Dewey among others,[59] and the Kellogg-Briand Pact of 1928, renouncing war. "Away with rifles, machine guns, and cannon!" said France's Foreign Minister, Aristide Briand,[60] co-author of the Kellogg-Briand Pact. In a letter to the *New Republic* in 1932, Romain Rolland urged, "Unite, all of you, against the common enemy. Down with war!"[61] Later, Georges Duhamel, looking back on the interwar pacifists in France, including himself, summarized their approach, which avoided seeing other nations as potential enemies:

> For more than twelve years Frenchmen of my kind, and there were many of them, spared no pains to forget what they knew about Germany. Doubtless it was imprudent, but it sprang from a sincere desire on our part for harmony and collaboration. We were willing to forget. And what were we willing to forget? Some very horrible things.[62]

The view of war itself, rather than other nations, as the enemy began shortly after the end of the First World War, as did the idea that patriotism must be superseded by internationalism, in the interests of peace. Addressing school teachers in 1919, Anatole France urged that they use the schools to promote pacifism and internationalism. "In developing the child, you will determine the future," he said. "The teacher must make the child love peace and its works; he must teach him to detest war; he will banish from education all that which excites hate for the stranger, even hatred of the enemy of yesterday," he added. Anatole France declared, "we must be citizens of the world or see all civilization perish."[63] Such ideas became dominant in French schools during the next two decades.

A key role in the spread of pacifism in France was played by the schools— more specifically, by the French teachers' unions, which began organized campaigns in the 1920s, objecting to postwar textbooks favorably depicting the French soldiers who had defended their country against German invaders in the First World War. Such textbooks were called "bellicose"— a verbal tactic still common among those with the vision of the anointed, of reducing views different from their own to mere emotions, as if in this case only pugnaciousness could account for resisting invaders or for praising those who had put their lives on the line to do so. The leading teachers' union, the *Syndicat national des instituteurs* (SN) launched a campaign against those textbooks "of bellicose inspiration" which it characterized as "a danger for the organization of peace." Since nationalism was said to be one of the causes of war, internationalism or "impartiality" among nations was considered to be a required feature of textbooks.[64]

This was not thought of as being against patriotism but, at the very least, it lessened the sense of obligation to those who had died to protect the nation, with its implicit obligation on members of generations that followed to do the same, if and when that became necessary again.

Leaders of the drive to rewrite history textbooks called their goal "moral disarmament" to match the military disarmament which many regarded as another key to peace. Lists of textbooks targeted for removal from the schools were made by Georges Lapierre, one of the SN leaders. By 1929, he was able to boast of all the "bellicose" books the SN campaign had gotten taken out of the schools, rewritten, or replaced. Faced with the threat of losing a share of the large textbook market, French publishers caved in to union demands that books about the First World War be revised to reflect "impartiality" among nations and to promote pacifism.

The once epic story of French soldiers' heroic defense at Verdun, despite the massive casualties they suffered, was now transformed into a story of horrible suffering by *all* soldiers at Verdun— from bullets, shells, poison gas, frostbite— presented in the much sought after spirit of impartiality: "Imagine the life of these combatants— French, allies, or enemies."[65] In short, men who had once been honored as patriotic heroes for having sacrificed their lives in a desperate struggle to hold off the invaders of their country were now verbally reduced to *victims*, and put on the same plane as other victims among the invaders. Ceremonies dedicating monuments to commemorate soldiers who had died in battle were sometimes turned into occasions for speeches promoting the pacifist ideology.[66]

Among those who tried to warn against "moral disarmament" was Marshal Philippe Pétain, the victor of the battle of Verdun, who in 1934 said that French teachers were out to "raise our sons in ignorance of or in contempt of the fatherland."[67] Years later, during the Second World War, one of the alerts issued to French soldiers said, "Remember the Marne and Verdun!"[68] But this was said to a generation that had been taught to see the Marne and Verdun *not* as historic sites of patriotic heroism by French soldiers but as places where soldiers on all sides had been victims alike.

France's behavior in the Second World War was in extraordinary contrast with its behavior in the First World War. France fought off the German invaders for four long years during the First World War, despite suffering horrendous casualties— more wartime deaths than a larger country like the United States has ever suffered in any war or in all its wars put together. Yet, during the Second World War, France surrendered after just six weeks of fighting in 1940. In the bitter moment of defeat, the head of the teachers' union was told: "You are partially responsible for the defeat."[69] Charles de Gaulle, François Mauriac, and many other Frenchmen blamed a lack of national will, or general moral decay, for the sudden and humiliating collapse of France in 1940.[70]

Although France's sudden collapse caught much of the world by surprise, Winston Churchill had said, as far back as 1932: "France, though armed to the teeth, is pacifist to the core."[71] Hitler was not surprised by France's sudden collapse, and had in fact predicted it.[72] When he pressed his generals to draw up plans for the invasion of France immediately after the swift German victory in Poland in the autumn of 1939, the generals' analyses of the various military and logistical factors involved led them to doubt that such a project could be undertaken, with any realistic hope of success, before 1941 or perhaps even 1942. But the most delay that Hitler would grant them was until the spring of 1940, which in fact was when the German invasion of France began. Hitler's reasons were wholly different from the objective factors which German generals had analyzed. It was based on his analysis of the French themselves.

Hitler said that France was no longer the same as the France that had fought doggedly through four years of the First World War, that the contemporary French were lacking in the personal strengths necessary for victory, and would falter and surrender.[73] That is in fact largely what happened. The objective factors, such as the number and quality of military equipment available to France and its British allies versus those available to the German invaders, led military leaders in both France and Germany at the time to conclude at the outset that France had the greater prospects of victory.[74] But Hitler had long made a study of public opinion, as well as official opinion, in France and Britain.[75] The words and deeds of both politicians and pacifists in those countries went into Hitler's calculations.

The invasion of France took place when it did only because Hitler adamantly insisted upon it, dismissing the advice of his own top generals. Decades later, scholarly studies in both France and Germany reached the same conclusion as that of French and German military leaders in 1940, that the objective military factors favored a French victory[76]— and certainly nothing like the swift and total collapse that occurred. How much of that collapse can be attributed to the large role of chance and misjudgments inherent in war, and how much to a fundamental inner erosion of morale, patriotism and resolution among the French themselves, is a question unlikely to be answered definitively.

What is clear, however is that the irresolution which marked French political responses to the German threat in the years leading up to the Second World War carried over into the war itself, beginning with the long months of the "phony war" from September 1939 to May 1940, during which France had overwhelming military superiority on Germany's western front, while German military forces were concentrated in the east, fighting Poland— and yet France did nothing. The German general responsible for defending the vulnerable western front said, "Every day of calm in the West is for me a gift from God."[77] In the earliest days of the war, when German military forces were most heavily concentrated on the eastern front, one of the generals under his command had informed him that, if the French attacked, he did not have enough resources to stop them for even one day.[78] Even a civilian like American foreign correspondent William L. Shirer was amazed as he observed the French inaction during the "phony war" and their irresolution and ineptness when the Germans attacked in 1940.[79]

While France was the most dramatic example of "moral disarmament" during the interwar years, it was by no means the only country in which such views prevailed among the intelligentsia. British pacifists likewise often depicted wars as being a result of national emotions or attitudes, rather than calculations of self-interest by aggressive rulers. In a 1931 editorial in the *New Statesman and Nation*, Kingsley Martin said that "modern war is the product of ignorance and idealism, not of far-sighted wickedness." Therefore what was needed to prevent a future war was "bringing up a new generation to recognise that martial patriotism is an out-of-date virtue" because taking part in a future war would be "something that is individually shameful as well as socially suicidal."[80] Bertrand Russell defined patriotism as "a willingness to kill and be killed for trivial reasons."[81]

In 1932, British author Beverley Nichols publicly declared himself in favor of peace at any price, and later wrote *Cry Havoc!*, one of the most prominent pacifist books of the decade.[82] In 1933, students at Oxford University publicly pledged themselves *not* to fight in defense of their country, and what became known as "the Oxford pledge" spread rapidly to other British universities, as well as being echoed in Britain by such intellectuals as Cyril Joad and A.A. Milne, famous author of *Winnie the*

Pooh, and in France by André Gide, who spoke of "the courageous students of Oxford."[83] Joad said that "the best way to ensure peace is to refuse in any circumstances to make war." He urged "an intensive campaign to induce the maximum number of young people to announce their refusal to fight in any war between nations."[84]

Joad was one of those who wrote graphically of the horrors and agonies of war, though Winston Churchill warned that Britain "cannot avoid war by dilating upon its horrors."[85] In Britain, as in France, patriotism was considered suspect as a cause of war. H.G. Wells, for example, declared himself against "the teaching of patriotic histories that sustain and carry on the poisonous war-making tradition of the past" and wanted British citizenship replaced by "world citizenship."[86] He regarded patriotism as a useless relic to be replaced by "the idea of cosmopolitan duty."[87] J.B. Priestley likewise saw patriotism as "a mighty force, chiefly used for evil."[88] A letter to *The Times* of London in 1936, signed by such prominent intellectuals as Aldous Huxley, Rebecca West, and Leonard Woolf, called for "the spread of the cosmopolitan spirit" and called for "writers in all countries" to "help all peoples to feel their underlying kinship."[89]

Meanwhile, Hitler was following such developments in Britain and France,[90] as he made his own plans and assessed the prospects of military victory.

Almost as remarkable as the lengths to which the pacifists of the 1930s went was the verbal virtuosity with which they downplayed the dangers of the pacifism they were advocating while Hitler was rearming on a massive scale in Germany and promoting the very patriotism among Germans that was being eroded by the intelligentsia in the democracies. Bertrand Russell used an argument that went as far back as 1793, when William Godwin claimed that a country which presented no military threat or provocation to other nations would not be attacked.[91] If Britain would reduce its armed forces, as Bertrand Russell advocated, "we should threaten no one, and no one would have any motive to make war on us." Russell explained further:

> When disarmament is suggested, it is natural to imagine that foreign conquest would inevitably follow, and would be accompanied by all the horrors that characterize warlike invasions. This is a mistake, as the

example of Denmark shows. Probably, if we had neither armaments nor Empire, foreign States would let us alone. If they did not, we should have to yield without fighting, and we should therefore not arouse their ferocity.[92]

According to Russell, if you declare "that you are prepared to be defenceless and trust to luck, the other people, having no longer any reason to fear you, will cease to hate you, and will lose all incentive to attack you." The reason for this conclusion was Lord Russell's claim: "In most civilized men, resistance is necessary to arouse ferocity."[93] From this it followed that fear of an impending war should lead to "unilateral disarmament."[94] Such reasoning was not peculiar to Bertrand Russell nor unique to Britain. In France, a book by the head of the French socialist party— and later premier— Léon Blum said:

> If a nation thus undertook to disarm, it would not in reality incur any risk, because the moral prestige which it would acquire would render it invulnerable to attack and the force of its example would induce all other States to follow.[95]

Another element in the pacifist case of the 1930s, in both France and Britain, was that even a victory in war would make no real difference. According to Bertrand Russell, "victory will be no less disastrous to the world than defeat would have been." Because of the need for tight wartime control of a panicked population, "anarchy will only be prevented by a military dictatorship, which may not prove to be temporary," so that the end result of even a victorious war "will be the substitution of an English Hitler for the German one."[96] Kingsley Martin likewise saw a new war as one "from which no one can emerge victorious,"[97] that "war would totally end civilisation."[98] In France, novelist Jean Giono asked what was the worst that could happen if the Germans invaded France. The French would become Germans, he said. "I prefer being a living German to being a dead Frenchman."[99] Literary figure Simone Weil argued along similar lines, asking "why is the possibility of German hegemony worse than French hegemony?"[100]

Just a little over two years after this abstract question about abstract countries, the Nazi conquest of France made the consequences of Hitler's hegemony much more painfully specific. In the aftermath of France's defeat,

Simone Weil, being of Jewish ancestry though a practicing Christian, fled the dangers of genocidal Nazi rule in France and died in England during the war. Georges Lapierre, who had spearheaded the drive against "bellicose" textbooks in French schools became, in the wake of France's defeat, part of the underground resistance to Nazi rule, but was captured and sent to the Dachau concentration camp, where he died.[101] Weil and Lapierre learned from experience, but too late to spare themselves or their country the consequences of the things they had advocated. Meanwhile, Jean Giono collaborated with the Nazi conquerors. Nor was he alone in this among French intellectuals.

Widespread pacifist sentiments among the intelligentsia in Britain during the interwar period were echoed in the political arena by leaders of the British Labor Party:

> In June 1933, at the East Fulham by-election, the Labour candidate received a message from the Labour Party leader, George Lansbury: 'I would close every recruiting station, disband the Army and disarm the Air Force. I would abolish the whole dreadful equipment of war and say to the world "do your worst".' Clement Attlee, who was to succeed him as leader, told the Commons, 21 December 1933: 'We are unalterably opposed to anything in the nature of rearmament.' Labour consistently voted, spoke and campaigned against rearmament right up to the outbreak of war.[102]

Two years later, Attlee said, "Our policy is not of seeking security through rearmament but through disarmament."[103] As late as 1937, Harold Laski said, "Are we really to support this reactionary Government. . . in rearming for purposes it refuses specifically to declare?"[104] The Labor Party's opposition to military preparedness did not change until the working class component of the Labor Party, represented by its unions, eventually overcame its intellectual component, represented by Laski and others with a doctrinaire opposition to military defense.[105]

A 1938 editorial in the *New Statesman and Nation* deplored the labor unions' "supporting rearmament" without getting some quid pro quo in the form of influence over the government's international policies or forcing the government "to limit effectively the profits of the arms industry."[106] In short, to intellectual supporters of the Labor Party, rearmament was still an ideological issue a year before the Second World War began, rather than a matter of national survival.

Similar anti-military and anti-armament views were common among the American intelligentsia. John Dewey, Upton Sinclair, and Jane Addams were among the American signers of a 1930 manifesto against military training for youths.[107] In 1934, Oswald Garrison Villard urged a "decrease by one-third of the United States army and the mustering out of 50 per cent of our reserve officers as evidence of our good faith."[108] Nor were such sentiments among intellectuals without influence upon holders of political power. When the Roosevelt administration cut the Army's budget, Army Chief of Staff General Douglas MacArthur had an angry confrontation with the President, offered his resignation, and was still so upset as he left the White House that he vomited on the steps.[109]

In such an atmosphere between the two World Wars, international disarmament conferences and agreements in which nations renounced war became very popular in the Western democracies. But, as with domestic gun-control laws, the real question is whether arms-limitation treaties actually limit the arms of anyone except those who respect the law, whether international or domestic. Both Japan and Germany violated armaments limitations agreements that they had signed, producing among other things larger battleships than these treaties allowed and larger than anything in either the British or American navies.

Violations of arms control treaties are not a happenstance. Such agreements are inherently one-sided. Leaders of democratic nations are under more pressure to sign such agreements than are leaders of dictatorships that can control, suppress or ignore public opinion. In democratic nations, neither academic nor media intellectuals are usually as concerned with scrutinizing the specifics of disarmament agreements as they are with celebrating the symbolism of the signing of such agreements and the "easing of international tensions" that they bring, as if emotional catharsis will deflect governments bent on military aggression. Thus intellectuals like John Dewey had cheered on the Washington Naval Agreements of 1921–1922,[110] and *The Times* of London praised the Anglo-German naval agreement of 1935 as "the outstanding fact in Anglo-German relations," as an "emphatic renunciation of hostile purpose towards this country" by Germany, and a "clear-sighted decision of HERR HITLER himself."[111]

Conversely, those with this vision roundly condemn leaders of their own country who refuse to compromise in order to reach such agreements. In addition to terms that explicitly tend to favor those nations whose intelligentsia are *not* free to criticize their governments, subsequent violations of these agreements by aggressor nations are more likely to be tolerated by leaders of democratic nations, who have no incentive to be quick to announce to their own citizens that they have been "had" in signing agreements that were widely publicized and widely celebrated when they were signed.

The intelligentsia do not need to convert political leaders to their own pacifist views in order to affect government policy. Leaders of democratic nations must always face the prospect of elections, and the atmosphere in which those elections are held is a fact of life to politicians seeking to keep their careers alive and their party in power. Thus, although clandestine German rearmament in violation of treaties began even before Hitler came to power in 1933, this was "secret" only in the sense that the German government did not acknowledge it and the general public in Western democratic countries were not made aware of it. But it was not secret from democratic leaders who received intelligence reports.[112]

British Conservative Party leader and later Prime Minister Stanley Baldwin, for example, was well aware of what was going on— but was also well aware of the political repercussions if he publicly announced German rearmament. In response to a speech in the House of Commons in 1936 by Winston Churchill, then a back-bencher, charging that the British government had engaged in "one-sided disarmament" and that the British army "lacks almost every weapon which is required for the latest form of modern war,"[113] Prime Minister Baldwin replied in terms of what the political realities were at the time of the 1933 elections:

> Supposing I had gone to the country and said that Germany was rearming, and that we must rearm, does anybody think that this pacific democracy would have rallied to that cry at that moment? *I cannot think*

of anything that would have made the loss of the election from my point of view more certain.[114]

Even a dozen years later, writing his monumental postwar, six-volume history, *The Second World War*, Churchill remained repelled by Baldwin's answer:

> This was indeed appalling frankness. It carried naked truth about his motives into indecency. That a Prime Minister should avow that he had not done his duty in regard to national safety because he was afraid of losing the election was an incident without parallel in our parliamentary history. Mr. Baldwin was, of course, not moved by any ignoble wish to remain in office. He was in fact in 1936 earnestly desirous of retiring. His policy was dictated by the fear that if the Socialists came into power, even less would be done than his Government intended. All their declarations and votes against defence measures are upon record.[115]

Here, as in many other situations, the intelligentsia's effect on the course of events did not depend upon their convincing the holders of power. All they had to do was convince enough of the public so that the holders of power became fearful of losing that power if they went against the prevailing vision— pacifism, in this case. If Baldwin had lost power, he would have lost it to those who would turn the pacifist vision into a reality potentially disastrous to the country. Britain, after all, narrowly escaped being invaded and conquered in 1940, and only because of a belated development of its interceptor fighter planes that shot down German bombers during the aerial blitz that was intended to prepare the way for the invasion force being mobilized across the English Channel. Had the pacifists in the Labor Party come to power in 1933, it is by no means clear that this narrow margin of survival would have been in place.

There was a similar reluctance among leaders in France to alert the public to danger, or perhaps even to acknowledge the dangers to themselves. Although French Foreign Minister Aristide Briand was well aware of the dramatically rising political support for the Nazis in the 1930 German elections, and what that portended in terms of a military threat to France, like Baldwin he was not prepared to alarm the public:

Briand was untroubled: Hitler will not go far, he assured the press while doing his best to keep news of German militarism reviving from the French public. Parades and demonstrations of the German Right were "completely suppressed in newsreels shown in French movie houses," reported the American military attaché.[116]

Even before Hitler came to power, French intelligence agents had already penetrated Germany's clandestine military buildup.[117] But neither the press nor the politicians wanted to tell the French public things that they did not want to hear, after all the traumas that they had been through during the First World War. Even after a further escalation of the vote for the Nazis in the 1932 elections brought Hitler into the German government, evasion or denial of the dangers to France continued:

> In the new German elections the Nazis became the largest party in the Reichstag, but the French press was not impressed. President Hindenburg had brought in General von Schleicher to hold the fort against the house painter-demagogue. Newspapers from Left to Right celebrated "the piteous end of Hitlerism" (*L'Œuvre*, January 1, 1933) and "the decadence of Hitler's movement" (*Paris-Soir*, January 1, 1933). The German Boulanger had missed the boat, exulted *L'Echo de Paris* (Nov. 7, 1932), forgetting how law-abiding the populist nineteenth-century general had been. The Socialist *Populaire* and the royalist *Action française* agreed: Hitler was henceforth excluded from power. But Schleicher resigned as January 1933 ended, and the demagogue found himself in power after all. A pacifist dedicated his latest book, *Peace on Earth* to Adolf Hitler.[118]

As in other times and in other contexts, it is worth noting in passing the know-it-all tone of condescension in the press, which is a corollary of self-exaltation among the intelligentsia.

However understandable the French desire to avoid a repetition of the horrors they had experienced in the First World War, their intellectuals' resolute denials of the dangers building up across the Rhine reached high levels of unreality. One of the early signs of this unreality was the celebration of the Kellogg-Briand pact of 1928, outlawing war. Named for an American Secretary of State and the French Foreign Minister, this pact received virtually unanimous approval in the French press.[119] Nothing is easier than to get peaceful people to renounce violence, even when they provide no concrete ways to prevent violence from others.

The French did not want to hear anything bad about Germany. Even Hitler's *Mein Kampf*, which spelled out his hostile intentions toward France, did not get through to the intelligentsia or to the public because a French court stopped its full translation, so that only expurgated versions were available to the few who were interested.[120] By the late 1930s, as refugees from Germany fled to France, bearing stories of the horrors of the Nazi regime, their stories were not only widely rejected but, because many of these refugees were Jewish, this provoked increased anti-Semitism, based on the notion that Jews were trying to provoke a war between France and Germany. Anti-Semitism was not confined to the masses, but was common among French intellectuals as well.[121]

In Britain, as in France, there was strong resistance among the intelligentsia to recognizing the nature of the Nazi regime within Germany or the external threat that it posed to Western democracies. The influential *Manchester Guardian* said that, despite the Nazis' radical ideas, they would act like "ordinary politicians" when they took office. Britain's largest circulation newspaper at the time, the *Daily Herald*, dismissed Hitler as a "clown" and opined that he would share the fate of his immediate predecessors as Chancellor of Germany, whose terms had lasted only a matter of weeks. The *Daily Telegraph* likewise said that Hitler was "done for" and would be gone before the end of 1932.[122] Harold Laski likewise declared in 1932 that "the Hitlerite movement has passed its apogee," that Hitler was "a cheap conspirator rather than an inspired revolutionary, the creature of circumstances rather than the maker of destiny."[123]

The most influential British newspaper, *The Times* of London, considered Hitler a "moderate," at least compared to other members of his party.[124] After Hitler and the Nazis achieved supreme power in Germany in 1933, *The Times* was especially resistant to letting news of the Nazis' domestic oppressions or international threats reach the public. Dispatches from *The Times'* own foreign correspondents in Germany were often filtered, rewritten, and sometimes rejected outright when they reported the raw reality of what was happening under Hitler. Complaints from these correspondents were unavailing, and some resigned in protest against the newspaper's filtering of their dispatches critical of the Nazi regime and reassigning them to places away from crucial events in Germany, while *The Times'* editorials supported Prime Minister Neville Chamberlain's appeasement policies toward Germany. *Times* editor Geoffrey Dawson wrote candidly to his Geneva correspondent:

> I do my utmost, night after night, to keep out of the paper anything that might hurt their [German] susceptibilities. . . . I have always been convinced that the peace of the world depends more than anything else upon our getting into reasonable relations with Germany.[125]

Here, as in other contexts, the harm done by the intelligentsia seems especially great when they step out beyond the bounds of their competence (in this case, gathering and reporting news) to seek a wider and greater role in shaping events (in this case, by filtering news to fit their vision).

Responses to International Crises

The ideas pervasive among the intelligentsia between the two World Wars would be no more than a footnote to the history of the times if these ideas did not have repercussions on the society at large, and indeed on the history of the world. But the influence of the ideas spread by the intelligentsia became apparent in the series of international crises that led up to the Second World War. The first of these crises involved the Rhineland in 1936.

After the shock of the First World War, the Treaty of Versailles sought to render Germany's huge military potential less dangerous through various restrictions, including limitations on the size of German military forces, a ban on military conscription in Germany and forbidding the German government from stationing troops in the Rhineland, the region of Germany where its industrial capacity was concentrated. This last provision meant that any future German attacks on other nations risked having its own undefended industrial sector seized by the French.

These otherwise objectionable limitations on national sovereignty were clearly based on *not* seeing Germany as an abstract nation in an abstract world, but as the most dangerous threat to the nations around it, both from the military prowess it had demonstrated in the First World War— inflicting casualties on its enemies at much higher than its own casualty rate— and from its industrial predominance in Europe and its central location on the continent, from which it could strike in any direction.

With the passage of time, however, the British intelligentsia by the 1930s were discussing these restrictions on Germany as if Germany were an abstract nation in an abstract world. The fact that Germany was being treated *unequally* under the Versailles Treaty was seen by much of the British intelligentsia as a reason why it would be wrong to forbid the German government from doing things that other governments did. As Winston Churchill noted, in his aptly titled book *The Gathering Storm*, when "in 1932 the German delegation to the Disarmament Conference categorically demanded the removal of all restrictions upon their right to rearm, they found much support in the British press." He added:

> *The Times* spoke of "the timely redress of inequality," and *The New Statesman* of "the unqualified recognition of the principle of the equality of states." This meant that the seventy million Germans ought to be allowed to rearm and prepare for war without the victors in the late fearful struggle being entitled to make any objection. Equality of status between victors and vanquished; equality between a France of thirty-nine millions and a Germany of nearly double that number![126]

In short, the mundane specifics— on which matters of life and death depended— were subordinated by the intelligentsia to abstract principles about abstract nations. Germany was to be treated just as if it were Portugal or Denmark, even though the restrictions imposed by the Treaty of Versailles were due precisely to the fact that Germany had *not* behaved like Portugal or Denmark, and had a military capacity vastly greater than that of Portugal or Denmark.

With the rise to power of Adolf Hitler in 1933, unrestricted German rearmament went from being a demand to becoming a reality— in stages, beginning cautiously and then continuing more boldly as the Western democracies did nothing to enforce the restricting provisions of the Treaty of Versailles. Because of the initially small size of the German military under those restrictions, these violations began at a time when France alone had overwhelming military superiority over Germany and could have intervened unilaterally to stop the buildup of the Nazi military machine— a fact of which Hitler was vividly aware, and German military leaders even more fearfully so.[127]

The crucial step, without which the Nazis' wars of aggression would be impossible, was the stationing of German troops in the country's industrial region, the Rhineland. Only after its own industry was secured could Germany attack other nations. Hitler clearly understood both how essential the stationing of German troops in the Rhineland was— and how risky it was, given the relative sizes of the French and German armies at the time:

> "The forty-eight hours after the march into the Rhineland," Paul Schmidt, his interpreter, heard him later say, "were the most nerve-racking in my life. If the French had then marched into the Rhineland, we would have had to withdraw with our tails between our legs, for the military resources at our disposal would have been wholly inadequate for even a moderate resistance."[128]

The stakes were the highest— military conquests abroad or the collapse of the Nazi regime within Germany. "A retreat on our part," Hitler later admitted, "would have spelled collapse."[129] Hitler bet everything on irresolution by the French. He won his bet and tens of millions of people later lost their lives as a result. Yet this action in the Rhineland, like others before it, continued to be viewed among the British intelligentsia as an abstract question about abstract nations. A phrase repeated again and again in the British press after Hitler sent troops into the Rhineland was that "After all, they are only going into their own back-garden."[130] A very similar view was taken in the French press.[131] Despite French military superiority, the lack of political will paralyzed them from using that military superiority to prevent Hitler from remilitarizing the Rhineland:

> Nowhere in France was there the slightest indication that the public wanted or would even tolerate military action on account of German remilitarization of the Rhineland. The satirical weekly *Le Canard enchaîné* expressed a common view when it said: "The Germans have invaded— Germany!" Communist leaders, supposedly in the forefront of opposition to Nazism, called stridently for preventing "the scourge of war from falling anew on us." They urged that the whole nation unite "against those who want to lead us to massacre." Socialist spokesmen termed "inadmissible any response that risked war," saying that even reinforcing the Maginot Line would be "provocative." The right-wing dailies *Le*

Matin and *Le Jour* declared that conflict with Germany would benefit only communist Russia.[132]

Nor were such views confined to France. When the French Foreign Minister, Pierre-Étienne Flandin, met with British Prime Minister Stanley Baldwin, to ask for British *political* support for action that France might take in response to German remilitarization of the Rhineland— France already having the *military* means to respond unilaterally— according to Flandin, Baldwin's response was: "You may be right, but if there is *even one chance in a hundred* that war would follow from your police operation, I have not the right to commit England."[133] This kind of thinking was commonplace at the time, as if there were no dangers from *inaction* to be weighed in the balance. In retrospect, we now know that Western democracies' inaction in response to Hitler's repeated provocations were crucial to his decisions to move toward war, confident that Western leaders were too timid to respond in time, or perhaps even at all.

This was especially clear in other international crises leading up to the Second World War. The West's half-hearted and ineffective response to Mussolini's invasion of Ethiopia in 1935, in defiance of the League of Nations, was one of the inactions which led Hitler to doubt their will. Their inaction in response to the German remilitarization of the Rhineland in 1936, and to both Germany's and Italy's interventions into the Spanish civil war that same year, followed by the Western democracies' inaction in response to Germany's annexation of Austria in 1938, all contributed to his contempt for Western leaders and his confidence that they would do nothing more than talk.

The crisis that most solidified that confidence on Hitler's part was the crisis over his demand to annex Czechoslovakia's Sudetenland, adjacent to Germany and populated mostly by people of German ancestry. At the Munich conference in 1938, France, Britain, and Italy concurred in Hitler's annexation of the Sudetenland, abandoning Czechoslovakia to its fate, despite France's mutual defense treaty with Czechoslovakia.

The power of the intelligentsia is demonstrated not only by their ability to create a general climate of opinion that strikes fear into those who oppose their agenda but also by their ability to create a climate of opinion which richly rewards those political leaders whose decisions are consonant with the vision of the intelligentsia. There has probably never been a leader of a democratic nation more widely or more enthusiastically acclaimed, by the public, in the press, and by members of opposition parties as well as his own, as British Prime Minister Neville Chamberlain was when he returned from the Munich conference of 1938, waving an agreement with Hitler which he characterized as producing "peace for our time."[134] Less than a year later, the biggest and most bloody war in all of human history began.

Seeing each of Hitler's successive demands as a separate issue (the perspective of one-day-at-a-time rationalism), the French press saw the 1938 demand for German annexation of Czechoslovakia's Sudetenland as a question of "Should the French get themselves killed for Beneš, the Free Mason?" as *Je Suis Partout* put it and, in 1939, as Hitler demanded German annexation of Poland's lone port of Danzig (Gdansk), the question was posed as "Do We Have to Die for Danzig?" as a headline in *L'Œuvre* put it.[135] The phrase "Why die for Danzig?" was considered a hallmark of sophistication among the intelligentsia at the time, but was instead a sign of their dangerous talent for verbal virtuosity, which can pose questions in ways that make the desired answer almost inevitable, whatever the substantive merits or demerits of the issue.

Contrary to one-day-at-a-time rationalism, the real question was not whether it was worth dying over the Rhineland, over Czechoslovakia, over Austrian annexation, or over the city of Danzig. The question was whether one recognized in the unfolding pattern of Hitler's actions a lethal threat. By 1939 the French public seemed to have reached a more realistic understanding of what Hitler was doing than some of the country's intelligentsia. A poll in France in 1939 showed 76 percent of the public willing to use force in defense of Danzig.[136] A history of this period noted that French premier Édouard Daladier "complained that he could not appear in an open place or in a bistro without seeing people stand up and cry, 'Lead! We will follow you!'"[137]

Still, this was very late in the day, just months before the outbreak of the Second World War. The pervasive pacifism of that era and its political consequences had left France backed into a corner, where it now faced the prospect of war after having lost potential allies whom it had thrown to the wolves, in the hope of being spared Hitler's wrath themselves. As noted in Chapter 2, among the military equipment used by the Germans when they invaded France in 1940 were tanks manufactured in Czechoslovakia.

The Outbreak of War

The aggressor Axis nations in the Second World War— Germany, Italy and Japan— did not have the resources, and were well aware that they did not have the resources, to match the combined resources of the democratic nations, including Britain, France, and the United States, in an arms race. Achieving the goals of the Axis powers depended on (1) the Western democracies not mobilizing their resources in time to stave off devastating defeats, which in fact the Axis inflicted time and again during the first three years of the Second World War, and (2) not having the fortitude to continue fighting in the face of an unbroken string of bloody losses and retreats, both in Europe and in Asia, until such time as their greater resources could eventually be mobilized to begin counter-attacks.

That strategy came dangerously close to success. It was November 1942— three years after Britain had entered the Second World War— before British Prime Minister Winston Churchill could say, after the battle of El Alamein in North Africa, "we have a new experience. We have victory."[138] There had been nothing but a steady stream of defeats and retreats for the British up to that point, both in Europe and in Asia, and few expected Britain itself to survive in 1940,[139] after France fell to defeat in just six weeks of fighting and the *Luftwaffe* launched its massive bombings of London and other British cities.[140] Americans also had their first military victory in 1942, with incredible good luck overcoming lopsided Japanese naval superiority at the battle of Midway.[141]

Intellectuals played a major role in bringing both Britain and the United States to such a desperate situation with a steady drumbeat of pacifist, anti-national-defense efforts between the two World Wars. In October 1938, a month after Munich and less than a year before the beginning of the Second World War, the influential British journal *New Statesman and Nation* described rearmament as "only an inefficient and wasteful form of subsidy to industries which can find no better employment for their capital" and declared that "we shall not regain self-respect by trebling the numbers of our aeroplanes."[142] Even in February 1939, just months before the outbreak of the Second World War, the *New Statesman and Nation* referred to "the international Bedlam rearmament race" and questioned the money being made by "makers of aircraft and munitions" who were described as "friends" of the "Tory Government."[143] We now know that those aircraft and munitions provided the narrow margin by which Britain survived Hitler's aerial onslaught a year later, despite a widespread view in 1940 that Britain would not survive. History also suggests that years of "arms race" and "merchants of death" rhetoric contributed to making that margin of survival so narrow and precarious.

Intellectuals played a major role in creating the atmosphere of both military weakness and political irresolution within democratic nations, which made a war against those nations look winnable to the leaders of the Axis dictatorships. In addition to thus helping bring on the most devastating war in human history, intellectuals so impeded the buildup and modernizing of military forces in democratic nations in the years leading up to that war— demonizing military equipment suppliers as "merchants of death," being a classic example— that this ensured that American and British armed forces would often be outgunned in battle,* until belated and desperate efforts, both in war industries and on the battlefields, narrowly avoided total defeat and later turned the tide that led ultimately to victory.

The wartime costs of prewar self-indulgences in pacifist moral preening and anti-military crusades by the intelligentsia were staggering in both blood and treasure. Had Hitler and his allies won the Second World War, the enduring costs for the whole human race would have been incalculable.

Neglect of history has allowed us today to forget how narrowly the Western democracies as a whole escaped the ultimate catastrophe of a victory by Hitler and his allies. More important, it has allowed us to forget

---

* As one example of what this meant, obsolete American torpedo bombers at the battle of Midway had a top speed of barely 100 miles an hour, and the much faster Japanese Zero fighter planes shot most of them out of the sky. Of the 82 Americans who flew into the battle of Midway on these planes, only 13 returned alive. Victor Davis Hanson, *Carnage and Culture: Landmark Battles in the Rise of Western Power* (New York: Doubleday, 2001), pp. 342-351.

what brought the Western democracies to such a perilous point in the first place— and the potential for the same notions and attitudes, promoted by today's intelligentsia as by the intelligentsia between the two World Wars, to bring us to the same perilous tipping point again, with no assurance that either the luck or the fortitude that saved us the first time will do so again.

Chapter 8

Intellectuals and War:
Repeating History

The timid civilized world has found nothing with which to oppose the onslaught of a sudden revival of barefaced barbarity, other than concessions and smiles.

Aleksandr Solzhenitsyn[1]

Many wars have been fought in many parts of the world since the Second World War but none thus far has been comparable in magnitude or in the range of its consequences. Like the First World War, the Second World War brought sweeping changes in the attitudes of Western intellectuals— but very different changes. As we have seen, many intellectuals who had rallied behind the Allied cause in the First World War, especially as that cause was articulated by Woodrow Wilson, turned to radical pacifism in the aftermath of that brutal and disillusioning carnage. By contrast, in the period immediately following the end of the Second World War, the tragic lessons of that war and of the years that had led up to it were too indelibly etched into people's consciousness for many to return to the naive and doctrinaire pacifism that had once been so common among intellectuals in the Western democracies.

The shocking differences between the behavior of democratic nations and totalitarian nations had been too recently, too graphically and too painfully demonstrated during the war for "moral equivalence" to be a widely saleable commodity, even among the intelligentsia. That would come later, as the mass atrocities of Nazi Germany and imperial Japan faded into the mists of memory and the similar mass atrocities of the Soviet Union remained largely concealed or ignored. But in the immediate aftermath of the Second World War, evil and danger were not things that could be ignored, viewed with an air of sophisticated detachment or verbally shrouded in euphemisms. *Time* magazine, for example, said in May 1945, at the end of the war in Europe:

> This war was a revolution against the moral basis of civilization. It was conceived by the Nazis in conscious contempt for the life, dignity and freedom of individual man and deliberately prosecuted by means of slavery, starvation and the mass destruction of noncombatants' lives. It was a revolution against the human soul.[2]

The difference between the hand-wringing and navel-gazing of the 1930s and the atmosphere in the immediate postwar era was epitomized in the way the decision was made by President Harry Truman to proceed with developing the hydrogen bomb, a weapon vastly more destructive than the atomic bombs that had devastated Hiroshima and Nagasaki. This was President Truman's consultation with his advisers:

> Lilienthal spoke of his fears of an arms race. Acheson countered by pointing out the growing public and political pressures on Truman. Lilienthal again spoke of his own "grave reservations." Truman cut him short. He did not, the President said, believe that an H bomb would ever be used, but because of the way the Russians were behaving, he had no other course. The meeting lasted only seven minutes. "Can the Russians do it?" Truman asked. All three men nodded yes. "In that case," Truman said, "we have no choice. We'll go ahead."[3]

The decade of the 1950s was still too close to the Second World War for the prewar notions, attitudes and blindspots of the intellectuals to make a strong comeback, or for the benefits of a free and decent society to be taken for granted and its human flaws to become a reason for sweeping rejections of its norms and institutions. That would begin in the 1960s, especially among people too young to have known what the Second World War was all about or what had led up to that catastrophe.

The difference between the immediate postwar period and the later period showed up in many ways. When visiting cemeteries and war memorials in Western Europe, decades later, distinguished American military historian Victor Davis Hanson noticed a difference between the messages at American cemeteries and the messages at European war memorials:

> The inscriptions at American graveyards admonish the visitor to remember sacrifice, courage, and freedom; they assume somebody bad once started a war to hurt the weak, only to fail when somebody better stopped them. In contrast, the "folly" of war— to paraphrase Barbara Tuchman— is what one gleans at most World War II museums in Europe. The displays, tapes, and guides suggest that a sudden madness once descended equally on normal-thinking Europeans and Americans at places like Nijmegen and Remagen. "Stupidity," a European visitor at Arnhem lectured me, best explains why thousands of young men killed each other for no good reason over "meaningless" bridges.[4]

Since the American commemorative sites were undoubtedly created first and the European war memorials later, after European economies had recovered from wartime devastations, the differences may reflect differences in time, rather than only differences between Americans and Europeans. In the later era, people living in safety purchased with other people's lives could loftily dismiss bridges as "meaningless," when in warfare the control of bridges can be a matter of life and death for armies and for the fate of whole nations.

A striking example of the wide mood swings to which some intellectuals have been subject was Bertrand Russell's postwar argument that Western nations should present the Soviet Union with an ultimatum to submit to a new world government, with its own armed forces, and— if the ultimatum was rejected, launch a preemptive war against the Soviet Union, while the United States had a nuclear bomb and the Soviets did not yet have one.[5] As reported in *The Observer* of London on November 21, 1948:

> "Either we must have a war against Russia before she has the atom bomb or we will have to lie down and let them govern us.". . . An atomic war would be one of extraordinary horror, but it would be "the war to end wars.". . . Fearing the horror of a future war was no way to prevent it. "Anything is better than submission."[6]

There could hardly be a greater contrast with Bertrand Russell's prewar advocacy of pacifism and unilateral disarmament— or with his subsequent return to that position. A decade later, Lord Russell said "I am for controlled nuclear disarmament." But, if it proved to be impossible to get the Soviet Union to agree to that, he was for "unilateral nuclear disarmament." He added:

> It is a bitter choice. . . . Unilateral disarmament is likely to mean, for a while, Communist domination of this world of ours. . . But if the alternatives are the eventual extinction of mankind and a temporary Communist conquest, I prefer the latter.[7]

After his return to his earlier pacifist and unilateral disarmament position, Bertrand Russell condemned those in the West who supported nuclear deterrence policies as people who "belong to the murderers' club." In this later period, Bertrand Russell described British Prime Minister Harold Macmillan and American President John F. Kennedy as "the wickedest people that ever lived in the history of man" and as "fifty times as wicked as Hitler" because Russell depicted their promotion of nuclear deterrence as "organizing the massacre of the whole of mankind."[8]

Whether as an advocate of preventive war or as a radical pacifist before and afterwards, Bertrand Russell sought sweeping and dramatic "solutions." While his particular solutions were unusual in both cases, what was far more common among intellectuals was to think of the world in terms of dramatic solutions of some sort, and to have their complete reversals of positions as to what specifically those solutions might be— as among intellectuals in general during and then after the First World War— leave them nevertheless confident that their superior wisdom and virtue should guide the masses and influence national policies. Clearly, at least one of their mutually incompatible positions had to be wrong, suggesting the old but apt phrase, "often wrong but never in doubt."

REPLAYING THE 1930s

The 1960s and the Vietnam war brought a more general return to the intellectual and ideological climate that had reigned during the 1920s and 1930s. Indeed, many of the very words and phrases of that earlier time reappeared in the 1960s, often put forth as if they were fresh new insights, instead of old notions already discredited by the course of history. For example, disarmament advocates once again called themselves "the peace movement" and called military deterrence an "arms race." Once again, the argument was made that "war solves nothing." Those who manufactured military equipment, who had been called "merchants of death" in the 1930s were now called "the military-industrial complex" and were once again regarded as a threat to peace, rather than suppliers of the means of deterring aggressor nations. The Oxford Pledge by young Englishmen of the 1930s, to refuse to fight for their country in war, was echoed during the 1960s by young Americans of military draft age who said, "Hell no, I won't go."

Graphic depictions of the horrors of war were once again seen as ways to promote peace, and a one-day-at-a-time rationalism was again considered to be the way to deal with issues that had the potential to escalate into war. Replacing the rhetoric of moral outrage with a more non-judgmental pragmatism and trying to see the other side's point of view were also part of this resurrected vision from the era between the two World Wars. Few who espoused these and other ideas from the 1930s recognized their antecedents, much less the disasters to which those antecedents had led. Most of the notions among the pacifist intelligentsia of the 1960s and later had appeared in British Prime Minister Neville Chamberlain's speeches back in the 1930s that were published as a collection in his book *In Search of Peace*, which appeared just months before the outbreak of the Second World War that these notions help bring on.[*]

More important, as too often happens, words became preemptive— disarmament being axiomatically equated with peace, for example. To disarmament advocates of his day, Churchill had said, "When you have

---

[*] Neville Chamberlain, *In Search of Peace* (New York: G.P. Putnam's Sons, 1939). These 1930s notions that reappeared in the 1960s and beyond include opposition to a "senseless competition in rearmament" (p. 45), the futility of war (140, 288), assertions that the peoples of all countries are "human beings like ourselves" (252) and desirous of peace (v, 192, 210), morally equating both sides in international conflicts (19, 27), the importance of seeing adversaries' viewpoint (53, 174), assertions that various kinds of psychological problems— enmities, fears, suspicions and misunderstandings— created a danger of war (5, 14, 50, 52, 53, 74, 97, 105, 106, 112, 133, 210, 212, 252), so that a relaxation of international tensions is crucial (158, 185), and for this "personal contacts" between heads of state are vital (34, 40, 120, 187, 209, 210, 216, 230, 242, 251-252, 271). What Chamberlain called "personal contacts" between heads of state would be renamed "summit meetings" in the later period but the reasoning and the conclusions were the same.

peace, you will have disarmament"[9]— not the other way around— but there was seldom even an attempt to test this hypothesis against that of those who automatically transformed disarmament advocates into "the peace movement."

The Vietnam War

Among the many implications of the war in Vietnam was that it once again illuminated the role of the intelligentsia in influencing the policies of a society and the course of history. That role was not the role that Machiavelli once sought, the role of directly influencing the thinking, beliefs or goals of those who wield power. In modern democratic nations, the intelligentsia can have influence— sometimes decisive influence— by creating a general climate of opinion in which it becomes politically impossible for the wielders of power to do what they believe needs to be done.

As already noted in Chapter 7, Stanley Baldwin— by his own later admission— dared not tell the British public that Germany was rearming in 1933 for fear of losing that year's election, because saying that Germany was rearming implied that Britain needed to rearm, and the dominant climate of opinion at the time would have rejected that conclusion and whoever was the messenger bringing that bad news. Baldwin dared not tell what he knew,* not simply to save his own political position, but because he knew that any attempt on his part to sound the alarm about impending dangers from Germany could bring to power the opposition Labor Party, which was totally opposed to military preparedness and would make the nation even more vulnerable than it was.

In short, the climate of opinion of the times made it politically difficult for Britain to rearm adequately, as either a deterrent to war or as a means of defending itself in the event of war, even though its highest officials were fully aware of the dangers of what was at that time clandestine German rearmament, at least in the sense that the general public was not aware of it. Thus the influence of the intelligentsia was decisive, even though they failed

---

* Baldwin's veiled public references to things he could say if his lips were not sealed brought him the popular nickname of "Old Sealed Lips" and caused famed British editorial cartoonist David Low to draw caricatures of Baldwin with tape over his mouth. David Low, *Years of Wrath: A Cartoon History 1932-1945* (London: Victor Gollancz, 1949), p. 37.

completely to convince the country's highest officials that what they said was correct.

Although the Vietnam war involved very different issues and different facts, its outcome reflected the same influence of the intelligentsia on public opinion. Whatever the merits or demerits of the decision of the United States to become a major participant in the war to prevent South Vietnam from being conquered by North Vietnam's Communist government, the stark fact is that more than 50,000 Americans died winning military victories in Vietnam that ended in political defeat because the climate of opinion created by the intelligentsia in the United States made it politically impossible not only to continue the involvement of American troops in the fighting there, but impossible even to continue to supply the resources needed by the South Vietnam government to defend itself after American troops were withdrawn. With one side receiving aid from outside and the other side not, the outcome was inevitable— the conquest of South Vietnam by North Vietnam.

The decisive turning point in the Vietnam war came with a massive 1968 uprising of Communist guerrillas in South Vietnam during a Vietnamese holiday called "Tet"— an uprising which became known as "the Tet offensive," launched during what was supposed to be a holiday truce. After many optimistic statements by American political and military leaders about how well the war was going, it came as a shock to the American public that the Communists were able to launch such a massive effort in the heart of South Vietnam.[10] Moreover, many in the media depicted what happened as a defeat for the United States, when in fact the Communist guerilla movement was decimated in the fighting and was never the same again.[11]

Communist leaders themselves, after taking over South Vietnam, openly admitted in later years that they had lost militarily in their war with American troops in Vietnam, including during their Tet offensive, but pointed out that they had won politically in America. During the war itself, American prisoner of war James Stockdale was told by his North Vietnamese captor, "Our country has no capability to defeat you on the battlefield," but that they expected to "win this war on the streets of New York."[12]

Legendary Communist military leader General Vo Nguyen Giap, who had defeated the French in the decisive battle of Dien Bien Phu in 1954, and who later commanded North Vietnamese forces against the Americans, said candidly in later years, "We were not strong enough to drive out a half-million American troops, but that wasn't our aim." His goal was political: "Our intention was to break the will of the American Government to continue the war. Westmoreland was wrong to expect that his superior firepower would grind us down. If we had focused on the balance of forces, we would have been defeated in two hours." As it was, the North Vietnamese lost "at least a million" troops killed, mostly by American troops, according to one of General Giap's aides— a death toll almost 20 times that of the Americans.[13] Looking back, years later, General Giap's aide called the Communist losses during the Tet offensive "devastating."[14]

A still later interview with a man who had served as a colonel on the staff of the North Vietnamese army, and who had received the surrender of South Vietnam in 1975, told a very similar story. A 1995 interview with Colonel Bui Tin produced these questions and answers:

Q: Was the American antiwar movement important to Hanoi's victory?

A: It was essential to our strategy. Support for the war from our rear was completely secure while the American rear was vulnerable. Every day our leadership would listen to world news over the radio at 9 a.m. to follow the growth of the American antiwar movement. Visits to Hanoi by people like Jane Fonda and former Attorney General Ramsey Clark and ministers gave us confidence that we should hold on in the face of battlefield reverses. We were elated when Jane Fonda, wearing a red Vietnamese dress, said at a press conference that she was ashamed of American actions in the war and that she would struggle along with us.

Q: Did the Politburo pay attention to these visits?

A: Keenly.

Q: Why?

A: Those people represented the conscience of America. The conscience of America was part of its war-making capability, and we were turning that power in our favor. America lost because of its democracy; through dissent and protest it lost the ability to mobilize a will to win.[15]

As regards the pivotal Tet offensive of 1968, the interviewer's question as to the purpose of that operation was answered plainly: "Tet was designed to influence American public opinion." As for the results of the Tet offensive: "Our losses were staggering and a complete surprise. Giap later told me that Tet had been a military defeat, though we had gained the planned political advantages when Johnson agreed to negotiate and did not run for re-election." Militarily, however, "Our forces in the South were nearly wiped out by all the fighting in 1968."[16]

This paradoxical combination of overwhelming American military victories in Vietnam and devastating political defeat in Washington was crucially dependent on the climate of opinion in the United States, a climate to which the intelligentsia made a major contribution.

One of the themes of contemporary critics of the Vietnam War, both before and after the Tet offensive, was that the war was unwinnable because it was essentially a "civil war" conducted by Communist guerrillas within South Vietnam, though aided and abetted by the Communist government of North Vietnam, rather than a war between these two nations. Well-known historian and contemporary commentator Arthur Schlesinger, Jr. opined that these guerrillas could "keep fighting underground for another 20 years."[17] The Tet offensive seemed to be in keeping with this view, especially when those widespread attacks were depicted as a "heavy blow" and a "setback" for American and South Vietnamese military forces and a "success" for the Communists in the *New York Times*,[18] among other places. Nationally syndicated columnist Drew Pearson said that the United States had taken a "shellacking."[19]

CBS anchor man Walter Cronkite said, "we are mired in stalemate"[20] and, while this was a less dire conclusion than some others, the size of Cronkite's audience and the fact that he had been shown in a poll to be the most trusted person in America, gave great weight to his conclusion that the war was militarily unwinnable. Aides to President Johnson later said that the Cronkite broadcast had convinced the president that he was losing the public support necessary to carry on the war to a military victory. A month later, Lyndon Johnson announced that he would not seek re-election and that he was seeking negotiations with North Vietnam.

As we now know, North Vietnamese Communist leaders in Hanoi had virtually the same military evaluation of the Tet offensive as American leaders in Washington— namely, that it was an overwhelming defeat for the Communist guerrillas. The Communists' political success consisted precisely in the fact that media outlets like the *New York Times* declared their military offensive successful. The *Wall Street Journal* likewise rejected the Johnson administration's contention that the Tet offensive was a "last gasp" of the Communist Vietcong guerilla movement in South Vietnam.[21] By this time, the Johnson administration's credibility had been squandered by its own previous words and actions,[22] so that what we now know to be the inaccurate military assessment by the media carried more weight in shaping public opinion than the accurate assessments made by national leaders in both Hanoi and Washington.

The key assumption of anti-war critics was that, in the words of distinguished columnist Walter Lippmann, "The Americans cannot exterminate the Viet Cong" guerrillas in South Vietnam— a view shared by historian Arthur Schlesinger, Jr. and by others.[23] Yet the Tet offensive virtually accomplished that supposedly impossible task, costing the Vietcong guerrillas such a loss of manpower and of areas they had previously controlled, as well as their ability to get new recruits, that what was called a civil war became afterwards more clearly a war between the armies of nations.[24] To Lippmann, writing in 1965, three years before the Tet offensive, what was happening in South Vietnam was a civil war in which "the rebels are winning."[25] Yet Lippmann later considered himself vindicated by the Tet offensive: "The Vietnamese war is, I have always believed, unwinnable."[26] *Washington Post* columnist Joseph Kraft was one of many others who echoed the theme that the Vietnam war was "unwinnable."[27] In a democracy, if enough people believe that a war is unwinnable, that can make it unwinnable.

Like many others, Walter Lippmann's solution from the beginning had been a "negotiated settlement." He paid as little attention to the actual viability of such a settlement as many other intellectuals have paid over the years to the viability of various international disarmament treaties and other agreements with totalitarian dictatorships. Nor was Lippmann alone.

Economist John Kenneth Galbraith was among many others who urged that course.[28] In the end, Lyndon Johnson's successor, President Richard Nixon, in fact made a negotiated settlement with North Vietnam— and that settlement proved to be simply a face-saving surrender on the installment plan to the North Vietnamese, who took over South Vietnam, and made clear to the world what had happened by renaming Saigon, the South Vietnamese capital, Ho Chi Minh City, in honor of the former ruler of North Vietnam.

In the aftermath of the Communist political victory in Vietnam, those in the Western democracies who had opposed American involvement in the Vietnam war on humanitarian grounds, because of the large casualties among civilians and soldiers alike, were now confronted by the fact that the end of the war did not put an end to the casualties. Military historian Victor Davis Hanson observed:

> A communist victory brought more death and even greater dislocation to the Vietnamese than did decades of war— more often slowly by starvation, incarceration, and flight, rather than by outright mass murder. . . Exact numbers are in dispute, but most scholars accept that well over 1 million left by boat; and hundreds of thousands of others crossed by land into neighboring Thailand and even China. . .Those who died in leaky boats or in storms numbered between 50,000 and 100,000. . . [29]

The Vietnam war also saw the revival in America of a pattern seen in France between the two World Wars— the downgrading of soldiers in battle from the role of patriotic heroes, no matter what acts of bravery and self-sacrifice they engaged in. During the Vietnam war, this tendency was carried even further. Collateral damage to Vietnamese civilians during American military operations, or even allegations of individual misconduct by American troops, led to sweeping moral condemnations of the U.S. military as a whole, often without any examination of the question whether such collateral damage was unusual in warfare or unusually extensive, or whether atrocities were authorized or condoned by authorities.[30] The most widely publicized atrocity against civilians— the "My Lai massacre" by an American military unit against a South Vietnamese village that was suspected of harboring Communist guerrillas— was stopped by other

American troops when they arrived on the scene, and the officer in charge was court-martialed for things that the Communist guerrillas did routinely and on a vastly larger scale.[31]

The image, filtered through the media, of those who served in the military during the Vietnam war, like the image of French soldiers who had served in the First World War, often became that of victims. "'Hero stories' were off the menu" in Vietnam, as the head of the *Washington Post*'s bureau in Vietnam later recalled the coverage of the war in the American media.[32] A common image of Vietnam veterans was that they were disproportionately the poor, the uneducated, the minorities— and that the trauma of combat drove them to widespread drug usage in Vietnam and to acts of violence upon returning home with "post-traumatic stress syndrome." Widely hailed motion pictures depicting that era dramatized such images.[33] Hard statistical data, however, contradicted such depictions[34] and some of the Vietnam "combat veterans" featured on television specials by Dan Rather and others later turned out to have never been in combat or never to have been in Vietnam.[35] But what they said fit the vision and that was often enough to get them on television and cited in newspapers and books.

Some among the American media and intelligentsia outdid the interwar French by depicting American combat veterans as villains. The only Pulitzer Prize awarded for coverage of the Tet offensive went to a reporter who wrote about the My Lai massacre without ever setting foot in Vietnam.[36] This tangential tragedy thus overshadowed innumerable battles across South Vietnam in which American troops won overwhelming victories. That much of this fighting against urban guerrillas in civilian clothes took place in residential neighborhoods made the task more difficult for American troops but presented the media with numerous opportunities to criticize those troops:

> Homes surrounding the track were stuffed with hundreds of snipers. It took a week of house-to-house fighting for American army troops and ARVN [South Vietnamese] forces to locate and expel the Vietcong, who rarely surrendered and had to be killed almost to the last man. Yet on television Americans were being blamed for blasting apart residences, as if no one noticed that urban snipers were shooting marines in the middle of a holiday truce.[37]

This battle in Saigon was not the only one reported in this one-sided way. The city of Hué, near the border with North Vietnam, was captured by a large force of Vietcong guerrillas and North Vietnamese troops, after which they massacred thousands of civilians, who were buried in mass graves. The American counter-attack that retook the city was heavily criticized in the media for its destruction of ancient historic structures, such criticisms often being made by journalists who had little or nothing to say about the mass atrocities committed by the Communists there.[38]

Long after the Vietnam war was over, CNN broadcast a story in 1998 suggesting an officially sanctioned American atrocity back in 1970. As the *Wall Street Journal* reported: "A former Green Beret sued Cable News Network and Time magazine for defamation over the now-retracted CNN broadcast, recounted in Time, that accused the U.S. military of using nerve gas to kill American defectors during the Vietnam War."[39] A co-author of that story, Peter Arnett, was also the sole source for a more famous but unsubstantiated remark supposedly made by an American military officer in Vietnam that "It became necessary to destroy the town to save it."[40] As military historian Victor Davis Hanson reported: "Yet there was little evidence— other than from Arnett himself— that any American officer said anything of the sort."[41]

The negative images of American troops filtered through the media were so pervasive and so powerful that Vietnam war veterans returning home were often openly disdained or insulted.

The Cold War

The Cold War between the United States and the Soviet Union began well before Americans' entry into the Vietnam war and continued well after it. If the Western democracies' recognition of the Soviet threat can be dated to a particular event, that event would be Winston Churchill's 1946 speech in Fulton, Missouri, when he pointed out how the Soviets' wartime commitment to providing free elections and independent governments in Eastern Europe had been violated, as part of a process of Soviet expansion and dictatorial rule:

> From Stettin in the Baltic to Trieste in the Adriatic, an iron curtain has descended across the Continent. Behind that line lie all the capitals of the ancient states of Central and Eastern Europe. Warsaw, Berlin, Prague, Vienna, Budapest, Belgrade, Bucharest and Sofia, all these famous cities and the populations around them lie in what I must call the Soviet sphere, and all are subject in one form or another, not only to Soviet influence but to a very high and, in many cases, increasing measure of control from Moscow.[42]

Among the many efforts to prevent that iron curtain from extending farther west were the Marshall Plan, to aid the rebuilding of Western Europe from the devastations of war, and the North Atlantic Treaty Organization (NATO) to present a united military front of European nations, including American troops in these nations and an American nuclear umbrella over them, with the threat of retaliation by all against a military attack on any one of the NATO member nations. None of this was done without large and continuing controversies within the Western democracies, in which the intelligentsia played major roles.

Churchill's "iron curtain" speech, for example, evoked much adverse reaction among the intelligentsia within both the United States and Britain. Nobel Prize-winning author Pearl Buck, for example, called the Churchill speech a "catastrophe."[43] A *Chicago Tribune* editorial opined that "Mr. Churchill loses a good deal of stature by this speech."[44] Columnist Marquis Childs lamented "the strong anti-Russia bias which ran through the body of the speech."[45] The *Boston Globe*, the *Washington Star* and various other American newspapers also reacted negatively to Churchill's speech, as did leading columnist Walter Lippmann, though the *New York Times* and the *Los Angeles Times* praised it.[46] In Britain, reactions ranged from that of the *Evening News*, which praised Churchill's warning, to George Bernard Shaw, who called the speech "nothing short of a declaration of war on Russia." There were similar conflicting reactions to the "iron curtain" speech in Paris.[47]

In the decades that followed, attempts to bolster Western Europe's military defenses against the Soviet bloc were similarly controversial among the intelligentsia, some of whom asked whether it was "better to be red than dead." Western Europe, however, was just one theater of the Cold War, and military defense was just one of the areas of conflict between the Soviet

Union and the United States, which extended into economic, political, social and ideological competition.

Although this was a non-military Cold War in the sense that American and Soviet troops did not fight battles directly against each other, there were many parts of the world in which military battles took place between troops backed respectively by the Soviets and the Americans. Vietnam was just one of those battlefronts. Moreover, even though the war between the United States and the Soviet Union was "cold" in the sense of lacking direct military conflict between these two countries, over it all hung the threat of the ultimate catastrophe of nuclear war.

During the Cold War, and especially after the escalating involvement of the United States in the Vietnam war, many among the intelligentsia began repeating the old notion that war "solves nothing," an echo from the 1930s, where the futility of war was proclaimed, among many others, by Neville Chamberlain, who said that war "wins nothing, cures nothing, ends nothing"[48]— and who was in turn echoing what many among the intelligentsia were saying in his day. But, like so much that has been said by the intelligentsia on so many subjects, the notion that "war solves nothing" had less to do with any empirical evidence than with its consonance with the vision of the anointed, which in turn has had much to do with the exaltation of the anointed. Had the battle of Lepanto in 1571 or the battle of Waterloo in 1815 gone the other way, this could be a very different world today. Had the desperate fighting at Stalingrad and on the beaches at Normandy gone the other way during the Second World War, life might not be worth living for millions of human beings today.

There have of course been futile wars in which all the nations on both sides ended up far worse off than before— the First World War being a classic example. But no one would make the blanket statement that medical science "solves nothing" because many people die despite treatment and some die because of wrong treatment or even from the remote risks of vaccinations. In short, mundane specifics are more salient in evaluating any particular war than are the sweeping, abstract and dramatic pronouncements so often indulged in by the intelligentsia.

The futility of an "arms race" was another staple of the 1930s that made a comeback in the 1960s, even though it was one-sided disarmament—moral as well as military— in the democratic nations after the First World War which made another war look winnable to the Axis powers, and thus led to the Second World War. The notion that an "arms race" would lead to war, which had been a staple of intellectuals during the interwar era, and which was also echoed in the political arena, notably by Neville Chamberlain,* was a notion that made a comeback during the second half of the twentieth century. Whatever the plausibility of this notion, what is crucial is that few intellectuals saw any reason to go beyond plausibility to seek hard evidence on this crucial assumption as an empirically verifiable proposition, but instead treated it as an unquestionable axiom.

Right after the Second World War had demonstrated tragically the dangers of disarmament and of half-hearted rearmament, the idea of the futility of an arms race receded. But when President John F. Kennedy invoked this lesson of the Second World War by saying in his inaugural address in 1961, "We dare not tempt them with weakness,"[49] despite his youth he was speaking for a passing generation and for ideas that would soon be replaced by opposite ideas, espoused ironically in later years by his own youngest brother in the United States Senate. The idea of military strength as a foundation of peace by deterring potential enemies faded rapidly from the 1960s on, at least among intellectuals. Instead, during the long years of the Cold War between the Soviet Union and the United States, arms limitation agreements were advocated by much, if not most, of the Western intelligentsia.

---

* "I must confess that the spectacle of this vast expenditure upon means of destruction instead of construction has inspired me with a feeling of revolt against the folly of mankind. The cost is stupendous, and the thought of the sacrifice that it must entail upon us, and upon those who come after us, drives the Government always to search for a way out, to seek to find some means of breaking through this senseless competition in rearmament which continually cancels out the efforts that each nation makes to secure an advantage over the others." Neville Chamberlain, *In Search of Peace* (New York: G.P. Putnam's Sons, 1939), p. 45. The fallacy in this is that not all nations were seeking to get an advantage by rearming. Some were rearming in order to prevent other nations from getting an advantage that would lead those other nations to attack them. Verbal equivalence once more concealed profound differences in the real world. Moreover, "mankind" is not a decision-making unit. Each nation is a decision-making unit and there is no "folly" in any nation's refusal to be disarmed when other nations are armed.

Treaties proclaiming peaceful intentions among nations, especially those limiting military weapons, were once more praised by the intelligentsia for "relaxing tensions" among nations. But international tensions had been relaxed by such agreements many times before, during the period between the two World Wars, by such things as the Washington Naval Agreements of 1921-1922, the Locarno Pact of 1925, the Kellogg-Briand Pact of 1928, the Anglo-German Naval Agreement of 1935 and the grand relaxation of all— the Munich agreement of 1938, in which Britain and France gave away an ally that they would desperately need in the war that began just one year later.

All this history vanished from memory, as if it had never happened, as the Western intelligentsia of the Cold War era repeated Neville Chamberlain's oft-reiterated emphasis on "personal contact"[50] between leaders of opposing nations by celebrating "summit meeting" after "summit meeting" between American and Soviet leaders, christening the afterglow of these meetings as "the spirit of Geneva," "the spirit of Camp David," and of other sites of similar meetings and pacts. It was as if the causes of war were hostile emotions that could be defused by a better understanding between peoples, or misunderstandings between governments that could be cleared up by meetings of opposing heads of state. But the desire of *A* to ruin *B* is not an "issue" that can be resolved amicably around a conference table.

Empirical questions about the mundane specifics of international agreements, such as the verifiability of their terms or whether their restrictions on the West were matched by comparable restrictions on the Soviets, seldom received much attention by the intelligentsia, who were too busy promoting euphoria over the fact that international agreements had been signed, to the accompaniment of lofty rhetoric.

The general asymmetry of international agreements between democratic and autocratic governments goes back well before the Cold War. Not only do the intelligentsia of democratic countries help create a climate of opinion eager for such agreements and uncritical of their specifics, that same public opinion forces democratic governments to live up to the terms of such agreements, while there is no comparable pressure on autocratic governments. Thus, as noted in Chapter 7, British and American governments restricted the size of their battleships to what was specified in the Washington Naval Agreements of 1921-1922, and the British also did the same as regards the Anglo-German Naval Agreement of 1935— with the net result during the Second World War being that both Japan and Germany had battleships larger than any in the British or American navy, because the totalitarian German and Japanese governments were free to violate those agreements.

Similarly, during the Vietnam war, a cease-fire negotiated in Paris had to be observed by South Vietnam because the South Vietnamese were dependent on American military supplies, and the United States was under the pressure of public opinion to see that the cease-fire was observed. Meanwhile, Communist North Vietnam was free to ignore the agreement that its representative had signed to such international fanfare, which culminated in a Nobel Prize for peace to both North Vietnamese representative Le Duc Tho and American Secretary of State Henry Kissinger.

With North Vietnam free to continue the fighting and South Vietnam inhibited from taking comparable countermeasures, the net result was that North Vietnam conquered South Vietnam. The Nixon administration was not naive when it made the agreements that led to this result. President Nixon wanted the war to be over and the Paris Accords created the short-run appearance of a peaceful resolution of the Vietnam war, the short run being what counts in politics.

Once again, the intellectuals' effect on the course of events did not depend on their convincing or influencing the holders of power. President Nixon had no regard for intellectuals. It was by helping shape the climate of public opinion that the intelligentsia influenced Nixon's foreign policy decision, at the cost of abandoning South Vietnam to its fate.

Among the many notions of the 1920s and 1930s that returned in the 1960s was the irrelevant claim that the peoples of all countries desire peace— as if what the German people desired mattered to Hitler[51] or what the Soviet peoples wanted mattered to Stalin. As a corollary to this notion, the old idea of more "people to people" contacts for the sake of peace, as urged by John Dewey back in the 1920s,[52] returned as if it were a new idea during the Cold War. It was as if war was a result of some insufficiency of empathy among peoples, or some mass psychological malaise that could be treated therapeutically.

John Dewey said in 1922: "If we succeed in really understanding each other, some way of cooperation for common ends can be found."[53] In the next decade, a similar sentiment was expressed by British Prime Minister Neville Chamberlain[54] and, decades after that, the same idea was revived and became the *leitmotif* of media and academic discourse during the decades of the Cold War. The idea that mutual understanding was the key to peace— and its corollary, that seeing the other side's point of view was crucial— were key to the 1930s diplomacy of Prime Minister Chamberlain.[55] But, like so much in the prevailing vision, it was taken as axiomatic, not as a hypothesis subject to empirical verification from history or from more contemporary events.

The election of Ronald Reagan as President of the United States in 1980 brought policies and practices directly the opposite of those favored by intellectuals. Instead of emphasizing, as Neville Chamberlain had, the importance of understanding an adversary nation's point of view,[56] President Reagan emphasized the importance of making sure that adversary nations understood the American point of view, as when he called the Soviet Union "an evil empire"— to the consternation of the intelligentsia.[57] In his first meeting with Soviet premier Mikhail Gorbachev in Geneva in 1985, Reagan was quite blunt: "We won't stand by and let you maintain weapon superiority over us. We can agree to reduce arms, or we can continue the arms race, which I think you know you can't win."[58] During a visit to West Berlin in 1987, Reagan was told that the Communists in East Berlin had long-range listening devices. This was his response, as recounted in his autobiography:

> "Watch what you say," one German official said. Well, when I heard that, I went out to a landing that was even closer to the building and began sounding off about what I thought of a government that penned in its people like farm animals.
>
> I can't remember exactly what I said, but I may have used a little profanity in expressing my opinion of Communism, hoping I would be heard.[59]

Later that day, he went to the infamous Berlin Wall, where he made a public statement that stunned the intelligentsia as much as his "evil empire" remark: "Mr. Gorbachev, tear down this wall!"[60] This was a double insult because, officially at least, it was the sovereign East German government that was responsible for the Berlin Wall. By publicly going over their heads directly to Soviet premier Gorbachev, he was in effect calling the East German regime a puppet government.

Another area in which Ronald Reagan marked a break with past practices of Western leaders was in refusing to make international agreements, when he did not consider the terms right, even if that meant that he came away from a summit meeting empty-handed and would be blamed by the media for not reaching an agreement. At a 1986 summit meeting in Iceland with Soviet leader Mikhail Gorbachev, there were many tentative agreements on arms reductions but, when time came to finalize an accord, Gorbachev said, "This all depends, of course, on you giving up SDI," the Strategic Defense Initiative, the missile defense program called "star wars" by its opponents. Later, recalling this sticking point at the eleventh hour in his autobiography, Reagan said:

> I was getting angrier and angrier.
> I realized he had brought me to Iceland with one purpose: to kill the Strategic Defense Initiative. He must have known from the beginning he was going to bring it up at the last minute.
> "The meeting is over," I said. "Let's go, George, we're leaving."[61]

With that, President Reagan and Secretary of State George Shultz walked out, even though the Soviets had indicated that they were prepared to stay for another day.* There would be later summits, but this summit let the Soviets know that Reagan, unlike previous Western leaders, did not feel a need to come away with an agreement at virtually any cost.

The fact that the Reagan approach, which many among the intelligentsia saw as likely to lead to war, led instead to the end of the Cold War, while the Chamberlain approach that was supposed to lead to peace

---

* "Gorbachev was stunned. The Soviets had already made it known they were willing to spend another day in Reykjavik. Gorbachev had more to say. As Reagan put his coat on, Gorbachev said to him, 'Can't we do something about this?' Reagan had had enough. 'It's too late,' he said." Lou Cannon, *President Reagan: The Role of a Lifetime* (New York: Public Affairs, 2000), p. 690.

led instead to the biggest war in history, has made no dent on the vision of the anointed.

The Cold War Intelligentsia

Verbal virtuosity was as much in evidence among the intelligentsia in the 1960s and afterwards as it was in the world of the 1920s and 1930s. Disarmament advocates called themselves "peace" movements in both eras, preempting the crucial question whether one-sided disarmament was more likely to lead to peace or to war, and whether "relaxing international tensions" was more likely to reduce the drive to war among all nations or to leave the intended victims less mindful of the dangers from aggressors. As in other contexts, the fatal talent of verbal virtuosity often served as a substitute for scrutinizing empirical evidence or engaging in analysis. It was not that the intelligentsia did these things badly. Their clever verbal formulations often made it unnecessary for them to do these things at all.

During the 1980s, when President Reagan met a Soviet nuclear missile buildup in Eastern Europe with an American nuclear missile buildup in Western Europe, this revived the "arms race" arguments of the 1920s and 1930s, polarizing public opinion in Western nations, including the United States. *Washington Post* columnist William Raspberry deplored "a protracted, expensive and dangerous nuclear arms race."[62] *New York Times* columnist Anthony Lewis said "it is not a rational response" to Soviet power "to intensify an arms race."[63] Fellow *New York Times* columnist Tom Wicker referred to "an arms race that has grown out of all reason."[64] "Better, surely, to concentrate on the effort to bring the arms race under control, thus keeping civilized life as we know it at least physically intact," said author and former diplomat George F. Kennan.[65] Nobel Peace Prize winner Alva Myrdal said, "I was never able to stop the search for the why's and how's of something so senseless as the arms race."[66]

Such views were echoed in the political arena. As already noted, President John F. Kennedy's youngest brother, Senator Edward M. Kennedy of Massachusetts, became a leading political figure making the same argument against an "arms race" as that of many, if not most, of the intelligentsia.

In 1982, Senator Kennedy was among those who objected to President Reagan's military buildup as "a dangerous new spiral in nuclear weapons competition" and called for "reversing the nuclear arms race."[67] In 1983, Senator Kennedy said, "We will seek to freeze the arms race which someday could make a cold wasteland of all the earth."[68] Later that same year, he said "We must stop the arms race before it stops us."[69] Senator Kennedy also joined other Senators in a statement in a letter to the *New York Times* declaring: "Experts and citizens across the country are embracing the freeze as the best way to end the nuclear arms race before it is too late."[70] In other words, once the Soviets' nuclear missile buildup in Eastern Europe gave them military superiority in Europe, we should freeze that superiority instead of restoring the balance. Attacking President Reagan's policies in the Senate, Kennedy called on his fellow Senators to "stop the nuclear arms race before it stops the human race."[71]

Though Senator Kennedy was a leading voice for a nuclear freeze, he was joined by many other prominent political figures and by many in the media who echoed their message. Those who resurrected the "arms race" argument against military deterrence that had been so pervasive in the era between the two World Wars proceeded on the implicit assumption of sufficient resources on all sides to permit indefinite escalation of mutually offsetting military buildups. That assumption was demonstrated to be false when President Reagan's military buildup in the 1980s proved to be more than the Soviet Union's economy could match— as Reagan knew.* The fact that the actual consequence of Reagan's policy was the direct opposite of what the "arms race" argument had predicted— that is, the consequence was the end of the Cold War, rather than the beginning of a nuclear war— has had as little effect on the prevailing vision as other facts which directly contradict other premises of that vision.

That more conciliatory policies had failed for decades to end the nuclear threat under which the world had lived during the Cold War decades was

---

* "At the start of 1986, we were getting more and more evidence that the Soviet economy was in dire shape. It made me believe that, if nothing else, the Soviet economic tailspin would force Mikhail Gorbachev to come around on an arms reduction agreement we both could live with. If we didn't deviate from our policies, I was convinced it would happen." Ronald Reagan, *An American Life* (New York: Simon and Schuster, 1990), p. 660.

likewise ignored. Most of the intelligentsia simply lavished praise on Soviet premier Mikhail Gorbachev for no longer following the policies of his predecessors.[72] The alternative was to admit that there might be something to be said for the Reagan emphasis on military strength and for his rejection of the "arms race" rhetoric which had been so central to the thinking of the intelligentsia for so long.

Some have contested the issue as to whether the end of the Cold War should be credited more to Reagan or to Gorbachev but for many, if not most, of the intelligentsia there was no issue to contest, since it was unthinkable that one of their fundamental assumptions could be wrong. Yet, after the end of the Cold War and the dissolution of the Soviet Union, former Soviet high officials said that Reagan's policies were a crucial factor. According to the *Washington Post*: "Speaking at a Princeton University conference on the end of the Cold War, the officials said former Soviet president Mikhail Gorbachev was convinced any attempt to match Reagan's Strategic Defense Initiative, which was launched in 1983 to build a space-based defense against missiles, would do irreparable harm to the Soviet economy."[73]

The "arms race" notion, as a characterization of military deterrence, was just one of the many ideas of the 1920s and 1930s that were resurrected during the Cold War era. Just as the French teachers' unions turned France's schools into indoctrination centers for pacifism in the 1920s and 1930s, with emphasis on the horrors of war, so in the United States during the Cold War American classrooms became places for indoctrination in the horrors of war. Dramatizations of the nuclear bombing of Japanese cities were one example:

> In grisly detail these generally well-off upper middle class kids were obliged to observe Japanese women and children being incinerated by the fire storm set in motion by the dropping of nuclear bombs. The youngsters sat riveted in their seats. Sobbing could be heard. By the conclusion the general mood of the class was well expressed by an emotional young lady who asked, "Why did we do it?" The teacher responded by saying, "We did it once; we can do it again. Whether these weapons of destruction are used depends on you." So began a unit on nuclear weapons.[74]

Reducing children to tears in the classroom, as part of the indoctrination process, had likewise been part of the *modus operandi* in France between the two World Wars:

> At a boys' school in Amiens, for example, teachers asked children whose fathers had been killed in combat to speak to the class. "More than one tear was shed," the headmaster reported. Similarly, a teacher from a girls' advanced primary school in Amiens noted that at her school, one student in six had lost a father between 1914 and 1918: "The roll call of the dead was carried out with the most moving reverence," the teacher reported, "and both teachers and students were united by their emotions." Yet another teacher, this time from a girl's school in Pont de Metz, reported that the solemn silence she called for upon the roll call of the dead "was broken by the sobs of many children whose fathers were killed in the war."[75]

It should be noted that here, as in other contexts, the fatal misstep of teachers was in operating beyond their competence— teachers having no professional qualifications for understanding the dangers of manipulating children's emotions, nor any special qualifications for understanding international political complications or what factors make wars less likely or more likely, much less what factors are likely to lead to collapse and defeat, as in France in 1940.

As in interwar France, the leading teachers' union— in America, the National Education Association— was a spearhead of pacifism and a fountainhead of ideas of the left in general. At its annual meetings, the NEA passed innumerable resolutions on subjects ranging far beyond education to issues involving migrant workers, voting laws, gun control, abortion, statehood for the District of Columbia, and many others, including issues of war and peace. Its resolutions, speeches and awards over the years have promoted the same combination of pacifism and internationalism that marked the efforts of the French teachers' unions between the two World Wars.

These resolutions have urged "disarmament agreements that reduce the possibility of war,"[76] urged "that the United States make every effort to strengthen the United Nations to make it a more effective instrument for world peace,"[77] called for "a halt to the arms race,"[78] and declared that "specific materials need to be developed for use in school classrooms in order to attain goals that focus on the establishment of peace and the understanding of nuclear proliferation."[79] The idea so much in vogue in the 1920s and 1930s, that war itself was the enemy, not other nations, reappeared in an NEA resolution that declared nuclear war "the common enemy of all nations and peoples."[80] Trophies were awarded at the NEA's meetings for schools that created programs to promote pacifism and internationalism, in the name of "peace."

In 1982, for example, the National Education Association at its annual meeting awarded a peace trophy to its affiliate in the city of St. Albans, Vermont, because its teachers had organized all sorts of pacifist activities, including having their students send letters to Senators on hunger and peace.[81] In 1985, the West Virginia Education Association was awarded a prize for developing an "educational" project on nuclear issues that had children contacting the White House and the Kremlin.[82] The people-to-people theme of the years between the two World Wars, when the French teachers' union established joint activities with German teachers,[83] was repeated by having school children making and sending symbolic gifts to Japan. In 1982, the Representative Assembly of the National Education Association called for a "freeze" on the development, testing or deployment of nuclear weapons.[84] That same year, NEA president Willard H. McGuire addressed a special session on disarmament held at United Nations headquarters in New York, and declared:

> If wars in the past left almost unimaginable death and destruction in their wake, a future war between the major world Powers could well mean the end of civilization on this planet. So it becomes imperative that we teachers, through our member organizations, work to prevent the precious instrument of education from ever again becoming the tool of irrational leaders who would pervert the world's youth into believing that there is nobility in militarism, that there can be peace only through deterrence, or that there is safety only if we live frightened lives behind nuclear shields for protection.
>
> We must educate the world's children to believe that real peace is possible, a peace free of nuclear threats and counter-threats, a peace where human life is something more than a list of numbers on some benighted general's chart. Such a peace can only be possible through world disarmament. The world's teachers must work toward this goal.[85]

What qualified him to sweepingly dismiss officials who had far more access to information, and far more experience in foreign affairs, as "irrational" and generals as "benighted," was a question never addressed. Nor was the question of his mandate for turning classrooms into indoctrination centers. But Willard H. McGuire was not unique. Two years later, a new NEA president, Mary Hatwood Futrell, excoriated the Reagan administration for having "escalated the arms race, and increased the risk of world incineration."[86]

In 1990, NEA president Keith Geiger called for putting "human needs above the arms race"[87] and, after Iraq invaded Kuwait, he urged President George H.W. Bush to "continue to pursue peaceful means to end the Iraqi occupation of Kuwait," so as to "avoid war while maintaining inviolable principles in the Persian Gulf."[88] There were no suggestions as to how this remarkable feat might be achieved, much less any discussion of the track record of attempts to undo military conquests through diplomacy or boycotts.

There has also been a repeat of media leaders taking a sympathetic view of nations opposed to their own. Columnist Robert Novak, for example, revealed a discussion he had with Cable News Network (CNN) founder Ted Turner who, as indicated by Novak's account, also repeated the 1920s and 1930s pattern of equating believers in military deterrence with advocates of war:

> As we walked across Lafayette Square on the way to my office, Turner said: "I can't understand, Novak, why you're in favor of all-out nuclear war." He then launched a defense of the Kremlin's arms control policies and lauded the people's paradise in Cuba. I tried to argue back, but it was tough getting a word in edgewise with Ted Turner. When we reached my thirteenth-floor office, I introduced him to a young woman in the Evans & Novak outer office whose main job was handling the phone calls. Turner looked her in the eye and asked: "How do you feel working for a man who is in favor of a nuclear holocaust?"
>
> The woman looked at Ted as though he were mad, and to a certain extent he was.[89]

The Iraq Wars

Two wars against Iraq, beginning respectively in 1991 and in 2003, were fought under the specter of the Vietnam war, with predictions of another "quagmire" in both cases, though the 1991 war in fact successfully drove Iraq out of Kuwait in short order, with minimal American casualties and overwhelming losses inflicted on Iraqi armed forces. Tom Wicker of the *New York Times*, for example, in 1990 foresaw "a bloody and ill-conceived war against Iraq," one with "devastating casualties for United States forces."[90] Anthony Lewis of the *New York Times* speculated that there might be "20,000 American casualties."[91] A *Washington Post* writer reported a mathematical model developed at the Brookings Institution that produced an "optimistic" estimate of more than a thousand American deaths in the 1991 Iraq war and a "pessimistic" estimate of more than four thousand deaths.[92] In reality, 148 Americans were killed in combat during the first Iraq war.[93]

The second Iraq war, beginning in 2003, was more like most wars, with unforeseen setbacks and unpredictable side effects, quite aside from debatable issues about the wisdom of the invasion or the nature of its goals. Despite the swift military defeat of the Iraqi armed forces, peace was not restored because of a reign of terror directed in part against American troops, but primarily against Iraqi civilians, by both domestic and foreign terrorists, determined to prevent a very different kind of government from being established in the Middle East under American auspices.

As in the case of the Vietnam war, much of the media and the intelligentsia in general declared what was happening in Iraq to be a "civil war" and "unwinnable," and many urged the immediate withdrawal of American troops. When instead there was in 2007 an increase in the number of American troops— called a "surge"— in order to suppress the rampant terrorism, this surge was widely condemned in advance as futile by the intelligentsia, in the media and in Congress.

In January 2007, *New York Times* columnist Maureen Dowd dismissed the idea as President Bush's "nonsensical urge to Surge."[94] *New York Times* columnist Paul Krugman said: "The only real question about the planned 'surge' in Iraq— which is better described as a Vietnam-style escalation— is whether its proponents are cynical or delusional."[95] In February 2007, the *Washington Post* said: "Mr. Bush's surge is unlikely to produce a breakthrough toward peace; in fact the violence may continue to worsen."[96] The *St. Louis Post-Dispatch* said "it's too little, too late."[97] An op-ed column in the *Philadelphia Tribune* called the war "unwinnable."[98] The *New Republic* asked rhetorically: "So who in Washington actually believes this surge will work?" Answering their own question, they said only "one man"— Vice President Dick Cheney. But, they added, "Sooner or later, even for Dick Cheney, reality must intrude."[99] Even the tone of utter certainty and condescension echoed that of the 1920s and 1930s intelligentsia.

Among those in politics who condemned the surge in advance was a future President of the United States, Senator Barack Obama, who said in January 2007 that the impending surge was "a mistake that I and others will actively oppose in the days to come." He called the projected surge a "reckless escalation," and introduced legislation to begin removal of American troops from Iraq no later than May 1, 2007, "with the goal of removing all United States combat forces from Iraq by March 31, 2008."[100] Senator Obama said: "Escalation has already been tried and it has already failed, because no amount of American forces can solve the political differences that lie at the heart of somebody else's civil war."[101] Another 20,000 American troops "will not in any imaginable way be able to accomplish any new progress."[102]

Senator Obama was not alone. Senator Edward Kennedy proposed requiring Congressional approval before there could be a surge.[103] Senate Majority Leader Harry Reid and Speaker of the House Nancy Pelosi sent a letter to President Bush, cautioning against the surge strategy: "Surging forces is a strategy that you have already tried and that has already failed," they said, and called the upcoming surge "a serious mistake."[104] Senator Hillary Clinton was also among those in Congress opposing the surge, and former Senator John Edwards called for an immediate withdrawal of American troops.[105]

A later (2009) Brookings Institution study of fatalities in 2007 among Iraqi civilians— the main target of terrorist attacks— showed such fatalities to have been an estimated 3,500 per month when predictions of failure for the surge were made in January 2007. In the wake of the surge, however, these fatalities fell to 750 per month by the end of the year. Fatalities among American troops in Iraq were 83 per month in January 2007, rose to a peak of 126 per month as military operations against terrorist strongholds increased, but fell to 23 per month by the end of the year, in the wake of the surge.[106]

At the time, however, there was fierce resistance among the intelligentsia to news that the surge was working. In June 2007, the *Los Angeles Times* said that there was "no evidence that the surge is succeeding."[107] In September 2007, under the title "Snow Job in the Desert," *New York Times* columnist Paul Krugman lamented the Bush administration's "remarkable success creating the perception that the 'surge' is succeeding, even though there's not a shred of verifiable evidence to suggest that it is."[108] *New York Times* columnist Frank Rich declared "The 'decrease in violence' fable" to be "insidious."[109]

Clearly, some people were determined to see this as another "unwinnable" war, another Vietnam. By 2009, however, even the *New York Times* was reporting— though not under banner headlines— that there had been large declines in fatalities among American troops in Iraq, Iraqi security forces and Iraqi civilians, to a fraction of what their fatalities had been two years earlier, before the surge. There had also been an increase in the number of Iraqi security forces and in the country's electricity output.[110]

While the surge was going on in 2007, however, it was something exceptional when two Brookings Institution scholars, identifying themselves as people who had previously criticized "the Bush administration's miserable handling of Iraq" nevertheless said after a visit to that country that "we were surprised by the gains we saw and the potential to produce not necessarily 'victory' but a sustainable stability that both we and the Iraqis could live with."[111] Other on-the-scene reports in 2007 likewise revealed substantial success against the terrorists in Iraq and a corresponding return to normalcy in Iraqi society, including a return of Iraqi expatriates who had fled the terrorism, and resident Iraqis who now frequented public places where they had been fearful of going before.

Those who were committed to the view that the war was "unwinnable," and a surge futile, remained unchanged despite the growing evidence that the surge was working. In September 2007, *New York Times* columnist Paul Krugman said: "To understand what's really happening in Iraq, follow the oil money, which already knows that the surge has failed."[112]

Insistence that the surge was a failure only escalated as signs of its success began to appear. As the September 2007 date neared for General David Petraeus' report to Congress on the surge which he commanded, there were growing outcries in the media and in politics that the general would only try to verbally spin the failure of the surge into success. Senator Dick Durbin, for example, said that "By carefully manipulating the statistics, the Bush-Petraeus report will try to persuade us that violence in Iraq is decreasing and thus the surge is working."[113] "We need to stop the surge and start to get our troops out," said Senator Joseph Biden in August 2007.[114]

These preemptive efforts at discrediting what Petraeus was about to report were climaxed by a full-page advertisement in the *New York Times*, on the opening day of his testimony, with a bold headline: "General Petraeus or General Betray Us?" sponsored by the political activist organization MoveOn.org.[115] The subtitle was "Cooking the Books for the White House." The *New York Times* charged MoveOn.org less than half the usual rate for a full-page ad and waived its policy against ads making personal attacks.[116]

In short, General Petraeus was accused of lying before he said anything— and in the face of growing evidence from a number of other sources that in fact the surge had substantially reduced violence in Iraq. The hostile atmosphere in which General Petraeus and U.S. ambassador Ryan Crocker testified before Congress was indicated by an account in *USA Today*:

> Following a day-long marathon Monday before two key House committees, they faced some of the Senate's most celebrated talkers— including five presidential candidates— in back-to-back hearings.
> In 10 hours of testimony, the two men got two bathroom breaks and less than 30 minutes for lunch.[117]

During these hearings, Senator Barbara Boxer said to General Petraeus: "I ask you to take off your rosy glasses."[118] Hillary Clinton said that the general's report required "the willing suspension of disbelief."[119] Congressman Rahm Emanuel said that General Petraeus' report could win "the Nobel Prize for creative statistics or the Pulitzer for fiction."[120] Congressman Robert Wexler declared that "among unbiased, non-partisan experts, the consensus is stark: The surge has failed." He compared General Petraeus' testimony to the discredited testimony of General William Westmoreland during the Vietnam war.[121] The same comparison was made by Frank Rich of the *New York Times*, who asserted that there were "some eerie symmetries between General Petraeus's sales pitch" and "General William Westmoreland's similar mission for L.B.J."[122] This was just one of the signs that the ghost of the Vietnam war still loomed over later wars. Even the tactics of opponents of the Vietnam war reappeared in many places. According to *USA Today*: "The testimony was punctuated by anti-war hecklers who rose one by one to shout slogans such as, "Generals lie, children die."[123]

Eventually, claims that the surge had failed as predicted faded away amid increasingly undeniable evidence that it had succeeded. But, far from causing a re-evaluation of the prevailing vision that had been so strident and so discredited by events, the success of the surge simply led to shrinking coverage of news from Iraq in much of the media. Unlike Vietnam, this time the military defeat of the enemy was prevented from being turned into a political surrender, though only at the eleventh hour, when the cries for immediate withdrawal were loudest.

These political developments reflected a prevailing vision of war growing out of the intelligentsia's perception of the Vietnam war which, among other things, left a legacy of catchwords such as the insistently repeated "unwinnable" and "quagmire." As in so many other areas, mundane facts to the contrary had little impact on the prevailing vision. Even when politicians said what they did for their own political purposes, those purposes could be served only because there were many others who sincerely believed the prevailing vision and would support those who espoused those beliefs. Once again, as in other times and places, the influence of the intelligentsia did not depend upon their convincing the holders of power, but only on their creating a climate of opinion providing incentives and constraints affecting what the holders of power could say and do.

Another throwback to the Vietnam war era was the highly publicized "combat veteran" who proclaimed his opposition to the war— and who later turned out not to have been a combat veteran at all. As the *New York Times* reported, after the truth about one of these "combat veterans" came out belatedly:

> The thick-muscled man with close-cropped hair who called himself Rick Duncan seemed right out of central casting as a prop for a Democratic candidate running against Bush administration policies last fall.
>
> A former Marine Corps captain who suffered brain trauma from a roadside bomb in Iraq and was at the Pentagon during the Sept. 11 attacks. An advocate for veterans rights who opposed the war. An Annapolis graduate who was proudly gay. With his gold-plated credentials, he commanded the respect and attention of not just politicians, but also police chiefs, reporters and veterans advocates for the better part of two years.
>
> Yet, except for his first name, virtually none of his story was true.[124]

That this man's easily checked lies passed muster in the media for two years suggests once again the receptivity of the intelligentsia to things that fit their vision, however unsubstantiated those things might be otherwise.

During the second Iraq war, the American intelligentsia repeated the patterns of the intelligentsia in France between the two World Wars— namely, the verbal reduction of combat soldiers from the status of patriotic heroes to that of pitiable victims. Even stories about the financial problems of reservists called away from their jobs to go on active duty in Iraq, or stories about the simple fact of sad goodbyes to friends or family members in the military being sent overseas, made the front pages of the *New York Times*,[125] while stories about the heroism of American troops in combat in Iraq or Afghanistan either went unreported or appeared on inside pages. Stories of extraordinary bravery of Americans under fire that won Congressional Medals of Honor— including men throwing themselves on enemy hand grenades, sacrificing their own lives to save the lives of those around them— were reported on pages 13 and 14, respectively, and one in the second section of the *New York Times*.[126] The *Washington Post* and the *Los Angeles Times* similarly buried these stories of extraordinary heroism on the inside pages and much of television news followed suit, either downplaying or completely ignoring such stories.

Negative stories, on the other hand, found instant prominence in the media, even when unsubstantiated. For example, much outrage was expressed in the media during the early days of the Iraq war when a claim was made that looters had pillaged precious artifacts from an Iraqi museum, which American soldiers had failed to protect.[127] That men fighting, with their lives on the line, were supposed to divert their attention to protecting museums was a remarkable enough premise. But the charge itself turned out to be false.[128] The artifacts in question had been secreted by the museum staff, in order to protect them from looters and from the dangers of war. Yet the media had not waited to substantiate the charges against the American military before bursting into print with these charges and bursting with indignation over them.

The American military's positive achievements in general, whether in battle or in restoring civil order or carrying out humanitarian activities, received little attention in the media. While the Iraq war began to disappear from the front pages of the *New York Times* as terrorist attacks declined in the wake of the surge, and coverage shrank similarly in other media, American casualties continued to be highlighted, even when those casualties were in single digits, and the cumulative casualties were constantly featured, even though these casualties were by no means high compared to other wars. In fact, all the Americans killed in the two Iraq wars put together were fewer than those killed taking the one island of Iwo Jima during the Second World War or *one day* of fighting at Antietam during the Civil War.[129]

Unless one believes that wars can be fought with no casualties, there was nothing unusual about the casualty rate in the first or second Iraq war, except for its being lower than in most wars. But casualties fit the constant theme of soldiers as victims, and verbal virtuosity has enabled this victimization message to be characterized as "supporting the troops" or even "honoring the troops." After the *New York Times* published photographs of dying and dead American soldiers in Iraq, its executive editor replied to criticisms by declaring that "death and carnage are part of the story, and to launder them out of our account of the war would be a disservice."[130] Such verbal virtuosity creates a straw man of "laundering out" the fact of deaths in war— which no one has ever doubted— and equates publishing photos of individual soldiers in the throes of death with just telling the story, while burying stories of soldiers' heroism deep inside the paper.

The same depiction of soldiers as victims dominated news stories of veterans returning home from combat. Problems of returning veterans, such as alcoholism or homelessness, were featured in the media, with no attempt to compare the incidence of such problems to the incidence of the same problems among the civilian population.[131] In other words, if all returning veterans were not completely immune to the problems that civilians experienced, that was presented as if it were a special problem brought on by military service. A front page article in the *New York Times* of January 13, 2008, for example, featured killings in the United States by veterans returning from the wars in Iraq and Afghanistan. "In many of those cases," it said, "combat trauma and the stress of deployment" were among the factors which "appear to have set the stage for a tragedy that was part destruction, part self-destruction."[132]

This particular attempt to picture veterans as victims failed to compare the homicide rate of returning veterans with the homicide rate among civilians of the same ages. Had they done so, it was pointed out in the *New York Post*, they would have found that the homicide rate among returning veterans was *one-fifth* that among civilians of the same ages.[133] Undaunted, the *New York Times* returned to the same theme in a front-page story a year later, in 2009— again going into gory details in individual cases, with no mention of the rate of homicides among military veterans compared to civilians of the same ages.[134]

Another promotion of the image of victimhood among military veterans was a story about suicide rates in the military having reached "the highest since the Army began keeping records," as the *New York Times* put it,[135] in a story echoed throughout the media. Yet, once again, there was no comparison with suicide rates among people of the same demographic characteristics in the civilian population— which was *higher* than among people in the military, as the Associated Press reported,[136] but which few media outlets mentioned. Once again, much of the media filtered out facts that went against their vision, leaving their readers with a wholly distorted picture. Like *The Times* of London in the 1930s, the *New York Times* in a later era took the lead in filtering and slanting news to fit its vision.

PATRIOTISM AND NATIONAL HONOR

No matter how much journalists, politicians or others undermine a war effort, anyone calling such actions unpatriotic is automatically met with the indignant response, "How dare you question my patriotism?" Just why patriotism is something that it is unreasonable or unworthy to question is something for which no argument is advanced, unless endless repetition is considered to be an argument.

This is not to say that anyone with whom one disagrees about a war or any other issue can be automatically called "unpatriotic." That is not a charge to be either automatically accepted or automatically rejected. Even actions detrimental to a country's self-defense are not automatically unpatriotic in intention. It is not necessary to assume that the intelligentsia of the 1930s, for example, deliberately set out to do such things as making their own countries vulnerable to military attack.

As noted in Chapter 7, Georges Lapierre— the leader of the French teachers' union's campaigns to promote pacifism in France's textbooks during the 1920s and 1930s, downplaying national pride and national defense— nevertheless, after the fall of France in 1940, joined the French underground resistance movement against the Nazi conquerors, and as a result ended up being captured and sent to his death in Dachau.[137] He was clearly not an unpatriotic man. But, whatever his intentions during the interwar years, the more important question is the ultimate effect of his efforts on a whole generation. Many other prewar pacifist teachers also ended up fighting in the French resistance movement after the vision they had promoted for so long led to opposite results from what they were seeking.

They had, in Burke's words from an earlier time, helped bring about the worst results "without being the worst of men."[138] In their own minds, the teachers "wove together patriotism and pacifism," according to an account of that era[139] but, regardless of what went on inside those educators' minds, the net result out in the real world was the same as if they had deliberately undermined the patriotism of a whole generation of their students, for whom they made internationalism as well as pacifism prime virtues, despite whatever passing mention there might be of love of country as a subordinate aspect of a love of humanity in general.

A much larger question than the patriotism or lack of patriotism of particular individuals or institutions is the question of how consequential patriotism itself is, and the related question of how consequential a sense of national honor is.

Patriotism has long been viewed by many intellectuals as a psychological phenomenon with no substantive basis. Back in the eighteenth century, William Godwin referred to patriotism as "high-sounding nonsense"[140] and "the unmeaning rant of romance."[141] As noted in Chapter 7, such views were still common in the twentieth century during the period between the two World Wars, among such prominent European intellectuals as Bertrand Russell, H.G. Wells, Romain Rolland, Kingsley Martin, Aldous Huxley, and J.B. Priestley, among others. In America, John Dewey decried patriotism as something that "degenerates into a hateful conviction of intrinsic superiority" and national honor as "a touchy and testy Honor" based on "emotion and fantasy."[142] But how consequential patriotism and national honor are cannot be determined *a priori* by how much either of them does or does not conform to the vision of the anointed.

As with many other things, how consequential they are can be discovered by what happens in their absence. When Hitler launched an invasion of France in 1940, against the advice of his top generals, it was because he was convinced that contemporary France was lacking in these supposedly irrelevant qualities[143]— and the sudden collapse of the French, despite their military advantages, suggests that these qualities are indeed consequential. What is called "national honor" is a long-run perspective on national decisions and their consequences, the opposite of the one-day-at-a-time rationalism by which France had declined to fight over the militarization of the Rhineland in 1936, or to live up to the French mutual defense treaty with Czechoslovakia in 1938, or to seriously engage the Germans militarily during the long months of the "phony war" following the formal declaration of war in 1939, despite France's large military superiority on the western front while Hitler's troops were concentrated in the east, conquering Poland.

A willingness to fight can be a deterrence to attack and, conversely, an unwillingness to meet a challenge or provocation can make a nation a target for an all-out assault. "National honor" is simply an idiomatic expression for this long-run perspective on national interest, as distinguished from a one-day-at-a-time perspective, which may serve the short-run interests of politicians, by sparing them from making the hard decisions which distinguish a politician from a statesman. But many intellectuals have tried to reduce a sense of national honor, like patriotism, to a psychological quirk and certainly "a very insufficient reason for hostilities," in Godwin's words.[144] However, even British Prime Minister Neville Chamberlain, the man most indelibly identified with the policy of appeasement of Hitler, belatedly seemed to acknowledge that national honor was consequential, just months before the Second World War began:

> I had the opportunity yesterday of exchanging a few words with M. Blum, the French Socialist leader and former Prime Minister, and he said to me that in his view, and in the view of all the Socialist friends with whom he had talked, there was only one danger of war in Europe, and that was a very real one: it was that the impression should get about that Great Britain and France were not in earnest and that they could not be relied upon to carry out their promises. If that were so, no greater, no more deadly mistake could be made— and it would be a frightful thing if Europe were to be plunged into war on account of a misunderstanding. [145]

In short, Europe and the world were on the brink of a catastrophic war because neither friend nor foe believed that Britain and France had national honor. That is, there was no sense of a firm resolve by the British or the French, on which friendly nations could stake their own survival by relying on allying themselves with Britain or France, at the cost of incurring the wrath of Nazi Germany.* Likewise, there was no sense among belligerent nations that they need fear anything more serious than temporizing words from Britain and France. What was lacking in Chamberlain's statement, on the eve of war, was any acknowledgment that it was his own policies, and similar policies in France, substituting talk for action, which had created this deadly misconception that all they would ever do was talk. Hitler was in fact quite surprised when his invasion of Poland led to declarations of war by Britain and France.[146]

If the Second World War grew out of a "misunderstanding," British and French sacrifice of national honor one year earlier, at Munich, fostered that misunderstanding and their belated refusal to sacrifice national honor a second time meant war.

The ultimate and bitter irony was that it was Neville Chamberlain's fate to make the declaration of war against Germany in 1939 which turned a regional invasion of Poland into the Second World War— the most catastrophic war in history— a war which he had striven to avoid at virtually all costs, brushing aside two years earlier "the old stand-upon-your-dignity methods"[147] that had once been part of the concept of national honor. Instead, Chamberlain operated on the basis of one-day-at-a-time rationalism in which, as he said in 1938, "we can remove the danger spots one by one," by "our willingness to face realities which we cannot change."[148] But, just one year later, Chamberlain abandoned that one-day-at-a-time-rationalism when he declared, "we are not prepared to sit by and see the independence of one country after another successively destroyed"[149]— even though he now had fewer potential allies left, after having abandoned Austria and Czechoslovakia to Nazi conquest, and was

---

* At the time of Hitler's militarization of the Rhineland, "France commanded the loyalty of the 'Little Entente,' namely, Czechoslovakia, Yugoslavia, and Rumania," according to Winston Churchill. (Winston Churchill, *The Second World War*, Vol. I: *The Gathering Storm* [Boston: Houghton Mifflin Co., 1983], p. 193.) But France's successive irresolution in the face of the Rhineland, Austrian and Munich crises made it necessary for these and other small nations in Europe to reassess their policies vis-à-vis Nazi Germany. German Foreign Minister Konstantin von Neurath informed American diplomat William Bullitt that, as Germany fortifies the Rhineland, "*the countries in Central Europe realise that France cannot enter German territory, all these countries will begin to feel very differently about their foreign policies, and a new constellation will develop.*"(Ibid., p. 206).

now in a weaker position from which to try to change the reality of Hitler's and Stalin's joint conquest of Poland.*

The ultimate issue was never Austria, Czechoslovakia, or Poland, as such. The issue was whether Hitler was to be allowed to upset the whole balance of power in Europe, on which peace depended, to the fatal disadvantage of Britain and France, simply by doing so in installments, with Britain and France posing the issue in each case in terms of one-day-at-a-time rationalism, while Hitler posed the issue explicitly in terms of "the national honour of a great people"[150]— in other words, a long run interest that he was willing to fight for.

As for Chamberlain's dismissal of "the old stand-upon-your-dignity methods," John Maynard Keynes saw the flaw in that:

> Our strength is great, but our statesmen have lost the capacity to appear formidable. It is in that loss that our greatest danger lies. Our power to win a war may depend on increased armaments. But our power to avoid a war depends not less on our recovering that capacity to appear formidable, which is a quality of will and demeanour.

Keynes said of Neville Chamberlain: "He is not escaping the risks of war. He is only making sure that, when it comes, we shall have no friends and no common cause."[151] Just two years later, these words became painfully prophetic, when Britain stood alone facing the wrath of Nazi Germany, as Hitler's *Luftwaffe* began bombing London and other places in the south of England, while a German invasion force was being assembled across the Channel on the coast of conquered France. The misconceptions on which Chamberlain had operated for years did not originate with him. They were part of the atmosphere of the times, an atmosphere to which intellectuals made a major contribution.

Despite a tendency in some intellectual circles to see the nation as just a subordinate part of the world at large— some acting, or even describing themselves, as citizens of the world— patriotism is, in one sense, little more than a recognition of the basic fact that one's own material well-being,

---

* Poland's independence was never restored until decades after the end of the Second World War, when the Soviet bloc in Eastern Europe dissolved in the last years of the Soviet Union itself.

personal freedom, and sheer physical survival depend on the particular institutions, traditions and policies of the particular nation in which one lives. There is no comparable world government and, without the concrete institutions of government, there is nothing to be a citizen of or to have enforceable rights, however lofty or poetic it may sound to be a citizen of the world. When one's fate is clearly recognized as dependent on the surrounding national framework— the institutions, traditions and norms of one's country— then the preservation of that framework cannot be a matter of indifference while each individual pursues purely individual interests.

Patriotism is a recognition of a shared fate and the shared responsibilities that come with it. National honor is a recognition that one-day-at-a-time rationalism is a delusion that enables politicians to escape the responsibilities of statesmanship.

Conditions may become so repugnant in one country that it makes sense to move to another country. But there is no such thing as moving to "the world." One may of course live in a country parasitically, accepting all the benefits for which others have sacrificed— both in the past and in the present— while rejecting any notion of being obliged to do the same. But once that attitude becomes general, the country becomes defenseless against forces of either internal disintegration or external aggression. In short, patriotism and national honor cannot be reduced to simply psychological quirks, to which intellectuals can consider themselves superior, without risking dire consequences, of which France in 1940 was a classic example. It was considered chic in some circles in France of the 1930s to say, "Rather Hitler than Blum."[152] But that was before they experienced living under Hitler or dying after dehumanization in Hitler's concentration camps.

Disdain for patriotism and national honor was just one of the attitudes among the intellectuals of the 1920s and 1930s to reappear with renewed force in Western democracies in the 1960s and afterwards. How far history will repeat itself, on this and other issues, is a question for the future to answer. Indeed, it is *the* question for the future of the Western world.

Chapter 9

Intellectuals and Society

The study of history is a powerful antidote to contemporary arrogance. It is humbling to discover how many of our glib assumptions, which seem to us novel and plausible, have been tested before, not once but many times and in innumerable guises; and discovered to be, at great human cost, wholly false.

Paul Johnson[1]

To understand the role of intellectuals in society, we must understand what they do— not what they say they do, or even what they may think they are doing, but what in fact are their actions and the social consequences of those actions. We can begin by trying to understand the incentives and constraints inherent in the role of intellectuals, as compared to people who are in other occupations. Individual intellectuals may say and do all sorts of things for all sorts of reasons but, when we try to understand general patterns among the intelligentsia as a whole, we need to examine the circumstances in which they operate, their track records and their impact on the larger society around them.

Among people whose occupations require high levels of mental ability— including mathematicians, chess grandmasters, scientists and others— we have defined as intellectuals those whose end products are ideas, as distinguished from tangible creations such as those of engineers, or services such as those of physicians and pilots. This dichotomy is not arbitrary. It conforms more or less to general usage and, more important, there are behavioral differences between intellectuals so defined and others whose work is likewise mentally demanding, and who may in many cases be academic colleagues on the same campuses.

These differences have much to do with both the supply and the demand for intellectuals in their roles as public intellectuals, people whose words contribute to the general atmosphere in which consequential decisions are made for society as a whole. Sometimes public intellectuals affect social outcomes by their direct advocacy of particular policies but sometimes their effect is indirect, when they simply explain their particular specialty— whether economics, criminology or some other subject— in a way that laymen can understand and which therefore influences public understanding and public opinion, whether or not these particular public intellectuals directly advocate one policy or another.

Perhaps more consequential than either of these roles of intellectuals is their creating a general set of presumptions, beliefs and imperatives— a vision— that serves as a general framework for the way particular issues and events that come along are perceived. For this, it is not necessary to be a "public intellectual" who addresses the population at large. Such disparate figures as Charles Darwin and Friedrich Hayek have had enormous influence over people who never read a word of theirs, but who absorbed their vision from others who had read them and received their direct impact. What John Maynard Keynes called "the gradual encroachment of ideas"[2] can change the way we see the world as it exists and change how we think the world ought to be.

While the word "intellectual" as a noun refers to a set of people in a given occupation, as an adjective it connotes a set of standards and achievements which may or may not characterize the actual behavior of most people in that occupation.

Certainly as public intellectuals, commenting on issues and events outside the realm of their respective specialties, intellectuals have not always exhibited intellectual standards, to put it mildly. Yet the many violations of those standards by intellectuals themselves have demonstrated repeatedly the distinction that they seek to blur between the noun and the adjective. These include such blatant examples of illogic as the one-observation "trend" (capitalism having made workers poor, as if they were more prosperous before) and the one-country international comparison, in which Professor Lester Thurow pronounced the United States the "worst" of the industrial nations when it comes to unemployment, by citing unemployment problems solely in the United States, while ignoring chronically worse unemployment problems in Western Europe and elsewhere. One of the most common violations of intellectual standards by intellectuals has been the practice of attributing an emotion (racism, sexism, homophobia, xenophobia, etc.) to those with different views, rather than answering their arguments.

Nevertheless, there is sufficient confusion between the meaning of the noun "intellectual" and the connotations of the same word as an adjective that critics of the behavior of intellectuals are often dismissed as people who are either hostile to intellectual endeavors or people who fail to appreciate intellectual processes or intellectual achievements. Richard Hofstadter's Pulitzer Prize-winning book *Anti-Intellectualism in American Life* perpetuated this confusion, both in its title and in its contents, where people who criticized intellectuals were depicted as people who exhibit "the national disrespect for mind" and a "dislike of specialists and experts."[3] Even the loss of an election by Adlai Stevenson— a man with only the image of an intellectual— was declared by Russell Jacoby in *The Last Intellectuals* to be an example of "the endemic anti-intellectualism of American society."[4]

Yet the American public honors intellectual achievements in science, engineering or the medical profession— which is to say, fields whose practitioners exhibit high intellectual ability but who are not intellectuals in the occupational sense defined here. As in many other contexts, imputing unworthy notions to others serves as a substitute for answering their arguments.

INCENTIVES AND CONSTRAINTS

When we define intellectuals as people whose end products are ideas whose validation process is the approval of peers, we uncover not only an ideological fault line between such people and others with high-level mental skills, but whose end products are technological, medical, scientific or other goods and services, we also discover a different set of incentives and constraints.

The Supply of Public Intellectuals

Ideologically, poll after poll has shown sociologists and scholars in the humanities, for example, to be more often liberal or left politically than are engineers or scientists. In addition to such ideological differences, there are differences in incentives and constraints between intellectuals in the sense defined here and other academic or other specialists in mentally demanding fields. For one thing, an engineer can become famous for his work *as an engineer* but the world's leading authority on French literature or the history of Mayan civilization is unlikely to be known, much less celebrated, beyond the confines of that specialty.

The incentives to become a "public intellectual"— that is, someone known for comments on issues of the day, whether within or outside that person's specialty— are obviously stronger for intellectuals, as defined here, than for others who can gain fame and/or fortune without ever bothering to either go beyond their own special expertise or even to explain their specialty in layman's language to the general public. A pioneer in heart surgery can gain national or even worldwide acclaim, without ever having to explain either the heart or surgery to a lay audience. But a pioneer in linguistics like Noam Chomsky would never become as widely known beyond the confines of his specialty as he has become by commenting on issues and events well beyond the realm of linguistics.

The intellectuals we have been studying have usually been public intellectuals, people whose comments help create a climate of opinion in which issues of the day are discussed and ultimately acted upon by those with political power. People in more utilitarian fields, whether in the academic world or not, may also choose as individuals to step outside the boundaries of their competence to comment on a range of issues at large, but there are fewer built-in incentives for them to do so.

Professor Richard A. Posner's landmark study *Public Intellectuals* points out that many individuals may become far better known, and more highly regarded, by the general public than they are by peers within their own respective professions. "Many public intellectuals are academics of modest distinction fortuitously thrust into the limelight" by their activities as public intellectuals, he asserts, noting a "tendency of a public intellectual's media celebrity to be inverse to his scholarly renown."[5]

While it would not be difficult to think of individuals who fit that description,[6] and who would therefore have incentives to seek recognition beyond their respective specialties that they have not achieved within those specialties, it would also not be difficult to think of other individuals of the highest levels of achievements within their own specialties who also chose either to write introductory textbooks for students or popular articles and books for the general public on subjects ranging from astronomy to economics. Intellectuals who popularize the field of their own expertise would include Nobel Prizewinning economists like Paul Samuelson, Milton Friedman, Gary Becker and others, and would include in the law such leading scholars as Robert Bork and Professor Posner himself. However, among the 100 public intellectuals mentioned most often in the media, Posner found only 18 who are also among the 100 intellectuals mentioned most often in the scholarly literature.[7]

Media celebrity and scholarly renown are indeed often areas that attract different people. Whatever the relative attractions of the two roles, to be a top scholar and a top popular public intellectual at the same time would require a rare ability to write at very different intellectual levels and in very different styles for a scholarly audience and for the general public. John Maynard Keynes, for example, was one of those with this rare ability. He was internationally known as a public intellectual, writing on issues inside and outside of economics, years before he became both the most famous and the most professionally influential economist of the twentieth century. Milton Friedman, so different from Keynes in other respects, likewise had that same rare ability to write at the highest intellectual level of his profession and at the same time write and speak in a way that made economics understandable to people with no background whatever in the subject. But people with the intellectual and literary versatility of Keynes and Friedman have been extremely rare.

While particular intellectually stellar individuals may choose to become public intellectuals for any of a variety of reasons, there are few *generally* compelling incentives for them to go outside the bounds of their specialty, except for those whom we have defined as intellectuals in the sense of people whose end products are ideas. For intellectuals in this sense, the choice may often be either accepting severe limits on the range of public recognition and public influence available to them, even when they are the best in the world at what they do, or to venture out beyond the bounds of their professional expertise— or even competence— to appeal to a vastly larger and much less discriminating audience.

The Demand for Public Intellectuals

Turning from the incentives that lead to a supply of public intellectuals to the demand for such people, we again find an important distinction between those people with high-level mental skills who are intellectuals in our sense and those who are in mentally demanding fields whose end products are more tangible or more empirically testable. There is a spontaneous demand from the larger society for the end products of engineering, medical, and scientific professions, while whatever demand there is for the end products of sociologists, linguists, or historians comes largely from educational institutions or is created by intellectuals themselves, mostly by stepping outside of whatever academic specialty they are in, to operate as "public intellectuals" offering "solutions" to social "problems" or by raising alarms over some dire dangers which they claim to have discovered.

In short, the demand for public intellectuals is largely manufactured by themselves. Otherwise, whatever the views of such intellectuals about the current state of the world, or about how it might be made better, such views are unlikely to make much difference to the public or to have any effect on government policy in a democracy. The general public contributes to the income of intellectuals in a variety of ways involuntarily as taxpayers who support schools, colleges, and various other institutions and programs subsidizing intellectual and artistic endeavors. Other occupations requiring great mental ability— engineers, for example— have a vast spontaneous market for their end products, such as airplanes, computers or buildings. But that is seldom true of people whose end products are ideas. There is neither a large nor a prominent role for them to play in society, unless they create such a role for themselves.

There could hardly be a set of incentives and constraints more conducive to getting people of great intellect to say sweeping, reckless or even foolish things. Some of those foolish and dangerous things have already been noticed here but, even so, these samples barely scratch the surface of a vast vein of reckless pronouncements by the intelligentsia, stretching back over the generations and no doubt stretching well into the future.

Among academic intellectuals especially, the spontaneous public appreciation and even acclaim for the work of their colleagues in the sciences, engineering, medicine and other fields provides yet another incentive to seek their own "place in the sun." So too does the prominence of many people outside of academia— people in business, courts, politics, sports and entertainment, for example. But most of these non-intellectuals first achieve public recognition or acclaim by their achievements within their respective areas of specialization, while many intellectuals could achieve comparable public recognition only by going outside their expertise or competence.

Who, besides professional philosophers and mathematicians, would have heard of Bertrand Russell, if he had not become a public intellectual, making inflammatory comments on things for which he had no qualifications? Similarly for linguist Noam Chomsky, entomologist Paul Ehrlich, and many others who have stood high within their own specialties but who attracted public attention only by going outside those specialties to make sweeping and attention-getting statements about things beyond their competence. They need not be outright charlatans, just people whose vast knowledge and understanding of one subject conceals from themselves and from others their fundamental ignorance of the things that bring them to public attention. Those among the academics or school teachers who lack either the inclination or the talent to become public intellectuals can vent their opinions in the classroom to a captive audience of students, operating in a smaller arena but in a setting with little chance of serious challenge.

Are whole societies to be put at risk for such vanities and conceits among a small segment of society? As we have already seen, especially in discussions of the role of Western intellectuals between the two World Wars, whole nations have already been put at risk and indeed led into disaster, by a climate of opinion to which the intelligentsia have made major contributions. Nor is this all simply a matter of history, as shown by the revival among the intelligentsia and the media of our own times of the attitudes, arguments and the very phrases of the period between the two World Wars.

THE INFLUENCE OF INTELLECTUALS

Before assessing the influence of intellectuals, we must define in what sense we consider influence. Professor Richard A. Posner, for example, considers public intellectuals to be not very influential and regards their predictions in particular as "generally not heeded."[8] He is no doubt correct in the terms in which he discusses the issue. That is, the public did not panic over Paul Ehrlich's predictions of impending economic and environmental disasters or George Orwell's fictional depictions of what to expect in 1984. However, we must distinguish the influence of particular intellectuals, with their own special agendas and predictions, from the influence of the intelligentsia as a whole on matters in which, as a group, they generally advance the same prevailing vision and filter out facts which go counter to that vision.

While the British public did not follow the specific prescriptions of Bertrand Russell to disband British military forces on the eve of the Second World War, that is very different from saying that the steady drumbeat of anti-military preparedness rhetoric among the intelligentsia in general did not impede the buildup of a military deterrence or defense to offset Hitler's rearming of Germany.

The impact of those whom we have defined as intellectuals— that is, people whose work begins and ends with ideas— has been growing over time, with the increasing numbers of intellectuals that more affluent societies are able to support, the increasing audience for their ideas provided by an ever wider spread of literacy and higher education, and with the vast increase in the reach of the mass media. Their influence has been felt in the law, in matters of national defense, and in its effects on the social cohesion without which a society cannot continue to remain a society. However, that influence has been largely confined to modern, democratic nations. A distinguished historian referred to "the thin sliver of the upper crust" of czarist Russian society "that constituted significant public opinion."[9] An even thinner sliver of those with consequential opinions has characterized modern totalitarian dictatorships, whether in Russia or in other countries around the world.

Intellectuals have every incentive to believe in the effectiveness of their own specialty— articulated ideas— and to correspondingly undervalue competing factors, such as the experience of the masses and especially the use of force by the police or the military. The unarticulated cultural distillations of mass experience over the generations are often summarily dismissed as mere prejudices. Force or the threat of force is likewise deemed far inferior to articulated reason, whether in dealing with criminals, children or hostile nations. "Military service is the remedy of despair— despair of the power of intelligence,"[10] as John Dewey put it.

Reason tends to be considered preferable *categorically*, with little consideration of differing circumstances in which one of these approaches— that is, reason or force— may be incrementally better than the other in some cases but not in other cases. The intelligentsia seem especially to reject the idea of private individuals using force in defense of themselves and their property or to have guns with which to do so.

In international issues of war and peace, the intelligentsia often say that war should be "a last resort." But much depends crucially on the context and the specific meaning of that phrase. War should of course be "a last resort"— but last in terms of preference, rather than last in the sense of hoping against hope while dangers and provocations accumulate unanswered, while wishful thinking or illusory agreements substitute for serious military preparedness— or, if necessary, military action. As Franklin D. Roosevelt said in 1941, "if you hold your fire until you see the whites of his eyes, you will never know what hit you."[11] The repeated irresolution of France during the 1930s, and on into the period of the "phony war" that ended in its sudden collapse in 1940, gave the world a painful example of how caution can be carried to the point where it becomes dangerous.

While the kinds of ideas prevalent among today's intellectuals have a long pedigree that reaches back at least as far as the eighteenth century, the *predominance* of those ideas in both intellectual circles and in the society at large, through their influence in the educational system, the media, the courts and in politics, is a much more recent phenomenon.

This is not to say that intellectuals had no influence at all in earlier eras, but in previous centuries there were fewer intellectuals and far fewer of their penumbra among the intelligentsia to carry their ideas into the schools, the media, the courts and the political arena. In earlier times, theirs was just one influence among many, and they had not yet acquired the ability to filter out what information and ideas reach the public through the media and through the educational system, or what ideas would become the touchstone of advanced thinking in the courts. For one thing, inherited traditional beliefs— both religious and secular— were more of a limitation on the influence of newly minted notions among the intellectuals.

More fundamentally, the influence of intellectuals on the course of events in society at large through their influence on the general public was less than today because, in most countries, the general public itself had far less influence on the direction of national policy in earlier eras. The American government was, after all, a major departure in the kinds of governments that existed in the world when the United States was founded in 1776. Before that— and in other countries long after that— even if the intelligentsia had had the kind of influence on the public that they have today, that would not have made nearly as much of a difference in government policies controlled by autocratic rulers. Moreover, neither the masses nor the elite expected intellectuals to have a major influence on governmental decisions. That influence grew in recent centuries with the spread of literacy and the spread of political power down the socioeconomic strata.

Although the United States presented the largest potential audience for intellectuals seeking political influence, Americans tended to be far less impressed by intellectuals than Europeans or some others were. American society began as a "decapitated" society, not only in the sense that the European aristocracy had far less incentive than others in their countries to brave the dangers of an Atlantic voyage and the hardships of pioneering in a new land, but also that there was not much incentive for European intellectuals to brave those dangers and hardships either. Moreover, American society remained for a long time in its formative period— which lasted in parts of the country as long as the frontier lasted— one in which mundane knowledge and mundane strengths and skills were more consequential for survival and progress than the special kinds of knowledge possessed by intellectuals.

The period from the 1960s to the 1980s was perhaps the high tide of the influence of the intelligentsia in the United States. Though the ideas of the intelligentsia still remain the prevailing ideas, their overwhelming dominance ideologically has been reduced somewhat by counter-attacks from various quarters— for example, by an alternative vision presented by Milton Friedman and the Chicago school of economists, by the rise of small but significant numbers of conservative and neo-conservative intellectuals in general, and by the rise of conservatives to a minority, but no longer negligible, role in the media, especially talk radio and the Internet, which have reduced the ability of the intelligentsia with the vision of the anointed to block from the public information that might undermine their vision.

Nevertheless, any announcement of the demise of the vision of the anointed would be very premature, if not sheer wishful thinking, in view of the continuing dominance of that vision in the educational system, television and in motion pictures that deal with social or political issues. In short, the intellectuals' vision of the world— as it is and as it should be— remains the dominant vision. Not since the days of the divine rights of kings has there been such a presumption of a right to direct others and constrain their decisions, largely through expanded powers of government. Everything from economic central planning to environmentalism epitomizes the belief that third parties know best and should be empowered to over-ride the decisions of others. This includes preventing children from growing up with the values taught them by their parents if more "advanced" values are preferred by those who teach in the schools and colleges.

The vision of the anointed is not just a vision of society; it is also a very self-flattering vision of the anointed themselves— a vision which they are very unlikely to give up. A "decent respect to the opinions of mankind"— the phrase used in the Declaration of Independence— has no place today in the vision of the anointed. On the contrary, defying "public clamor" has become a badge of honor and a certification as a member of the anointed. Angry outcries from the masses are not treated as warnings to be heeded but as further evidence of one's own superior insight, shared by other "thinking people." This is one of the many ways in which the vision seals itself off from challenges coming from the mundane experiences of millions. Moreover, the sweeping presumptions and aspirations of the anointed are still widely regarded by themselves and by others as idealism, rather than as ego indulgences.

That the world must present a tableau matching their preconceptions— or else there is something wrong with the world— is not just a fancy of the intelligentsia, but a basis for quotas by corporations and universities seeking to create such a tableau, and part of the law of the land in cases where discrimination is charged when the reality does not match the envisioned tableau.

While academic intellectuals are by no means the only intellectuals, in our times they are the quintessential intellectuals, whose careers are most independent of the outside world and of any accountability for the consequences of what they say and do, most insulated by tenure, and who have the most power to control the institutions in which they work, even in matters beyond their specialties, such as whether students can enroll in R.O.T.C. or have their free speech rights restricted by campus speech codes.

Intellectuals outside of academia may have careers in independent research organizations ("think tanks") or support themselves by their writings, but such intellectuals are not nearly as numerous as academic intellectuals and do not have the same lifetime security that tenure provides. Yet they too are little restricted by the values or beliefs of the population at large, or by any tests of logic or evidence, so long as what they say is consonant with the views of their colleagues or, in the case of free-lance writers, consonant with a sufficient constituency to support them financially and acclaim what they say.

Intellectuals not affiliated with an academic institution may or may not have much visibility to the general public. Opinion journalists— columnists, editorial writers, and television commentators— of course have ready access to a mass audience by virtue of their jobs. But the far larger number of journalists who are reporters catch the public eye only in so far as they go beyond being reporters to become people who filter, slant or sensationalize what they write. Like academics, they attract little or no personal attention when they stick to doing the job for which they are qualified, without embellishments, even if some of the stories that they report may be about momentous events that attract worldwide attention. Few people remember who reported that a man had landed on the moon or even who the reporter was from whom they first heard of the beginning or the end of a major war.

Even for columnists, editorial writers, and television journalists, there are no real qualifications required, other than an ability to attract an audience for the spoken or written word, whether or not those words have logical coherence or empirical validity. There are likewise no specific qualifications required for various other occupations among the intelligentsia, such as being a "consumer advocate," or heading a "public interest" organization— certainly no requirement of hard evidence that consumers or the public are in fact benefitted on net balance by one's activities, or even that the public are not harmed by those activities. For members of the intelligentsia who engage in such activities, qualifications are irrelevant, except for the ability to attract attention through whatever means are available.

Similarly with leaders and members of protest groups, many of whom are also part of the intelligentsia. The ability to organize large and strident protests, with or without violence, likewise guarantees not only television coverage of the protests themselves but also coverage of the particular rationales for the protest. While the incentives of the protest leaders are to acquire free publicity for their ideas, the incentives of the media are to fill television news programs with eye-catching events and colorful, sound-bite statements.

Neither the factual accuracy nor the logical consistency of those statements is decisive to either the media or to the members of the movement who are protesting. "What counts is the arrogant gesture, the complete disregard of the opinion of others, the singlehanded defiance of the world,"[12] as Eric Hoffer put it in his analysis of mass movements. In short, with both academic and non-academic intellectuals, the validation of their ideas or their status need not depend on the empirical verification of what they say. In that sense, they are unaccountable— and unaccountability means no constraint against irresponsibility.

School teachers are one of the elements of the intelligentsia in the penumbra surrounding the inner core of intellectuals. Like many others, the school teachers' role is quite modest and little noticed, and their influence on the course of national policy virtually nil, so long as they remain within the confines of their competence in their assigned role as transmitters of the cultural achievements of the past to the younger generation. Only by stepping outside that role to take on responsibilities for which they have neither qualifications nor accountability do they greatly expand their influence— whether by ideological indoctrination of students or by psychological manipulation of students in order to change the values which those students received from their parents.[13]

In either case, the teachers are unaccountable for the consequences, either to the students or to the society. For example, when the long downward trend in teenage pregnancy and venereal disease suddenly reversed after "sex education" was introduced into American schools in the 1960s,[14] it was the parents who were left to pick up the pieces when a teenage daughter became pregnant or an adolescent son caught some venereal disease. No teacher had to pay anything toward the financial costs or to lose a moment's sleep over what had happened, and verbal virtuosity enabled the changed values which "sex education" promoted to not only escape censure but even to continue to foster the notion that what was called "sex education" was the solution, rather than an aggravation of the problem. Like so much else, it fit the vision, which exempted it from the requirement of fitting the facts. Moreover, because these indoctrination exercises in promoting different values were called "education," who could be against them?

Not only do the intelligentsia themselves have incentives to venture far beyond any special expertise they may have, in order to influence public policy, their example and— in the case of teachers— their practice encourages similar venturesomeness and even zealotry among their students. In these cases as well, there are few, if any, constraints.

As early as elementary school, students have been encouraged or recruited to take stands on complex policy issues ranging up to and including policies concerning nuclear weapons, on which whole classes have been assigned to write to members of Congress or to the President of the United States. College admissions committees may give weight to various forms of environmentalism or other activism in considering which applicants to admit, and it is common for colleges to require "community service" as a prerequisite for applicants to be considered at all— with the admissions committee arbitrarily defining what is to be considered a "community service," as if, for example, it is unambiguously clear that aiding and abetting vagrancy ("the homeless") is a service rather than a disservice to a community.

In these and other ways, intellectual prerequisites for reaching serious policy conclusions are, ironically, undermined by the intelligentsia themselves. By encouraging or even requiring students to take stands when they have neither the knowledge nor the intellectual training to seriously examine complex issues, teachers promote the expression of unsubstantiated opinions, the venting of uninformed emotions, and the habit of acting on those opinions and emotions while ignoring or dismissing opposing views, without having either the intellectual equipment or the personal experience to weigh one view against another in any serious way.

In short, at all levels of the intelligentsia, and in a wide range of specialties, the incentives tend to reward going beyond whatever expertise the particular members of the intelligentsia may have, and the constraints against falsity are few or non-existent. It is not that most of the intelligentsia deliberately lie in a cynical attempt to gain notoriety or to advance themselves or their cause in other ways. However, the general ability of people to rationalize to themselves, as well as to others, is certainly not lacking among the intelligentsia.

Sweeping claims, alarming predictions, and heated moral crusades can generate a sense of importance for intellectuals in the mind of the public, as well as in their own minds. But to sustain that sense of importance, continuing and often strenuous efforts are necessary. In short, public intellectuals "cannot operate at room temperature,"[15] as Eric Hoffer put it.

It is hard to think of any decade within the past century when the intelligentsia were not embarked on some urgent crusade to save the world from some great danger to which ordinary folk were considered to be oblivious. In the early twentieth century, it was eugenics to prevent the national intelligence from declining as a result of higher birth rates among people with lower IQs, though in fact national scores on IQ tests *rose* substantially during that century.[16] In the 1920s, the crusade du jour was the promotion of disarmament and international treaties renouncing war; in the 1930s, there were too many crusades to count, as there were in the postwar world.

One of the many arrogant assumptions of the intelligentsia is that outsiders have to bring meaning into the lives of ordinary people, mobilize them behind some common cause and give them a sense of importance. Anyone who thinks that a mother is not important to a child or a child to a mother has no understanding of human beings. There are few things as important to lovers as each other. Most people already have someone to whom they are enormously important and whose lives would never be the same without them. That such people may seem unimportant to intellectuals says more about intellectuals than about them. And to project that sense of their unimportance onto the people themselves is one of the many violations of fundamental intellectual standards by intellectuals.

Constraints

Unlike engineers, physicians, or scientists, the intelligentsia face no serious constraint or sanction based on empirical verification. None could be sued for malpractice, for example, for having contributed to the hysteria over the insecticide DDT, which led to its banning in many countries around the world, costing the lives of literally millions of people through a resurgence of malaria. By contrast, doctors whose actions have had a far more tenuous connection with the medical complications suffered by their patients have had to pay millions of dollars in damages— illustrating once again a fundamental difference between the circumstances of the intelligentsia and the circumstances of people in other mentally demanding professions.

Even the liability of journalists under the laws against slander and libel has been reduced almost to the vanishing point in the case of slandered or libeled individuals who are considered to be "public figures." Yet, in terms of social consequences, slander or libel against individuals holding or aspiring to high government offices harms the general public as well as the particular individuals who are targeted. If voters are persuaded to abandon someone whom they were otherwise prepared to vote for, as a result of false charges spread by the media, that is as harmful as any other voter fraud. If nominees to be federal judges, including Supreme Court justices, can find their nominations derailed by false charges of racism or sexual harassment spread by the media, that can deprive the public not only of the services of those particular individuals but also the services of many others later, who refuse to jeopardize their reputations, built up over a lifetime, by entering a confirmation process where reckless and inflammatory accusations, spread nationwide through the media, have become the norm and proving oneself innocent is virtually impossible.

Not only the external world, but even their professional peers, impose few constraints on intellectuals— so long as those intellectuals are propounding the prevailing vision of the anointed, especially to a lay audience. Nor is the ultimate constraint— one's own personal standards— a constraint that is at all difficult to escape. As Jean-François Revel has observed:

> Each of us should realize that one possesses within oneself the formidable capacity to construct an explanatory system of the world and along with it a machine for rejecting all facts contrary to this system.[17]

Intellectuals are certainly not lacking in the ability to rationalize and, if anything, are likely to be more gifted with that talent than are most other people. Given the incentives and the constraints— or lack of constraints— many of the things said and done by the intelligentsia are understandable, however detrimental or even disastrous those things have been for the societies around them.

Government

Many of the incentives and constraints behind the patterns of intellectuals apply to another group— politicians— whose decisions as government officials can greatly magnify the influence of intellectuals. It is virtually axiomatic that, in an era when governments legislate, regulate and finance an ever more sweeping range of activities, there is no given individual with the amount or depth of consequential knowledge to competently make such a range of decisions. The net result is that politicians, like intellectuals, achieve public recognition when they go beyond the bounds of their competence, which they must do at least as often as public intellectuals, especially when many politicians have no special area of expertise, except in the art of getting elected.

The availability of experts for government officials to consult is by no means an adequate substitute for the knowledge that these officials lack, since there are usually experts on both sides— or many sides— of each issue, and choosing among those experts can also be a decision beyond the bounds of a politician's competence. Moreover, the real expertise of professional politicians— creating a good impression with the voting public— can make it unnecessary to know what they are talking about, so long as their words resonate with the voters. To the extent that politicians say and do things consonant with the prevailing vision, they are likely to achieve that, no matter how near or far the vision itself may be from reality.

Federal judges with lifetime tenure are even less constrained by reality. Legislators not only have larger staffs than judges have to collect information, but are also subject to consequential feedback— that is, feedback which they cannot ignore or dismiss— from the public on the actual effects of their legislation. Judges lack both these sources of information and correction, so that the ideas of the intelligentsia that judges accept have very little corrective feedback, and the importance of legal precedents makes corrections difficult, even when there are misgivings among judges themselves about the consequences of what they or their judicial colleagues have done.

Judges who respond to the prevailing vision of the intelligentsia of their times have little to constrain their indulgence in that vision and are likely to be lionized, rather than criticized, by the intelligentsia in the media or the law schools, when they step beyond their judicial expertise in applying existing laws, in order to "innovate" with decisions making social policies consistent with the vision of the anointed. By contrast, the most that can be expected by judges who confine their decisions within the circle of their legal expertise is being ignored. In many cases, such judges can expect to be attacked for standing in the way of progress when they decline to enact the vision of the anointed from the judicial bench and refuse to go along with colleagues who seek to do so.

Federal bureaucrats do not have quite the permanence of federal judges, nor quite the range of decision-making authority of members of Congress, but they have a combination of the two things that makes them a powerful "fourth branch of government"— and a branch of government which is not only outside the framework established by the Constitution, but one which often combines the legislative, judicial and executive powers so carefully separated by the Constitution. Although bureaucracies' policies, regulations and expenditures of money are technically not legislation, they often have much the same effect as legislation, without the Constitutional restrictions to which Congress is subject. Voting a member of Congress out of office requires far less effort from ordinary citizens than trying to get a decision of a federal bureaucracy reversed by going into the federal courts.

Vast sums of money dispensed by bureaucracies also give them great leverage with experts in their particular areas of operation. Bureaucracies' arbitrary choices of which particular academic or other researchers to finance not only enable them to influence public opinion in the direction of the policies favored by the bureaucrats, it can have a chilling effect on experts who know that expressing views opposed to that of the cash dispensers, whether on autism, global warming or numerous other issues, jeopardizes their own access to the large sums of money necessary to finance major research.

Since research funding can be crucial to the experts' own careers and that of their colleagues, a discreet silence may seem the better part of valor when an expert is unable to believe or advocate the position taken by a large bureaucracy. Not only will openly expressed skepticism, much less opposition, reduce the chances of getting research funding on that particular subject, to the extent that going against the grain of the bureaucracy reduces the favorable light in which the whole institution— which may be an academic department or a consulting firm— is viewed, the individual expert can be subjected to the displeasure (and its consequences) of day-to-day colleagues as well.

In short, bureaucracies are often able to turn the visions of the intelligentsia into the law of the land, at least within their own respective jurisdictions, subject to little correction by consequential feedback from those who know better or by those members of the public who suffer the consequences. In so far as the media think within the framework of the same vision, there may be little awareness conveyed to the general public that there are other views on the issues, much less informed criticism. Instead, the public may hear that "all the experts agree" on the issue.

Government in general— that is, all three Constitutionally established branches, as well as the bureaucratic "fourth branch"— is able to act on the basis of whatever notions or unsubstantiated assumptions prevail among the intelligentsia. Other views may exist but those discordant views face an uphill struggle, just to get noticed, much less examined. Empirical evidence may exist, going counter to the prevailing vision, but such evidence may be much like the tree that falls in an empty forest, as far as such empirical evidence reaching a large part of the general public. Modern, expansive government thus tends to magnify the influence of the intelligentsia, since government as a decision-making institution means essentially legislators, judges, executives and bureaucrats, none of whom is constrained to stay within the area of their own competence in making decisions.

THE TRACK RECORD OF INTELLECTUALS

What have the intellectuals actually done for society— and at what cost?

Many great advances in medicine, science, and technology have come out of the universities, research institutes, and industrial development departments of businesses, benefitting society at large and ultimately people around the world. Many of these benefits have been produced by individuals of extraordinary mental abilities— but seldom have these individuals been intellectuals in our sense of people whose end products are ideas whose only validation process is the approval of peers. What is striking about intellectuals in this latter sense is how difficult it is to think of benefits they have conferred on anyone outside their own circles— and how painfully apparent it is how much they have in fact cost the rest of society at large, not only economically but in many other ways.

While virtually anyone can name a list of medical, scientific, or technological things that have made the lives of today's generation better in some way than that of people in the past, including people just one generation ago, it would be a challenge for even a highly informed person to name three ways in which our lives today are better as a result of the ideas of sociologists or deconstructionists. One could, of course, define "better" as being aware of sociology, deconstruction, etc., or carrying out their policy agendas, but this circular reasoning would amount to just another of the arguments without an argument.

There have been landmark writings, even works of genius, in what are called the social sciences, though so many of these have been implicitly or explicitly attacks on things said by other writers in the social sciences that it is not at all clear how much net loss the society would have suffered if none of them in the whole profession had said anything. For example, the writings of James Q. Wilson on crime have been enormously valuable, but primarily by rebutting the prevailing ideas of other criminologists, which had produced social disasters on both sides of the Atlantic. In short, it was other intellectuals— not the general public— who were the source of the fashionable notions behind counterproductive policies on crime, as well as on other social issues. Prior to the ascendancy of those notions in the criminal justice system of the United States, murder rates had been going down for decades, under the traditional ideas and practices so much disdained by the intelligentsia.

Something similar could be said of other outstanding writings which rebutted other intellectual fashions, but which would have been unnecessary had not those fashions arisen and prevailed among the intelligentsia and found their way into public policy. However, even assuming that there has been a net benefit from the work of contemporary intellectuals, it is hard to believe that it has approached the benefits from such fields as engineering, medicine or agriculture.

There is an old saying that even a clock that is stopped is right twice a day. Intellectuals can claim credit for largely supporting the civil rights revolution of the 1960s but much of the credit must go to those who put themselves in danger in the South, rather than those who cheered them on from editorial offices in the North. Those who put their political careers on the line for the sake of civil rights, beginning with President Harry Truman in the 1940s, were ultimately the ones who made the legal changes which began the breaking down of state-sponsored racial discrimination. But whatever contributions the intelligentsia made as regards racial progress must be balanced off against their role in justifying or rationalizing the undermining of law and order, whether in racial or non-racial contexts, with blacks being the primary victims of the increased violence, including in some years more blacks than whites being murdered, in absolute numbers, despite the large differences in the sizes of the two populations.

In an earlier era, intellectuals in France, led by Émile Zola, exposed the fraudulence of the charges that had sent Captain Alfred Dreyfus to a Devil's Island prison. In fact, the very term "intellectual" has been said to have originated in that episode.[18] Though others— in the military and Georges Clemenceau in politics— had taken up the cause of Captain Dreyfus, even before Zola's famous article "J'accuse,"[19] nevertheless the Dreyfus episode was something to be put on the credit side of the ledger for intellectuals. But we have already seen how much was on the other side of that ledger, especially in France.

While it is difficult to put together a case that intellectuals as producers of ideas have created major and lasting benefits for the vast majority of people at all comparable to what people in other professions, or even in some mundane occupations, have created, what would be far less of a challenge would be to name things made *worse* by intellectuals, both in our own times and in other times.

Social Cohesion

One of the things intellectuals have been doing for a long time is loosening the bonds that hold a society together. They have sought to replace the groups into which people have sorted themselves with groupings created and imposed by the intelligentsia. Ties of family, religion, and patriotism, for example, have long been treated as suspect or detrimental by the intelligentsia, and new ties that intellectuals have created, such as class— and more recently "gender"— have been projected as either more real or more important.

Working class solidarity was among the notions once enjoying a vogue among intellectuals on the left. The First World War was a shock to such intellectuals, who had decided among themselves that working class people would not wage war against other working class people in other countries, presumably because intellectuals believed that country was less important than class. As in other cases, however, these intellectuals did not bother to find out whether working class people themselves shared that view. In short, the primacy of class over country, like so much else in the vision of the anointed, was not a hypothesis to be tested but an axiom to be proclaimed.

We have seen in Chapter 7 some of the ways in which leading intellectuals in Western democracies undermined their own countries' national security between the two World Wars. But before there can be national defense in a military sense, there has to be some feeling that the nation is worth defending, whether in a social, cultural or other sense. Most modern intellectuals seldom contribute toward that feeling. Some have even made statements such as this by George Kennan:

Show me first an America which has successfully coped with the
problems of crime, drugs, deteriorating educational standards, urban
decay, pornography and decadence of one sort or another— show me an
America that. . . is what it ought to be, then I will tell you how we are
going to defend ourselves from the Russians.[20]

Not all intellectuals are as blunt as this but it is by no means uncommon
for some among the intelligentsia to depict the United States as being on
trial and needing to prove its innocence— a standard seldom applied to
other countries— before it can claim the public's allegiance in its defense
against other nations, or perhaps even before its laws and social norms can
expect voluntary compliance at home. Nor is the United States unique in
this respect. The intelligentsia in some European nations have gone
further— being apologetic to Muslims at home and abroad, and have
acquiesced in the setting up of de facto Muslim enclaves with their own
rules and standards in Europe, as well as overlooking violations of the laws
in the European countries in which Muslim immigrants have settled.[21]

Fictitious images of foreign countries are just one of the ways in which
many intellectuals undermine their own. In other ways as well, many
intellectuals erode or destroy a sense of the shared values and shared
achievements that make a nation possible, or a sense of national cohesion
with which to resist those who would attack it from within or without. To
condemn their country's enemies would be to be like the masses but to
condemn their own society itself sets the anointed apart as moral exemplars
and incisive minds— at least to like-minded peers. Given the incentives and
constraints, it is hard to see how they could do otherwise, when whatever
significance that they might have in the larger society so often depends on
their criticisms of that society and their claims to have special "solutions" to
whatever they define as its "problems."

This is not to say that intellectuals cynically play on the gullibility of the
public in order to parlay their professional expertise into social acclaim or
political influence. They may sincerely believe what they say but those
beliefs often have no substance behind them nor— more important— any
test in front of them. After one of their ideas or policies is adopted, the
intelligentsia almost never ask the follow-up question: What has gotten
better as a result? Often things have gotten demonstrably worse,[22] and then

the verbal virtuosity of the intelligentsia is deployed to claim that the evidence doesn't prove anything because it was not necessarily what they did that caused things to go wrong. While it is fine to warn against the *post hoc* fallacy, what intellectuals seldom do is accept the burden of proof on themselves to show what has gotten better when their ideas were put into practice.

Under the influence of the intelligentsia, we have become a society that rewards people with admiration for violating its own norms and for fragmenting that society into jarring segments. In addition to explicit denigrations of their own society for its history or current shortcomings, intellectuals often set up standards for their society which no society of human beings has ever met or is ever likely to meet.

Calling those standards "social justice" enables intellectuals to engage in endless complaints about the particular ways in which society fails to meet their arbitrary criteria, along with a parade of groups entitled to a sense of grievance, exemplified in the "race, class and gender" formula today, though the same kind of thinking behind that particular formula has also been used to depict children as victims of their parents and illegal immigrants as victims of a calloused or xenophobic society in the country they enter. In short, many of the intelligentsia are engaged in the production and distribution of formulaic grievances and resentments, mining history when they cannot find enough contemporary grievances to suit their vision.

The kind of society to which that leads is one in which a newborn baby enters the world supplied with prepackaged grievances against other babies born the same day. It is hard to imagine anything more conducive to internal strife and a weakening of the bonds that hold a society together.

"The creation of nations out of tribes, in early modern times in Europe and in contemporary Asia and Africa, is the work of intellectuals," according to distinguished scholar Edward Shils.[23] But whatever their historic role in various other times and places, intellectuals in Western nations today are largely engaged in creating tribes out of nations. What Peter Hitchens in Britain has called "The atomization of society," which has "sundered many of the invisible bonds which once held our society together"[24] is a pattern which has not been confined to Britain or even to Western nations.

The positive achievements of the society in which intellectuals live seldom receive attention even remotely comparable to the amount of attention paid to grievances. This asymmetry, together with factual and logical deficiencies of many laments made in the name of "social justice," can create the image of a society not worth preserving, much less defending. The benefits of existing social arrangements are taken for granted as things that happen more or less automatically— even when they seldom happen in some other countries— and not as things for which sacrifice (or at least forbearance) is required, much less things that can be jeopardized by some of the zeal for "change" promoted without regard to the repercussions of those changes.

The Localization of Evil

Many among the intelligentsia see themselves as agents of "change," a term often used loosely, almost generically, as if things are so bad that "change" can be presupposed to be a change for the better. The history of changes that turned out to be for the worse, even in countries that were pretty bad to begin with— czarist Russia or Cuba under Batista, for example— receives remarkably little attention. But for an agenda of comprehensive and beneficial social change even to seem plausible, it must implicitly assume a localization of evil in some class, institution or officials, since sins and shortcomings universally present in human beings would leave little reason to hope for something dramatically better in a rearranged society, so that even a revolution could be much like rearranging the deck chairs on the *Titanic*.

Incremental reforms, evolving out of trial-and-error experience, may over the course of time amount to a profound change in society, but this is wholly different from the kind of sweepingly imposed prepackaged changes to smite the wicked and exalt the anointed, in keeping with the invidious and dramatic vision of the intellectuals. That vision requires villains, whether individuals or groups or a whole society permeated by wrong ideas that can be corrected by those with right ideas. Nor will it do if these villains are in some distant place, oblivious to the exhortations or condemnations of the intelligentsia. Home-grown villainy is much more accessible and a more attackable target, with more probability of being overthrown by the home audience for the vision of the intelligentsia.

In short, what must be attacked is "our society," to be subjected to the particular "change" favored by the intellectual elite. Society's sins, past and present, must be the focus. For example, a study of global poverty pointed out the contrast between the vastly unequal prospects of a black child born in rural South Africa and the prospects of a white child born the same day in Capetown, calling these differences "the legacy of apartheid's unequal opportunities."[25] There is no question that apartheid was evil or that the invasion and conquest of South Africa by whites, whose subjugation of the indigenous Africans allowed apartheid to be imposed, was evil. There is no moral ambiguity. But the *causal* connection with current-day poverty and inequality is by no means clear.

Was poverty less in those parts of sub-Saharan Africa ruled by blacks? Even in the worst days of apartheid, there was a net migration of indigenous Africans *into* South Africa, where poverty was less than in other parts of sub-Saharan Africa ruled by blacks. Was the contrast between the poverty of South African blacks and the whites who came to conquer them *less* back before the invasion, when both blacks and whites were living in their own indigenous lands? History shows that the answer to both questions must be "No." Are such drastic economic contrasts unique to Africa or even unusual on the world stage? Are these contrasts peculiar to different racial groups? The answer to both these questions must be "No" as well. The same author pointed out in the same book— indeed, on the previous page— what extreme contrasts in incomes there are within various African countries, far more so than in the United States, for example,[26] though apparently the implications did not carry over from one page to the next.

Another scholar has pointed out how one could draw a line through Europe and discover that a baby born east of that line had far less promising prospects than a baby born west of that line.[27] This contrast went back for centuries and persisted through all sorts of changes in regimes on both sides of that line. Social evils were not unknown on either side of that line through Europe, but gliding from moral condemnation to causal explanation is no more valid in Europe than in Africa or elsewhere.

Slavery has been a pervasive evil around the world for thousands of years but confusing morality with causation— and seeking a localization of evil— has led to the history of slavery being stood on its head throughout our educational system, as well as in the media and by the intelligentsia in general. Thus slavery has been depicted as if it were a peculiarity of white people against black people in the United States, or in Western societies. No one dreams of demanding reparations from North Africans for all the Europeans brought there as slaves by Barbary Coast pirates, even though these European slaves greatly outnumbered the African slaves brought to the United States and to the thirteen colonies from which it was formed.[28]

Because the West has not been immune to the evils, errors and shortcomings of the human race around the world, the intelligentsia have been able to document these failings in a way that makes them look like peculiarities of "our society." In the case of slavery, what was peculiar about the West was that it was the first civilization to turn *against* slavery, beginning in the eighteenth century, and that it destroyed slavery around the world, beginning in the nineteenth century, not only within its own societies but also in non-Western societies it controlled, influenced or threatened. Yet there is virtually no interest among today's intelligentsia in how a worldwide phenomenon like slavery was ended after thousands of years, for it did not simply die out of its own accord, but was forcibly suppressed by the West in campaigns around the world that lasted for more than a century, often over the bitter opposition of Africans, Asians and others who wanted slavery preserved. But that story seldom makes it through the filters.

What is highlighted is that the West had slavery, as if that was peculiar to the West. What is also highlighted is that black people were enslaved by white people in the West. But, even in the West, white people were enslaved by other white people for centuries before the first African was brought to the Western Hemisphere in chains. The very fact that these Africans were called "slaves" reflected the fact that a white group which had been enslaved for centuries before were Slavs— since the word for slave was derived from the name for Slavs, not only in English but in other European languages and in Arabic.[29] Distinguished historian Daniel Boorstin pointed out, "Now for the first time in Western history, the status of slave coincided with a difference of race."[30]

By and large, for most of history, Europeans enslaved other Europeans, Africans enslaved other Africans and Asians enslaved other Asians. As the mass enslavement of Europeans became a less viable option, the mass purchase of Africans enslaved by other Africans was resorted to. Racism grew out of this situation but racism cannot explain slavery, which preceded it by centuries. Yet the impression left by many among the intelligentsia is that racism explains white people enslaving black people. It is an impression too much in keeping with the prevailing vision to be scrutinized closely— and leaving out the rest of the story of slavery around the world makes the prevailing vision seem plausible.

Imperialism has been approached in much the same way by much of the intelligentsia, as an evil of "our society." But it is impossible to read much of the history of the world, ancient or modern, without encountering the bloody trail of conquerors and the sufferings they inflicted on the conquered. Like slavery, imperialism encompassed every branch of the human race, both as conquerors and conquered. It was an evil that was never localized in fact, however much some conquered peoples have been portrayed as noble victims by intellectuals— even on the eve of those victims assuming the role of victimizers when they got the chance, as many did after Woodrow Wilson's right of "self-determination" of peoples led to oppressed minorities in the dismembered Habsburg and Ottoman Empires acquiring their own nations, in which one of the first orders of business was the oppression of other minorities now living under their thumb.

Yet the story of conquest today is wholly disproportionately told as the story of brutal Europeans conquering innocent native peoples, the latter often depicted as "living in harmony with nature" or some other version of what Jean-François Revel has aptly called "the lyricism of Third World mythology."[31] This localization of evil is made to seem plausible by the fact that Europeans have in recent centuries had more wealth, more technology and more firepower with which to do what everyone else had done for thousands of years. But Europeans have not always been in the vanguard of technology or wealthier than other peoples— and during the centuries that preceded the rise of Europe on the world stage, millions of Europeans were subjugated by conquerors invading from Asia, the Middle East, and North Africa.

It took centuries of fighting before Spain finally expelled the last of its North African conquerors— in the very same year in which it sent Christopher Columbus on the voyage that would open a whole new hemisphere to conquest by Spaniards and other Europeans. Both slavery and brutal conquest were already common in the Western Hemisphere, long before Columbus' ships appeared on the horizon. Indeed, the emergence of the idea that conquest *per se* was wrong—as slavery *per se* was wrong— regardless of who did it to whom, was a slowly evolving notion, as a corollary to a sense of universalism pioneered by Western civilization. Yet today this history, too, is often stood on its head in depictions of peculiar Western evil, inheritable guilt and— not incidentally— liability for reparations.

The Propagation of the Vision

A survey of all the other issues on which the same spin and twist has been placed, whether with history or with contemporary events, by intellectuals would fill volumes. More important, it fills our schools and colleges.

The ideology of today's leading teachers' union in the United States— the National Education Association— is very much like the ideology of the French teachers' unions that spent many years undermining national defense for a whole generation of French students, equating courage with bellicosity and transforming the history of the heroes who had saved the country from invaders in the First World War into a history of mere victims, on a par with enemy troops seeking to devastate and subjugate the nation.

Imperfections or inefficiency can seldom destroy a nation. But the disintegration of its social bonds and the demoralization of its people's confidence and allegiance can. Intellectuals contribute greatly to both these processes. Setting group against group by arbitrarily viewing innumerable situations through the prism of "race, class, and gender," setting unreachable standards of "social justice," and setting impossible goals of redressing the wrongs of history, guarantee never-ending strife and an undermining of any society with a crusading intelligentsia and a public uncritically accepting the intellectuals' view of society and of themselves. So long as sweeping presumptions are accepted as knowledge and lofty rhetoric is regarded as idealism, intellectuals can succeed in projecting themselves as vanguards of generic "change"— for whose consequences they remain unaccountable.

A full record of the effects of the intelligentsia, in countries around the world, would require a book much larger than this one, if not multiple volumes. Here it is possible to list only some of their most prominent effects, and in summary form, since some of the specifics have already been discussed in previous chapters.

The intelligentsia have changed the high achievements and rewards of some members of society from an inspiration to others into a source of resentment and grievance for others.

The intelligentsia have largely ignored or downplayed the things in which Americans lead the world— including philanthropy, technology, and the creation of life-saving medicines— and treated the errors, flaws and shortcomings that Americans share with human beings around the world as special defects of "our society."

They encourage people who are contributing nothing to the world to complain, and even organize protests, because others are not doing enough for them.

They have rationalized the breaking of laws by those who choose to picture themselves as underdogs fighting an oppressive "system," even when these are college students from affluent homes.

They have, both in America and in France, verbally turned military heroes who put their lives on the line for their country into victims of war, people whom one might pity but never want to emulate.

In the schools and colleges, the intelligentsia have changed the role of education from equipping students with the knowledge and intellectual skills to weigh issues and make up their own minds into a process of indoctrination with the conclusions already reached by the anointed.

They have put the people whose work creates the goods and services that sustain a rising standard of living on the same plane as people who refuse to work, but who are depicted as nevertheless entitled to their "fair share" of what others have created— this entitlement being regardless of whether they observe even common decency on the streets or in the parks.

The intelligentsia have treated the conclusions of their vision as axioms to be followed, rather than hypotheses to be tested.

Some among the intelligentsia have treated reality itself as subjective or illusory, thereby putting current intellectual fashions and fads on the same plane as verified knowledge and the cultural wisdom distilled from generations of experience.

Intellectuals give people who have the handicap of poverty the further handicap of a sense of victimhood.

They have acted as if they are anointed to decide which segments of society to favor, who should be allowed to pick their own associates and who should not, which small risks people should be forbidden to take and which larger risks are all right.

They have romanticized cultures that have left people mired in poverty, violence, disease and chaos, while trashing cultures that have led the world in prosperity, medical advances and law and order. In doing so they have often disregarded, or even filtered out, the fact that masses of people were fleeing the societies intellectuals romanticized to go to the societies they condemned.

The intelligentsia have been quick to find excuses for crime and equally quick to attribute wrong-doing to police, even when discussing things for which they have neither expertise nor experience, such as shootings.

They have encouraged the poor to believe that their poverty is caused by the rich— a message that may be a passing annoyance to the rich but a lasting handicap to the poor, who may see less need to make fundamental changes in their own lives that could lift themselves up, instead of focusing their efforts on tearing others down.

The intelligentsia have acted as if their ignorance of why some people earn unusually high incomes is a reason why those incomes are either suspect or ought not to be permitted.

The utterly un-self-critical attitude of many intellectuals has survived many demonstrably vast, and even grotesque, contrasts between their notions and the realities of the world. For example, many leading American intellectuals in 1932 were publicly calling for a vote for the Communist Party of the United States, and many other leading intellectuals in the Western democracies in general were throughout the 1930s holding up the Soviet Union as a favorable contrast to American capitalism, at a time when people were literally starving to death by the millions in the Soviet Union and many others were being shipped off to slave labor camps.

The notion that disarmament and concessions were the way to avoid war has survived the reality that it was precisely these kinds of policies which led to the most catastrophic war of all time. The very same policies were resurrected by the intelligentsia during the first generation born after that war and proclaimed with at least equal zeal, self-righteousness and demonization of those who dared to think that a different approach was more likely to preserve peace. Nor was there much reconsideration when opposite policies led to the end of the Cold War.

Intellectuals have— on issues ranging across the spectrum from housing policies to laws governing organ transplants— sought to have decision-making discretion taken from those directly involved, who have personal knowledge and a personal stake, and transferred to third parties who have neither, and who pay no price for being wrong.

They have filtered information in the media, in the schools, and in academia, to leave out things that threaten their vision of the world.

Above all, they exalt themselves by denigrating the society in which they live and turning its members against each other.

SUMMARY AND IMPLICATIONS

The characteristics of intellectuals and the roles that they seek to play mesh well together. That applies both to intellectuals proper— people whose occupation is producing ideas as end products— and to the intelligentsia as a whole, including the large surrounding penumbra of those whose views reflect the views of the intellectuals.

The revealed preference of the intelligentsia— whether the specific subject is crime, economics or other things— is not only to be conspicuously different from society at large but also, and almost axiomatically, superior to society, either intellectually or morally, or both. Their vision of the world is not only a vision of causation in the world as it exists and a vision of what the world ought to be like, it is also a vision of *themselves* as a self-anointed vanguard, leading toward that better world.

Those whose specific ideas or general vision are different— the benighted— are often treated as unworthy obstacles to progress, nuisances to be disregarded, circumvented, or discredited, rather than as people on the same moral and intellectual plane, whose arguments are to be engaged factually and logically. The widespread and casual use of such phrases as "raising the consciousness" of others or assertions that opponents "just don't get it" reveal a preference for avoiding a confrontation on equal terms, which would itself mean surrendering part of the vision of the anointed. College speech codes with subjective criteria and often "re-education" provisions for those expressing benighted opinions emphasize the same preference in academic institutions, where intellectuals have their greatest direct control.

Perhaps most important of all, the vision of the anointed represents a huge investment of ego in a particular set of opinions, and therefore a major obstacle to reconsideration of those opinions in the light of evidence and experience. No one likes to admit being wrong but few have such a large personal stake in a set of beliefs as those with the vision of the anointed— or so few countervailing incentives to reconsider. The ruthlessness with which the anointed assail others and the doggedness with which they cling to their beliefs, in defiance of ever mounting evidence against the "root causes" of crime and other social theories, for example, is evidence of that large personal investment in a set of social or political opinions.

Intellectuals have no monopoly on dogmatism or ego, or on the power to rationalize. But the institutional constraints facing people in business, science, athletics, and many other fields confront those people with high and often ruinous costs for persisting in ideas that turn out not to work in practice.*

Similarly, the history of prevailing beliefs among scientists that they were forced to abandon in the face of contrary evidence is a major part of the entire history of science. In athletics, whether professional or collegiate, no theory or belief can survive incessant losses and neither can any manager or coach.

No such inescapable constraints confront people whose end products are ideas and whose ideas face only the validation of like-minded peers. That is especially the case with academic intellectuals, who control their own institutions and select their own colleagues and successors. No tenured professor can be fired because he voted for campus policies that turned out to be either economically or educationally disastrous for his college or university, or advocated policies that turned out to be catastrophic for society as a whole.

This unaccountability to the external world is not a happenstance but a deeply rooted principle enshrined under the title of "academic freedom." From unaccountability to irresponsibility can be a very short step. Other members of the intelligentsia, including both broadcast media and entertainment media, likewise have very wide latitude as far as checks on the validity of what they say is concerned, with their main constraint being whether they can draw an audience, whether with truth or falsehoods, and whether with constructive or destructive effects on the society at large.

Much as newly hatched turtles head instinctively toward the sea, those whose end products are ideas tend to gravitate toward institutions where their ideas are less subject to the dangers of factual discrediting. In addition to academic institutions and the media, the intelligentsia tend to gravitate toward non-profit organizations in general and foundations in particular.

---

* For example, the world's two largest retailers of the early twentieth century— Sears and Montgomery Ward— had both operated exclusively and prosperously as mail order houses for decades, and only began to operate as department stores after the rise of J.C. Penney and other department store chains created a competition which turned their decades of profitable business as mail order houses into millions of dollars in losses that threatened their very existence. Sears and Montgomery Ward, like many other businesses, were subjected to consequential feedback which they could neither ignore nor turn aside with clever phrases, even if those clever phrases had resonance among their peers.

The money needed to sustain foundations depends primarily on persuasive words— one of the fundamental talents of the intelligentsia— that will keep donations coming in, whether by alarms of impending disasters or by promises of social "solutions."

Foundations with their own endowments do not have even the modest requirement of attracting donations for survival, so that they can pursue the vision of those who run these foundations, without having to be concerned about anything beyond influencing the public in ways that will be pleasing to themselves and win the approval of their peers.

These places to which intellectuals tend to gravitate tend to be places where sheer *intellect* counts for much and where *wisdom* is by no means necessary, since there are few consequences to face or prices to be paid for promoting ideas that turn out to be disastrous for society at large.

However few are the constraints on what the intelligentsia choose to do in their work, the role that they aspire to play in society at large can be achieved by them only to the extent that the rest of society accepts what they say uncritically and fails to examine their track record. Despite formidable weapons wielded by the intelligentsia in their crusades for cultural, moral, and ideological hegemony, they are not always able to neutralize the countervailing force of facts, experience and common sense. That is especially so in the United States, where intellectuals have never gotten the kind of deference they have long received in Europe and in some other parts of the world. Yet, even among Americans, the steady encroachment of policies, practices, and laws based on the notions and ideologies prevalent among the intelligentsia has steadily narrowed the scope of the freedoms traditionally enjoyed by ordinary people to run their own lives, much less to shape government policy.

Intellectuals' downplaying of objective reality and objective criteria extends beyond social, scientific, or economic phenomena into art, music, and philosophy. The one over-riding consistency across all these disparate venues is the self-exaltation of the intellectuals. Unlike great cultural achievements of the past, such as magnificent cathedrals, which were intended to inspire kings and peasants alike, the hallmark of self-consciously "modern" art and music is its inaccessibility to the masses and often even deliberate offensiveness to, or mockery of, the masses.

Just as a physical body can continue to live, despite containing a certain amount of microorganisms whose prevalence would destroy it, so a society can survive a certain amount of forces of disintegration within it. But that is very different from saying that there is no limit to the amount, audacity and ferocity of those disintegrative forces which a society can survive, without at least the will to resist.

NOTES

PREFACE

1. J.A. Schumpeter, *History of Economic Analysis* (New York: Oxford University Press, 1954), p. 475.
2. Mark Lilla, *The Reckless Mind: Intellectuals in Politics* (New York: New York Review Books, 2001), p. 198.

CHAPTER 1: INTELLECT AND INTELLECTUALS

1. Alfred North Whitehead, "December 15, 1939," *Dialogues of Alfred North Whitehead as Recorded by Lucien Price* (Boston: Little, Brown and Company, 1954), p. 135.
2. Michael St. John Packe, *The Life of John Stuart Mill* (New York: The Macmillan Company, 1954), p. 315.
3. For example, according to the *Chronicle of Higher Education*: "Conservatives are rarest in the humanities (3.6 percent) and social sciences (4.9 percent), and most common in business (24.5 percent) and the health sciences (20.5 percent)." Among faculty in the social sciences and humanities at elite, Ph.D.-granting universities, "not a single instructor reported voting for President Bush in 2004," when the President received a majority of the popular vote in the country at large. See David Glenn, "Few Conservatives but Many Centrists Teach in Academe," *Chronicle of Higher Education*, October 19, 2007, p. A10. In the health sciences, a study showed that the proportion of the faculty who called themselves conservative was the same as the proportion who called themselves liberal (20.5 percent), with the remainder calling themselves moderate. In business there were slightly more self-styled conservatives than self-styled liberals (24.5 percent versus 21.3 percent). Neil Gross and Solon Simmons, "The Social and Political Views of American Professors," Working Paper, September 24, 2007,

p. 28. But in the social sciences and humanities, people who identified themselves as liberals were an absolute majority, with moderates outnumbering conservatives several times over among the remainder. See also Howard Kurtz, "College Faculties A Most Liberal Lot, Study Finds," *Washington Post*, March 29, 2005, p. C1; Stanley Rothman, S. Robert Lichter, and Neil Nevitte, "Politics and Professional Advancement Among College Faculty," *The Forum*, Vol. 3, Issue 1 (2005), p. 6; Christopher F. Cardiff and Daniel B. Klein, "Faculty Partisan Affiliations in All Disciplines: A Voter-Registration Study," *Critical Review*, Vol. 17, Nos. 3–4, pp. 237–255.

4.   Oliver Wendell Holmes, "The Profession of the Law," *Collected Legal Papers* (New York: Peter Smith, 1952), p. 32.

5.   George J. Stigler, *Essays in the History of Economics* (Chicago: University of Chicago Press, 1965), p. 21.

6.   See Thomas Sowell, *On Classical Economics* (New Haven: Yale University Press, 2006), pp. 143–146.

7.   Eric Hoffer, *Before the Sabbath* (New York: Harper & Row, 1979), p. 3. Richard Posner also said that public intellectuals "who do not expect to undergo the close scrutiny of a biographer pay little cost in reputation even for being repeatedly proved wrong by events." Richard A. Posner, *Public Intellectuals: A Study of Decline* (Cambridge, Massachusetts: Harvard University Press, 2001), p. 63.

8.   Paul R. Ehrlich, *The Population Bomb* (New York: Ballantine Books, 1968), p. xi.

9.   The results of the government study of the safety of the Corvair were reported in the *Congressional Record: Senate*, March 27, 1973, pp. 9748–9774.

CHAPTER 2: KNOWLEDGE AND NOTIONS

1.   Daniel J. Flynn, *Intellectual Morons: How Ideology Makes Smart People Fall for Stupid Ideas* (New York: Crown Forum, 2004), p. 4.

2.   Bertrand Russell, *Which Way to Peace?* (London: Michael Joseph, Ltd., 1937), p. 146.

3. League of Professional Groups for Foster and Ford, *Culture and the Crisis: An Open Letter to the Writers, Artists, Teachers, Physicians, Engineers, Scientists and Other Professional Workers of America* (New York: Workers Library Publishers, 1932), p. 32.

4. "Shaw Bests Army of Interviewers," *New York Times*, March 25, 1933, p. 17.

5. "G.B. Shaw 'Praises' Hitler," *New York Times*, March 22, 1935, p. 21.

6. Letter to *The Times* of London, August 28, 1939, p. 11.

7. George J. Stigler, *Memoirs of an Unregulated Economist* (New York: Basic Books, 1988), p. 178. "A full collection of public statements signed by laureates whose work gave them not even professional acquaintance with the problem addressed by the statement would be a very large and somewhat depressing collection." Ibid., p. 89.

8. Roy Harrod, *The Life of John Maynard Keynes* (New York: Augustus M. Kelley, 1969), p. 468.

9. Brad Stone, "The Empire of Excess," *New York Times*, July 4, 2008, p. C1. Wal-Mart has likewise put much emphasis on choosing the locations of its stores. Richard Vedder and Wendell Cox, *The Wal-Mart Revolution: How Big-Box Stores Benefit Consumers, Workers, and the Economy* (Washington: AEI Press, 2006), pp. 53–54.

10. F.A. Hayek, *The Constitution of Liberty* (Chicago: University of Chicago Press, 1960), p. 26.

11. Robert L. Bartley, *The Seven Fat Years: And How To Do It Again* (New York: The Free Press, 1992), p. 241.

12. John Dewey, *Human Nature and Conduct: An Introduction to Social Psychology* (New York: The Modern Library, 1957), p. 148.

13. Edmund Morris, *The Rise of Theodore Roosevelt* (New York: Modern Library, 2001), p. 466.

14. Eligio R. Padilla and Gail E. Wyatt, "The Effects of Intelligence and Achievement Testing on Minority Group Children," *The Psychosocial Development of Minority Group Children*, edited by Gloria Johnson Powell, et al (New York: Brunner/Mazel, Publishers, 1983), p. 418.

15. Stuart Taylor, Jr. and K.C. Johnson, *Until Proven Innocent: Political Correctness and the Shameful Injustices of the Duke Lacrosse Rape Case* (New York: St. Martin's Press, 2007), pp. 12–13, 186, 212, 233–234.

16. Jeff Schultz, "Wrong Message for Duke Women," *Atlanta Journal-Constitution*, May 27, 2006, p. C1; Harvey Araton, "At Duke, Freedom of Speech Seems Selective," *New York Times*, May 26, 2006, pp. D1 ff; John Smallwood, "School Should Ban 'Innocent' Sweatbands," *Philadelphia Daily News*, May 26, 2006, Sports, p. 107; Stephen A. Smith, "Duke Free-Falling from Grace," *Philadelphia Inquirer*, May 28, 2006, p. D1.

17. See Thomas Sowell, *Basic Economics: A Common Sense Guide to the Economy*, third edition (New York: Basic Books, 2007), pp. 275–281 for a discussion of resource allocation over time and pp. 20–23 and 28–29 for a discussion of resource allocation as of a given time.

18. See, for example, Ibid., p. 275.

19. Randal O'Toole, *The Best-Laid Plans: How Government Planning Harms Your Quality of Life, Your Pocketbook, and Your Future* (Washington: Cato Institute, 2007), p. 190.

20. Ibid., p. 194.

21. See, for example, Thomas Sowell, *The Vision of the Anointed: Self-Congratulation as a Basis for Social Policy* (New York: Basic Books, 1995), Chapter 2.

22. Sidney E. Zion, "Attack on Court Heard by Warren," *New York Times*, September 10, 1965, pp. 1 ff.

23. U. S. Bureau of the Census, *Historical Statistics of the United States: Colonial Times to 1970* (Washington: Government Printing Office, 1975), Part 1, p. 414.

24. James Q. Wilson and Richard J. Herrnstein, *Crime and Human Nature* (New York: Simon and Schuster, 1985), p. 409.

25. Michael J. Hurley, *Firearms Discharge Report*, Police Academy Firearms and Tactics Section, New York, 2006, p. 10. See also Al Baker, "A Hail of Bullets, a Heap of Uncertainty," *New York Times*, December 9, 2007, Week in Review section, p. 4.

26. Oliver Wendell Holmes, *Collected Legal Papers* (New York: Peter Smith, 1952), p. 197.

27. "The life of the law has not been logic: it has been experience. The felt necessities of the time, the prevalent moral and political theories, intuitions of public policy, avowed or unconscious, even the prejudices which judges share with their fellow-men, have had a good deal more to do than the syllogism in determining the rules by which men should be governed." Oliver Wendell Holmes, Jr., *The Common Law* (Boston: Little, Brown and Company, 1923), p. 1.

28. Eugene Davidson, *The Unmaking of Adolf Hitler* (Columbia, Missouri: University of Missouri Press, 1996), p. 198.

29. Winston Churchill, *Churchill Speaks 1897–1963: Collected Speeches in Peace & War*, edited by Robert Rhodes James (New York: Chelsea House, 1980), p. 552.

30. Ibid., pp. 642–643.

CHAPTER 3: INTELLECTUALS AND ECONOMICS

1. George J. Stigler, *The Economist as Preacher and Other Essays* (Chicago: University of Chicago Press, 1982), p. 61.

2. Quoted in Arthur C. Brooks, "Philanthropy and the Non-Profit Sector," *Understanding America: The Anatomy of An Exceptional Nation*, edited by Peter H. Schuck and James Q. Wilson (New York: Public Affairs, 2008), pp. 548–549.

3. "Class and the American Dream," *New York Times*, May 30, 2005, p. A14.

4. Evan Thomas and Daniel Gross, "Taxing the Super Rich," *Newsweek*, July 23, 2007, p. 38.

5. Eugene Robinson, "Tattered Dream; Who'll Tackle the Issue of Upward Mobility?" *Washington Post*, November 23, 2007, p. A39.

6. Janet Hook, "Democrats Pursue Risky Raising-Taxes Strategy," *Los Angeles Times*, November 1, 2007.

7. Andrew Hacker, *Money: Who Has How Much and Why* (New York: Scribner, 1997), p. 10.

8. See, for example, David Wessel, "As Rich-Poor Gap Widens in the U.S., Class Mobility Stalls," *Wall Street Journal*, May 13, 2005, pp. A1 ff.

9. "Movin' On Up," *Wall Street Journal*, November 13, 2007, p. A24.

10. David Cay Johnston, "Richest Are Leaving Even the Rich Far Behind," *New York Times*, June 5, 2005, section 1, pp. 1 ff.

11. U.S. Department of the Treasury, "Income Mobility in the U.S. from 1996 to 2005," November 13, 2007, p. 12.

12. W. Michael Cox & Richard Alm, "By Our Own Bootstraps: Economic Opportunity & the Dynamics of Income Distribution," *Annual Report, 1995*, Federal Reserve Bank of Dallas, p. 8.

13. Peter Saunders, "Poor Statistics: Getting the Facts Right About Poverty in Australia," *Issue Analysis* No. 23, Centre for Independent Studies (Australia), April 3, 2002, p. 5; David Green, *Poverty and Benefit Dependency* (Wellington: New Zealand Business Roundtable, 2001), pp. 32, 33; Jason Clemens & Joel Emes, "Time Reveals the Truth about Low Income," *Fraser Forum*, September 2001, pp. 24–26.

14. U.S. Department of Labor, Bureau of Labor Statistics, *Characteristics of Minimum Wage Workers: 2004* (Washington: Department of Labor, Bureau of Labor Statistics, 2005), p. 1 and Table 1.

15. U.S. Department of the Treasury, "Income Mobility in the U.S. from 1996 to 2005," November 13, 2007, p. 2.

16. Computed from Carmen DeNavas-Walt, et al., "Income, Poverty, and Health Insurance Coverage in the United States: 2005," *Current Population Reports*, P60–231 (Washington: U.S. Bureau of the Census, 2006), p. 4.

17. See, for example, "The Rich Get Richer, and So Do the Old," *Washington Post*, National Weekly Edition, September 7, 1998, p. 34; John Schmitt, "No Economic Boom for the Middle Class," *San Diego Union-Tribune*, September 5, 1999, p. G3.

18. Computed from *Economic Report of the President* (Washington: U.S. Government Printing Office, 2009), p. 321.

19. Herman P. Miller, *Income Distribution in the United States* (Washington: U.S. Government Printing Office, 1966), p. 7.

20. Robert Rector and Rea S. Hederman, *Income Inequality: How Census Data Misrepresent Income Distribution* (Washington: The Heritage Foundation, 1999), p. 11.

21. Data on numbers of heads of household working in high-income and low-income households in 2000 are from Table HINC–06 from the *Current Population Survey*, downloaded from the Bureau of the Census web site.

22. Alan Reynolds, *Income and Wealth* (Westport, CT: Greenwood Press, 2006), p. 28.

23. Michael Harrington, *The Other America: Poverty in the United States* (New York: Penguin Books, 1981), pp. xiii, 1, 12, 16, 17.

24. Alan Reynolds, *Income and Wealth*, p. 67.

25. Andrew Hacker, *Money*, p. 31.

26. Steve DiMeglio, "With Golf Needing a Boost, Its Leading Man Returns," *USA Today*, February 25, 2009, pp. 1A ff.

27. Jeffrey S. Gurock, *When Harlem Was Jewish: 1870–1930* (New York: Columbia University Press, 1979).

28. Conor Dougherty, "States Imposing Interest-Rate Caps to Rein in Payday Lenders," *Wall Street Journal*, August 9–10, 2008, p. A3.

29. "Pay Pals," *New York Times*, June 10, 2009, p. A26.

30. John Dewey, *Liberalism and Social Action* (Amherst, N.Y.: Prometheus Books, 2000), p. 43.

31. Bernard Shaw, *The Intelligent Woman's Guide to Socialism and Capitalism* (New York: Brentano's Publishers, 1928), p. 208.

32. Bertrand Russell, *Sceptical Essays* (New York: W.W. Norton & Co., Inc., 1928), p. 230.

33. John Dewey, *Liberalism and Social Action*, p. 65.

34. Aida D. Donald, *Lion in the White House: A Life of Theodore Roosevelt* (New York: Basic Books, 2007), p. 10.

35. Karl Marx, *Capital: A Critique of Political Economy* (Chicago: Charles H. Kerr & Co., 1909), Vol. III, pp. 310–311.

36. Karl Marx, "Wage Labour and Capital," section V, Karl Marx and Frederick Engels, *Selected Works* (Moscow: Foreign Languages Publishing House, 1955), Vol. I, p. 99. See also Karl Marx, *Capital*, Vol. III, pp. 310–311.

37. Karl Marx, *Theories of Surplus Value: Selections* (New York: International Publishers, 1952), p. 380.

38. Karl Marx and Frederick Engels, *Selected Correspondence 1846–1895*, translated by Dona Torr (New York: International Publishers, 1942), p. 476.

39. Ibid., p. 159.

40. John Dewey, *Liberalism and Social Action*, p. 73. "Unless freedom of individual action has intelligence and informed conviction back of it, its manifestation is almost sure to result in confusion and disorder." John Dewey, *Intelligence in the Modern World: John Dewey's Philosophy*, edited by Joseph Ratner (New York: Modern Library, 1939), p. 404.

41. John Dewey, *Human Nature and Conduct: An Introduction to Social Psychology* (New York: Modern Library, 1957), p. 277.

42. John Dewey, *Liberalism and Social Action*, p. 56.

43. Ibid., p. 50.

44. Ibid., p. 65.

45. Ronald Dworkin, *Taking Rights Seriously* (Cambridge, Mass.: Harvard University Press, 1980), p. 147.

46. See, for example, Adam Smith, *An Inquiry Into the Nature and Causes of the Wealth of Nations* (New York: Modern Library, 1937), pp. 98, 128, 249–250, 460, 537. When I was teaching, I offered to give an A to any student who could find a single positive characterization of businessmen in Adam Smith's 900-page book. None ever did.

47. Ibid., p. 423.

48. My own sketch of these arguments can be found in Chapters 2 and 4 of my *Basic Economics: A Common Sense Guide to the Economy*, third edition (New York: Basic Books, 2007). More elaborate and more technical accounts can be found in more advanced texts.

49. Herbert Croly, *The Promise of American Life* (Boston: Northeastern University Press, 1989), pp. 44, 45.

50. See, for example, Nikolai Shmelev and Vladimir Popov, *The Turning Point: Revitalizing the Soviet Economy* (New York: Doubleday, 1989), pp. 141, 170; Midge Decter, *An Old Wife's Tale: My Seven Decades in Love and War* (New York: Regan Books, 2001), p. 169.

51. Frederick Engels, "Introduction to the First German Edition," Karl Marx, *The Poverty of Philosophy* (New York: International Publishers, 1963), p. 19.

52. Karl Marx, *Capital: A Critique of Political Economy* (Chicago: Charles H. Kerr and Co., 1919), Vol. I, p. 15.

53. Harold J. Laski, Letter to Oliver Wendell Holmes, September 13, 1916, *Holmes-Laski Letters: The Correspondence of Mr. Justice Holmes and Harold J. Laski 1916–1935*, edited by Mark DeWolfe Howe (Cambridge, Massachusetts: Harvard University Press, 1953), Vol. I, p. 20.

54. Holman W. Jenkins, Jr., "Business World: Shall We Eat Our Young?" *Wall Street Journal*, January 19, 2005, p. A13.

55. Lester C. Thurow, *The Zero-Sum Society: Distribution and the Possibilities for Economic Change* (New York: Basic Books, 2001), p. 203.

56. Beniamino Moro, "The Economists' 'Manifesto' On Unemployment in the EU Seven Years Later: Which Suggestions Still Hold?" *Banca Nazionale del Lavoro Quarterly Review*, June-September 2005, pp. 49–66; *The Economic Report of the President*, pp. 326–327.

57. Theodore Caplow, Louis Hicks and Ben J. Wattenberg, *The First Measured Century: An Illustrated Guide to Trends in America, 1900–2000* (Washington: AEI Press, 2001), p. 47.

58. Lester C. Thurow, *The Zero-Sum Society*, p. 203.

59. "The Turning Point," *The Economist*, September 22, 2007, p. 35.

60. John Dewey, *Liberalism and Social Action*, p. 53. See also p. 88.

61. Ibid., p. 89.

62. Ibid., p. 44.

63. Ibid., p. 78.

64. Edward Bellamy, *Looking Backward: 2000–1887* (New York: Modern Library, 1917), p. 43.

65. V.I. Lenin, *The State and Revolution* (Moscow: Progress Publishers, 1969), p. 92.

66. V.I. Lenin, "The Role and Functions of the Trade Unions Under the New Economic Policy," *Selected Works* (Moscow: Foreign Languages Publishing House, 1952), Vol. II, Part 2, p. 618.

67. V.I. Lenin, "Ninth Congress of the Russian Communist Party (Bolsheviks)," ibid., p. 333.

68. Edmund Morris, *Theodore Rex* (New York: Modern Library, 2002), p. 360.

69. Ibid., pp. 10–11.

70. Loc. cit.

71. John Maynard Keynes, *The General Theory of Employment Interest and Money* (New York: Harcourt, Brace and Company, 1936), p. 19.

72. Woodrow Wilson, *Woodrow Wilson: Essential Writings and Speeches of the Scholar-President*, edited by Mario R. DiNunzio (New York: New York University Press, 2006), p. 342.

73. Charles F. Howlett, *Troubled Philosopher: John Dewey and the Struggle for World Peace* (Port Washington, N.Y.: Kennikat Press, 1977), p. 31.

74. John Kenneth Galbraith, *American Capitalism: The Concept of Countervailing Power*, Sentry edition (Boston: Houghton Mifflin Co., 1956), p. 113.

75. Ibid., pp. 114–115.

76. Ibid., p. 136.

77. Ibid., p. 137.

78. Ibid., p. 44.

79. Ibid., p. 26.

80. Jim Powell, *Bully Boy: The Truth About Theodore Roosevelt's Legacy* (New York: Crown Forum, 2006), pp. 82, 89–90.

81. Theodore Roosevelt, *The Rough Riders: An Autobiography* (New York: The Library of America, 2004), p. 692.

82. Ibid., p. 685.

83. Ibid., p. 691.

84. Jim Powell, *Bully Boy*, p. 112.

85. Ibid., p. 111.

86. Ibid., pp. 109–110.

87. Edmund Morris, *Theodore Rex*, p. 427.

88. Jim Powell, *Bully Boy*, p. 135.

89. "Spare a Dime? A Special Report on the Rich," *The Economist*, April 4, 2009, p. 4 of special report.

90. Richard Vedder and Lowell Gallaway, *Out of Work: Unemployment and Government in Twentieth-Century America* (New York: Holmes & Meier, 1993), p. 77.

91. Milton Friedman and Anna Jacobson Schwartz, *A Monetary History of the United States: 1867–1960* (Princeton: Princeton University Press, 1963), p. 407; John Kenneth Galbraith, *The Great Crash, 1929* (Boston: Houghton Mifflin, 1961), p. 32.

92. Richard Vedder and Lowell Gallaway, *Out of Work*, p. 77.

93. Loc. cit.

94. Jim Powell, *FDR's Folly: How Roosevelt and His New Deal Prolonged the Great Depression* (New York: Crown Forum, 2003), p. 92.

95. "Reagan Fantasies, Budget Realities," *New York Times*, November 5, 1987, p. A34.

96. Mary McGrory, "Fiddling While Wall St. Burns," *Washington Post*, October 29, 1987, p. A2.

97. "What the US Can Do," *Financial Times* (London), October 28, 1987, p. 24.

98. Roger C. Altman, "If Reagan Were F.D.R.," *New York Times*, November 20, 1987, p. A39.

99. "The Turning Point," *The Economist*, September 22, 2007, p. 35.

100. Jim Powell, *FDR's Folly*, pp. xv–xvi.

CHAPTER 4: INTELLECTUALS AND SOCIAL VISIONS

1. Walter Lippmann, *Public Opinion* (New York: The Free Press, 1965), p. 80.

2. Paul Johnson, *Enemies of Society* (New York: Atheneum, 1977), p. 145.

3. Joseph A. Schumpeter, *History of Economic Analysis* (New York: Oxford University Press, 1954), p. 41.

4. John Stuart Mill, "Utilitarianism," *Collected Works of John Stuart Mill* (Toronto: University of Toronto Press, 1969), Vol. X, p. 215.

5. John Stuart Mill, "De Tocqueville on Democracy in America [I]," *Collected Works of John Stuart Mill* (Toronto: University of Toronto Press, 1977), Vol. XVIII, p. 86; John Stuart Mill, "Civilization," ibid., pp. 121, 139; John Stuart Mill, "On Liberty," ibid., p. 222.

6. Jean-Jacques Rousseau, *The Social Contract,* translated by Maurice Cranston (New York: Penguin Books, 1968), p. 49.

7. Donald Kagan, *On the Origins of War and the Preservation of Peace* (New York: Doubleday, 1995), p. 414.

8. Mark DeWolfe Howe, editor, *Holmes-Laski Letters: The Correspondence of Mr. Justice Holmes and Harold J. Laski 1916–1935* (Cambridge, Massachusetts: Harvard University Press, 1953), Volume I, p. 12.

9. See my *A Conflict of Visions*, second edition (New York: Basic Books, 2007).

10. Ibid., pp. 9–17, 166–167, 198–199.

11. Ibid., pp. 147–153.

12. See, for example, William Godwin, *Enquiry Concerning Political Justice and Its Influence on Morals and Happiness* (Toronto: University of Toronto Press, 1946), Vol. II, Chapter XVI; John Dewey, *Human Nature and Conduct: An Introduction to Social Psychology* (New York: Modern Library, 1957), pp. 114–115; Bernard Shaw, *The Intelligent Woman's Guide to Socialism and Capitalism* (New York: Brentano's Publishers, 1928), pp. 158–160.

13. Donald Kagan, *On the Origins of War and the Preservation of Peace,* p. 212.

14. Will and Ariel Durant, *The Lessons of History* (New York: Simon and Schuster, 1968), p. 81.

15. Alexander Hamilton et al., *The Federalist Papers* (New York: New American Library, 1961), p. 87.

16. Ibid., p. 46.

17. Richard A. Epstein, *Overdose: How Excessive Government Regulation Stifles Pharmaceutical Innovation* (New Haven: Yale University Press, 2006), p. 15.

18. Ian Ayres, *Super Crunchers: Why Thinking-by-Numbers Is the New Way to Be Smart* (New York: Bantam Books, 2007), p. 3.

19. Ibid., pp. 1–9. See also Mark Strauss, "The Grapes of Math," *Discover*, January 1991, pp. 50–51; Jay Palmer, "Grape Expectations," *Barron's*, December 30, 1996, pp. 17–19.

20. Ian Ayres, *Super Crunchers*, pp. 82–83.

21. Tom Wicker, "Freedom for What?" *New York Times*, January 5, 1990, p. A31.

22. Richard A. Epstein, *Overdose*, p. 15.

23. Joseph Epstein, "True Virtue," *New York Times Magazine*, November 24, 1985, p. 95.

24. Thomas Robert Malthus, *Population: The First Essay* (Ann Arbor: University of Michigan Press, 1959), p. 3.

25. William Godwin, *Of Population* (London: Longman, Hurst, Rees, Orme and Brown, 1820), pp. 520, 550, 554.

26. Edmund Burke, *The Correspondence of Edmund Burke*, edited by R. B. McDowell (Chicago: University of Chicago Press, 1969), Vol. VIII, p. 138.

27. F.A. Hayek, *The Road to Serfdom* (Chicago: University of Chicago Press, 1944), pp. 55, 185.

28. Winston Churchill, *Churchill Speaks 1897–1963: Collected Speeches in Peace & War*, edited by Robert Rhodes James (New York: Chelsea House, 1980), p. 866.

29. See my *A Conflict of Visions*, second edition, pp. 58–60, 256–260.

30. Andrew Hacker, *Two Nations: Black and White, Separate, Hostile, Unequal* (New York: Charles Scribner's Sons, 1992), p. 52.

31. Arthur C. Brooks, *Who Really Cares: The Surprising Truth About Compassionate Conservatism* (New York: Basic Books, 2006), pp. 21–22, 24.

32. Bertrand Russell, *Which Way to Peace?* (London: Michael Joseph, Ltd., 1937), p. 179.

33. John Dewey, "Outlawing Peace by Discussing War," *New Republic*, May 16, 1928, p. 370.

34. Loc. cit.

35. John Dewey, "If War Were Outlawed," *New Republic*, April 25, 1923, p. 234.

36. Ibid., p. 235.

37. J.B. Priestley, "The Public and the Idea of Peace," *Challenge to Death*, edited by Storm Jameson (New York: E.P. Dutton & Co., Inc., 1935), p. 313.

38. Ibid., p. 309.

39. See, for example, William Godwin, *Enquiry Concerning Political Justice*, Vol. I, pp. 456–457.

40. T.S. Eliot, "The Cocktail Party," *The Complete Poems and Plays* (New York: Harcourt, Brace and Company, 1952), p. 348.

41. Alfred Lief, editor, *Representative Opinions of Mr. Justice Holmes* (Westport, CT: Greenwood Press, 1971), pp. 160, 282.

42. Mark DeWolfe Howe, editor, *Holmes-Laski Letters*, Vol. II, p. 888.

43. Ibid., pp. 822–823. Holmes' original statement that the "common law is not a brooding omnipresence in the sky" is from the U.S. Supreme Court case of *Southern Pacific Co. v. Jensen*. He also used the phrase in a letter to British jurist Sir Frederick Pollock. Mark DeWolfe Howe, editor, *Holmes-Pollock Letters: The Correspondence of Mr. Justice Holmes and Sir Frederick Pollock 1874–1932* (Cambridge, Massachusetts: Harvard University Press, 1942), Vol. 2, p. 215.

44. Alfred Lief, editor, *The Dissenting Opinions of Mr. Justice Holmes* (New York: The Vanguard Press, 1929), p. 33.

45. Jonah Goldberg, *Liberal Fascism: The Secret History of the American Left from Mussolini to the Politics of Meaning* (New York: Doubleday, 2008), pp. 17, 25–26.

46. See, for example, G. Kinne, "Nazi Stratagems and their Effects on Germans in Australia up to 1945," *Royal Australian Historical Society*, Vol. 66, Pt. 1 (June 1980), pp. 1–19; Jean Roche, *La Colonisation Allemande et Le Rio Grande Do Sul* (Paris: Institut des Hautes Études de L'Amérique Latine, 1959), pp. 541–543.

47. Valdis O. Lumans, *Himmler's Auxiliaries* (Chapel Hill: University of North Carolina Press, 1993), pp. 77–87.

48. Hélène Carrère d'Encausse, *Decline of an Empire: The Soviet Socialist Republics in Revolt* (New York: Newsweek Books, 1980), pp. 146, 150–151.

49. Jonah Goldberg, *Liberal Fascism*, pp. 45–46, 410–413.

50. Ibid., pp. 324–325, 344–357.

51. See, for example, Chapter 3 of my *Inside American Education: The Decline, the Deception, the Dogmas* (New York: The Free Press, 1993).

52. Lewis A. Coser, *Men of Ideas: A Sociologist's View* (New York: The Free Press, 1970), p. 141.

53. "The statesman, who should attempt to direct private people in what manner they ought to employ their capitals, would not only load himself with a most unnecessary attention, but assume an authority which could safely be trusted, not only to no single person, but to no council or senate whatever, and which would nowhere be so dangerous as in the hands of a man who had folly and presumption enough to fancy himself fit to exercise it." Adam Smith, *An Inquiry into the Nature and Causes of the Wealth of Nations* (New York: Modern Library, 1937), p. 423.

54. Oliver Wendell Holmes, Jr., *The Common Law* (Boston: Little, Brown and Company, 1923), p. 1.

55. Jonah Goldberg, *Liberal Fascism*, p. 52.

56. Jean-Jacques Rousseau, *The Social Contract*, translated by Maurice Cranston, p. 89.

57. William Godwin, *Enquiry Concerning Political Justice*, Vol. I, p. 446; Antoine-Nicolas de Condorcet, *Sketch for a Historical Picture of the Progress of the Human Mind*, translated by June Barraclough (London: Weidenfeld and Nicolson, 1955), p. 114.

58. Karl Marx and Frederick Engels, *Selected Correspondence 1846–1895*, translated by Dona Torr (New York: International Publishers, 1942), p. 190.

59. Bernard Shaw, *The Intelligent Woman's Guide to Socialism and Capitalism*, p. 456.

334 Intellectuals and Society

60. Edmund Wilson, *Letters on Literature and Politics 1912–1972*, edited by Elena Wilson (New York: Farrar, Straus and Giroux, 1977), p. 36. Nor was this due to the racism of Southern whites, for Wilson himself referred to how distasteful Chattanooga was to him because of "the niggers and the mills." Ibid., pp. 217, 220. Years later, upon seeing the poverty of Italy at the end of World War II, Wilson said, "that isn't the way that white people ought to live." Ibid., p. 423.

61. Quoted in Jonah Goldberg, *Liberal Fascism*, p. 38.

62. Lincoln Steffens, "Stop, Look, Listen!" *The Survey*, March 1, 1927, pp. 735–737, 754–755.

63. Jonah Goldberg, *Liberal Fascism*, pp. 28–29.

64. Ibid., p. 21. A year later, after Hitler had come to power, Wells characterized him as "a clumsy lout" with "his idiotic symbols" and "his imbecile cruelties." "H.G. Wells Scores Nazis as 'Louts,'" *New York Times*, September 22, 1933, p. 13. By 1939 he was attacking both Mussolini and Hitler, though he exempted the Soviet Union from his condemnation. See "Wells Sees in U.S. Hope for Mankind," *New York Times*, August 4, 1939, p. 3.

65. Jonah Goldberg, *Liberal Fascism*, pp. 100–101, 103–104.

66. Ibid., pp. 26–27.

67. Ibid., p. 103.

68. Ibid., p. 10.

69. Daniel J. Flynn, *Intellectual Morons: How Ideology Makes Smart People Fall for Stupid Ideas* (New York: Crown Forum, 2004), p. 173.

70. Jonah Goldberg, *Liberal Fascism*, p. 140.

71. Ibid., pp. 122–123, 146–148.

72. John Dewey, *Liberalism and Social Action* (Amherst, N.Y.: Prometheus Books, 2000), p. 13.

73. Edmund Burke, "A Letter to the Right Hon. Henry Dundas, One of His Majesty's Principal Secretaries of State with the Sketch of a Negro Code," Edmund Burke, *The Works of the Right Honorable Edmund Burke*, third edition (Boston: Little, Brown, and Company, 1869), Vol. VI, pp. 256–289.

74. Adam Smith, *The Theory of Moral Sentiments* (Indianapolis: Liberty Classics, 1976), p. 337.

75. John Dewey, *Liberalism and Social Action*, p. 66.

76. John Larkin, "Newspaper Nirvana?" *Wall Street Journal*, May 5, 2006, p. B1; Tim Harford, *The Undercover Economist* (New York: Oxford University Press, 2005), p. 3.

77. Raymond Aron, *The Opium of the Intellectuals* (London: Secker & Warburg, 1957), p. 227.

78. See, for example, Abigail and Stephan Thernstrom, *No Excuses: Closing the Racial Gap in Learning* (New York: Simon & Schuster, 2003), pp. 43–50; Thomas Sowell, "Patterns of Black Excellence," *The Public Interest*, Spring 1976, pp. 26–58.

79. William Godwin, *Enquiry Concerning Political Justice*, Vol. I, p. 107.

80. Ibid., p. 47.

81. William Godwin, *The Enquirer: Reflections on Education, Manners, and Literature* (London: G. G. and J. Robinson, 1797), p. 70.

82. Ibid., p. 67.

83. Adam Smith, *The Theory of Moral Sentiments*, p. 529.

84. Edmund Burke, *Speeches and Letters on American Affairs* (New York: E.P. Dutton & Co., Inc., 1961), p. 203.

85. Woodrow Wilson, "What is Progress?" *American Progressivism: A Reader*, edited by Ronald J. Pestritto and William J. Atto (Lanham, MD: Lexington Books, 2008), p. 48.

86. Mark DeWolfe Howe, editor, *Holmes-Laski Letters*, Vol. II, p. 974.

87. Elizabeth Wiskemann, *Czechs & Germans: A Study of the Struggle in the Historic Provinces of Bohemia and Moravia* (London: Oxford University Press, 1938), pp. 142, 148.

88. Thomas Sowell, *The Housing Boom and Bust* (New York: Basic Books, 2009), pp. 97–102.

89. Malcolm Gladwell, *Outliers: The Story of Success* (Boston: Little, Brown and Co., 2008), p. 112.

90. Padma Ramkrishna Velaskar, "Inequality in Higher Education: A Study of Scheduled Caste Students in Medical Colleges of Bombay," Ph.D. dissertation, Tata Institute of Social Sciences (Bombay), 1986.

CHAPTER 5: OPTIONAL REALITY IN THE MEDIA AND ACADEMIA

1. Jean-François Revel, *The Flight from Truth: The Reign of Deceit in the Age of Information*, translated by Curtis Cate (New York: Random House, 1991), p. 34.

2. J.A. Schumpeter, *History of Economic Analysis* (New York: Oxford University Press, 1954), p. 43n.

3. Daniel J. Flynn, *A Conservative History of the American Left* (New York: Crown Forum, 2008), p. 214.

4. Jean-François Revel, *The Flight from Truth*, translated by Curtis Cate, p. 259.

5. Carmen DeNavas-Walt, et al., "Income, Poverty, and Health Insurance Coverage in the United States: 2006," *Current Population Reports*, P60–233 (Washington: U.S. Bureau of the Census, 2007), p. 5; Glenn B. Canner, et al., "Home Mortgage Disclosure Act: Expanded Data on Residential Lending," *Federal Reserve Bulletin*, November 1991, p. 870; Glenn B. Canner and Dolores S. Smith, "Expanded HMDA Data on Residential Lending: One Year Later," *Federal Reserve Bulletin*, November 1992, p. 808; Rochelle Sharpe, "Unequal Opportunity: Losing Ground on the Employment Front," *Wall Street Journal*, September 14, 1993, pp. A1 ff.

6. Bernard Goldberg, *Bias: A CBS Insider Exposes How the Media Distort the News* (Washington: Regnery Publishing Inc., 2002), p. 63.

7. Brian C. Anderson, *South Park Conservatives: The Revolt Against Liberal Media Bias* (Washington: Regnery Publishing Inc., 2005), p. 14. An earlier study found that more than half of all corporate heads in television dramas "do something illegal, ranging from fraud to murder." Paul Hollander, *Anti-Americanism: Critiques at Home and Abroad 1965–1990* (New York: Oxford University Press, 1992), p. 231.

8. Bernard Goldberg, *Bias*, p. 81.

9. Daniel Golden, "Aiming for Diversity, Textbooks Overshoot," *Wall Street Journal*, August 19, 2006, pp. A1 ff.

10. Walter Duranty, "All Russia Suffers Shortage of Food; Supplies Dwindling," *New York Times*, November 25, 1932, p. 1.

11. S. J. Taylor, *Stalin's Apologist: Walter Duranty, The New York Times's Man in Moscow* (New York: Oxford University Press, 1990), p. 182.

12. Ibid., p. 205.

13. Gregory Wolfe, *Malcolm Muggeridge: A Biography* (Grand Rapids: William B. Eerdmans Publishing Co., 1997), p. 119.

14. Robert Conquest, *The Harvest of Sorrow: Soviet Collectivization and the Terror-Famine* (New York: Oxford University Press, 1986), p. 303.

15. See, for example, Michael Ellman, "A Note on the Number of 1933 Famine Victims," *Soviet Studies*, Vol. 43, No. 2 (1991), p. 379; R.W. Davies and Stephen G. Wheatcroft, *The Years of Hunger: Soviet Agriculture, 1931–1933* (New York: Palgrave Macmillan, 2004), p. 415; Steve Smith, "Comment on Kershaw," *Contemporary European History*, February 2005, p. 130; James E. Mace, "The Politics of Famine: American Government and Press Response to the Ukrainian Famine, 1932–1933," *Holocaust and Genocide Studies*, Vol. 3, No. 1 (1988), p. 77; Hiroaki Kuromiya, *Stalin* (Harlow, England: Pearson Education Limited, 2005), pp. 103–104. Even Soviet publications carried reports for the country as a whole "that the number of victims of hunger and terror during the 1930s and during the war, according to the no longer tongue-tied Soviet demographers, far exceeded the harshest evaluations of anti-communist historiography." Jean-François Revel, *The Flight from Truth*, translated by Curtis Cate, p. 208.

16. S. J. Taylor, *Stalin's Apologist*, p. 206.

17. James E. Mace, "The Politics of Famine: American Government and Press Response to the Ukrainian Famine, 1932–1933," *Holocaust and Genocide Studies*, Vol. 3, No. 1 (1988), p. 82.

18. Ronald Dworkin, "Affirming Affirmative Action," *New York Review of Books*, October 22, 1998, pp. 91 ff; Alan Wolfe, "Affirmative Action: The Fact Gap," *New York Times*, October 25, 1998, Book Review section, p. 15; Richard Flacks, "Getting to Yes; The Shape of the River," *Los Angeles Times*, July 4, 1999, Book Review section, p. 7; Ellis Cose, "Cutting Through Race Rhetoric," *Newsweek*, September 28, 1998, p. 75; David Karen, "Go to the Head of the Class," *The Nation*, November 16, 1998, pp. 46 ff.

19. Stephan Thernstrom and Abigail Thernstrom, "Reflections on The Shape of the River," *UCLA Law Review*, Vol. 46, No. 5 (June 1999), p. 1589.

20. Gail Heriot, "Affirmative Action Backfires," *Wall Street Journal*, August 24, 2007, p. A15; "Race Data for Bar Admissions Research Stays Under Wraps," *California Bar Journal*, December 2007, pp. 1 ff.

21. Peter Hitchens, *A Brief History of Crime: The Decline of Order, Justice and Liberty in England* (London: Atlantic Books, 2003), p. 168.

22. Gary Mauser, "Some International Evidence on Gun Bans and Murder Rates," *Fraser Forum*, October 2007, p. 24.

23. Jeffrey A. Miron, "Violence, Guns, and Drugs: A Cross-Country Analysis," *Journal of Law and Economics*, Vol. 44, No. 2, Part 2 (October 2001), p. 616.

24. Joyce Lee Malcolm, *Guns and Violence: The English Experience* (Cambridge, Massachusetts: Harvard University Press, 2002), p. 225.

25. James Q. Wilson, "Criminal Justice," *Understanding America: The Anatomy of an Exceptional Nation*, edited by Peter H. Schuck and James Q. Wilson (New York: Public Affairs, 2008), p. 479.

26. James B. Jacobs, *Can Gun Control Work?* (New York: Oxford University Press, 2002), p. 13.

27. William McGowan, *Coloring the News: How Crusading for Diversity Has Corrupted American Journalism* (San Francisco: Encounter Books, 2001), pp. 99–100.

28. For example, in a report from the Family Research Institute in June 2005 titled "Homosexual Child Molestation: Part 2" and another report from the same organization titled "Domestic Violence Higher Among Homosexuals?" in August 2008.

29. William McGowan, *Coloring the News*, p. 105.

30. Ibid., pp. 235, 236.

31. Jennifer Harper, "To Be 'Illegal' or Not to Be: Newsroom Question," *Washington Times*, March 6, 2009, p. A1.

32. William McGowan, *Coloring the News*, p. 89.

33. Ibid., p. 90.

34. Loc. cit.

35. Ibid., pp. 90–94.
36. David Murray, Joel Schwartz, and S. Robert Lichter, *It Ain't Necessarily So: How Media Make and Unmake the Scientific Picture of Reality* (Lanham, Maryland: Rowman & Littlefield, 2001), p. 71.
37. "Media Eat Up Hunger Study," *Media Watch*, April 1991, p. 1.
38. Loc. cit.
39. Robert E. Rector, "Hunger and Malnutrition Among American Children," *Backgrounder* No. 843 (August 2, 1991), The Heritage Foundation, p. 2.
40. Jonah Goldberg, *Liberal Fascism: The Secret History of the American Left from Mussolini to the Politics of Meaning* (New York: Doubleday, 2008), pp. 127–128.
41. See, for example, John Kenneth Galbraith, *The Great Crash, 1929* (Boston: Houghton Mifflin, 1961), pp. 143–146; Arthur M. Schlesinger, *Paths to the Present* (Boston: Houghton Mifflin, 1964), p. 237.
42. Amity Shlaes, *The Forgotten Man: A New History of the Great Depression* (New York: HarperCollins, 2007), pp. 148–149.
43. Paul Johnson, *A History of the American People* (New York: HarperCollins, 1997), p. 757.
44. Herbert Hoover, *The Memoirs of Herbert Hoover: The Great Depression 1929–1941* (New York: The Macmillan Company, 1952), p. 29.
45. Herbert Hoover, *The Memoirs of Herbert Hoover: The Cabinet and the Presidency 1920–1933* (New York: The Macmillan Company, 1952), pp. 99, 103–104.
46. Amity Shlaes, *The Forgotten Man*, p. 131.
47. Herbert Hoover, *The Memoirs of Herbert Hoover: The Great Depression 1929–1941*, pp. 43–46.
48. Oswald Garrison Villard, "Pity Herbert Hoover," *The Nation*, June 15, 1932, p. 669.
49. "Wanted— A Government," *New Republic*, March 4, 1931, p. 58.
50. Edmund Wilson, *The Shores of Light: A Literary Chronicle of the Twenties and Thirties* (New York: Farrar, Straus and Young, Inc., 1952), p. 498.

51. Edmund Wilson, *The American Jitters: A Year of the Slump* (New York: Charles Scribner's Sons, 1932), p. 296.

52. Robert S. Allen and Drew Pearson, *Washington Merry-Go-Round* (New York: Horace Liveright, 1931), p. 55.

53. Harold Laski, "Persons and Personages: President Hoover," *Living Age*, June 1931, p. 367.

54. "Ickes Says Hoover Let Needy 'Starve,'" *New York Times*, April 7, 1936, p. 5.

55. Robert S. McElvaine, *The Great Depression: America, 1929–1941* (New York: Times Books, 1993), p. 52.

56. Paul Krugman, "Fifty Herbert Hoovers," *New York Times*, December 29, 2008, p. A25.

57. David McCullough, *Truman* (New York: Simon & Schuster, 1992), pp. 389–390.

58. Merle Miller, *Plain Speaking: An Oral Biography of Harry S. Truman* (New York: Berkley Publishing Corp., 1974), p. 220.

59. "Adlai E. Stevenson," *New York Times*, July 15, 1965, p. 28.

60. Russell Jacoby, *The Last Intellectuals: American Culture in the Age of Academe* (New York: Basic Books, 2000), p. 81.

61. Michael Beschloss, "How Well-Read Should a President Be?" *New York Times*, June 11, 2000, section 4, p. 17.

62. David McCullough, "Harry S. Truman: 1945–1953," *Character Above All: Ten Presidents from FDR to George Bush*, edited by Robert A. Wilson (New York: Simon & Schuster, 1995), p. 58.

63. Robert H. Ferrell, *Harry S. Truman: A Life* (Columbia, Missouri: University of Missouri Press, 1994), p. 19.

64. Glen Jeansonne, *A Time of Paradox: America from the Cold War to the Third Millennium, 1945–Present* (Lanham, Maryland: Rowman & Littlefield, 2007), p. 225.

65. Ron Suskind, *A Hope in the Unseen: An American Odyssey from the Inner City to the Ivy League* (New York: Broadway Books, 1998), p. 116.

66. Jeffrey Toobin, "The Burden of Clarence Thomas," *The New Yorker*, September 27, 1993, p. 43.

67. Carl T. Rowan, "Thomas is Far From 'Home,'" *Chicago Sun-Times*, July 4, 1993, p. 41.

68. Mary McGrory, "Thomas Walks in Scalia's Shoes," *Washington Post*, February 27, 1992, p. A2.

69. Kevin Merida, et al., "Enigmatic on the Bench, Influential in the Halls," *Washington Post*, October 10, 2004, pp. A1 ff.

70. Loc. cit.

71. Ken Foskett, *Judging Thomas: The Life and Times of Clarence Thomas* (New York: William Morrow, 2004), pp. 274–276.

72. Kevin Merida and Michael A. Fletcher, *Supreme Discomfort: The Divided Soul of Clarence Thomas* (New York: Doubleday, 2007), p. 340.

73. David C. Lipscomb, "Thomas Inspires Boys School Grads," *Washington Times*, May 30, 2008, p. A1.

74. Jan Crawford Greenburg, *Supreme Conflict: The Inside Story of the Struggle for Control of the United States Supreme Court* (New York: Penguin Press, 2007), p. 117.

75. Edmund Wilson, *Travels in Two Democracies* (New York: Harcourt, Brace and Company, 1936), p. 321.

76. "After the Slaughter, What Hope?" *The Economist*, March 9, 2002, p. 45.

77. "Caste and The Durban Conference," *The Hindu* (India), August 31, 2001 (online).

78. "Reservation Policy Not Implemented in Full," *The Hindu* (India), November 18, 2001 (on-line).

79. Tom O'Neill, "Untouchable," *National Geographic*, June 2003, pp. 2–31.

80. Winston Churchill was one of those who was not taken in by benign depictions of India by Western or Indian intellectuals. "These Brahmins who mouth and patter the principles of Western Liberalism, and pose as philosophic and democratic politicians, are the same Brahmins who deny the primary rights of existence to nearly sixty millions of their own fellow countrymen whom they call 'untouchable,' and whom they have by thousands of years of oppression actually taught to accept this sad position." Winston Churchill, *Churchill Speaks*

1897–1963: Collected Speeches in Peace & War, edited by Robert Rhodes James (New York: Chelsea House, 1980), p. 536.

81. Paul Hollander, *Political Pilgrims: Travels of Western Intellectuals to the Soviet Union, China, and Cuba 1928–1978* (New York: Oxford University Press, 1981), p. 13.

82. "A Reaffirmation of Principle," *New York Times*, October 26, 1988, p. A21.

83. Richard Hofstadter, *Anti-Intellectualism in American Life* (New York: Vintage Books, 1963), pp. 3, 24.

84. Nicholas D. Kristof, "Obama and the War on Brains," *New York Times*, November 9, 2008, Week in Review section, p. 10.

85. Jacques Barzun, *The House of Intellect* (New York: Perennial Classics, 2002), p. 2.

86. Clark Hoyt, "Keeping Their Opinions to Themselves," *New York Times*, October 19, 2008, Week in Review section, p. 12.

87. J.A. Schumpeter, *History of Economic Analysis*, p. 43.

88. Jean-François Revel, *The Flight from Truth*, translated by Curtis Cate, p. 241.

89. Jonah Goldberg, *Liberal Fascism*, p. 343.

90. Arnold P. Hinchliffe, *Harold Pinter* (New York: Twayne Publishers, Inc., 1967), p. 101.

91. Paul Johnson, *Enemies of Society* (New York: Atheneum, 1977), p. 230.

92. Will Rogers, *A Will Rogers Treasury: Reflections and Observations*, edited by Bryan B. Sterling and Frances N. Sterling (New York: Crown Publishers, 1982), p. 88.

93. Jacques Barzun, *The House of Intellect*, p. 15.

94. Nikolai Shmelev and Vladimir Popov, *The Turning Point: Revitalizing the Soviet Economy* (New York: Doubleday, 1989), p. 170.

95. Eric Hoffer, *First Things, Last Things* (New York: Harper & Row, 1971), p. 117.

96. H.G. Wells, *The Anatomy of Frustration: A Modern Synthesis* (New York: The Macmillan Company, 1936), p. 115.

97. Ibid., p. 100.

98. George J. Stigler, *Essays in the History of Economics* (Chicago: University of Chicago Press, 1965), pp. 20–22, *passim.*

99. Tim Harford, *The Undercover Economist* (New York: Oxford University Press, 2005), p. 3.

100. Paul Johnson, *Intellectuals* (New York: Harper & Row, 1988), p. 319.

101. Ibid., p. 246.

102. Eric Hoffer, *First Things, Last Things,* p. 117.

CHAPTER 6: INTELLECTUALS AND THE LAW

1. Richard A. Epstein, *How Progressives Rewrote the Constitution* (Washington: The Cato Institute, 2006), p. viii.

2. Oliver Wendell Holmes, Jr., *The Common Law* (Boston: Little, Brown and Company, 1923), p. 1.

3. *Lauren Hill Cemetery v. City and County of San Francisco,* 216 U.S. 358 (1910), at 366.

4. Oliver Wendell Holmes, *Collected Legal Papers* (New York: Peter Smith, 1952), p. 194.

5. Antoine-Nicolas de Condorcet, *Sketch for a Historical Picture of the Progress of the Human Mind,* translated by June Barraclough (London: Weidenfeld and Nicolson, 1955), p. 112.

6. Ronald Dworkin, *Taking Rights Seriously* (Cambridge, Massachusetts: Harvard University Press, 1980), p. 147.

7. Ibid., p. 145.

8. Ibid., p. 239.

9. Theodore Roosevelt, *The Rough Riders: An Autobiography* (New York: The Library of America, 2004), p. 614. See also p. 721.

10. Edmund Morris, *Theodore Rex* (New York: The Modern Library, 2002), p. 165.

11. Woodrow Wilson, *Constitutional Government in the United States* (New Brunswick, N.J.: Transaction Publishers, 2006), p. 158.

12. Ibid., p. 167.

13. Ibid., p. 169.

14. *Roe v. Wade,* 410 U.S. 113 (1973).

15. *Engel v. Vitale*, 370 U.S. 421 (1962).

16. *Miranda v. Arizona*, 384 U.S. 436 (1966).

17. *Brown v. Board of Education of Topeka, Kansas*, 347 U.S. 483 (1954).

18. *Furman v. Georgia*, 408 U.S. 238 (1972).

19. *Lynch v. Donnelly*, 465 U.S. 668 (1984); *Allegheny County v. American Civil Liberties Union*, 492 U.S. 573 (1989); *Rosenberger v. Rector and Visitors of University of Virginia*, 515 U.S. 819 (1995); *McCreary County, Kentucky v. American Civil Liberties Union*, 545 U.S. 844 (2005); *Van Orden v. Perry*, 545 U.S. 677 (2005).

20. *Baker v. Carr*, 369 U.S. 186 (1962).

21. Herbert Croly, *The Promise of American Life* (Boston: Northeastern University Press, 1989), pp. 35–36.

22. Ibid., p. 200.

23. Roscoe Pound, "Mechanical Jurisprudence," *Columbia Law Review*, Vol. 8 (December 1908), p. 615.

24. Ibid., pp. 605, 609, 612.

25. Ibid., pp. 612, 614.

26. Roscoe Pound, "The Need of a Sociological Jurisprudence," *The Green Bag*, October 1907, pp. 611, 612.

27. Roscoe Pound, "Mechanical Jurisprudence," *Columbia Law Review*, Vol. 8 (December 1908), p. 614.

28. Roscoe Pound, "The Need of a Sociological Jurisprudence," *The Green Bag*, October 1907, pp. 614, 615.

29. Ibid., pp. 612, 613.

30. Roscoe Pound, "Mechanical Jurisprudence," *Columbia Law Review*, Vol. 8 (December 1908), pp. 605, 606, 610, 612, 613, 618, 620, 622.

31. Richard A. Epstein, *How Progressives Rewrote the Constitution*, pp. 4–5, 39.

32. Louis D. Brandeis, "The Living Law," *Illinois Law Review*, February 1916, p. 461.

33. Ibid., p. 462.

34. Ibid., p. 464.

35. Loc cit.

36. Loc cit.

37. Ibid., p. 471.

38. John Dewey, *Liberalism and Social Action* (Amherst, New York: Prometheus Books, 2000), p. 68.

39. *Dred Scott v. Sandford*, 60 U.S. 393 (1857), at 407.

40. Ibid., at 562, 572–576.

41. *Wickard v. Filburn*, 317 U.S. 111 (1942), at 114.

42. Ibid., at 118.

43. Ibid., at 128.

44. *United Steelworkers v. Weber*, 443 U.S. 193 (1979), at 201, 202.

45. Ibid., at 222.

46. Oliver Wendell Holmes, *Collected Legal Papers*, p. 307.

47. *Adkins v. Children's Hospital*, 261 U.S. 525 (1923), at 570.

48. *Day-Brite Lighting, Inc. v. Missouri*, 342 U.S. 421 (1952), at 423.

49. *Griswold v. Connecticut*, 381 U.S. 479 (1965), at 484.

50. Michael Kinsley, "Viewpoint: Rightist Judicial Activism Rescinds a Popular Mandate," *Wall Street Journal*, February 20, 1986, p. 25.

51. Linda Greenhouse, "Justices Step In as Federalism's Referee," *New York Times*, April 28, 1995, pp. A1 ff.

52. Ruth Colker and James J. Brudney, "Dissing Congress," *Michigan Law Review*, October 2001, p. 100.

53. "Federalism and Guns in School," *Washington Post*, April 28, 1995, p. A26.

54. Joan Biskupic, "Top Court Ruling on Guns Slams Brakes on Congress," *Chicago Sun-Times*, April 28, 1995, p. 28.

55. Linda Greenhouse, "Farewell to the Old Order in the Court," *New York Times*, July 2, 1995, section 4, pp. 1 ff.

56. Cass R. Sunstein, "Tilting the Scales Rightward," *New York Times*, April 26, 2001, p. A23.

57. Cass R. Sunstein, "A Hand in the Matter," *Legal Affairs*, March-April 2003, pp. 26–30.

58. Jeffrey Rosen, "Hyperactive: How the Right Learned to Love Judicial Activism," *New Republic*, January 31, 2000, p. 20.

59. Adam Cohen, "What Chief Justice Roberts Forgot in His First Term: Judicial Modesty," *New York Times*, July 9, 2006, section 4, p. 11.

60. "The Vote on Judge Sotomayor," *New York Times*, August 3, 2009, p. A18.
61. Cass R. Sunstein, "Tilting the Scales Rightward," *New York Times*, April 26, 2001, p. A23.
62. "Inside Politics," CNN Transcripts, July 11, 2005.
63. See, for example, Anthony Lewis, "A Man Born to Act, Not to Muse," *New York Times Magazine*, June 30, 1968, pp. 9 ff.
64. Jack N. Rakove, "Mr. Meese, Meet Mr. Madison," *Atlantic Monthly*, December 1986, p. 78.
65. Antonin Scalia, *A Matter of Interpretation: Federal Courts and the Law* (Princeton: Princeton University Press, 1997), pp. 17, 45.
66. William Blackstone, *Commentaries on the Laws of England* (New York: Oceana Publications, 1966), Vol. 1, p. 59.
67. Oliver Wendell Holmes, *Collected Legal Papers*, p. 204.
68. Ibid., p. 207.
69. Mark DeWolfe Howe, editor, *Holmes-Pollock Letters: The Correspondence of Mr. Justice Holmes and Sir Frederick Pollock 1874–1932* (Cambridge, Massachusetts: Harvard University Press, 1942), Vol. 1, p. 90.
70. *Northern Securities Company v. United States*, 193 U.S. 197 (1904), at 401.
71. Robert H. Bork, *Tradition and Morality in Constitutional Law* (Washington: American Enterprise Institute, 1984), p. 7.
72. Jack N. Rakove, "Mr. Meese, Meet Mr. Madison," *Atlantic Monthly*, December 1986, p. 81.
73. Ibid., pp. 81, 82.
74. Ibid., p. 84.
75. Ronald Dworkin, *A Matter of Principle* (Cambridge, Massachusetts: Harvard University Press, 1985), pp. 40, 43, 44.
76. Ibid., p. 42.
77. Jack N. Rakove, "Mr. Meese, Meet Mr. Madison," *Atlantic Monthly*, December 1986, p. 78.
78. Stephen Macedo, *The New Right v. The Constitution* (Washington: Cato Institute, 1986), p. 10.

79. Ronald Dworkin, *A Matter of Principle*, p. 318.

80. Ibid., p. 331.

81. "The High Court Loses Restraint," *New York Times*, April 29, 1995, section 1, p. 22.

82. Mark DeWolfe Howe, editor, *Holmes–Laski Letters: The Correspondence of Mr. Justice Holmes and Harold J. Laski 1916–1935* (Cambridge, Massachusetts: Harvard University Press, 1953), Volume I, p. 752.

83. *Abrams v. United States*, 250 U.S. 616 (1919), at 629.

84. Mark DeWolfe Howe, editor, *Holmes–Laski Letters*, Volume I, p. 389.

85. Mark DeWolfe Howe, editor, *Holmes–Laski Letters*, Volume II, p. 913.

86. R.R. Palmer, *Twelve Who Ruled: The Year of the Terror in the French Revolution* (Princeton: Princeton University Press, 1989), pp. 132–133.

87. See, for example, Charles Murray, *Human Accomplishment: The Pursuit of Excellence in the Arts and Sciences, 800 B.C. to 1950* (New York: HarperCollins, 2003), pp. 92, 99, 100, 101, 258, 279, 282, 301–304, 356; Malcolm Gladwell, *Outliers: The Story of Success* (New York: Little, Brown and Co., 2008), Chapter 1; Thomas Sowell, *The Vision of the Anointed: Self-Congratulation as a Basis for Social Policy* (New York: Basic Books, 1995), pp. 35–37.

88. Linda Greenhouse, "The Year the Court Turned Right," *New York Times*, July 7, 1989, pp. A1 ff.

89. Linda Greenhouse, "Shift to Right Seen," *New York Times*, June 13, 1989, pp. A1 ff.

90. Tom Wicker, "Bush and the Blacks," *New York Times*, April 16, 1990, p. A19.

91. "A Red Herring in Black and White," *New York Times*, July 23, 1990, p. A14.

92. William T. Coleman, Jr., "A False 'Quota' Call," *Washington Post*, February 23, 1990, p. A23.

93. "A Gentler Civil Rights Approach," *Boston Globe*, August 3, 1991, p. 18.

94. "A Civil Rights Setback," *Boston Globe*, June 9, 1989, p. 16.

95. Ronald Dworkin, *Freedom's Law: The Moral Reading of the American Constitution* (Cambridge, Massachusetts: Harvard University Press, 1996), p. 157.

96. Tamar Jacoby, "A Question of Statistics," *Newsweek*, June 19, 1989, p. 58.

97. Reginald Alleyne, "Smoking Guns Are Hard to Find," *Los Angeles Times*, June 12, 1989, p. 5.

98. Howard Eglit, "The Age Discrimination in Employment Act, Title VII, and the Civil Rights Act of 1991: Three Acts and a Dog That Didn't Bark," *Wayne Law Review*, Spring 1993, p. 1190.

99. Alan Freeman, "Antidiscrimination Law: The View From 1989," *The Politics of Law: A Progressive Critique,* revised edition, edited by David Kairys (New York: Pantheon Books, 1990), p. 147.

100. Candace S. Kovacic-Fleischer, "Proving Discrimination After *Price Waterhouse* and *Wards Cove*: Semantics as Substance," *American University Law Review*, Vol. 39 (1989–1990), p. 662.

101. U.S. Equal Employment Opportunity Commission, *Legislative History of Titles VII and XI of Civil Rights Act of 1964* (Washington, D.C.: U.S. Government Printing Office, no date), pp. 3005, 3006–3007, 3160, and *passim.*

102. Ibid., p. 3015.

103. Edwin S. Mills, "The Attrition of Urban Real-Property Rights," *The Independent Review*, Fall 2007, p. 209.

104. Laurence H. Tribe, *Constitutional Choices* (Cambridge, Massachusetts: Harvard University Press, 1985), p. 187.

105. Loc. cit.

106. Will Oremus, "Bay Meadows Vote to Have Broad Repercussions," *Inside Bay Area*, April 21, 2008.

107. Leslie Fulbright, "S.F. Moves to Stem African American Exodus," *San Francisco Chronicle*, April 9, 2007, pp. A1 ff; Bureau of the Census, *1990 Census of Population: General Population Characteristics California*, 1990 CP–1–6, Section 1 of 3, pp. 27, 28, 30, 31; U.S. Census Bureau, *Profiles of General Demographic Characteristics 2000:*

2000 Census of Population and Housing, California, Table DP–1, pp. 2, 20, 39, 42.

108. See, for example, William Godwin, *Enquiry Concerning Political Justice and Its Influence on Morals and Happiness* (Toronto: University of Toronto Press, 1946), Vol. II, p. 462; John Dewey, *Human Nature and Conduct: An Introduction to Social Psychology* (New York: Modern Library, 1957), p. 18; Edward Bellamy, *Looking Backward: 2000–1887* (Boston: Houghton Mifflin, 1926), pp. 200–201.

109. James Q. Wilson and Richard J. Herrnstein, *Crime and Human Nature* (New York: Simon and Schuster, 1985), p. 409.

110. Joyce Lee Malcolm, *Guns and Violence: The English Experience* (Cambridge, Massachusetts: Harvard University Press, 2002), pp. 164–165.

111. James Q. Wilson and Richard J. Herrnstein, *Crime and Human Nature,* pp. 423–425; Joyce Lee Malcolm, *Guns and Violence,* pp. 166–168, 171–189; David Fraser, *A Land Fit for Criminals: An Insider's View of Crime, Punishment and Justice in England and Wales* (Sussex: Book Guild Publishing, 2006), pp. 352–356; Theodore Dalrymple, "Protect the Burglars of Bromsgrove!" *City Journal,* October 20, 2008.

112. Joyce Lee Malcolm, *Guns and Violence,* p. 184.

113. C. H. Rolph, "Guns and Violence," *New Statesman,* January 15, 1965, pp. 71, 72.

114. C. H. Rolph, "Who Needs a Gun?" *New Statesman,* January 16, 1970, p. 70.

115. Peter Hitchens, *A Brief History of Crime: The Decline of Order, Justice and Liberty in England* (London: Atlantic Books, 2003), p. 151.

116. Ibid., p. 166.

117. Joyce Lee Malcolm, *Guns and Violence,* p. 168.

118. Franklin E. Zimring, *The Great American Crime Decline* (New York: Oxford University Press, 2008), pp. 6, 15.

119. Department of the Treasury, Bureau of Alcohol, Tobacco & Firearms, "Commerce in Firearms in the United States," February 2000, p. 6.

120. Joyce Lee Malcolm, *Guns and Violence,* pp. 5, 204.

121. Ibid., p. 184.

122. Chris Henwood, "Council Tells Gardener: Take Down Barbed Wire In Case It Hurts Thieves Who Keep Burgling You," *Birmingham Evening Mail*, October 11, 2008, p. 9.

123. Stephan Thernstrom and Abigail Thernstrom, *America in Black and White: One Nation, Indivisible* (New York: Simon and Schuster, 1997), p. 162.

124. Joyce Lee Malcolm, *Guns and Violence*, pp. 90–91.

125. See, for example, Franklin E. Zimring, *The Great American Crime Decline*, p. 55.

126. Sidney E. Zion, "Attack on Court Heard by Warren," *New York Times*, September 10, 1965, pp. 1 ff.

127. Tom Wicker, "In the Nation: Which Law and Whose Order?" *New York Times*, October 3, 1967, p. 46.

128. "The Unkindest Cut," *The Economist*, January 3, 2009, p. 42.

129. See, for example, David Fraser, *A Land Fit for Criminals*, especially Chapters 3, 6, 7.

130. Ibid., p. xviii.

131. Fox Butterfield, "Crime Keeps on Falling, but Prisons Keep on Filling," *New York Times*, September 28, 1997, p. WK1. Earlier, Fox Butterfield said: "Oddly, during the 1960's, as crime rose, the number of Americans in prison actually declined." Fox Butterfield, "U.S. Expands Its Lead in the Rate of Imprisonment," *New York Times*, February 11, 1992, p. A16. In other words, the inverse relationship between crime and punishment seemed puzzling in both eras.

132. "Prison Nation," *New York Times*, March 10, 2008, p. A16.

133. Tom Wicker, "The Punitive Society," *New York Times*, January 12, 1991, p. 25.

134. Dirk Johnson, "More Prisons Using Iron Hand to Control Inmates," *New York Times*, November 1, 1990, p. A18.

135. David Fraser, *A Land Fit for Criminals*, p. 97; Peter Saunders and Nicole Billante, "Does Prison Work?" *Policy* (Australia), Vol. 18, No. 4 (Summer 2002–03), pp. 3–8.

136. David Fraser, *A Land Fit for Criminals*, pp. 71–73.

137. "A Nation of Jailbirds," *The Economist*, April 4, 2009, p. 40.

138. David Fraser, *A Land Fit for Criminals*, p. 72.

139. "A Nation of Jailbirds," *The Economist*, April 4, 2009, p. 40.

140. David Fraser, *A Land Fit for Criminals*, p. 109.

141. Daniel Seligman and Joyce E. Davis, "Investing in Prison," *Fortune*, April 29, 1996, p. 211.

142. David Fraser, *A Land Fit for Criminals*, p. 38; "Criminal Statistics 2004," *Home Office Statistical Bulletin*, November 2005, Table 1.2.

143. David Barrett, "Thousands of Criminals Spared Prison Go on to Offend Again," *Daily Telegraph* online (London), 20 December 2008.

144. David Fraser, *A Land Fit for Criminals*, pp. 7–8, 277–278.

145. Ibid., pp. 13–14.

146. Ibid., Chapters 6, 7.

147. James Q. Wilson and Richard J. Herrnstein, *Crime and Human Nature*, pp. 428–434.

148. Jaxon Van Derbeken, "Homicides Plummet as Police Flood Tough Areas," *San Francisco Chronicle*, July 6, 2009, pp. C1 ff.

CHAPTER 7: INTELLECTUALS AND WAR

1. Eugen Weber, *The Hollow Years: France in the 1930s* (New York: W.W. Norton, 1994), p. 5.

2. Donald Kagan, *On the Origins of War and the Preservation of Peace* (New York: Doubleday, 1995), pp. 132–133.

3. Martin Gilbert, *The First World War: A Complete History* (New York: Henry Holt, 1994), pp. 29, 34; Barbara W. Tuchman, *The Guns of August* (New York: Bonanza Books, 1982), pp. 125, 127.

4. Jonah Goldberg, *Liberal Fascism: The Secret History of the American Left from Mussolini to the Politics of Meaning* (New York: Doubleday, 2008), p. 83.

5. William E. Leuchtenburg, "Progressivism and Imperialism: The Progressive Movement and American Foreign Policy, 1898–1916," *Mississippi Valley Historical Review*, Vol. 39, No. 3 (December 1952), pp. 483–504; Jonah Goldberg, *Liberal Fascism*, pp. 106–111.

6. Herbert Croly, *The Promise of American Life* (Boston: Northeastern University Press, 1989), p. 259.

7. Ibid., p. 256.

8. William E. Leuchtenburg, "Progressivism and Imperialism: The Progressive Movement and American Foreign Policy, 1898–1916," *Mississippi Valley Historical Review*, Vol. 39, No. 3 (December 1952), pp. 486, 487, 497.

9. Herbert Croly, *The Promise of American Life*, pp. 302, 303.

10. Ibid., p. 169.

11. Jonah Goldberg, *Liberal Fascism*, p. 107.

12. Jim Powell, *Wilson's War: How Woodrow Wilson's Great Blunder Led to Hitler, Lenin, Stalin, and World War II* (New York: Crown Forum, 2005), pp. 80–81. See also Arthur S. Link, *Woodrow Wilson and the Progressive Era: 1910–1917* (New York: Harper & Brothers, 1954), Chapters 4, 5.

13. The great economist Alfred Marshall saw in Britain's attempt to starve the German population a lasting source of bitterness and a future war. Writing in 1915 to his most famous student, John Maynard Keynes, Marshall said: "I shall not live to see our next war with Germany; but you will, I expect." *Memorials of Alfred Marshall*, edited by A.C. Pigou (New York: Kelley & Millman, Inc., 1956), p. 482.

14. Woodrow Wilson, "Address to a Joint Session of Congress Calling for a Declaration of War," *Woodrow Wilson: Essential Writings and Speeches of the Scholar-President*, edited by Mario R. DiNunzio (New York: New York University Press, 2006), p. 401.

15. Ibid., p. 402.

16. Jim Powell, *Wilson's War*, p. 136.

17. Jonah Goldberg, *Liberal Fascism*, p. 105.

18. Ibid., p. 63.

19. Charles F. Howlett, *Troubled Philosopher: John Dewey and the Struggle for World Peace* (Port Washington, N.Y.: Kennikat Press, 1977), p. 20.

20. Thomas J. Knock, *To End All Wars: Woodrow Wilson and the Quest for a New World Order* (New York: Oxford University Press, 1992), pp. 77–78. Intellectuals were not alone in idolizing Woodrow Wilson.

"Across Europe there were squares, streets, railway stations and parks bearing Wilson's name." Margaret MacMillan, *Paris 1919: Six Months That Changed the World* (New York: Random House, 2002), p. 15.

21. Quoted in Daniel Patrick Moynihan, *Pandaemonium: Ethnicity in International Politics* (Oxford: Oxford University Press, 1993), pp. 81, 82.

22. Ibid., p. 83.

23. David C. Smith, *H.G. Wells: Desperately Mortal* (New Haven: Yale University Press, 1986), p. 221.

24. H.G. Wells, *The War That Will End War* (New York: Duffield & Company, 1914), p. 54.

25. Daniel Patrick Moynihan, *Pandaemonium*, p. 100.

26. Woodrow Wilson, "Address to a Joint Session of Congress Calling for a Declaration of War," *Woodrow Wilson*, edited by Mario R. DiNunzio, p. 402.

27. Daniel J. Flynn, *A Conservative History of the American Left* (New York: Crown Forum, 2008), p. 178.

28. Jonah Goldberg, *Liberal Fascism*, pp. 108–111, *passim*.

29. Ibid., pp. 112–113.

30. John Dewey, *Characters and Events: Popular Essays in Social and Political Philosophy*, edited by Joseph Ratner (New York: Henry Holt and Company, 1929), Vol. II, p. 517.

31. Eugen Weber, *The Hollow Years*, p. 11.

32. Alistair Horne, *To Lose A Battle: France 1940* (New York: Penguin Books, 1990), p. 49.

33. Eugen Weber, *The Hollow Years*, pp. 13, 14.

34. Ibid., pp. 18, 24.

35. Derek W. Lawrence, "The Ideological Writings of Jean Giono (1937–1946)," *The French Review*, Vol. 45, No. 3 (February 1972), p. 589.

36. Robert Shepherd, *A Class Divided: Appeasement and the Road to Munich, 1938* (London: Macmillan, 1988), p. 17.

37. Martin Ceadel, *Semi-Detached Idealists: The British Peace Movement and International Relations, 1854–1945* (Oxford: Oxford University Press, 2000), p. 242.

38. Harold J. Laski, *A Grammar of Politics* (London: George Allen & Unwin, Ltd., 1925), p. 587.

39. John Dewey, "Outlawing Peace by Discussing War," *New Republic*, May 16, 1928, p. 370; John Dewey, "If War Were Outlawed," *New Republic*, April 25, 1923, p. 235

40. Robert Shepherd, *A Class Divided*, p. 50.

41. Martin Ceadel, *Semi-Detached Idealists*, p. 359.

42. Martin Ceadel, *Pacifism in Britain 1914–1945: The Defining of a Faith* (Oxford: Clarendon Press, 1980), p. 253.

43. Robert Skidelsky, *John Maynard Keynes*, Vol. 3: *Fighting for Britain 1937–1946* (New York: Viking Penguin, 2001), p. 34.

44. Bertrand Russell, *Which Way to Peace?* (London: Michael Joseph, Ltd., 1937), p. 179.

45. H.G. Wells, *The Anatomy of Frustration: A Modern Synthesis* (New York: The Macmillan Co., 1936), p. 102.

46. Kingsley Martin, "Russia and Mr. Churchill," *New Statesmanship: An Anthology*, edited by Edward Hyams (London: Longmans, 1963), p. 70.

47. Kingsley Martin, "The Educational Role of the Press," *The Educational Role of the Press*, edited by Henry de Jouvenel, et al (Paris: International Institute of Intellectual Co–Operation, 1934), pp. 29–30.

48. When Churchill in 1937— two years before the beginning of the Second World War— advocated doubling the size of the Royal Air Force, the leader of the Liberal Party declared this to be the language of Malays "running amok." A year later, when Churchill again rose in Parliament to chastise the government for not rearming, this was the response: "An embarrassed silence greeted Churchill as he ended. Then members anxious to turn to more pleasant thoughts rattled their papers, stood, and shuffled out to the lobby, many heading for tea. One member told his Visitor's Gallery guest, Virginia Cowles, "It was the usual Churchill filibuster— he likes to rattle the saber and he does it

jolly well but you have to take it with a grain of salt." This was one year before the Second World War began. James C. Humes, *Churchill: Speaker of the Century* (New York: Stein and Day, 1982), p. 175.

49. David James Fisher, **Romain Rolland and the Politics of Intellectual Engagement** (Berkeley: University of California Press, 1988), pp. 61–65.

50. "Ask League to Act to End Army Draft," *New York Times*, August 29, 1926, p. E1.

51. The book was written by H.C. Engelbrecht and F.C. Hanighen. See Robert Skidelsky, **John Maynard Keynes**, Vol. 3: **Fighting For Britain 1937–1946**, p. 34.

52. Charles F. Howlett, *Troubled Philosopher*, p. 134.

53. "Romain Rolland Calls for a Congress against War," *New Republic*, July 6, 1932, p. 210.

54. H.G. Wells, *The Work, Wealth and Happiness of Mankind* (Garden City, N.Y.: Doubleday, Doran & Co., Inc., 1931), Vol. II, p. 669.

55. Harold J. Laski, "If I Were Dictator," *The Nation*, January 6, 1932, p. 15.

56. Aldous Huxley, *Aldous Huxley's Hearst Essays*, edited by James Sexton (New York: Garland Publishing, Inc., 1994), pp. 9–10.

57. J.B. Priestley, "The Public and the Idea of Peace," *Challenge to Death*, edited by Storm Jameson (New York: E.P. Dutton & Co., Inc., 1935), p. 319.

58. E.M. Forster, "Notes on the Way," *Time and Tide*, June 2, 1934, p. 696; E.M. Forster, "Notes on the Way," *Time and Tide*, November 23, 1935, p. 1703.

59. Charles F. Howlett, *Troubled Philosopher*, pp. 55–56.

60. Donald Kagan, *On the Origins of War and the Preservation of Peace*, p. 314.

61. "Romain Rolland Calls for a Congress against War," *New Republic*, July 6, 1932, p. 210.

62. Georges Duhamel, *The French Position*, translated by Basil Collier (London: Dent, 1940), p. 107.

63. "A Speech by Anatole France," *The Nation*, September 6, 1919, p. 349.

64. Mona L. Siegel, *The Moral Disarmament of France: Education, Pacifism, and Patriotism, 1914–1940* (Cambridge: Cambridge University Press, 2004), pp. 127, 132.

65. Ibid., p. 146.

66. Daniel J. Sherman, *The Construction of Memory in Interwar France* (Chicago: University of Chicago Press, 1999), p. 300.

67. Mona L. Siegel, *The Moral Disarmament of France*, p. 160.

68. Ernest R. May, *Strange Victory: Hitler's Conquest of France* (New York: Hill and Wang, 2000), p. 283.

69. Mona L. Siegel, *The Moral Disarmament of France*, p. 217.

70. Malcolm Scott, *Mauriac: The Politics of a Novelist* (Edinburgh: Scottish Academic Press, 1980), p. 79.

71. Winston Churchill, *Churchill Speaks 1897–1963: Collected Speeches in Peace & War*, edited by Robert Rhodes James (New York: Chelsea House, 1980), p. 554.

72. Alistair Horne, *To Lose A Battle*, p. 189.

73. Ernest R. May, *Strange Victory*, pp. 18–23.

74. See, for example, B.H. Liddell Hart, *History of the Second World War* (New York: Paragon Books, 1979), pp. 35–36; Ernest R. May, *Strange Victory*, pp. 5–6, 278.

75. Ernest R. May, *Strange Victory*, pp. 103–106. See also Winston S. Churchill, *The Second World War*, Vol. I: *The Gathering Storm* (Boston: Houghton Mifflin Co., 1983), p. 168.

76. Ernest R. May, *Strange Victory*, pp. 215, 220, 245, 252, 276–277, 278, 287, 289, 439, 454, 455, 456.

77. Ibid., p. 17.

78. Ibid., pp. 17, 280.

79. William L. Shirer, *Berlin Diary: The Journal of a Foreign Correspondent 1934–1941* (Tess Press, 2004), pp. 167, 189, 201, 219, 242, 260, 332–333, 345, 347, 348, 349, 372. Hitler shrewdly anticipated and encouraged French quiescence. Shirer in Berlin wrote in his diary on September 3: "The High Command lets it be known that on the western front the Germans won't fire *first* against the French." Ibid., p. 163.

80. Kingsley Martin, "War and the Next Generation," *New Statesman and Nation*, April 11, 1931, p. 240.

81. Bertrand Russell, *Sceptical Essays* (New York: W.W. Norton & Co., Inc., 1928), p. 184.

82. Martin Ceadel, *Pacifism in Britain 1914–1945*, p. 105.

83. Ibid., pp. 106, 131; André Gide, *The André Gide Reader*, edited by David Littlejohn (New York: Alfred A. Knopf, 1971), pp. 804–805.

84. Martin Ceadel, *Pacifism in Britain 1914–1945*, p. 137.

85. Winston Churchill, *Churchill Speaks 1897–1963*, edited by Robert Rhodes James, p. 645. Earlier Churchill said: "Many people think that the best way to escape war is to dwell upon its horrors, and to imprint them vividly upon the minds of the younger generation. They flaunt the grisly photographs before their eyes. They fill their ears with tales of carnage. They dilate upon the ineptitude of generals and admirals. They denounce the crime and insensate folly of human strife." Ibid., p. 586.

86. David C. Smith, *H.G. Wells*, pp. 317, 321.

87. H.G. Wells, *The Anatomy of Frustration*, p. 98.

88. J.B. Priestley, "The Public and the Idea of Peace," *Challenge to Death*, edited by Storm Jameson, p. 316.

89. "Spreading the Spirit of Peace," *The Times* (London), August 28, 1936, p. 8.

90. Ernest R. May, *Strange Victory*, pp. 103–106.

91. William Godwin, *Enquiry Concerning Political Justice and Its Influence on Morals and Happiness* (Toronto: University of Toronto Press, 1946), Vol. II, pp. 144–145.

92. Bertrand Russell, *Which Way to Peace?*, p. 139.

93. Ibid., pp. 140, 144.

94. Ibid., pp. 144–145.

95. Raymond Leslie Buell, "Even in France They Differ on Armaments," *New York Times*, February 21, 1932, Book Review section, pp. 10 ff.

96. Bertrand Russell, *Which Way to Peace?*, pp. 99, 122.

97. Kingsley Martin, "Dictators and Democrats," *New Statesman and Nation*, May 7, 1938, p. 756.

98. Kingsley Martin, "The Inescapable Facts," *New Statesman and Nation*, March 19, 1938, p. 468.

99. Richard J. Golsan, *French Writers and the Politics of Complicity: Crises of Democracy in the 1940s and 1990s* (Baltimore: Johns Hopkins University Press, 2006), p. 83.

100. Simone Weil, *Formative Writings 1929–1941*, edited and translated by Dorothy Tuck McFarland and Wilhelmina Van Ness (Amherst: University of Massachusetts Press, 1987), p. 266.

101. Mona L. Siegel, *The Moral Disarmament of France*, pp. 218–219. The teachers' union encouraged other teachers to join the resistance. Among other things, this indicated that these teachers were not lacking in personal patriotism, even though they had for years attempted to blend internationalism and patriotism when teaching the young, producing the effect of the proverbial trumpet that makes an uncertain sound.

102. Paul Johnson, *Modern Times: The World From the Twenties to the Nineties* (New York: Perennial Classics, 2001), p. 348.

103. Robert Shepherd, *A Class Divided*, p. 41.

104. Harold Laski, "The People Wait for a Lead," *Daily Herald*, January 4, 1937, p. 10.

105. Talbot C. Imlay, *Facing the Second World War: Strategy, Politics, and Economics in Britain and France 1938–1940* (New York: Oxford University Press, 2003), pp. 199, 303–304; Robert Shepherd, *A Class Divided*, pp. 102–103; Robert Paul Shay, Jr., *British Rearmament in the Thirties: Politics and Profits* (Princeton: Princeton University Press, 1977), pp. 217–218; Tom Buchanan, *Britain and the Spanish Civil War* (New York: Cambridge University Press, 1997), pp. 78–79.

106. "Trade Unionism and Democracy," *New Statesman and Nation*, September 10, 1938, p. 369.

107. Charles F. Howlett, *Troubled Philosopher*, p. 77.

108. Oswald Garrison Villard, "Issues and Men: The President's Disarmament Opportunity," *The Nation*, January 31, 1934, p. 119.

109. William Manchester, *American Caesar: Douglas MacArthur 1880–1964* (Boston: Little, Brown and Company, 1978), pp. 154, 156; Matthew F.

Holland, *Eisenhower Between the Wars: The Making of a General and Statesman* (Westport, CT: Praeger, 2001), pp. 171–172.

110. Charles F. Howlett, *Troubled Philosopher*, pp. 55–56.

111. "The Way of Appeasement," *The Times* (London), November 25, 1937, p. 15.

112. Eugen Weber, *The Hollow Years*, p. 241.

113. Winston Churchill, *Churchill Speaks 1897–1963*, edited by Robert Rhodes James, pp. 624, 627.

114. Winston S. Churchill, *The Second World War*, Vol. I: *The Gathering Storm*, p. 216.

115. Ibid., pp. 216–217.

116. Eugen Weber, *The Hollow Years*, p. 126.

117. Ernest R. May, *Strange Victory*, p. 138.

118. Eugen Weber, *The Hollow Years*, p. 127.

119. Ibid., p. 126.

120. Ibid., p. 128.

121. Ibid., pp. 102, 107–108.

122. Ian Kershaw, *Making Friends with Hitler: Lord Londonderry, the Nazis and the Road to World War II* (New York: Penguin Press, 2004), pp. 28, 30, 31.

123. H.J. Laski, "Hitler— Just a Figurehead," *Daily Herald*, November 19, 1932, p. 8.

124. Ian Kershaw, *Making Friends with Hitler*, pp. 29–30.

125. John Evelyn Wrench, *Geoffrey Dawson and Our Times* (London: Hutchinson, 1955), p. 361. In 1935, American foreign correspondent William L. Shirer recorded in his diary that a *Times* of London correspondent "has complained to me in private that the *Times* does not print all he sends, that it does not want to hear too much of the bad side of Nazi Germany and apparently has been captured by the pro-Nazis in London." William L. Shirer, *Berlin Diary*, p. 33. Dawson's filtering of the news extended to his coverage of German troops marching into Czechoslovakia's Sudetenland in 1938, where the predominantly German population warmly greeted them, while the Czechs fled from Nazi rule. "Every day there were photographs of the

triumphant German troops marching into the Sudetenland. . . In the photographs the joyful welcome accorded to the German soldiers bore witness to the apparent justice of the Munich settlement. Photographs of refugees *had* reached *The Times*. Dawson refused to print them." Martin Gilbert and Richard Gott, *The Appeasers* (Boston: Houghton Mifflin Co., 1963), p. 191.

126. Winston S. Churchill, *The Second World War*, Volume I: *The Gathering Storm*, p. 73.

127. William L. Shirer, *The Rise and Fall of the Third Reich: A History of Nazi Germany* (New York: Simon and Schuster, 1960), pp. 292–294. See also William L. Shirer, *Berlin Diary*, pp. 44–45.

128. William L. Shirer, *The Rise and Fall of the Third Reich*, p. 293.

129. Loc. cit. The conclusion that a German retreat could have spelled the end of the Nazi regime was also shared by Winston Churchill. See Winston S. Churchill, *The Second World War*, Vol. I: *The Gathering Storm*, p. 194. Although a later historian questioned this conclusion (Ernest R. May, *Strange Victory*, pp. 36–38), William L. Shirer pointed out, contrary to Professor May, that the German troops in the Rhineland were to be ordered to beat a hasty retreat back over the Rhine in the event that French troops intervened. The mere concentration of French troops near the German border, to reinforce the Maginot Line, caused the top German generals to urge Hitler to pull their troops back out of the Rhineland, which Hitler refused to do. (William L. Shirer, *The Rise and Fall of the Third Reich*, pp. 290–291, 293).

130. Winston S. Churchill, *The Second World War*, Vol. I: *The Gathering Storm*, pp. 196–197.

131. Eugen Weber, *The Hollow Years*, p. 23; Ernest R. May, *Strange Victory*, pp. 142–143.

132. Ernest R. May, *Strange Victory*, pp. 142–143.

133. Winston S. Churchill, *The Second World War*, Vol. I: *The Gathering Storm*, p. 197.

134. "Harold Macmillan later observed of the period immediately following Munich, 'The whole world seemed united in gratitude to the man who had prevented war. No wonder the Prime Minister lived in an exalted, almost intoxicated mood. To question his authority was treason; to deny his inspiration almost blasphemy.'" Robert Shepherd, *A Class Divided*, p. 225. See also pp. 1–5.

135. Eugen Weber, *The Hollow Years*, pp. 175, 260.

136. Ibid., p. 261.

137. Ernest R. May, *Strange Victory*, p. 7.

138. Winston Churchill, *Churchill Speaks 1897–1963*, edited by Robert Rhodes James, p. 809.

139. "Washington in August, I'm told, had almost given Britain up as lost and was in a state of jitters for fear the British navy would fall into Hitler's hands and thus place the American eastern seaboard in great danger." William L. Shirer, *Berlin Diary*, pp. 444–445. Winston Churchill himself had warned President Franklin D. Roosevelt in May 1940 that if he— Churchill— and his government were replaced by others who would "parley amid the ruins" with a victorious Germany, the British fleet would be "the sole remaining bargaining counter" they could use to try to win "the best terms they could for the surviving inhabitants." Winston S. Churchill, *The Second World War*, Vol. II: *Their Finest Hour* (Boston: Houghton Mifflin, 1949), pp. 56–57.

140. "At the climax of what he called the Battle of Britain, Churchill, on a September Sunday afternoon, drove with his wife from the prime minister's country residence at Chequers to Uxbridge, the underground nerve center of the Royal Air Force. On the wall were electronic maps revealing the disposition of the twenty-five squadrons of the RAF. As discs began to dot the electrified chart indicating each successive wave of German aircraft swooping in from France, the Fighter Command released its squadrons one by one to meet each onslaught. Soon the red lights signaled that all 25 squadrons were in the air. By then the British

fighters were winging on their last ounce of fuel and firing their last round of ammunition.

"'What other reserves have we?' asked Churchill.
"'There are none,' the air marshal answered.
"Silence descended on the room."

James C. Humes, *Churchill*, p. 191.

141. Victor Davis Hanson, *Carnage and Culture: Landmark Battles in the Rise of Western Power* (New York: Doubleday, 2001), Chapter 9.

142. "Policy for a National Opposition," *New Statesman and Nation*, October 22, 1938, p. 596.

143. "Passing the Buck," *New Statesman and Nation*, February 25, 1939, p. 272.

CHAPTER 8: INTELLECTUALS AND WAR: REPEATING HISTORY

1. A. Solzhenitsyn, "Nobel Lecture in Literature, 1970," *Literature 1968–1980: Nobel Lectures Including Presentation Speeches and Laureates' Biographies*, edited by Tore Frangsmyr and Sture Allen (Singapore: World Scientific, 1993), p. 42.

2. "Victory in Europe," *Time*, May 14, 1945, p. 17.

3. David Halberstam, *The Fifties* (New York: Random House, 1993), p. 46.

4. Victor Davis Hanson, "If the Dead Could Talk," *Hoover Digest*, 2004, No. 4, pp. 17–18.

5. Bertrand Russell, "The International Bearings of Atomic Warfare," *United Empire*, Vol. XXXIX, No. 1 (January–February 1948), p. 21. See also Bertrand Russell, "International Government," *The New Commonwealth*, January 1948, p. 80.

6. "Fight Before Russia Finds Atom Bomb," *The Observer* (London), November 21, 1948, p. 1. After his comments were reported on both sides of the Atlantic, Bertrand Russell in a letter to *The Times* of London said: "I did not, as has been reported, urge immediate war with Russia. I did urge that the democracies should be *prepared* to use force if necessary, and that their readiness to do so should be made perfectly

clear to Russia, for it has become obvious that the Communists, like the Nazis, can only be halted in their attempts to dominate Europe and Asia by determined and combined resistance by every means in our power, not excluding military means if Russia continues to refuse all compromise." "Lord Russell's Address," *The Times* (London), November 30, 1948, p. 5.

7. Joseph Alsop, "Matter of Fact," *Washington Post and Times Herald*, February 19, 1958, p. A15.

8. Paul Johnson, *Intellectuals* (New York: Harper & Row, 1988), pp. 208, 209, 210.

9. Steven F. Hayward, *Greatness: Reagan, Churchill, and the Making of Extraordinary Leaders* (New York: Crown Forum, 2005), p. 147.

10. Peter Braestrup, *Big Story: How the American Press and Television Reported and Interpreted the Crisis of Tet 1968 in Vietnam and Washington* (Garden City, NY: Anchor Books, 1978), pp. 49–54.

11. Ibid., pp. ix–xi.

12. Jim and Sybil Stockdale, *In Love and War: The Story of a Family's Ordeal and Sacrifice During the Vietnam Years* (New York: Harper & Row, 1984), p. 181.

13. Stanley Karnow, "Giap Remembers," *New York Times Magazine*, June 24, 1990, p. 36.

14. Ibid., p. 62.

15. "How North Vietnam Won the War," *Wall Street Journal*, August 3, 1995, p. A8.

16. Loc. cit.

17. Arthur Schlesinger, Jr., "A Middle Way Out of Vietnam," *New York Times*, September 18, 1966, p. 112.

18. "Needed: A Vietnam Strategy," *New York Times*, March 24, 1968, section 4, p. 16.

19. Drew Pearson, "Gen. Westmoreland Ouster Is Urged," *Washington Post, Times Herald*, February 10, 1968, p. B11.

20. Kathleen J. Turner, *Lyndon Johnson's Dual War: Vietnam and the Press* (Chicago: University of Chicago Press, 1985), p. 231.

21. "The Logic of the Battlefield," *Wall Street Journal*, February 23, 1968, p. 14.

22. Peter Braestrup, *Big Story*, pp. 465–468; Victor Davis Hanson, *Carnage and Culture: Landmark Battles in the Rise of Western Power* (New York: Doubleday, 2001), pp. 404–405.

23. Walter Lippmann, "Negotiated Settlement in Vietnam— It Makes Sense," *Los Angeles Times*, February 12, 1967, p. F7; Arthur Schlesinger, Jr., "A Middle Way Out of Vietnam," *New York Times*, September 18, 1966, pp. 111–112.

24. Peter Braestrup, *Big Story*, pp. ix–xi.

25. Walter Lippmann, "The Vietnam Debate," *Washington Post, Times Herald*, February 18, 1965, p. A21.

26. Walter Lippmann, "'Defeat,'" *Newsweek*, March 11, 1968, p. 25.

27. Joseph Kraft, "Khesanh Situation Now Shows Viet Foe Makes Strategy Work," *Washington Post, Times Herald*, February 1, 1968, p. A21.

28. Richard Parker, *John Kenneth Galbraith: His Life, His Politics, His Economics* (Chicago: University of Chicago Press, 2005), pp. 432–433.

29. Victor Davis Hanson, *Carnage and Culture*, p. 425.

30. See, for example, Peter Braestrup, *Big Story*, Chapter 6; Victor Davis Hanson, *Carnage and Culture*, pp. 393, 395.

31. "The My Lai Massacre," *Time*, November 28, 1969, pp. 17–19; "Cite Pilot for Valor at My Lai," *Chicago Tribune*, November 29, 1969, p. 8.

32. Peter Braestrup, *Big Story*, p. 24.

33. B.G. Burkett and Glenna Whitley, *Stolen Valor: How the Vietnam Generation Was Robbed of Its Heroes and Its History* (Dallas: Verity Press, 1998), p. 44.

34. Victor Davis Hanson, *Carnage and Culture*, pp. 422–423.

35. B.G. Burkett and Glenna Whitley, *Stolen Valor*, Chapters 4–5, 19.

36. Victor Davis Hanson, *Carnage and Culture*, p. 393.

37. Loc. cit.

38. Ibid., pp. 394–398.

39. Leslie Cauley and Milo Geyelin, "Ex-Green Beret Sues CNN, Time Over Retracted Nerve-Gas Report," *Wall Street Journal*, August 7, 1998, p. 1.

40. Albert L. Kraus, "Two Kinds of Warfare," *New York Times*, February 14, 1968, p. 61.

41. Victor Davis Hanson, *Carnage and Culture*, p. 418.

42. Winston Churchill, *Churchill Speaks 1897–1963: Collected Speeches in Peace & War*, edited by Robert Rhodes James (New York: Chelsea House, 1980), p. 881.

43. "Churchill Visit Scored," *New York Times*, March 7, 1946, p. 5.

44. "Mr. Churchill's Plea," *Chicago Daily Tribune*, March 7, 1946, p. 18.

45. Marquis Childs, "Churchill's Speech," *Washington Post*, March 6, 1946, p. 8.

46. "Press Reaction to Churchill Plan For Closer U.S. Ties With Britain," *United States News*, March 15, 1946, p. 39; Walter Lippmann, "Mr. Churchill's Speech," *Washington Post*, March 7, 1946, p. 11; "Let's Hang Together— Churchill," *Los Angeles Times*, March 7, 1946, p. A4.

47. "Europe's Capitals Stirred by Speech," *New York Times*, March 7, 1946, p. 5; "Mr. Churchill's Speech," *The Times* (London), March 6, 1946, p. 5.

48. Neville Chamberlain, *In Search of Peace* (New York: G.P. Putnam's Sons, 1939), p. 288.

49. John F. Kennedy, *John F. Kennedy: Containing the Public Messages, Speeches, and Statements of the President, 1961* (Washington: United States Government Printing Office, 1962), p. 2.

50. Neville Chamberlain, *In Search of Peace*, pp. 34, 40, 120, 209, 216, 230, 240, 242, 250, 271. The same idea, in different words, recurs repeatedly elsewhere in the same book.

51. Writing in his diary on August 31, 1939— the day before the German invasion of Poland that set off the Second World War— American foreign correspondent in Berlin, William L. Shirer, said: "Everybody against the war. People talking openly. How can a country go into a major war with a population so dead against it?" William L. Shirer,

Berlin Diary: The Journal of a Foreign Correspondent 1934–1941 (Tess Press, 2004), p. 153.

52. Charles F. Howlett, *Troubled Philosopher: John Dewey and the Struggle for World Peace* (Port Washington, NY: Kennikat Press, 1977), p. 53.

53. John Dewey, *Characters and Events: Popular Essays in Social and Political Philosophy*, edited by Joseph Ratner (New York: Henry Holt and Company, 1929), Vol. I, pp. 199, 201. (This was a reprint of an essay by Dewey that was first published in 1922).

54. Neville Chamberlain, *In Search of Peace*, pp. 119, 132, 198.

55. Ibid., pp. 53, 174, 208, 251–252.

56. Loc. cit.

57. See, for example, Tom Wicker, "2 Dangerous Doctrines," *New York Times*, March 15, 1983, p. A25; Strobe Talbott, "Behind the Bear's Angry Growl," *Time*, May 21, 1984, pp. 24, 27; Anthony Lewis, "Onward, Christian Soldiers," *New York Times*, March 10, 1983, p. A27; Colman McCarthy, "The Real Reagan: Can He See the Forest for the Trees?" *Washington Post*, March 27, 1983, p. G7; TRB, "Constitutional Questions," *New Republic*, March 28, 1983, p. 4; "The Lord and the Freeze," *New York Times*, March 11, 1983, p. A30.

58. Dinesh D'Souza, *Ronald Reagan: How an Ordinary Man Became an Extraordinary Leader* (New York: The Free Press, 1997), p. 189.

59. Ronald Reagan, *An American Life* (New York: Simon and Schuster, 1990), pp. 680–681.

60. Ibid., p. 683.

61. Ibid., pp. 677, 679.

62. William Raspberry, "Why the Freeze Is on the Ballot," *Washington Post*, October 29, 1982, p. A29.

63. Anthony Lewis, "The Diabolical Russians," *New York Times*, November 18, 1985, p. A21.

64. Tom Wicker, "30 Years of Futility," *New York Times*, November 22, 1985, p. A35.

65. George F. Kennan, "First Things First at the Summit," *New York Times*, November 3, 1985, section 4, p. 21.

66. Colman McCarthy, "The Disarming, Modest Manner of Alva Myrdal," *Washington Post*, October 24, 1982, p. H8.

67. "Voters' Real Opportunity to Help Stop the Nuclear Arms Race," *New York Times*, November 1, 1982, p. A18.

68. Adam Clymer, "Strong 1984 Role Vowed by Kennedy," *New York Times*, February 6, 1983, p. 28.

69. Margot Hornblower, "Votes Arms Freeze; 27 For, 9 Against Resolution," *Washington Post*, March 9, 1983, pp. A1 ff.

70. "'The Best Way to End the Nuclear Arms Race,'" *New York Times*, March 16, 1983, p. A26.

71. Helen Dewar, "Senate Rejects Arms Freeze; Debt Ceiling Rise Voted Down," *Washington Post*, November 1, 1983, pp. A1 ff.

72. See, for example, Mona Charen, *Useful Idiots: How Liberals Got It Wrong in the Cold War and Still Blame America First* (New York: Perennial, 2004), pp. 110–115.

73. "SDI, Chernobyl Helped End Cold War, Conference Told," *Washington Post*, February 27, 1993, p. A17.

74. Herbert I. London, *Armageddon in the Classroom: An Examination of Nuclear Education* (Lanham, MD: University Press of America, 1987), p. vii.

75. Mona L. Siegel, *The Moral Disarmament of France: Education, Pacifism, and Patriotism, 1914–1940* (Cambridge: Cambridge University Press, 2004), p. 80.

76. National Education Association, *NEA Handbook 1999–2000* (Washington: National Education Association, 1999), p. 343.

77. National Education Association, *NEA Handbook 1980–81* (Washington: National Education Association, 1980), p. 244.

78. National Educational Association, *NEA Handbook 1982–83* (Washington: National Education Association, 1982), p. 237.

79. National Education Association, *NEA Handbook 1985–86* (Washington: National Education Association, 1985), p. 247.

80. Loc. cit.

81. National Education Association, *Proceedings of the Sixty–First Representative Assembly, 1982* (Washington: National Education Association, 1983), p. 62.

82. National Education Association, *Proceedings of the Sixty–Fourth Representative Assembly, 1985* (Washington: National Education Association, 1986), pp. 107–108; Carl Luty, "Thinking the Unthinkable. . . Thoughtfully," *NEA Today*, March 1983, pp. 10–11.

83. Mona L. Siegel, *The Moral Disarmament of France*, p. 136.

84. National Education Association, *NEA Handbook 1982–83*, p. 237.

85. "Statement of Mr. Willard McGuire," *Twelfth Special Session, United Nations General Assembly*, June 25, 1982, A/S–12/AC.1/PV.7, p. 12.

86. National Education Association, *Proceedings of the Sixty-Third Representative Assembly, 1984* (Washington: National Education Association, 1985), p. 10.

87. Keith Geiger, "The Peace Dividend: Meeting America's Needs," *NEA Today*, March 1990, p. 2.

88. Keith Geiger, "A Time for Hope," *Washington Post*, December 23, 1990, p. C4.

89. Robert D. Novak, *The Prince of Darkness: 50 Years Reporting in Washington* (New York: Crown Forum, 2007), p. 432.

90. Tom Wicker, "The War Option," *New York Times*, October 31, 1990, p. A25.

91. Anthony Lewis, "The Argument for War," *New York Times*, December 14, 1990, p. A39.

92. Barton Gellman, "How Many Americas Would Die in War with Iraq?" *Washington Post*, January 6, 1991, p. A21.

93. Donald Kagan, "Colin Powell's War," *Commentary*, June 1995, p. 45.

94. Maureen Dowd, "Monkey on a Tiger," *New York Times*, January 6, 2007, p. A15.

95. Paul Krugman, "Quagmire of the Vanities," *New York Times*, January 8, 2007, p. A19.

96. "A Detached Debate; Have the Senators Arguing over Iraq War Resolutions Read the National Intelligence Estimate?" *Washington Post*, February 6, 2007, p. A16.

97. "The One that Brung Him," *St. Louis Post-Dispatch*, July 5, 2007, p. B8.

98. Ron Walters, "Bush Won't Face Truth about the War in Iraq," *Philadelphia Tribune*, January 21, 2007, p. 6A.

99. "Funeral Surge," *New Republic*, February 12, 2007, p. 7.

100. Jon Ward, "Democrats Ready to Fight New War Plan," *Washington Times*, January 11, 2007, p. A1; *Congressional Record: Senate*, January 30, 2007, p. S1322; Shailagh Murray, "Obama Bill Sets Date for Troop Withdrawal," *Washington Post*, January 31, 2007, p. A4.

101. Jon Ward, "Democrats Ready to Fight New War Plan," *Washington Times*, January 11, 2007, p. A1.

102. *Congressional Record: Senate*, January 18, 2007, p. S722.

103. Jon Ward, "Kennedy Proposal Uncovers Party Rift; Leave Iraq Now vs. Slow Retreat," *Washington Times*, January 10, 2007, p. A1.

104. Eric Pfeiffer, "Pelosi Threatens to Reject Funds for Troop Surge," *Washington Times*, January 8, 2007, p. A1.

105. Jon Ward, "Democrats Ready to Fight New War Plan," *Washington Times*, January 11, 2007, p. A1.

106. Michael E. O'Hanlon and Jason H. Campbell, *Iraq Index: Tracking Variables of Reconstruction & Security in Post-Saddam Iraq* (http://www.brookings.edu/iraqindex), May 28, 2009, pp. 5, 14.

107. "Peace Talks Now," *Los Angeles Times*, June 12, 2007, p. A20.

108. Paul Krugman, "Snow Job in the Desert," *New York Times*, September 3, 2007, p. A13.

109. Frank Rich, "As the Iraqis Stand Down, We'll Stand Up," *New York Times*, September 9, 2007, section 4, p. 14.

110. Jason Campbell, et al., "The States of Iraq and Afghanistan," *New York Times*, March 20, 2009, p. A27.

111. Michael E. O'Hanlon and Kenneth M. Pollack, "A War We Just Might Win," *New York Times*, July 30, 2007, p. A17.

112. Paul Krugman, "A Surge, and Then a Stab," *New York Times*, September 14, 2007, p. A21.

113. Alan Nathan, "Slamming the Messenger," *Washington Times*, September 18, 2007, p. A17.

114. Farah Stockman, "Intelligence Calls Iraq's Government Precarious," *Boston Globe*, August 24, 2007, p. A1.

115. Advertisement, "General Petraeus or General Betray Us?" *New York Times*, September 10, 2007, p. A25.

116. Howard Kurtz, "New York Times Says It Violated Policies Over MoveOn Ad," *Washington Post*, September 24, 2007, p. A8.

117. Kathy Kiely, "Senators Have Their Say During Marathon Hearings; 'Take Off Your Rosy Glasses,' General Told in 10 Hours of Inquiries," *USA Today*, September 12, 2007, p. 6A.

118. Loc. cit.

119. Elisabeth Bumiller, "A General Faces Questions from Five Potential Bosses," *New York Times*, September 12, 2007, p. A10.

120. S. A. Miller, "Petraeus' Integrity under Fire on Hill," *Washington Times*, September 10, 2007, p. A1.

121. Susan Page, "A Mixed Reception, with No Sign of Consensus on War," *USA Today*, September 11, 2007, p. 1A.

122. Frank Rich, "Will the Democrats Betray Us?" *New York Times*, September 16, 2007, section 4, p. 11.

123. Susan Page, "A Mixed Reception, with No Sign of Consensus on War," *USA Today*, September 11, 2007, p. 1A.

124. Dan Frosch and James Dao, "A Military Deception, Made Easier by a Reluctance to Ask Questions," *New York Times*, June 8, 2009, p. A10.

125. Diana B. Henriques, "Creditors Press Troops Despite Relief Act," *New York Times*, March 28, 2005, pp. A1 ff; Dan Barry, "A Teenage Soldier's Goodbyes on the Road to Over There," *New York Times*, March 4, 2007, section 1, pp. 1 ff.

126. Eric Schmitt, "Medal of Honor to Be Awarded to Soldier Killed in Iraq, a First," *New York Times*, March 30, 2005, p. A13; Sarah Abruzzese, "Bush Gives Medal of Honor to Slain Navy Seals Member," *New York Times*, April 9, 2008, p. A14; Raymond Hernandez, "A Protector As a Child, Honored As a Hero," *New York Times*, October 22, 2007, p. B1.

127. See, for example, John F. Burns, "Pillagers Strip Iraqi Museum of Its Treasure," *New York Times*, April 13, 2003, pp. A1 ff; "Lawlessness in

Iraq Puts U.S. Military Gains at Risk," *USA Today*, April 14, 2003, p. 12A; Maria Puente, "The Looting of Iraq's Past," *USA Today*, April 15, 2003, p. 7D; Douglas Jehl and Elizabeth Becker, "Experts' Pleas to Pentagon Didn't Save Museum," *New York Times*, April 16, 2003, p. B5; Constance Lowenthal and Stephen Urice, "An Army for Art," *New York Times*, April 17, 2003, p. A25; Frank Rich, "And Now: 'Operation Iraqi Looting,'" *New York Times*, April 27, 2003, section 2, pp. 1 ff; Andrew Gumbel and David Keys, "The Iraq Conflict: U.S. Blamed for Failure to Stop Sacking of Museum," *The Independent* (London), April 14, 2003, p. 6.

128. William Booth and Guy Gugliotta, "All Along, Most Iraqi Relics Were 'Safe and Sound,'" *Washington Post*, June 9, 2003, p. A12; Charles Krauthammer, "Hoaxes, Hype and Humiliation," *Washington Post*, June 13, 2003, p. A29; Matthew Bogdanos, "The Casualties of War: The Truth About the Iraq Museum," *American Journal of Archaeology*, Vol. 109, No. 3 (July 2005), pp. 477–526.

129. *WWII: Time-Life Books History of the Second World War* (New York: Prentice Hall Press, 1989), p. 401; *The Columbia Encyclopedia*, fifth edition (New York: Columbia University Press, 1993), p. 116.

130. Clark Hoyt, "The Painful Images of War," *New York Times*, August 3, 2008, Week in Review section, p. 10.

131. See, for example, Christian Davenport, "From Serving in Iraq to Living on the Streets; Homeless Vet Numbers Expected to Grow," *Washington Post*, March 5, 2007, pp. B1 ff. The problems of returning Iraq war veterans going to college were headlined in the *New York Times'* education section: "Crowded classrooms can send them into a panic. They have trouble focusing. They can't remember facts. And no one around them understands what they've seen. . . These new students will need help. Are campuses ready?" *New York Times*, November 2, 2008, Education Life section, p. 1. Despite how radically this differs from the experience of veterans going to college after World War II, where troops had longer individual tours in combat and higher fatality rates, isolated anecdotes were all that were offered to substantiate these sweeping claims in the story itself. See Lizette Alvarez, "Combat to College," Ibid., pp. 24 ff.

132. Deborah Sontag and Lizette Alvarez, "Across America, Deadly Echoes of Foreign Battles," *New York Times*, January 13, 2008, section 1, pp. 1, 14.

133. Ralph Peters, "Smearing Soldiers," *New York Post,* January 15, 2008.

134. Lizette Alvarez and Dan Frosch, "A Focus on Violence by G.I.'s Back from War," *New York Times*, January 2, 2009, pp. A1 ff.

135. "Suicide Rate for Soldiers Rose in '07," *New York Times*, May 30, 2008, p. A18.

136. Pauline Jelinek, "Soldier Suicides Hit Highest Rate–115 Last Year," Associated Press Online, May 30, 2008.

137. Mona L. Siegel, *The Moral Disarmament of France*, pp. 218–219.

138. Edmund Burke, *The Correspondence of Edmund Burke*, edited by R. B. McDowell (Chicago: University of Chicago Press, 1969), Vol. VIII, p. 138.

139. Mona L. Siegel, *The Moral Disarmament of France*, p. 167.

140. William Godwin, *Enquiry Concerning Political Justice and Its Influence on Morals and Happiness* (Toronto: University of Toronto Press, 1946), Vol. II, p. 180.

141. Ibid., p. 146.

142. John Dewey, *Characters and Events*, edited by Joseph Ratner, Vol. II, pp. 800, 801.

143. Alistair Horne, *To Lose A Battle: France 1940* (New York: Penguin Books, 1990), p. 189.

144. William Godwin, *Enquiry Concerning Political Justice*, Vol. II, p. 151.

145. Neville Chamberlain, *In Search of Peace*, pp. 307–308.

146. William L. Shirer, *The Rise and Fall of the Third Reich: A History of Nazi Germany* (New York: Simon and Schuster, 1960), pp. 595–596.

147. Neville Chamberlain, *In Search of Peace*, p. 33. It should be noted that Hitler presented his position in terms of "the national honour of a great people" in a letter to Chamberlain. Ibid., p. 170.

148. Ibid., p. 107.

149. Ibid., p. 305.

150. Ibid., p. 170.

151. J.M. Keynes, "A Positive Peace Programme," *New Statesman and Nation*, March 26, 1938, pp. 509, 510.

152. Alistair Horne, *To Lose A Battle*, p. 129.

CHAPTER 9: INTELLECTUALS AND SOCIETY

1. Paul Johnson, *The Quotable Paul Johnson: A Topical Compilation of His Wit, Wisdom and Satire*, edited by George J. Marlin, et al (New York: Farrar, Straus and Giroux, 1994), p. 138.

2. John Maynard Keynes, *The General Theory of Employment Interest and Money* (New York: Harcourt, Brace and Company, 1936), p. 383.

3. Richard Hofstadter, *Anti-Intellectualism in American Life* (New York: Vintage Books, 1963), pp. 3, 14. Hofstadter's caveat jeopardizes the main thrust of his argument: "It seems clear that those who have some quarrel with intellect are almost always ambivalent about it: they mix respect and awe with suspicion and resentment; and this has been true in many societies and phases of human history. In any case, anti-intellectualism is not the creation of people who are categorically hostile to ideas. Quite the contrary: just as the most effective enemy of the educated man may be the half-educated man, so the leading anti-intellectuals are usually men deeply engaged with ideas, often obsessively engaged with this or that outworn or rejected idea." Ibid., p. 21. Because this caveat still does not distinguish intellectual processes and achievements, on the one hand, from the behavior of people in one subset of those whose work involves such processes and achievements, on the other, it perpetuates the confusion that hostility to one is hostility to the other. Admitting that many of the critics of intellectuals are themselves men of ideas, Hofstadter can dispose of their ideas by characterizing these ideas as "outworn or rejected"— which is to say, ideas with which he disagrees. In short, an ideological disagreement has been verbally transformed by Hofstadter into an issue of hostility to intellectual processes, even though he admits evidence to the contrary, including the fact that Edison "was all but canonized by the American public." Ibid., p. 25.

4. Russell Jacoby, *The Last Intellectuals: American Culture in the Age of Academe* (New York: Basic Books, 2000), p. 81.

5. Richard A. Posner, *Public Intellectuals: A Study of Decline* (Cambridge, Massachusetts: Harvard University Press, 2001), pp. 5, 7.

6. Among economists, for example, data in Posner's study showed Lester Thurow to have been mentioned more than twice as often as Nobel Prizewinner Gary Becker in the media, while Becker was cited more than eight times as often as Thurow in scholarly publications. Ibid., pp. 194, 205.

7. Ibid., pp. 174, 194–206, 209–214.

8. Ibid., p. 135.

9. Donald Kagan, *On the Origins of War and the Preservation of Peace* (New York: Doubleday, 1995), p. 104.

10. Charles F. Howlett, *Troubled Philosopher: John Dewey and the Struggle for World Peace* (Port Washington, N.Y.: Kennikat Press, 1977), p. 73.

11. In a broadcast on May 27, 1941, President Roosevelt said:

    "Nobody can foretell tonight just when the acts of the dictators will ripen into attack on this hemisphere and us. But we know enough by now to realize that it would be suicide to wait until they are in our front yard.
    "When your enemy comes at you in a tank or a bombing plane, if you hold your fire until you see the whites of his eyes, you will never know what hit you. Our Bunker Hill of tomorrow may be several thousand miles from Boston." Franklin D. Roosevelt, *The Public Papers and Addresses of Franklin D. Roosevelt*, 1941 Volume, edited by Samuel I. Rosenman (New York: Harper & Brothers, 1950), p. 189.

12. Eric Hoffer, *The True Believer: Thoughts on the Nature of Mass Movements* (New York: Harper Perennial, 1989), p. 116.

13. See, for example, Chapter 3 of my *Inside American Education: The Decline, the Deception, the Dogmas* (New York: The Free Press, 1993).

14. See Thomas Sowell, *The Vision of the Anointed: Self-Congratulation as a Basis for Social Policy* (New York: Basic Books, 1995), pp. 15–21.

15. Eric Hoffer, *First Things, Last Things* (New York: Harper & Row, 1971), p. 117.

16. James R. Flynn, "Massive IQ Gains in 14 Nations: What IQ Tests Really Measure," *Psychological Bulletin*, Vol. 101, No. 2 (1987), pp. 171–191.

17. Jean-François Revel, *The Flight from Truth: The Reign of Deceit in the Age of Information*, translated by Curtis Cate (New York: Random House, 1991), p. 361.

18. Lewis A. Coser, *Men of Ideas: A Sociologist's View* (New York: The Free Press, 1970), p. 215.

19. Ibid., p. 216.

20. Paul Hollander, *Anti-Americanism: Critiques at Home and Abroad 1965–1990* (New York: Oxford University Press, 1992), p. 242.

21. See, for example, Theodore Dalrymple, *Our Culture, What's Left of It: The Mandarins and the Masses* (Chicago: Ivan R. Dee, 2005), pp. 296–310; Bruce Thornton, *Decline and Fall: Europe's Slow-Motion Suicide* (New York: Encounter Books, 2007), Chapter 3; Christopher Caldwell, *Reflections on the Revolution in Europe: Immigration, Islam, and the West* (New York: Doubleday, 2009).

22. See, for example, Chapter 2 of my *The Vision of the Anointed*.

23. Edward Shils, *The Constitution of Society* (Chicago: University of Chicago Press, 1982), p. 182.

24. Peter Hitchens, *The Abolition of Britain: From Winston Churchill to Princess Diana* (San Francisco: Encounter Books, 2002), pp. 4, 7.

25. Bradley R. Schiller, *The Economics of Poverty and Discrimination*, tenth edition (Upper Saddle River, N.J.: Pearson Education, Inc., 2008), p. 72.

26. Ibid., p. 71.

27. Angelo M. Codevilla, *The Character of Nations: How Politics Makes and Breaks Prosperity, Family, and Civility* (New York: Basic Books, 1997), p. 50.

28. See Robert C. Davis, *Christian Slaves, Muslim Masters: White Slavery in the Mediterranean, the Barbary Coast, and Italy, 1500–1800* (New York: Palgrave Macmillan, 2003), p. 23; Philip D. Curtin, *The Atlantic Slave Trade: A Census* (Madison: University of Wisconsin Press, 1969), pp. 72, 75, 87.

29. Orlando Patterson, *Slavery and Social Death: A Comparative Study* (Cambridge, Mass.: Harvard University Press, 1982), pp. 406–407; W. Montgomery Watt, *The Influence of Islam on Medieval Europe* (Edinburgh: Edinburgh University Press, 1972), p. 19; Bernard Lewis, *Race and Slavery in the Middle East: An Historical Inquiry* (New York: Oxford University Press, 1990), p. 11; Daniel Evans, "Slave Coast of Europe," *Slavery & Abolition*, Vol. 6, Number 1 (May 1985), p. 53, note 3; William D. Phillips, Jr., *Slavery from Roman Times to the Early Transatlantic Trade* (Minneapolis: University of Minnesota Press, 1985), p. 57.

30. Daniel J. Boorstin, *The Americans*, Vol. II: *The National Experience* (New York: Random House, 1965), p. 203.

31. Jean-François Revel, *The Flight from Truth*, translated by Curtis Cate, p. 16.

INDEX